CONTENTS

PART TWO

UNEMPLOYMENT, NATIONAL OUTPUT, AND FISCAL POLICY

PART THREE

MONEY, MONETARY POLICY, AND INCOMES POLICY

PART FOUR

ECONOMIC GROWTH AND THE ENVIRONMENT

PART FIVE

INTERNATIONAL ECONOMICS

PREFACE

to the Second Edition

This book is intended for use in courses in the principles of economics. It is designed to supplement, not substitute for, a textbook presenting the principles of economics. Although meant to be a companion to my volume, *Principles of Macroeconomics,* Second Edition (Norton, 1977), it can be used with any standard textbook. It attempts to present a balanced blend of both theory and applications—and to do this within a reasonable length. Moreover, it provides a wide spectrum of views—conservative, liberal, and radical—concerning the important public policy issues of the day. By presenting conflicting points of view, this book attempts to heighten the student's interest and to show how the principles of economics can be applied to important social problems.

The papers contained in this volume cover the full range of macroeconomics. In each area, I have included some classic *theoretical* and *policy* papers, as well as papers that illustrate the *measurement* and *empirical* usefulness of theoretical constructs, and papers that provide interesting *case studies.* The emphasis is on the blending of theory, applications, and case studies. Also, the emphasis is on relatively fresh articles, over a third of the selections having been published in the 1970s.

To my mind, the most effective way to teach elementary economics is to demonstrate how it can be, and has been, used to shed light on important real-world problems. If one takes the trouble to show students the relevance and power of the principles of economics, they usually are motivated to learn the material more thoroughly. Throughout this book, articles are included that demonstrate the application and applicability of these basis principles. In most cases the applications are to problems of public policy;

but their application to private decision-making is not overlooked.

I have tried to keep this book at a level commensurate with the background and abilities of the typical student. Of course, there are advantages in including some articles that will appeal to the most capable, and I have done so. But the bulk of the selections can be read and comprehended by those of average competence. Fortunately, it is possible, I believe, to acquaint students with classic papers by the great names of present-day economics—Samuelson, Friedman, Stigler, Tobin, Heller, Wallich, Solow, and many others—without expecting them to perform intellectual feats beyond their capacities or training. Also, one can introduce them to the giants of the past, such as Adam Smith and Thomas Malthus, and focus their attention on the reports of government agencies and congressional hearings on vital current problems, without taxing their capacities unreasonably.

In this second edition, I have tried to alter the book's contents in the light of the reactions of the many instructors who have used the book in their courses. New articles have been included on inflation, monetary policy, divestiture of the oil firms, planning, East-West trade, ITT, income inequality, welfare programs, productivity, and many other topics. About one-fifth of the articles in this edition are new.

I would like to thank Michael Taussig of Rutgers University and Fred Westfield of Vanderbilt University for comments and suggestions, as well as the many teachers who gave me the benefits of their experiences using the first edition. Also, I would like to thank my wife for her help in assembling some of these materials.

E. M.

PART ONE

Economics and the American Economy

Economics, like any discipline aimed at social understanding and social betterment, should pull its weight in man's struggle to achieve a better lot. How relevant is economics to the great social problems facing modern society? In the opening selection, Charles Schultze, Chairman of President Carter's Council of Economic Advisers, discusses the aims and achievements of economics, and points out that economics plays a major role in the solution of important problems of public and private policy. He concludes that there "is a need for both the pragmatist who would harness in the public service man's drive for worldly goods and the idealist who would lift man's drive to more lofty goals. Neither is irrelevant."

The American economy is a mixed capitalistic system; and like any capitalistic system, it depends heavily on the price system, which is described concisely and simply by W. Allen Wallis. His brief essay indicates how the price system solves the basic problems of what should be produced, how it should be produced, and who should receive the output. Even in prisoner-of-war camps during World War II, the price system sprang up, in a spontaneous way, to allocate the supplies of food and commodities received by prisoners. The next selection, by R. A. Radford, is a classic account of how the price system functioned behind enemy lines in World War II.

Of course, the advantages of the price system have long been recognized, as indicated by the next item, which is an excerpt from Adam Smith's *The Wealth of Nations*. Smith argues that: "As every individual . . . endeavors as much as he can . . . to employ his capital [so that] its produce may be of greatest value," he is "led by an invisible hand" to promote the public interest. Marxists Paul Baran and Paul Sweezy, in the following article, make a sweeping

1

indictment of capitalism on the grounds that the capitalistic division of labor has a dehumanizing effect on workers. Needless to say, their analysis would not be accepted by most American economists. Robert L. Heilbroner then analyzes the future of capitalism. In his view, "the next phase of capitalism must be an increasingly planned system, and the drift of business society will be toward a business-government state." This view, like that of Baran and Sweezy, is highly controversial.

While the American economy is capitalistic, it is a mixed capitalistic system, which means that the government, as well as the price system, plays an important role in determining how society's resources are used, and for what purpose. No question is debated more hotly than the proper economic role of the government. Some, like George J. Stigler, are skeptical about the efficiency or effectiveness of the government, and favor a reduction in government controls over economic life. In his witty and provocative paper, Stigler asks that, despite the fact that "no method of displaying one's public spiritedness is more popular than to notice a problem and pass a law," close studies be made of the comparative performance of public and private enterprises to determine what activities can in fact be carried out more efficiently by government.

Paul Samuelson, on the other hand, is much less concerned about the growth of government intervention in economic matters. Although he agrees with Adam Smith about the undesirability of certain types of government intervention, he goes on to point out that Smith's "invisible hand" maximizes social welfare only if "the state intervenes to make the initial distribution of dollar votes ethically proper." In Samuelson's view, the price system, no less than the government, is a method of coercion; and he concludes that: "There are no rules concerning the proper role of government that can be established by a priori reasoning."

1

Is Economics Obsolete?
No, Underemployed

CHARLES L. SCHULTZE

Charles L. Schultze is chairman of President Carter's Council of Economic Advisers. This article is from the Saturday Review, *January 22, 1972.*

The current disenchantment, particularly among the young, with the optimistic, problem-solving approach to social issues that characterized the 1960s not surprisingly has rubbed off on economics. Many members of the economics profession now question the relevance and meaning of the fundamental assumptions underlying the economics that is currently taught and practiced. Some of the critics have been saying these things for several years but have only lately found someone to listen. A few are recent converts from orthodoxy. And among the younger members of the profession, these critical views are becoming fairly widespread.

There is merit in some of the criticism, but little in the general notion that economics has grown obsolete or irrelevant. The indictment against it should read not that economics is irrelevant but that its very relevant tools have been too sparingly applied to the kinds of problems now confronting us. In some instances, economics is a victim of its own highly relevant successes.

One of the major counts in the indictment is that Keynesian economics is incapable of handling the central policy issue of the era: how to make full employment compatible with reasonable price stability. Yet, in the twenty-five years since the Second World War, a period during which Keynesian fiscal policy emerged from advanced theory courses to become the conventional wisdom of Presidents, unemployment in no year averaged more than 7 percent, compared with the 1930s, during which unemployment never fell below 14 percent. The major depressions and massive financial panics that sporadically afflicted industrial economies for the century-and-a-half before 1940 are no longer even a dim threat. And aside from the brief aftermath of World War II, the inflations that quite rightly gave Americans cause for worry have not exceeded 5 or 6 percent per year at their worst, a far cry from the persistent rates of 10 and 20 percent per year with which some nations of the world have been living for decades.

Modern economics can and has successfully prescribed the means of preventing large-scale unemployment without bringing on major inflation. It can devise, and has devised, ways of preventing major inflation without precipitating serious depressions. Although the prescriptions of economists are not solely responsible for the sharply improved postwar performance of the Western economies, they surely played a major role. What we now label a failure of theory and policy has been a roaring success by pre-Keynesian standards.

The puzzle economics has not yet solved, and which critics quite properly point to, is the worrisome, but far from catastrophic, inflation that appears when overall demand and supply come into balance during periods of high, but not excessive, prosperity. Yet this failure may stem not so much from shortcomings of the basic theoretical apparatus as from the difficulty of making precise measurements. Economics has little difficulty in prescribing counterbalances to large swings in prices and employment. But in recent years we have been dealing with variations in the employment rate between 3.5 and 6 percent and with differences of 2 to 3 percent in the rate of inflation. And within these ranges the analysis of how wages and prices interact and the prescribing of policy require more precise and complex measurements than we have yet devised. Still, a good carpenter can make a perfectly satisfactory joint with instruments that would be useless for calibrating the tolerances in an Apollo guidance mechanism. Which is by no means to say that the carpenter should throw away his tools as being irrelevant to modern society.

A better understanding of the inflation that accompanies high (even though not excessively high) employment may not ultimately rest on some radical new breakthrough in economic theory. Rather it may well result from gradual improvement in our knowledge about labor markets, about the role of people's expectations during inflation, and about how the market power of unions and business is translated into specific wage and price decisions. Policy instruments to deal with the problem may correspondingly be found in improvements in manpower training programs and antitrust policy, and in the gradual development of wage-price standards sufficiently flexible to avoid smothering the economy in regulation, yet tough enough to influence a key decision when it counts.

Whatever the outcome, any successful prescription for jointly achieving full employment and price stability will undoubtedly contain a large dose of what I may loosely call Keynesian economics—extended, modified, and supplemented, but not abandoned.

Another major indictment against contemporary economics runs approximately like this: Because economics ignores the substantial economic power now concentrated in large firms and unions, and because on a larger scale it accepts the fundamental status quo of current power relationships in society and ignores the relationship between the distribution of power and the distribution of income, it either has no policy prescriptions for pressing social problems or offers ameliorative remedies that only scratch the surface.

To some extent, the charge that modern economics has produced little in the way of remedies for the current siege of social problems is valid, but paradoxically this is so for reasons precisely opposite to those advanced by economics' critics. Economics may be faulted, not because it possesses a theoretical apparatus of no relevance to current social problems, but because in many cases it has failed to apply, or only recently begun to apply, an apparatus that is particularly well suited to dealing with a large segment of those problems.

Much of economics deals with the problem of how a decentralized decision-making system can be made to provide proper incentives so that individual decision-makers, apparently pursuing their own ends, nevertheless tend to act in a way consistent with the public good—the "invisible hand" of Adam Smith. Since time immemorial it has been too often assumed that the apparatus of analysis which dealt with this problem applied only to the private market and that the public sector of the economy must operate by a completely different set of rules. Yet, a little reflection will demonstrate that many of the major social problems with which government is now seized require solutions under which the decisions of thousands of communities and millions of individuals are somehow channeled toward nationally desired objectives.

Cleaning up environmental pollution, changing the delivery structure of an ineffective and inequitable medical-care system, providing compensatory educational programs, and offering training and labor market opportunities to the previously disadvantaged depend for their success or failure on day-to-day decisions made by particular communities, business firms, and individuals throughout the nation. No program that merely seeks to transfer these hundreds of thousands, indeed millions, of decisions to a few officials in Washington can hope to be effective. Nor, conversely, can any program that simply shovels federal revenues to state and local governments, and then hopes for the best. Somehow institutional frameworks and incentives that guide a multitude of particular decisions toward national ends have to be developed.

And here, traditional economics and its incentive-oriented apparatus suggest a number of approaches. The major problems of environmental pollution, for instance, stem from the fact that air and water are given free to all comers, and like any good that is given away these commodities will be overused; with no incentives to conserve them, neither individuals nor business firms will lend their talents toward developing and using new conservation technology. But old-fashioned economic analysis suggests that placing a stiff charge on the dumping of pollutants into the air or water will marvelously stimulate the discovery of production methods that reduce pollution, just as the rising cost of labor has promoted a steady growth in techniques to increase output per man-hour, at a rate that roughly doubles the efficiency of labor every twenty-five years. Economics also brings into question whether it makes any more sense to rely solely on detailed regulation and court decision for minimizing pollution than it would to use these devices for minimizing other industrial costs.

As for health care, conventional economics indicates that the nation can hardly hope to have an efficient use of scarce medical resources when the current health care system provides a powerful set of incentives to waste and misdirect those resources: insurance plans that cover hospitalization but not office visits, thereby encouraging excessive use of hospitals; private and governmental insurance that reimburses hospitals on a cost-plus basis, penalizing the efficient and rewarding the inefficient; financial rewards keyed to dramatic intervention (the cardiac surgeon) but quite niggardly for the practice of preventive medicine; etc.

In the area of public education, economic analysis points to the difficulty of getting superior performances from a monopoly with a captive market (the public school system of the inner city) and can help design means of introducing incentives for improvement and innovations. It also emphasizes the impossibility of designing and enforcing urban land-use plans in an economic environment where many aspects of the tax laws and land laws provide large positive incentives for urban sprawl. It provides insights into the problem of urban congestion by showing how most auto users are not now required to pay the real social costs that their ride imposes on other citizens

and how this fact provides incentives for socially excessive use of crowded highways.

As these examples indicate, many of our social problems arise because the current system of markets, laws, and customs provides positive incentives for individuals, business firms, and local communities to engage in what can objectively be called antisocial conduct. Correspondingly, substantial improvement in these areas is most unlikely to come from governmental programs that rely principally on traditional, centralized decision-making, but must rest in part on a restructuring of incentives and institutions—a task for which economics, far from being obsolete, has been too little used.

In terms of social problems, economic analysis also has a relevant role to play as a bearer of unpleasant truths—that in some areas of social policy the nation is seeking to pursue conflicting goals. It is literally impossible, for example, to design a welfare program that simultaneously meets four often-sought goals: providing a generous minimum income to the poor; preserving incentives for productive work by avoiding a rapid reduction in welfare benefits as recipients begin to earn outside money; instituting welfare reform in a way that does not reduce the income of any beneficiaries under the current system; and preventing such large budgetary costs that those not far above the poverty line have to be taxed heavily to support those just below it. No program can do all of these things simultaneously.

In the same vein, a public service job program must seek a compromise between two conflicting objectives: to provide wages and working conditions sufficiently attractive to appeal to the unemployed and the low-paid casual worker and to avoid drawing workers away from productive jobs elsewhere. A national medical program cannot at one and the same time guarantee virtually all the medical care private citizens can demand regardless of income, provide a financial mechanism and a set of incentives that hold down escalation of costs, and avoid comprehensive detailed regulation of medical care by Washington bureaucrats.

Pointing out relevant truths of this sort, however, appears to be one of the factors underlying the charges of irrelevancy leveled against economics. Such observations about conflicting objectives imply the need for compromise. But to those for whom compromise is inherently evil, and for whom most problems fundamentally trace back to the greed of the power structure, calling attention to the technical difficulties that would face even a liberated world seems to be irrelevant at best and obstructionist at worst.

A similar reaction, perhaps, will greet the assertion that there are many social issues in which economics should not be expected to play a central role. Economists can seek to ferret out the economic consequences of racial discrimination and help in devising means to expand opportunities for racial minorities. But the eradication of discrimination itself will necessarily depend heavily on a combination of legal steps, education, and political leadership. Economists can trace many of the causes of financial crisis now afflicting large central cities. But the job of rationalizing the archaic jumble of local government in metropolitan areas, thereby providing a viable economic base for large cities, is a task beyond what should be expected of economists. While many of our social ills have major economic consequences, there are some that will yield only to political solutions.

One area in which the economics profession has a decidedly mixed record is the field of income distribution. The problem is not so much a deficiency in economic theory as it relates to income distribution but rather a tendency on the part of the profession to exhibit an excessive concern for efficiency as compared with equity in dealing with situations where the two are in conflict.

An economic system can be very efficient in providing private and public goods to meet the demands generated by a very lopsided income distribution—fine mansions, good public protection, and rapid mass transit for affluent suburbanites while the poor live in hovels, are victimized by crime, and spend inordinate amounts of time getting to work. The formal structure of economics recognizes that its rules for an efficient allocation of resources are blind with respect to the distribution of income; that efficiency considerations alone cannot justify policies which have significant effects on that distribution; and, conversely, that policies which redistribute income in a direction society thinks more just may be warranted even when those policies reduce efficiency. Most economists working in the field of taxation have paid close attention to matters of distribution, and the large majority have raised their voices in favor of strengthening the redistributive features of the tax system. On the other hand, in many areas of public policy, economists as a body have had a bias toward letting efficiency considerations rule.

Higher efficiency, however, is often secured at the expense of particular groups of workers and individual communities. It is not so much that the remedies for these problems need be sought in protectionism, subsidies to dying industries, or rigid featherbedding work rules. Rather, an affluent society might well be expected to provide better income guarantees to workers than ours now does, particularly to older workers, whose skills have been rendered obsolete by economic change and growth. Economists have generally been much more active in pointing to the efficiency gains of unimpeded economic change than in devising means of minimizing its impact on particular workers and communities. In a similar vein, it is only recently that economists and statisticians have begun to look deeply into the often perverse income distribution consequences of many public programs—farm subsidies, low tuition at state universities, urban highway building, irrigation and flood control projects, and the like.

Paying more attention to the problems of income distribution, however, would not rescue conventional economics from attack. To the Western economist, income distribution problems can be approached through such pragmatic measures as reforming the tax system, restructuring welfare programs, and providing more equal educational opportunities. But to radical critics, these are Band-Aid measures. The basic cause of maldistribution of income, they say, is the maldistribution of power that inevitably accompanies a market-oriented free enterprise system. Any pragmatic measures will eventually be perverted by the holders of economic power to their own ends. Only the demise of the market system itself will make it possible to provide a just distribution of the fruits of man's productive activity.

Here indeed is a fundamental difference in approach. An evaluation of the merits of the case would go far beyond the scope of this article, and, in any event, logical argument seldom makes converts in this controversy. I cannot resist pointing out, however, that in any complex society, whatever its original structure, there is a tendency for power, influence, and wealth to become concentrated in relatively few hands, and this is particularly true whenever societies seek to provide incentives for abundant production. Eternal vigilance is the price of an egalitarian distribution of income. Even in the "post-revolutionary state," the old pragmatic measures of progressive taxation, transfer payments such as welfare benefits, and equal educational opportunities would still be important tools for securing a just distribution of income.

There remain two major areas in which even the most sympathetic view of modern economics would have to concede that charges against the state of the art do strike home. One involves the behavior of producers, the other, that of consumers.

The panoply of tools with which economics seeks to explain how resources are allocated in the private market relies quite heavily on the premise of profit-maximizing firms, each responding to but not controlling the market in which it operates and making decisions subject to reasonably good knowledge about the future consequences of those decisions. For purposes of analyzing the long-run effects of economic policy actions, this "model" of the world is quite serviceable. In the long run, firms do seek to maximize profits; they cannot control basic changes in their economic environment; and there is sufficient feedback from their decisions to provide reasonably accurate information. But in the short run, the behavior of firms with respect to modest changes in prices, wages, and investment policy is much less predictable. They can insulate their own markets against moderate threats; their search for long-run profits is roughly consistent with a number of alternative short-term strategies; and before the feedback from their decisions reaches them, they are faced with great uncertainty.

The inability of economic theory to predict the short-run behavior of firms might not be so important except for the problem of inflation. The long-run allocation of resources, and the shift in price relationships that brings it about, probably does proceed much in the manner explained by economic theory. But it may take place around a generally rising price trend. And unlike market shares, inflation is generally irreversible. A series of short-term decisions on the part of many firms and unions can lead to continuing inflation. The weakness of current economics in predicting the short-run behavior of modern firms and unions thus turns into a serious deficiency in terms of the ability of economists to explain today's inflation *cum* unemployment.

The second charge hits home in the sensitive area of consumer preference theory. Traditional economics takes consumer tastes and preferences as given. It neither looks behind them nor seeks to weigh their relative merits. This approach has two consequences. First, the economist has little to say about the social implications of advertising practices that create and destroy preferences, nor about the social waste represented by the resources devoted to the satisfaction of manipulated tastes. Nor does he have anything to contribute to the deeper problem of the way in which basic preferences themselves respond to economic development, except to note that "yes, this does indeed happen, and the sociologists better get to work."

Second, and perhaps more important, the economist, by taking individual preferences as given and absolute, sharply limits the field of his analysis when it comes to many matters of public policy. The tools of economics are designed to show how resources can best be deployed to meet society's wants. By its assumption that the relevant social wants are based on the existing preferences of individuals, and that those preferences cannot be questioned, economics has erected a barrier against the use of its analysis in some of the most important matters of public policy. The economist can give advice on the efficiency of the policy instruments chosen to meet an objective. But when it comes to choosing among different objectives, the economist qua economist must be silent. Personal tax cuts that increase society's consumption of beer and whitewall tires hold equal status with increased public expenditures for education. Choice between the two is a "value judgment," which he must eschew.

One promising line of research has been suggested as a means of breaking this impasse. Individual tastes and preferences are themselves hierarchical. Many of our wants are means to a higher set of goals. The demand for the services of physicians and hospitals is itself a means of attaining a higher end, the maintenance of health. The demand for automobiles is (in part, at least) a demand for transportation. To the extent that preferences are considered means to an end, rather than ends themselves, they can be judged in terms of their efficiency—how well does the satisfaction of a particular "lower-order" preference contribute to the attainment of the "higher-order" goal. At least some preferences can be looked at critically and not accepted unquestionably. Once the question of efficiency is introduced, economics is back on familiar ground. It is peculiarly suited to analyze matters of efficiency.

No one has pursued this line of approach at any great length. Whether it will pay off, in terms of providing a more solid footing for economic theory than the shifting sands of "absolute preferences," cannot be foretold. Barring some progress in this area, economics must stand guilty on part of one count of the indictment against it.

Reflecting on the nature of radical criticism of

economics leads to one further comment. Economics is fundamentally a discipline that deals with man as he is. At its best, economics seeks to harness man's very human motivations to the public interest. Much of the New Left is interested in changing man, elevating his motives, reducing his greed, and intensifying his love for his fellow man. Economics is a social science, but love is a religion. They are both relevant, but they are not on the same plane of discourse. The economist, for example, generally thinks it naive to hope that pollution will somehow be conquered by bringing public pressure on corporations to exercise "social responsibility." But he does advocate changes in the structure of incentives and the network of contract laws to create a situation in which it becomes a corporation's own self-interest to act "responsibly."

To the young radical, such technical solutions, which accept and play upon man's drive for material advancement, seem shabby and mean. The evangelism of love and understanding mingle curiously with an intolerant hate for institutions built on the search for money and wealth. But they mingle no more curiously than in the Epistles of St. Paul. There is need for both the pragmatist who would harness in the public service man's drive for worldly goods and the idealist who would lift man's drive to more lofty goals. Neither is irrelevant.

2

The Price System

W. ALLEN WALLIS

W. Allen Wallis is Chancellor of the University of Rochester. This article appeared in The Freeman, *in 1957.*

Almost everyone says he's in favor of free enterprise but hardly anyone really is. Slogans like "Make free enterprise work" or "Preserve capitalism" are the usual rallying cries of all kinds of programs to impair freedom of enterprise. A lot of this is disingenuous.

These disingenuous slogans of the false friends of free enterprise don't bother me nearly as much as the fact that many real friends of free enterprise have hazy notions about how such a system is supposed to work. Even they fail to understand that most so-called "welfare" objectives can be achieved better by free enterprise than by collectivism. In debate they are too often easy pushovers for the collectivists.

I am continually impressed by the fact that most individualists and most collectivists are surprisingly close together in their general objectives of social welfare—elimination of poverty, reduction of inequality, and provision for hardship. The differences between the individualists and the collectivists are differences not in values but in technical analysis of the means of attaining these values.

For this reason, I shall make an attempt to picture in very broad strokes the basic mechanism of a free enterprise economy—to describe the way it should—and mostly does—work.

200 Million Individuals

Here in the United States is an area of about three million square miles containing 200 million people. Suppose you were asked how to organize these people to utilize the resources available to them for their material satisfactions. You can imagine you have a fairly detailed inventory of the natural resources of the country, of the people and their knowledge, energies, and abilities, and of their wants. Imagine that all these resources are as unorganized as a set of chessmen just poured out of their box and awaiting organization on the chessboard. Your problem is to organize the resources so that wants will be filled as well as possible.

Organization Problems

If you can get your head working at all in the face of so staggering a prospect, it will occur to you that one of the first things you are going to need is some way of establishing goals and measuring achievement. Which of the many things wanted are going to be produced, in what quantities, and with what priorities?

And after you establish these goals and priorities, you will need a method of assigning the various pieces of capital, the various natural resources, and the various people to particular activities. Each will have several alternative uses; you will need a method of coordinating the resources assigned to cooperate in each task.

Then, third, you will have to have some system for dividing the product among the people; who gets how much of what, and when?

Fourth, you will probably realize that for one reason or another your system will not work perfectly but will sometimes have overproduced some things and underproduced others. You will need some system of adjustment to these temporary shortages and abundances, until your method of measuring achievement and your method of allocating resources can get the basic situation corrected.

A fifth kind of problem you may worry about is that of providing for the expansion and improvement of your capital equipment and technological knowledge.

These five functions have to be provided for when you establish any organization, even a small and relatively simple one. When we consider the large and complex organization of an entire economy, what are some of the alternative ways of arranging for them?

Alternative Systems

The most obvious way to arrange things is the way an army does. You set up a commander or a general staff. They decide on goals, they decide who shall do what to attain them, they decide how to apportion the product, and they issue orders accordingly. Another method is that used in beehives and ant colonies in which caste and custom determine who does what. Things go on in the same way, generation after generation.

A third way is to introduce money and let each person decide which he will perform of the activities that others will pay for, and what he will buy of the things that others offer for money.

Under this system, goals are set by the money offers of individuals for goods and services. Resources are allocated to one activity or another by the desires of their owners for money income. Goods are distributed to individuals according to their willingness and ability to pay the prices. Thus prices become the crucial organizing element in such an economy. Indeed, this system is often called the "price system."

Efficient and Voluntary

The price system has two outstanding features. First, it is by all odds the most efficient system of social organization ever conceived. It makes it possible for huge multitudes to cooperate effectively, multitudes who may hardly know of each other's existence, or whose personal attitudes toward one another may be indifference or hostility. Second, it affords a maximum of individual freedom and a minimum of coercion. And since people can cooperate effectively in production even when their attitudes on other issues are hostile, there is no need for unity and conformity in religion, politics, recreation, and language—or even in patriotism and good will except in the very broadest sense.

Although one of the big features of the price system that commends it is the voluntary nature of individual actions, the system nevertheless exerts powerful inducements and even compulsions.

Guides to Action

A consumer who has it in mind to use up a lot of a scarce commodity highly prized by others is forced to forego consuming other commodities to an extent judged by others to be equivalent. A producer who tries to get more income than his services are judged by others to be worth is prevented from doing so by the freedom of buyers to buy elsewhere and of other sellers to underprice him. A business manager who tries to waste labor, capital, and raw materials is prevented from doing so because he will find himself taking in less money than he pays out. As long as he can make good the deficit, by giving up his own right to consume, this can continue; but when he can no longer make good—that is when he can no longer pay for the labor, capital, and raw materials—he is forced to stop wasting them just as firmly as if a cease and desist order were issued by a Federal Bureau of Efficiency. Maybe more firmly, for his congressman may be more influential with the federal bureau than with his creditors.

The freedom of the system produces inducements or compulsions for individuals to act efficiently in the general interest. It is not by any means true that each enterprise is free to do what it pleases. It is restricted by the freedom of consumers to buy elsewhere; of the owners of labor, capital, and raw materials to sell elsewhere; and of business managers to enter the same business in competition with it.

Price Communications

This freedom of others to compete for advantages is effective in checking individual self-aggrandizement because economic information is effectively disseminated by prices. Prices represent one of the most efficient communication devices ever invented.

Indeed, we might look on the problem of organization as hinging on communication. The problem is to bring to bear on each decision two very different kinds of information. On one hand, any decision depends on general, over-all economic data; for example, how much a certain product is wanted, and how abundant the resources are from which it could be made. On the other hand, it depends on minute special knowledge; for example, knowledge of peculiar abilities, of unused resources, of possible changes in ways of doing things.

Centralize or Disperse?

Now the problem is whether to transmit the detailed knowledge of special circumstances to a central agency, or to transmit the general information to the individuals who have the detailed knowledge. The detailed knowledge is too voluminous and nebulous for transmittal or for assimilation, and no one could know what parts should be selected. The general information, however, is summarized in prices.

Just that part of the general data that is relevant to an individual's decision is summarized in prices. If a price goes up, that tells him everything he needs to know to guide his action; he does not need to know why the price went up; the fact that it did go up tells him to try to use a little less or it tells him to produce more of the commodity, and how far to go in his efforts.

Not only do prices convey information on how an individual *should* act, but they provide at the same time a powerful inducement for him to do so.

An understanding of the theory of a price system is essential to any efforts to improve our economic organization or to any comparison of alternative modes of economic organization. To me, the most depressing thing about the prospects for a free society is not the hydrogen bomb, or international politics, or communist agitation; it is the fact that so very few have any understanding of economics.

3

The Economic Organisation of a P.O.W. Camp

R. A. RADFORD

This well-known article by R. A. Radford first appeared in Economica, *in 1945, the last year of World War II.*

Although a P.O.W. camp provides a living example of a simple economy which might be used as an alternative to the Robinson Crusoe economy beloved by the textbooks, and its simplicity renders the demonstration of certain economic hypotheses both amusing and instructive, it is suggested that the principal significance is sociological. True, there is interest in observing the growth of economic institutions and customs in a brand new society, small and simple enough to prevent detail from obscuring the basic pattern and disequilibrium from obscuring the working of the system. But the essential interest lies in the universality and the spontaneity of this economic life; it came into existence not by conscious imitation but as a response to the immediate needs and circumstances. Any similarity between prison organisation and outside organisation arises from similar stimuli evoking similar responses.

The following is as brief an account of the essential data as may render the narrative intelligible. The camps of which the writer had experience were Oflags

and consequently the economy was not complicated by payments for work by the detaining power. They consisted normally of between 1,200 and 2,500 people, housed in a number of separate but intercommunicating bungalows, one company of 200 or so to a building. Each company formed a group within the main organisation and inside the company the room and the messing syndicate, a voluntary and spontaneous group who fed together, formed the constituent units.

Between individuals there was active trading in all consumer goods and in some services. Most trading was for food against cigarettes or other foodstuffs, but cigarettes rose from the status of a normal commodity to that of a currency. Our supplies consisted of rations provided by the detaining power and (principally) the contents of Red Cross food parcels—tinned milk, jam, butter, biscuits, bully, chocolate, sugar, etc., and cigarettes. So far the supplies to each person were equal and regular. Private parcels of clothing, toilet requisites, and cigarettes were also received, and here equality ceased owing to the different numbers despatched and the vagaries of the post. All these articles were the subject of trade and exchange.

The Development and Organisation of the Market

Very soon after capture people realised that it was both undesirable and unnecessary, in view of the limited size and the equality of supplies, to give away or to accept gifts of cigarettes or food. "Goodwill" developed into trading as a more equitable means of maximising individual satisfaction.

We reached a transit camp in Italy about a fortnight after capture and received one-quarter of a Red Cross food parcel each a week later. At once exchanges, already established, multiplied in volume. Starting with simple direct barter, such as a nonsmoker giving a smoker friend his cigarette issue in exchange for a chocolate ration, more complex exchanges soon became an accepted custom. Stories circulated of a padre who started off round the camp with a tin of cheese and five cigarettes and returned to his bed with a complete parcel in addition to his original cheese and cigarettes; the market was not yet perfect. Within a week or two, as the volume of trade grew, rough scales of exchange values came into existence. Sikhs, who had at first exchanged tinned beef for practically any other foodstuff, began to insist on jam and margarine. It was realised that a tin of jam was worth one-half pound of margarine plus something else; that a cigarette issue was worth several chocolate issues, and a tin of diced carrots was worth practically nothing.

In this camp we did not visit other bungalows very much and prices varied from place to place; hence the germ of truth in the story of the itinerant priest. By the end of a month, when we reached our permanent camp, there was a lively trade in all commodities and their relative values were well known, and expressed not in terms of one another—one didn't quote bully in terms of sugar—but in terms of cigarettes. The cigarette became the standard of value. In the permanent camp people started by wandering through the bungalows calling their offers—"cheese for seven" (cigarettes)—and the hours after parcel issue were bedlam. The inconveniences of this system soon led to its replacement by an Exchange and Mart notice board in every bungalow, where under the headings "name," "room number," "wanted" and "offered" sales and wants were advertised. When a deal went through, it was crossed off the board. The public and semipermanent records of transactions led to cigarette prices being well known and thus tending to equality throughout the camp, although there were always opportunities for an astute trader to make a profit from arbitrage. With this development everyone, including nonsmokers was willing to sell for cigarettes, using them to buy at another time and place. Cigarettes became the nonmal currency, though, of course, barter was never extinguished.

The unity of the market and the prevalence of a single price varied directly with the general level of organisation and comfort in the camp. A transit camp was always chaotic and uncomfortable: people were overcrowded, no one knew where anyone else was living, and few took the trouble to find out. Organisation was too slender to include an Exchange and Mart board, and private advertisements were the most that appeared. Consequently a transit camp was not one market but many. The price of a tin of salmon is known to have varied by two cigarettes in 20 between one end of a hut and the other. Despite a high level of organisation in Italy, the market was morcellated in this manner at the first transit camp we reached after our removal to Germany in the autumn of 1943. In this camp—Stalag VIIA at Moosburg in Bavaria—there were up to 50,000 prisoners of all nationalities. French, Russians, Italians, and Yugoslavs were free to move about within the camp: British and Americans were confined to their compounds, although a few cigarettes given to a sentry would always procure permission for one or two men to visit other compounds. The people who first visited the highly organised French trading centre, with its stalls and known prices, found coffee extract—relatively cheap among the tea-drinking English—commanding a fancy price in biscuits or cigarettes, and some enterprising people made small fortunes that way. (Incidentally we found out later that much of the coffee went "over the wire" and sold for phenomenal prices at black market cafés in Munich: some of the French prisoners were said to have made substantial sums in RMk.s. This was one of the few occasions on which our normally closed economy came into contact with other economic worlds.)

Eventually public opinion grew hostile to these monopoly profits—not everyone could make contact with the French—and trading with them was put on a regulated basis. Each group of beds was given a quota of articles to offer and the transaction was carried out by accredited representatives from the British compound, with monopoly rights. The same method was used for trading with sentries elsewhere, as in this trade secrecy and reasonable prices had a peculiar importance, but as is ever the case with regulated companies, the interloper proved too strong.

The permanent camps in Germany saw the highest level of commercial organisation. In addition to the Exchange and Mart notice boards, a shop was organised as a public utility, controlled by representatives of the Senior British Officer, on a no profit basis. People left their surplus clothing, toilet requisites, and food there until they were sold at a fixed price in cigarettes. Only sales in cigarettes were accepted— there was no barter—and there was no higgling. For food at least there were standard prices: clothing is less homogeneous and the price was decided around a norm by the seller and the shop manager in agreement; shirts would average say 80, ranging from 60 to 120 according to quality and age. Of food, the shop carried small stocks for convenience; the capital was provided by a loan from the bulk store of Red Cross cigarettes and repaid by a small commission taken on the first transactions. Thus the cigarette attained its fullest currency status, and the market was almost completely unified.

The Cigarette Currency

Although cigarettes as currency exhibited certain peculiarities, they performed all the functions of a metallic currency as a unit of account, as a measure of value and as a store of value, and shared most of its characteristics. They were homogeneous, reasonably durable, and of convenient size for the smallest or, in packets, for the largest transactions. Incidentally, they could be clipped or sweated by rolling them between the fingers so that tobacco fell out.

Cigarettes were also subject to the working of Gresham's Law. Certain brands were more popular than others as smokes, but for currency purposes a cigarette was a cigarette. Consequently buyers used the poorer qualities and the Shop rarely saw the more popular brands: cigarettes such as Churchman's No. I were rarely used for trading. At one time cigarettes hand-rolled from pipe tobacco began to circulate. Pipe tobacco was issued in lieu of cigarettes by the Red Cross at a rate of twenty-five cigarettes to the ounce and this rate was standard in exchanges, but an ounce

would produce thirty homemade cigarettes. Naturally, people with machine-made cigarettes broke them down and rerolled the tobacco, and the real cigarette virtually disappeared from the market. Hand-rolled cigarettes were not homogeneous and prices could no longer be quoted in them with safety: each cigarette was examined before it was accepted and thin ones were rejected, or extra demanded as a make-weight. For a time we suffered all the inconveniences of a debased currency.

Machine-made cigarettes were always universally acceptable, both for what they would buy and for themselves. It was this intrinsic value which gave rise to their principal disadvantage as currency, a disadvantage which exists, but to a far smaller extent, in the case of metallic currency—that is, a strong demand for nonmonetary purposes. Consequently our economy was repeatedly subject to deflation and to periods of monetary stringency. While the Red Cross issue of fifty or twenty-five cigarettes per man per week came in regularly, and while there were fair stocks held, the cigarette currency suited its purpose admirably. But when the issue was interrupted, stocks soon ran out, prices fell, trading declined in volume and became increasingly a matter of barter. This deflationary tendency was periodically offset by the sudden injection of new currency. Private cigarette parcels arrived in a trickle throughout the year, but the big numbers came in quarterly when the Red Cross received its allocation of transport. Several hundred thousand cigarettes might arrive in the space of a fortnight. Prices soared, and then began to fall, slowly at first but with increasing rapidity as stocks ran out, until the next big delivery. Most of our economic troubles could be attributed to this fundamental instability.

Price Movements

Many factors affected prices, the strongest and most noticeable being the periodical currency inflation and deflation described in the last paragraphs. The periodicity of this price cycle depended on cigarette and, to a far lesser extent, on food deliveries. At one time in the early days, before any private parcels had arrived and when there were no individual stocks, the weekly issue of cigarettes and food parcels occurred on a Monday. The nonmonetary demand for cigarettes was great, and less elastic than the demand for food: consequently prices fluctuated weekly, falling towards

Sunday night and rising sharply on Monday morning. Later, when many people held reserves, the weekly issue had no such effect, being too small a proportion of the total available. Credit allowed people with no reserves to meet their nonmonetary demand over the weekend.

The general price level was affected by other factors. An influx of new prisoners, proverbially hungry, raised it. Heavy air raids in the vicinity of the camp probably increased the nonmonetary demand for cigarettes and accentuated deflation. Good and bad war news certainly had its effect, and the general waves of optimism and pessimism which swept the camp were reflected in prices. Before breakfast one morning in March of this year, a rumour of the arrival of parcels and cigarettes was circulated. Within ten minutes I sold a treacle ration for four cigarettes (hitherto offered in vain for three), and many similar deals went through. By 10 o'clock the rumour was denied, and treacle that day found no more buyers even at two cigarettes.

More interesting than changes in the general price level were changes in the price structure. Changes in the supply of a commodity, in the German ration scale or in the makeup of Red Cross parcels, would raise the price of one commodity relative to others. Tins of oatmeal, once a rare and much sought after luxury in the parcels, became a commonplace in 1943, and the price fell. In hot weather the demand for cocoa fell, and that for soap rose. A new recipe would be reflected in the price level: the discovery that raisins and sugar could be turned into an alcoholic liquor of remarkable potency reacted permanently on the dried fruit market. The invention of electric immersion heaters run off the power points made tea, a drug on the market in Italy, a certain seller in Germany.

In August, 1944, the supplies of parcels and cigarettes were both halved. Since both sides of the equation were changed in the same degree, changes in prices were not anticipated. But this was not the case: the nonmonetary demand for cigarettes was less elastic than the demand for food, and food prices fell a little. More important however were the changes in the price structure. German margarine and jam, hitherto valueless owing to adequate supplies of Canadian butter and marmalade, acquired a new value. Chocolate, popular and a certain seller, and sugar, fell. Bread rose, several standing contracts of bread for cigarettes were broken, especially when the bread ration was reduced a few weeks later.

In February, 1945, the German soldier who drove the ration wagon was found to be willing to exchange loaves of bread at the rate of one loaf for a bar of chocolate. Those in the know began selling bread and buying chocolate, by then almost unsaleable in a period of serious deflation. Bread, at about forty, fell slightly; chocolate rose from fifteen; the supply of bread was not enough for the two commodities to reach parity, but the tendency was unmistakable.

The substitution of German margarine for Canadian butter when parcels were halved naturally affected their relative values, margarine appreciating at the expense of butter. Similarly, two brands of dried milk, hitherto differing in quality and therefore in price by five cigarettes a tin, came together in price as the wider substitution of the cheaper raised its relative value.

Public opinion on the subject of trading was vocal if confused and changeable, and generalisations as to its direction are difficult and dangerous. A tiny minority held that all trading was undesirable as it engendered an unsavoury atmosphere; occasional frauds and sharp practices were cited as proof. Certain forms of trading were more generally condemned; trade with the Germans was criticised by many. Red Cross toilet articles, which were in short supply and only issued in cases of actual need, were excluded from trade by law and opinion working in unshakable harmony. At one time, when there had been several cases of malnutrition reported among the more devoted smokers, no trade in German rations was permitted, as the victims became an additional burden on the depleted food reserves of the hospital. But while certain activities were condemned as antisocial, trade itself was practiced, and its utility appreciated, by almost everyone in the camp.

More interesting was opinion on middlemen and prices. Taken as a whole, opinion was hostile to the middleman. His function, and his hard work in bringing buyer and seller together, were ignored; profits were not regarded as a reward for labour, but as the result of sharp practices. Despite the fact that his very existence was proof to the contrary, the middleman was held to be redundant in view of the existence of an official Shop and the Exchange and Mart. Appreciation only came his way when he was willing to advance the price of a sugar ration, or to buy goods spot and carry them against a future sale. In these cases the element of risk was obvious to all, and the convenience of the service was felt to merit some reward. Particularly unpopular was the middleman with an element of monopoly, the man who contacted the ration wagon driver, or the man who utilised his knowledge of Urdu. And middlemen as a group were blamed for reducing prices. Opinion notwithstanding, most people dealt with a middleman, whether consciously or unconsciously, at some time or another.

There was a strong feeling that everything had its "just price" in cigarettes. While the assessment of the just price, which incidentally varied between camps, was impossible of explanation, this price was nevertheless pretty closely known. It can best be defined as the price usually fetched by an article in good times when cigarettes were plentiful. The "just price" changed slowly; it was unaffected by short-term variations in supply, and while opinion might be resigned to departures from the "just price," a strong feeling of resentment persisted. A more satisfactory definition of the "just price" is impossible. Everyone knew what it was, though no one could explain why it should be so.

As soon as prices began to fall with a cigarette shortage, a clamor arose, particularly against those who held reserves and who bought at reduced prices. Sellers at cut prices were criticised and their activities referred to as the black market. In every period of dearth the explosive question of "should nonsmokers receive a cigarette ration?" was discussed to profitless length. Unfortunately, it was the nonsmoker, or the light smoker with his reserves, along with the hated middleman, who weathered the storm most easily.

The popularity of the price-fixing scheme, and such success as it enjoyed, were undoubtedly the result of this body of opinion. On several occasions the fall of prices was delayed by the general support given to the recommended scale. The onset of deflation was marked by a period of sluggish trade; prices stayed up but no one bought. Then prices fell on the black market, and the volume of trade revived in that quarter. Even when the recommended scale was revised, the volume of trade in the Shop would remain low. Opinion was always overruled by the hard facts of the market.

Curious arguments were advanced to justify price fixing. The recommended prices were in some way related to the calorific values of the foods offered: hence some were overvalued and never sold at these prices. One argument ran as follows: not everyone has private cigarette parcels—thus, when prices were high and trade good in the summer of 1944, only the lucky rich could buy. This was unfair to the man with few cigarettes. When prices fell in the following winter, prices should be pegged high so that the rich, who had enjoyed life in the summer, should put many cigarettes circulation. The fact that those who sold to the rich in the summer had also enjoyed life then, and the fact that in the winter there was always someone willing to sell at low prices were ignored. Such arguments were hotly debated each night after the approach of Allied aircraft extinguished all lights at 8 P.M. But prices moved with the supply of cigarettes, and refused to stay fixed in accordance with a theory of ethics.

4

The Invisible
Hand of Free Enterprise

ADAM SMITH

Adam Smith, one of the giants of economics, was Professor of Moral Philosophy at the University of Glasgow. This piece comes from his great work The Wealth of Nations, *published in 1776.*

Every individual who employs his capital in the support of domestic industry, necessarily endeavours so to direct that industry, that its produce may be of the greatest possible value.

The produce of industry is what it adds to the subject or materials upon which it is employed. In proportion as the value of this produce is great or small, so will likewise be the profits of the employer. But it is only for the sake of profit that any man employs a capital in the support of industry, and he will always, therefore, endeavour to employ it in the support of that industry of which the produce is likely to be of the greatest value, or to exchange for the greatest quantity either of money or of other goods.

But the annual revenue of every society is always precisely equal to the exchangeable value of the whole annual produce of its industry, or rather is precisely the same thing with that exchangeable value. As every individual, therefore, endeavours as much as he can both to employ his capital in the support of domestic industry, and so to direct that industry that its produce may be of the greatest value, every individual necessarily labours to render the annual revenue of the society as great as he can. He generally, indeed, neither intends to promote the public interest, nor knows how much he is promoting it. By preferring the support of domestic to that of foreign industry, he intends only his own security; and by directing that industry in such a manner as its produce may be of the greatest value, he intends only his own gain, and he is in this, as in many other cases, led by an invisible hand to promote an end which was no part of his intention. Nor is it always the worse for the society that it was no part of it. By pursuing his own interest he frequently promotes that of the society more effectually than when he really intends to promote it. I have never known much good done by those who affected to trade for the public good. It is an affectation, indeed, not very common among merchants, and very few words need be employed in dissuading them from it.

What is the species of domestic industry which his capital can employ, and of which the produce is likely to be of the greatest value, every individual, it is evident, can, in this local situation, judge much better than any statesman or lawgiver can do for him. The statesman, who should attempt to direct private people in what manner they ought to employ their capitals, would not only load himself with a most unnecessary attention, but assume an authority which could safely be trusted to no single person, to no council or senate whatever, and would nowhere be so dangerous as in the hands of a man who had folly and presumption enough to fancy himself fit to exercise it.

To give the monopoly of the home market to the produce of domestic industry, in any particular art or manufacture, is in some measure to direct private people in what manner they ought to employ their capitals, and must, in almost all cases, be either a useless or a hurtful regulation. If the produce of domestic can be brought there as cheap as that of foreign industry, the regulation is evidently useless. If it cannot, it must generally be hurtful. It is the maxim of every prudent master of a family, never to attempt to make at home what it will cost him more to make than to buy. The tailor does not attempt to make his own shoes, but buys them of the shoemaker. The shoemaker does not attempt to make his own clothes, but employs a tailor. The farmer attempts to make neither the one nor the other, but employs those different artificers. All of them find it for their interest to employ their whole industry in a way in which they have some advantage over their neighbours, and to purchase with a part of its produce, or with the price of a part of it, whatever else they have occasion for.

What is prudence in the conduct of every private family, can scarce be folly in that of a great kingdom.

If a foreign country can supply us with a commodity cheaper than we ourselves can make it, better buy it of them with some part of the produce of our own industry, employed in a way in which we have some advantage. The general industry of the country, being always in proportion to the capital which employs it, will not thereby be diminished, no more than that of the above-mentioned artificers; but only left to find out the way in which it can be employed with the greatest advantage. It is certainly not employed with the greatest advantage when it is thus directed towards an object which it can buy cheaper than it can make. The value of its annual produce is certainly more or less diminished, when it is thus turned away from producing commodities evidently of more value than the commodity which it is directed to produce. According to the supposition, that commodity could be purchased from foreign countries cheaper than it can be made at home. It could, therefore, have been purchased with a part only of the commodities, or, what is the same thing, with a part only of the price of the commodities, which the industry employed by an equal capital would have produced at home, had it been left to follow its natural course. The industry of the country, therefore, is thus turned away from a more, to a less advantageous employment, and the exchangeable value of its annual produce, instead of being increased, according to the intention of the lawgiver, must necessarily be diminished by every such regulation.

5

Capitalism: An Irrational System

PAUL BARAN and PAUL SWEEZY

Paul Baran and Paul Sweezy are two of America's best-known Marxist economists. This piece is taken from their book, Monopoly Capital, *published in 1966.*

Adam Smith saw in the division of labor the key to the wealth of nations, and he was of course right. Many before and after him saw a darker side, and they were right too. In Marx's words, "the division of labor seizes upon not only the economic but every other sphere of society and everywhere lays the foundation of that all-engrossing system of specializing and sorting men, that development in a man of one single faculty at the expense of all other faculties, which caused A. Ferguson, the master of Adam Smith, to exclaim: 'We make a nation of helots, and have no free citizens.'"

The great social critics of the nineteenth century, from Owen and Fourier through Marx and Engels, were all moved by a sense of outrage at this profoundly dehumanizing effect of the capitalist division of labor. And much as their visions of the good society differed, they all had one thing in common: conditions must be created to foster the development of whole human beings, "free citizens," in possession of all their faculties and capable of realizing their full potentialities. Some thought in romantic terms, of a return to a supposedly lost Golden Age. Others, of whom Marx and Engels were by far the most influential, saw the

solution in the maximum development through scientific and technological advance of the productivity of human labor. As Marx expressed it in a well known passage in the *Critique of the Gotha Program,* it would be only

> when the enslaving subordination of the individual to the division of labor, and with it the antithesis between mental and physical labor, has vanished; when labor is no longer merely a means of life but has become life's principal need; when the productive forces have also increased with the all-round development of the individual, and all the springs of cooperative wealth flow more abundantly—only then will it be possible completely to transcend the narrow outlook of bourgeois right and only then will society be able to inscribe on its banners: From each according to his ability, to each according to his needs!

Marx thought that such a high degree of labor productivity could be realized only in a "higher stage of communist society." We can now see that this was an illusion, that from the point of view of raising the productivity of labor, capitalism had a much greater potential than Marx, or for that matter contemporary bourgeois social scientists, imagined. The giant

19

corporation has proved to be an unprecedentedly effective instrument for promoting science and technology and for harnessing them to the production of goods and services. In the United States today the means already exist for overcoming poverty, for supplying everyone with the necessities and conveniences of life, for giving to all a genuinely rounded education and the free time to develop their faculties to the full—in a word for escaping from that all-engrossing system of specializing and sorting men of which Marx wrote.

In fact, of course, nothing of the sort has happened. Men are still being specialized and sorted, imprisoned in the narrow cells prepared for them by the division of labor, their faculties stunted and their minds diminished. And a threat to their security and peace of mind which already loomed large in Marx's day has grown in direct proportion to the spreading incidence and accelerated speed of technological change under monopoly capitalism.

> Modern industry never looks upon or treats the existing form of a production process as final. The technical basis of industry is therefore revolutionary, while all earlier modes of production were essentially conservative. By means of machinery, chemical processes, and other methods, it leads to continual changes not only in the technical basis of production, but also in the function of the laborer, and in the social combinations of the labor-process. At the same time, therefore, it revolutionizes the division of labor within the society, and incessantly transfers masses of capital and of work-people from one branch of production to another. Large-scale industry by its very nature therefore necessitates changes in work, variability of function, universal mobility of the laborer; on the other hand, in its capitalistic form, it reproduces the old division of labor with its ossified particularities. We have seen how this insurmountable contradiction robs the worker's situation of all peace, permanence, and security; how it constantly threatens, by taking away the instruments of labor, to snatch from his hands his means of subsistence, and, by suppressing his particular subdivided task, to make him superfluous. We have seen, too, how this contradiction works itself out through incessant sacrifices by the working class, the most reckless squandering of labor power, and the devastations caused by social anarchy.

To bring this statement up to date one need only add that the scale of industry has grown incomparably bigger during the past century, that with the advent of automation and cybernation its technical basis has become far more revolutionary, and that the suppression of particular subdivided tasks has never taken place in so many areas of industry and with such startling speed. If it were not for the expansion of jobs in the so-called service sector of the economy (including government), the plight of the worker who must sell his labor power in order to earn his livelihood would indeed be desperate.

While the growth of the service sector has partially compensated for the job-destroying effects of modern technology, it and related developments have added a new dimension to the dehumanization of the labor process under capitalism. There is no need to repeat here what has been so much emphasized in earlier chapters, that a large and growing part of the product of monopoly capitalist society is, judged by genuine human needs, useless, wasteful, or positively destructive. The clearest illustration is the tens of billions of dollars worth of goods and services which are swallowed up every year by a military machine the only purpose of which is to keep the people of the world from solving their problems in the only way they can be solved, through revolutionary socialism. But it is not only those who man and supply the military machine who are engaged in an anti-human enterprise. The same can be said in varying degrees of many millions of other workers who produce, and create wants for, goods and services which no one needs. And so interdependent are the various sectors and branches of the economy that nearly everyone is involved in one way or another in these antihuman activities: the farmer supplying food to troops fighting against the people of Vietnam, the tool and die makers turning out the intricate machinery needed for a new automobile model, the manufacturers of paper and ink and TV sets whose products are used to control and poison the minds of the people, and so on and on and on.

"There is," Paul Goodman writes, "'nearly full employment' (with highly significant exceptions), but there get to be fewer jobs that are necessary and unquestionably useful; that require energy and draw on some of one's best capacities; and that can be done keeping one's honor and dignity." Goodman is certainly right to stress that his "simple objective fact" is important in explaining the troubles of young people in this society. But it is more than that: it is important in explaining the alienation from work, the cynicism, the corruption which permeate every nook and cranny of monopoly capitalism and which anyone with a sense of history cannot fail to recognize as characteristic features of a society in full decline.

6

The Future of Capitalism

ROBERT L. HEILBRONER

Robert L. Heilbroner is Norman Thomas Professor of Economics at the New School for Social Research. This article is taken from his book, Business Civilization in Decline, *published by W. W. Norton in 1976.*

Capitalism is drifting into planning. Is there anyone who would deny the fact? The problem is to interpret it, to place the drift in the perspective of a larger historic movement. It will be my major thesis that the political apparatus within capitalism is steadily growing, enhancing its power, and usurping functions formerly delegated to the economic sphere—not to undo, but to preserve that sphere. In the end, I think this same political expansion will be a major factor in the extinction of the business civilization.

Let us begin, then, by considering the present. Everyone agrees that business has contracted its place within society over the last fifty years, crowded out by a growing government presence. Hence our first task is to gain some understanding of this basic shift. Does the enlargement of the political apparatus of the state in itself mean that business civilization is declining? Need we go no further than a recognition of this change to concede that capitalism is disappearing?

This central problem has been discussed many times. I would like to bring some freshness to the issue by considering the matter in an impressionistic, but I think not unrealistic way, from the points of view of two New Yorkers, both conveniently named Smith, one a conservative businessman, the other a professor of radical leanings.

Arising early one morning, Conservative Smith glances at the headlines, which feature the Government's latest incursions into the economy (whatever they may be), and groans: They are out to destroy the business system. As he reads the details of these Government rulings and forays, he is moved to reflect on the invasion of Government into every facet of private life. Even his breakfast is touched by its ubiquitous presence—the orange juice container, the wrapper on his loaf of bread, the tin that holds his coffee, all bear descriptive labels imposed by Government decree.

Indeed, as he goes about his day, it seems to Smith that it is impossible to escape from the presence of Government. The taxi he takes to Pennsylvania Station charges a fare set by Government. The train he boards for Washington (Government city) is owned and operated by the Government. Once in Washington, Smith learns that a proposed merger in which his company is interested will be forbidden by a Government ruling. Telephoning the news to New York at rates set by a Government agency, he decides to return immediately, boarding an aircraft whose route, maintenance, equipment, operating procedures, and fare have all been Government-determined. On the trip home Smith figures how much of his year-end bonus will go to the Government in taxes, ruefully calculating the rate at 50 percent: how can a man make any money, he asks, when he works as much for the Government as for himself?

Home again, he relaxes in his apartment, whose construction was partly subsidized by Government, and idly watches a Government-licensed television station dutifully complying with a Government regulation to devote a portion of its prime time to public-interest broadcasting. His son, who attends a Government-supported university, comes in to borrow the family's car, which has been designed to meet certain Government specifications. Before retiring, Smith looks over his mail, which includes a bill from the Government for the Social Security payments he must make for his maid. Switching off the lights, for which he has been paying at Government-established rates, he settles into his bed, from whose mattress dangles the Government-decreed tag ("Do not Remove Under Penalty of Law"), and as he finally dozes off, he asks himself: "Is this still capitalism? God, no!"

This is the sort of scenario that delights the guardians of economic conservatism. But consider it again, this time from the viewpoint of our other Smith, of radical political leanings.

Shaking his head over the paper at breakfast (once again the Government has acted as a front for business), Smith also observes the compulsory labels on his foods, but reflects on how little faith one can repose in them, given the sorry record of the Food and Drug Administration's responsiveness to industry pressure. Paying his cab fare downtown, Radical Smith muses that the taxi industry is controlled by a public agency more ready to boost fares than to increase the number of licensed cabs. Boarding the Amtrak train, he recalls that the railroad was taken over by Government only as a last resort to shore up a sagging industry. Arriving in Government city, he is struck by the ease with which business executives communicate their views to the Government and the difficulty with which the "working man" communicates his views: could this be, he wonders, why the tax laws so outrageously favor the rich and propertied, why a national health insurance plan is still lacking, why wage incomes suffer but dividends rise, despite the worst depression since 1929?

During his rounds, Smith hears of the failure of his namesake to pull off the merger he was seeking. Radical Smith is not much impressed, because he knows that Conservative Smith's experience was the exception rather than the rule. Largely because of mergers, the top 100 industrial corporations today own a larger percentage of total corporate assets than did the top 200 industrial firms only twenty years ago. So, too, Smith is not so impressed by the Government regulation of the plane on which he flies home as by the fact that regulation has largely been used to suppress competition: not a single new trunk line has been authorized since regulation began in 1938. Again, Radical Smith does not worry about Conservative Smith's tax burden, because he knows that the top 1 percent of taxpayers (with incomes of roughly $50,000 and up) pay an average of only 26 percent of their total incomes, including capital gains, to the Internal Revenue Services. He would point out as well that the expensive apartment house in which the other Smith lives was built with money provided for "low-cost" housing that somehow got diverted into high-cost housing; that the safety specifications on Smith's car are generally regarded as inadequate, thanks to industry protestations; that the Social Security payments going to the maid are insufficient to support her above the poverty level, whereas the electric light rates established by Government were intended to provide utility companies with profits of about 10 percent on sales. "Is this capitalism?" asks Radical Smith. "Of course. What else?"

Thus both Smiths would impatiently dismiss the question "Is this capitalism?" although each would answer it differently. Nevertheless, I think it is useful to pose the question in all seriousness. For I am inclined to think that neither the stereotyped conservative nor radical conceptions of capitalism shed enough light on the economic and political reality that surrounds us, much less on the destination toward which we may be headed.

Let me begin with the conservative's picture of capitalism. Like the radical's, it is founded on what we might call a minimal structural definition: capitalism is an economic system in which the means of production—factories, farms, mines, etc.—are owned by private individuals or firms, and in which the primary method of distributing incomes is the competition of the marketplace. We shall have an opportunity later to discuss how useful this minimal definition is. But also like the radical, the conservative sees more in capitalism than a bare institutional structure. He also sees capitalism as a larger social system, but a social system with a particular (although usually unacknowledged) characteristic. This is its essentially static nature. By this the conservative does not rule out change, above all the change of economic improvement. But the change affects economic magnitudes and not social relationships. Capitalism is thus conceived as a dynamic economic process contained in a basically fixed social setting, especially with regard to its class differences.

We shall return to this vision of a fundamentally fixed society. But one disturbing trend bedevils the conservative's static conception of capitalism. It is the trend we have already noticed—the steadily growing presence of Government. From decade to decade, government looms ever larger in the economic framework. No wonder, then, that the conservative pictures the intrusion of government as disruptive—even subversive—of the stable social milieu that capitalism implies to him.

Has the steady entry of government meant the subversion of capitalism? Let us try to answer the question by dividing the long history of government intervention into three distinct, although overlapping, periods. The first can be traced back to colonial America and probably reached its heyday in the early to middle decades of the nineteenth century. This is the period when government intruded into the economy as a direct stimulus for economic expansion itself. It is the era during which federal and state money made possible the network of early roads, canals, and railroads (not to mention public schools) that played an important role in imparting the momentum of growth to the formative system. To be sure, it is difficult to measure exactly the contribution made by government, but it seems indisputable that undertakings such as the Erie Canal, the transcontinental railroads, or later the Panama Canal, were at least as important for the expansion of capitalism in their time as the federal highway system, the airline network, or the armaments industry have been for the growth of the economy in more recent times. Need I add that these examples testify that the role of the government as a propulsive force for economic expansion has certainly not come to an end?

A second period of government's relation to capitalism began after the Civil War, vastly accelerated during the New Deal, and is perhaps peaking in our own time. This is the phase during which the main form of government intervention appears in the proliferation of agencies such as the Interstate Commerce Commission, the Federal Trade Commission, the Federal Reserve System, and the alphabet array that arose under Franklin Roosevelt to supervise the operation of agriculture, the securities industry, utilities, and the like.

What was the common element in this new insinuation of government power? I think most historians would agree that it was the regulation of markets. In one manner or another, the new agencies sought to bring order to markets in which the competitive process was threatening to bankrupt an industry (farming), or to undermine its reliability (banking), or to demoralize its operations (utilities). Indeed, one of the insights that radical historians have given us is the recognition of the role played by leading businessmen in actively promoting regulation in order to stave off the cut-throat competition and other evils they were unable to police by themselves. In 1911 Judge Elbert Gary, the arch-conservative head of the United States Steel Corporation, actually told a dumfounded Congressional Committee that "I believe we must come to enforced publicity and government control . . . even as to prices, and, so far as I am concerned . . . I would be very glad if we knew exactly where we stand . . . and if we had some place where we could go, to a responsible governmental authority, and to say to them, 'Here are our facts and figures . . . now you tell us what we have the right to do and what prices we have the right to charge.'"[1]

Whatever the responsibility of the business community in originating the legislation designed to control its own operations, there is little doubt that, once enacted, the regulatory laws were used to stabilize industrial operations. Here we can witness the long, solicitous history of ICC railroad rate-setting, or the aforementioned refusal of the CAB to license an additional competitive trunk line. This does not mean that businessmen have "liked" being regulated, or that regulation has not to some extent served the public as well as the private interest. But the history of regulation makes it difficult to contend that the power of government has been used to "destroy" any sector over which it was appointed to keep order. On the contrary, the evidence is overwhelming that regulation has been used mainly to protect the regulated sector against competition, from within or without, or to ameliorate abuses threatening to undermine it.

A third phase of government-business interaction opens with the New Deal and is still very much with us. This is the active use of central government's pow-

---

[1]Quoted in Gabriel Kolko, *The Triumph of Conservatism* (Glencoe, Ill.: The Free Press, 1963), p. 174.

ers to bring the economy to an acceptable level of employment, growth, and welfare.

Of all changes in business-government relations, this is probably the one most attended with feelings of "socialistic" betrayal on the part of conservatives. Indeed, in the late 1930s the Veritas Society was founded at Harvard University to expunge the teaching of Keynesian economics from the curriculum. I suspect that the Society is now defunct, for with the general embrace of Keynesian principles by the Republican Party there is no longer any respectable opposition to the use of the government's fiscal and monetary powers to counteract a deficiency in aggregate demand, or to bring individual incomes above some minimum poverty line. How conservative—how conserving of the business system—does not the New Deal look in retrospect!

But just as the dust has settled in this area of government intervention, it is stirred up in another, brought about by a condition that was quite unforeseen by Keynes—namely, the stubborn persistence of inflation despite the presence of a very high level of unemployment.

Many efforts have been made in various countries to control inflation—tightening the money supply, deliberately deflating the economy, applying wage and price controls, formulating a concerted "incomes policy." None has yet been successful. There seems to be a chronic and deep-seated pressure for rising prices built into the operations of contemporary capitalism—a pressure that resides ultimately in a changed balance of power between capital and labor, tilting the balance in favor of the latter.

Whatever the differences in the attempted cures for inflation, there is a marked common feature to the responses to the problem. *In one manner or another, public responsibility for the working of the system has been extended.* The economic aims of government have now been broadened to include the attainment of socially acceptable levels of price stability. Moreover, just because the various measures so far tried have not succeeded, I believe the reach of government intervention will be forced to expand still further, probably through controls that cover not only prices and wages, but also dividends and profits. If, as I shall contend, inflation is basically an endemic consequence of the operation of the economic mechanism, what possible remedy is there other than the assertion of a political will over the unwanted outcome of that mechanism?

This is a diagnosis that is today advanced by only a few economists and advocated by still fewer, John Kenneth Galbraith being a principal exception. But I believe the number of adherents for extended government intervention will grow if the underlying condition continues to be intractable to milder medicines, as has been the case to date in every capitalist nation. Moreover, despite the general distaste with which controls are viewed today, I presume it will not come as a surprise if I declare that their eventual imposition will be accepted as a measure needed to save, not to destroy, the business system.

Is the conservative wholly wrong, then, in his conception of capitalism? Clearly, I think he is indeed mistaken with regard to the "subversive" intent of government. Yet, oddly enough, I believe the conservative is right in his underlying picture of capitalism as a static social system. But it is not the institutional framework—and certainly not the business-state relationship—that is static. It is the social core of the system, its structure of privilege.

The most obvious and important form of this privilege is the continuous creation and allocation of a highly disproportionate share of income to two groups within capitalist society—those who own substantial quantities of property and those who man the command posts within the business world. Capitalism has always rewarded these strata generously. Going back to 1910, admittedly on the basis of somewhat shaky data, we find that the top 10 percent of income recipients, whose incomes were mainly derived from property and management, got just over one-third of the nation's total individual income. In recent years, the top 10 percent of family units received about 30 percent of all income. The change, if any, has been miniscule. Moreover, on the basis of much firmer data, it seems certain that the share of the top 10 percent has been unchanged since 1960.

Income statistics are deceptive, because changes in the tax laws cause high-income receivers to rearrange the manner in which they get income, exchanging outright compensation for capital gains, or causing large payments to be deferred into installments over future years. However, when examining more substantial data with respect to the ownership of wealth, we find that here too the irrefutable impression is one of stability rather than change. Estimates based on studies by Robert Lampman and others indicate that the share of private wealth held by the top 2 percent of all families declined from 33 percent in 1922 to 25 percent in 1949, but thereafter rose again to 32 percent in 1958. There is no evidence that the concentration of wealth has diminished since then.

The point of these well-known statistics is obvious. Despite fifty years of increased government intervention, supposedly "confiscatory" taxation, welfare statism, and the rest, nothing like a dramatic change has marked the distribution of income or wealth within American capitalism. This in no way denies that the system has generated a steadily rising standard of living for most of the population. But there remains a vast gulf between the quality of life of the "middle" classes—the 15 million-odd American families that enjoy, in the mid-1970s, incomes of more than about $10,000 but less than about $15,000—and the very small group of Americans—perhaps some 200,000 families in all—who enjoy an annual income of $100,000 or more. It is this stratum of privilege that capitalism protects, and whose persistence confirms, albeit from an unexpected angle, the conservative's view of capitalism as a system that grows but that does not fundamentally change.

Not surprisingly, the radical sees things from a diametrically opposite vantage point. Like the conservative, the radical also fastens on the pillars of private property and the market as the critical and distinctive institutions of capitalism. But unlike the conservative, who sees in these institutions the foundation for a static social system, the radical sees in them the source of a pervasive and ultimately irresistible dynamics.

In fact, to the radical the most striking attribute of capitalism is precisely its inherent tendency for revolutionary change, brought about by the irrepressible contradictions of its economic processes. The very problems that we have noted as generative of government intervention—the need to support and advance economic growth, the need to control markets, the need to assure a minimum of social provisioning, the need to repress inflation—appear to the radical as the outcome of the peculiar economic institutions and mechanisms of capitalism, and the intervention of government therefore appears to him to be part of the inherent self-preservative reaction of a system threatened with self-destruction.

I think the radical is essentially correct in this diagnosis. Nonetheless, I find a weakness in the radical view. It is a tendency to assume a subservience of the political apparatus to the economic interests of the system—a subservience that ultimately defines too narrowly the independent power of government or the independent shaping influence of social institutions.

As I have put it elsewhere, the radical view sees the economy as the engine and the government as the caboose in the evolution of capitalism—indeed, perhaps of all socio-economic systems. I believe the process is more accurately likened to a train in which there are two engines, one economic, one political, capable of pulling in different directions as well as coordinating their efforts.

Only such a conception, I think, can help us understand the extraordinary variety of institutions that we find when we survey the spectrum of countries with private property and market bases. How else are we to account for the differences between Japan, where the large corporations guarantee lifetime employment to their workers and where it is difficult to distinguish, at the apex, government from business, and the United States, where the indignities of unemployment are considered no part of a corporation's responsibilities and where government and business intermingle but preserve their respective identities? How shall we explain the severe taxation of upper-income groups in Norway with the easy enforcement of tax laws in Italy? How shall we understand the difference between Sweden, where the public sector, as such, is very small but the degree of public control over the economy is considerable, and France, where the public sector is formidable but its effectiveness small?

All these nations have economic structures that rest on private property and economic systems that depend on market forces. All display similar tendencies of instability, inflation, business concentration, and the like. But from nation to nation the degree and manner of public correction of these problems varies, largely as a consequence of differing capacities to create and maintain strong and effective political authorities willing to set themselves "against" as well as side by side with the business community.

This is a problem to which we shall return in due course. Here I wish to do no more than emphasize the existence of a political sphere whose composition, coherence, and will vary enormously from one capitalism to the next. The political engine in some capitalist economies is extremely powerful. In others it is weak. The defeiency of the radical view of capitalism lies in its failure to explain—or even to consider—this problem. The world of politics and power remains unexamined in the radical perspective, or worse, assumes the character of a passive accompaniment to changes in the economic structure. The tacit assumption is therefore that there can be no exercise of political power for ends that lie beyond those of the maintenance of privilege. The possibility that the very preservation of society may require changes that will profoundly alter the social relationships of capitalism or the still more heretical possibility that government may "detach" itself from the economic base and assert control for the ultimate purpose of preserving a system of political power are not part of the radical scheme of things. Yet it is precisely such tendencies that I think underlie the long-term evolution of the system, in ways that we shall examine in the chapters to come.

But [here] we are considering only the immediate future—the next ten years or so of capitalist history. Is it possible to venture a general prognosis for this period? From what I have written, it should follow that the relationship between business and state will be affected primarily by the nature and severity of the difficulties generated by the economic workings of the system. And here I think we can discern three kinds of difficulties, present in varying degrees in all capitalist economies:

1. *There is the continued propensity of capitalism to develop generalized disorders that require government intervention.* Inflation is only the latest of these "macro" problems. Depression persists as a dangerous social malady. At the very least, these ills require a continuation of the existing levels of public intervention. If, as I shall maintain, inflation is deeply rooted in the economic system, or if the deflationary "cure" for inflation becomes worse than the disease, then we can expect further intervention along the lines I have indicated.

2. *There is a tendency to develop serious localized disorders.* The near-breakdown of the mass transportation system in the United States, the near-collapse of the financial structure in Europe and the United States in the early 1970s, the near-insolvency of many cities at home and abroad, are all instances of recent "micro" failures within the economy. They have brought increasing government involvement in the rescue of the affected areas, for it is evident that railroads, large banks, or vital cities cannot go bankrupt without creating a vast wreckage. This is a consequence of an ever more tightly knit economic mechanism. I therefore suspect that the trend toward government ownership of unprofitable private activities, and responsibility for failing local public activities, will increase further in the future.

3. *There are the dangers imposed by a constricting environment.* During the past few years, we have become aware of the possibility of overrunning our resource base before technological remedies can be found. There is also a growing unease over the damage that unconstrained industrial expansion works on the life-carrying capabilities of the planet. These new elements add an imperious force for the monitoring, direction, and, if needed, forceful suppression of economic activity. Much has been written about these environmental challenges, and I shall refer to them many times. I shall therefore say no more at this stage than to point to their obvious implications with respect to the extension of the government's role within the economic system.

Thus the general prognosis for the immediate future seems very clear. The next phase of capitalism must be an increasingly planned system, and the drift of business society will be toward a business-government state.

7

The Government of the Economy

George J. Stigler is Walgreen Professor of American Institutions at the University of Chicago. This article, together with the following one by Paul Samuelson, was published by the Graduate School of Business of the University of Chicago in 1963.

No doubt this is the best of all possible worlds, for the time being. But even in the best of possible worlds, a good many things happen that displease us. Without exception we are shocked when a tranquilizer is sold, and its use by pregnant women leads to tragic deformities in babies. We are all distressed when there is extensive unemployment and personal suffering. Most of us are displeased when a strike closes down a railroad or a port or the airlines. Some of us are deeply annoyed when the price of soybeans falls. A few of us are outraged when an increase is announced in the price of steel, but this particular few is not unimportant. And I, if no one else, am incensed with an industry that bribes assistant professors to be learned on TV quiz shows. Some of us full professors could have memorized the answers, and anyway it should be necessary to bribe a professor only to be stupid.

There was an age when social dissatisfaction was kept in the house. All evils were ancient evils, and therefore necessary evils which served at least to keep men humble and patient. This resignation to imperfection has almost vanished in modern times—the

hereafter in which all problems are solved has been moved up to two months after the next election. And government has become the leading figure in almost every economic reform. I propose to discuss what governments can do in economic life, and what they should do.

The question of what governments can do, what they are capable of doing, will strike many Americans, and for that matter most non-Americans, as an easy one. For it is a belief, now widely held and strongly held, that the government can, if it really puts its mind and heart to a task, do anything that is not palpably impossible. The government, we shall all admit, cannot really turn the number π into a simple fraction by legislative mandate, nor can a joint resolution of the houses of Congress confer immortality. But with a will, the government can see to it that fully 85 per cent of the male population, and a few women, are taught several infinite series for calculating π, and with a will, the government can prolong human life appreciably by suitable medical and social insurance programs.

An Article of Faith

This acceptance of the omnipotence of the state does not represent a generalization of experience; it is not a product of demonstrated effectiveness in bending events to the wise or foolish designs of policy. On the contrary, the belief is an article of faith, indeed an article of almost desperate faith. It is not an intrinsically absurd belief; there is no rigorous logical demonstration that the state cannot turn sows' ears into silken purses. There is also no logical demonstration that all men cannot become saints, but the number of saintly men has not yet risen to the level where the census makes it a separate statistical category.

Our faith in the power of the state is a matter of desire rather than demonstration. When the state undertakes to achieve a goal, and fails, we cannot bring ourselves to abandon the goal, nor do we seek alternative means of achieving it, for who is more powerful than a sovereign state? We demand, then, increased efforts of the state, tacitly assuming that where there is a will, there is a governmental way.

Yet we know very well that the sovereign state is not omnipotent. The inability of the state to perform certain economic tasks could be documented from some notorious failures. Our cotton program, for example, was intended to enrich poor cotton farmers, increase the efficiency of production, foster foreign markets, and stabilize domestic consumption. It is an open question whether twenty-eight years of our farm program have done as much for poor cotton farmers as the trucking industry. Again, the Federal Trade Commission is the official guardian of business morals, including advertising morals. I am reasonably confident that more would have been achieved if one of the F.T.C.'s forty-eight years of appropriations had been devoted to a prize for the best exposé of sharp practices.

That there should be failures of governmental policy is not surprising, nor will the failures lead us to a blanket condemnation of governmental activity in economic life. Invariable success, after all, is found in only a few places—one, by the way, being the recapitulation of the previous year by college presidents. What is surprising is how little we know about the degree of success or failure of almost all governmental intervention in economic life. And when I say how little we know, I expressly include the people whose business it should be to measure the achievements, the professional economists.

When we have made studies of governmental controls that are sufficiently varied in scope and penetrating in detail, we may be able to construct a set of fairly useful generalizations about what the state can do. But society will not wait upon negligent scholars before meeting what seem to be pressing issues. The remainder of my article cannot wait either, so I am driven to present what I consider plausible rules concerning feasible economic controls.

There is a great danger, as you well know, that the lessons one draws from experience will be those which one seeks. From 1940 to 1942 I worked for an agency that eventually became the Office of Price Administration. I ask you to be forgiving; I was young, and at least I was eventually eased out for opposing price controls.

What economic tasks can a state perform? I propose a set of rules which bear on the answer to the question, but I shall not attempt a full argument in support of them—it must suffice to give an illustrative case, a plausible argument. It must suffice partly because full proofs have not been accumulated, but partly also because I wish to have time to discuss what the state should do, which is considerably less than what it can do.

RULE 1: *The state cannot do anything quickly.*

It would be unseemly to document at length the glacial pace of a bureaucracy in double step. Suffice it to say that if tomorrow a warehouse full of provisions labelled *"For General Custer: Top Priority"* were found, no one would have to be told whether the warehouse was publicly or privately owned. That warehouse is still lost, but consider this report on the Federal Trade Commission by the Select Committee on Small Business of the House of Representatives:

From a large number of individual cases studied, one has been selected to indicate the tortuous movement of a case through the complicated mechanism of the Commission. The *Florida Citrus* case (Docket 5640), although in other respects reasonably typical, was chosen for three specific reasons: (1) It is one in which prompt action was highly desirable; (2) it involved no novel questions of law; and (3) it required no lengthy hearings before trial examiners, as all allegations of fact were admitted by the respondent. The chronology in this case in brief is as follows:

Apr. 23, 1946	*Docketing of the application for complaint.*
Sept. 30, 1947	*Recommendation that complaint*

	be issued upon completion of investigation.
Jan. 23, 1948	*Approval of examiner's recommendation by chief examiner.*
Feb. 3, 1948	*Consideration by Commission and assignment to Commissioner for preliminary review.*
Oct. 13, 1948	*Recommendation of Commissioner that case be referred to Bureau of Litigation.*
Oct. 29, 1948	*Request to Department of Justice for certain information.*
Do	*Assignment to trial attorneys for review and recommendation.*
Dec. 15, 1948	*Report of trial attorney submitting draft of complaint.*
Dec. 21, 1948	*Memorandum to Commission by Chief of Division of Antimonopoly Trials that complaint be issued.*
Dec. 27, 1948	*Referral to Commissioner.*
Feb. 11, 1949	*Recommendation by Commissioner that complaint be issued.*
Feb. 18, 1949	*Complaint issued. Beginning of formal action.*
Apr. 11, 1949	*Filing of answer by respondents admitting allegations of fact.*
Sept. 8, 1949	*Granting of respondent's request for leave to file substitute answer.*
Oct. 10, 1949	*Filing of respondent's brief on questions of law.*
Oct. 18, 1949	*Filing of reply brief.*
Dec. 30, 1949	*Assignment to Commissioner.*
Jan. 10, 1950	*Reassignment to another Commissioner.*
June 30, 1950	*Recommendation of Commissioner that matter be referred to Bureau of Industry Cooperation. So ordered by Commission.*

So passed fifty months; I must in candor add that twenty-five months later an order was issued. A decent respect for due process lies behind some of the procedural delays, and poses a basic issue of the conflicting demands of justice and efficiency in economic regulation. But deliberation is intrinsic to large organizations: not only does absolute power corrupt absolutely; it delays fantastically. I would also note that initiative is the least prized of a civil servant's virtues, because the political process allots much greater penalties for failure than rewards for success.

Size vs. Control

RULE 2: When the national state performs detailed economic tasks, the responsible political authorities cannot possibly control the manner in which they are performed, whether directly by governmental agencies or indirectly by regulation of private enterprise.

The lack of control is due to the impossibility of the central authority either to know or to alter the details of a large enterprise. An organization of any size—and I measure size in terms of personnel—cannot prescribe conduct in sufficient detail to control effectively its routine operations: it is instructive that when the New York City subway workers wish to paralyze their transportation system, they can do so as effectively by following all the operating instructions in literal detail as by striking.

Large organizations seek to overcome the frustrating problems of communication and command by seeking and training able executives, who could be described more accurately as able subordinates. But to get a good man and to give him the control over and responsibility for a set of activities is of course another way of saying that it is impossible for the central authorities to control the activities themselves. As the organization grows, the able subordinate must get able subordinates, who in turn must get able subordinates, who in turn must get able subordinates, who in turn—well, by the time the organization is the size of the federal government, the demands for ability begin to outstrip the supply of even mediocre genes.

I estimate, in fact, that the federal government is at least 120 times as large as any organization can be and still keep some control over its general operations. It is simply absurd to believe that Congress could control the economic operations of the federal government; at most it can sample and scream. Since size is at the bottom of this rule, two corollaries are:

1. *Political control over governmental activity is diminishing.*
2. *The control exercised by a small city is much greater than the control exercised over General Motors by its Board of Directors.*

Uniformity of Treatment

RULE 3: The democratic state strives to treat all citizens in the same manner; individual differences are ignored if remotely possible.

The striving for uniformity is partly due to a desire for equality of treatment, but much more to a desire for administrative simplicity. Thus men with a salary of $100,000 must belong to the Social Security system; professors in New York must take a literacy test to vote; the new automobile and the 1933 Essex must be inspected; the most poorly coordinated driver and the most skillful driver must obey the same speed limits; the same minimum wage must be paid to workers of highly different productivities; the man who gives a vaccination for smallpox must have the same medical credentials as a brain surgeon; the three-week-old child must have the same whiskey import allowance as a grown Irishman; the same pension must be given to the pilot who flew 100 dangerous missions as to the pilot who tested a Pentagon swivel chair; the same procedure must be passed through to open a little bank in Podunk and the world's largest bank in New York; the same subsidy per bale of cotton must be given to the hillbilly with two acres and the river valley baron with 5,000 acres. We ought to call him Uncle Same.

RULE 4: The ideal public policy, from the viewpoint of the state, is one with identifiable beneficiaries, each of whom is helped appreciably, at the cost of many unidentifiable persons, none of whom is hurt much.

The preference for a well-defined set of beneficiaries has a solid basis in the desire for votes, but it extends well beyond this prosaic value. The political system is not trustful of abstract analysis, nor, for that matter, are most people. A benefit of $50 to each of one million persons will always seem more desirable than a $1 benefit to each of 150 million people, because one can see a $50 check, and hence be surer of its existence. In fact, it is worth mentioning one corollary of Rule 4: no politician will worry much about anything that can't be photographed. Another corollary is: if Texas wants it, give it.

The suspicion of abstract theory is of course well-founded: most abstract theories recorded in history have been false. Unfortunately it is also an abstract theory, and a silly one, that says one should believe only what he can see, and if the human race had adhered to it we would still be pushing carts with square wheels.

You do not need to be told that someone is always hurt by an economic policy, which is only a special case of the basic economic theorem that there is no such thing as a free lunch. On the other hand, I do not say that all political lunches are priced exorbitantly.

RULE 5: The state never knows when to quit.

One great invention of a private enterprise system is bankruptcy, an institution for putting an eventual stop to costly failure. No such institution has yet been conceived of in the political process, and an unsuccessful policy has no inherent termination. Indeed, political rewards are more closely proportioned to failure than to success, for failure demonstrates the need for larger appropriations and more power. This observation does not contradict my previous statement that a civil servant must avoid conspicuous failure at all costs, for his failure is an unwise act, not an ineffectual policy.

The two sources of this tenacity in failure are the belief that the government must be able to solve a social problem, and the absence of objective measures of failure and success. The absence of measures of failure is due much more to the lack of enterprise of economists than to the nature of things. One small instance is the crop forecasting service of the Department of Agriculture. This service began shortly after the Civil War, and it eventually involved thousands of reporters and a secrecy in preparation of forecasts that would thwart Central Intelligence. It was not until 1917 that a Columbia professor, Henry Moore, showed that the early season forecasts were almost as good as flipping a coin, and the later season forecasts were almost as good as running a regression equation on rainfall. But as I have remarked, most public policies simply have not been studies from this viewpoint.

Let me emphasize as strongly as I can that each of these characteristics of the political process is a source of strength in some activities, as well as a limitation in other activities. If the state could move rapidly, contrary to Rule 1, and readily accepted abstract notions, contrary to Rule 4, our society would become the victim of every fad in morals and every popular fallacy in philosophy. If the state could effectively govern the details of our lives, no tyranny would ever have been overthrown. If the state were to adapt all its rules to individual circumstances, contrary to Rule 3, we would live in a society of utter caprice and obnoxious favoritism. If the state knew when to quit, it would never have engaged in such unpromising ventures as the American Revolution, not that I personally consider this our best war. But what are virtues in the preservation of our society and its basic liberties are not necessarily virtues in fixing the wages of labor or the number of channels a television set can receive.

These rules, and others that could be added, do not say that the state cannot socialize the growing of wheat or regulate the washing of shirts. What the rules say is that political action is social action, that political action displays reasonably stable behavioral characteristics, and that prescriptions of political behavior which disregard these characteristics are simply irresponsible. To say, after describing a social economic problem, that the state must do something about it, is equivalent in rationality to calling for a dance to placate an angry spirit. In fact the advantage is with the Indians, who were sure to get some useful exercise. The state can do many things, and must do certain absolutely fundamental things, but it is not an Alladin's lamp.

State's Proper Economic Role

I turn now to our subject, the proper economic role for the state.

A tolerably adequate discussion of this subject would involve a fairly detailed statement of the major values of American society, either as we think they are or as we think they should be. In the course of such a statement we would have to decide on the comparative importances of national defense, personal freedom, benevolence and humanitarianism, egalitarianism, and other civilized values.

After completing this large task, probably to no one person's satisfaction, we should then have to take up each of the incredibly numerous economic activities now undertaken by the state or currently proposed to it, and examine this activity in the light of these basic social values, of the probable capacity of governments to perform tasks, and of the detailed economic effects of the policies. This may be a suitable syllabus for a four-year course, but borders on the ambitious as a program for the remainder of this hour.

I therefore propose merely to sketch what I believe is the proper treatment of certain classes of important economic problems. Even a much wiser man would have to court the charge of dogmatism by so cursory a

treatment, but at least a basis will be provided for our subsequent discussion.

Class 1: Monopoly

The fear of monopoly exploitation underlies a vast network of public regulation—the control over the so-called public utilities, including the transportation and communication industries and banking institutions, as well as traditional antitrust policies. The proper methods of dealing with monopoly, in their order of acceptability, are three:

1. The maintenance or restoration of competition by the suitable merger prevention policies, which we now fail to use in areas such as rail and air transport, and by the dissolution of monopolies. The method of once-for-all intervention provides the only really effective way of dealing with monopoly.

It will be said that for technological reasons even a modest amount of competition is unattainable in many areas. I believe these areas are very few in number. Even when a community can have only one electric company, that company is severely limited by the long-run alternatives provided by other communities.

2. Where substantial competition cannot be achieved—and I do not ask for perfect competition—the entry into the field is often controlled by the state—for example the TV channels are allocated by the FCC. Here auctioning off the channels seems the only feasible method of capturing the inherent monopoly gains. The history of regulation gives no promise that such gains can be eliminated.

3. In the few remaining cases in which monopoly cannot be eliminated or sold to the monopolist, monopolies should be left alone, simply because there is no known method of effective control.

Class 2: Poverty

A community does not wish to have members living in poverty, whatever the causes of the poverty may be. The maximum level of socially tolerable poverty will vary with the society's wealth, so poor societies will stop short at preventing plain starvation, but Texans will demand, through the oil embargoes that Presidents Eisenhower and Kennedy found expedient to accept, also Cadillacs and psychiatrists in their minimum poverty budget. I consider treatment of poverty a highly proper function of the state, but would propose that it be dealt with according to two principles:

1. Direct aid should take the form of direct grants of money, and only this form. The present methods involve an unending chain of *ad hoc* grants in kinds: some subsidized housing, some subsidized medical care, some subsidized food, some rigging of selling prices of cotton and wheat, some lunches for children, and so on. Not only are many of these policies grossly inefficient, as when a farm support program hurts tenants and helps landowners or a minimum wage law leads to the discharge of the neediest workers, but also the policies impose gross limitations on the freedom of the poor. If the poor would rather spend their relief checks on food than on housing, I see no reason for denying them the right. If they would rather spend the money on whiskey than on their children, I take it that we have enforceable laws to protect children.

2. The basic problem of poverty from the social viewpoint, however, is not the alleviation of current need but equipping the people to become self-supporting. Here we have been extraordinarily phlegmatic and unimaginative in acquiring understanding of the basic problem of low productivity and in devising methods of increasing the skills and opportunities of the poor. The old English settlement laws sought to tie the poor to their native parish, and this utter perversity is presently approached by a relief and old age system which at times imposes marginal taxes in excess of 100 percent on earnings. We have become so single-minded in worshipping the curriculum of the good liberal arts college that we have only a primitive system of industrial training. We tolerate widespread restrictionism on entry by unions, when it is the excluded entrants we should be worrying about.

In fact, so-called liberal policies in this area often seem to me to be almost studied in their callousness and contempt for the poor. Many ameliorative policies assume that the poor are much poorer in intelligence than in worldly goods, and must be cared for like children. Few people ask of a policy: What will be the effects on the poor who are not beneficiaries? If we tear down a slum, and rehouse half the people better at public cost, the only response to a query about the other half will be—we must do this for them too. Much of our welfare program has the macabre humor of a game of musical chairs.

Class 3: Economic Distress

I define economic distress as experiencing a large fall in income, or failing to share in a general rise, but without reaching some generally accepted criterion of poverty—of course the two differ only in degree. Much of our farm program, our oil program, our protective tariff system, our regional development schemes, our subsidies for metals and soon for commuters, are so motivated. Here my prescriptions would be:

1. Compensation for losses in the cases in which the distress is clearly and directly caused by governmental policy.
2. Exactly the same kind of treatment of distress as of poverty in other respects: Direct grants in the short-run; policies to foster the mobility of resources in the long-run. I do not conceal the belief that many of these special aid programs are so indefensible that an open subsidy program could not survive.

Class 4: Consumer and Worker Protection

Since unpunished fraud is profitable, it must be punished. I doubt whether many people realize how strong are the remedies provided by traditional law, and in particular how effective the actions of people who have been defrauded. I am confident that research in this area would suggest methods of vastly increasing the role of self-policing in the economy.

It is otherwise with the alleviation of consumer incompetence: The belief is becoming strong that there is much fraud, or at least indefensible waste, that consumers are incompetent to discover. An illustration may be taken from the hearings on the "Truth in Lending" bill which Senator Douglas has been seeking:

The following actually took place on the weekend of February 5, 1960, in the city of Chicago. It was a chill winter's day when William Rodriguez wandered from movie house to movie house, his mind desperately seeking the illusions of the great silver screen.

Finally, the projectors were still and William once more walked the now silent streets. Before returning to his wife, Nilda, and their four children, he stopped at a drugstore to make a purchase. Then, as he slowly trudged through the rain and snow, he began to eat rat poison.

At 2:00 A.M., he reached home and told his wife what he had done. Nilda called the police who came to take her husband to the hospital. As they carried him into the street, a letter dropped from his pocket. The letter had been sent by a Chicago firm that had sold William a second-hand TV set on time. The set had broken down the day after he received it. The firm threatened to garnishee his wages if he did not pay some of the money he owed. William Rodriguez received the bill on Thursday. He had until Saturday, the day he died, to make payment.

William Rodriguez had two failings. He simply would not listen to advice if it meant giving up something for Nilda and the children. Further, he would always take anybody's word for anything when buying things. At the time of his death, William Rodriguez owed about $700. Part of his debt included a religious medal he had bought for his wife on Mother's Day. The medal cost William $30. It was later valued at 50 cents.

It even reached the point where William was charged for goods he never purchased. Once a stranger came to Nilda's door and left a bedspread. The stranger said it was for a neighbor and that he would pick it up the next day. He never came. Shortly thereafter, William's pay was garnisheed for $34.

Although his wages had been garnisheed three times previously, there was no judgment against William Rodriguez when he died. This time, though, he feared new garnishments might mean the loss of his job. And he knew, too, that even if he was not fired, the garnishments would mean endless hardship to his family.

I assume this tragic tale is true—what shall we do? My basic answer to this painful problem is: In order to preserve the dignity and freedom of the individual in my society, I shall if I must pay the price of having some fail wholly to meet the challenge of freedom. I find it odd that a society which once a generation will send most of its young men against enemy bullets to defend freedom, will capitulate to a small handful of citizens unequal to its challenge.

This basic position does not imply that we should accept the institutions of 1900, or 1963, or any other year, as ideal in the protection they have given to men against fraud and danger. We should be prepared to examine any existing institution, or any proposal for change, with an open mind.

We should not, however, accept dramatic episodes as a measure of need; we should not simply assume that there is a useful law for every problem; and we should not lazily accept remedies which take freedom from ninety-seven men in order to give protection to three.

I should add, since I introduced the question, that I am in favor of truth in lending, and also in borrowing, and in selling, and in campaigning for office, and in lecturing to Swarthmore students, but not in courtship. Senator Douglas' bill has my support the day he shows me, first, that it will achieve any significant results, and second, that these results are worth at least 10 percent of the social costs of enforcing the statute.

These classes do not exhaust the range of functions undertaken by modern states, but they will suffice to illustrate the positions that seem to me to best meet the values of our society and the known limitations on its political processes.

And now I close. I consider myself courageous, or at least obtuse, in arguing for a reduction in governmental controls over economic life. You are surely desirous of improving this world, and it assuredly needs an immense amount of improvement. No method of displaying one's public-spiritedness is more popular than to notice a problem and pass a law. It combines ease, the warmth of benevolence, and a suitable disrespect for a less enlightened era. What I propose is, for most people, much less attractive: Close study of the comparative performance of public and private economy, and the dispassionate appraisal of special remedies that is involved in compassion for the community at large. I would urge you to examine my views in the most critical spirit, if I thought it necessary; I do urge you to attempt the more difficult task of exercising your critical intelligence in an appraisal of the comfortable wishfulness of contemporary policy.

8

The Economic
Role of Private Activity

PAUL A. SAMUELSON

*Paul A. Samuelson is Institute Professor at Massachusetts
Institute of Technology. This article, together with the
previous one by George Stigler, was published by the Graduate
School of Business of the University of Chicago in 1963.*

Introduction: Matter and Antimatter

Thoreau, disapproving of the Mexican War, would
not pay his taxes and was put in jail for civil
disobedience. His Concord neighbor, Emerson, went
to visit him down at the hoosegow and called out:
"Henry, what are you doing in there?" Thoreau
replied, "Waldo, what are you doing out there?"

Illustrative of the same point was a conversation I
had once with an economist for one of the great
international oil companies. I was astonished to learn
from him that their crews and engineers did not drill
for oil in the Middle East. He explained the paradox as
follows: "The Sheiks there are always anxious to make
us sell immediately more oil than the market will bear;
and they would take a dim view if we slackened on the
job of exploration. So, we drill in the hope of getting
dry holes, but follow a research procedure that will
mark off for us where oil really is to be found."

By now you will have perceived my point. One way
of approaching the question, "What is the proper role
of Government?" is to ask, "What is the proper role of
non-Government?" While you cannot be confident

that the man who is most proficient in playing regular
checkers (or tic-tac-toe) will also be best at playing
"give-away" (or cot-cat-cit in which the loser is made
to have three of his symbols in a linear array),
conventional wisdom or logic does ensure that by
finding the optimal role for nongovernment, you can
thereby define the proper role for government. Not
taking the bull by the horns should at least give us a
fresh perspective on the animal.

Lincoln's Formula

Some people begin the discussion of a concept by
telling you how it is defined in Webster's dictionary. I
follow the other fork and quote Abraham Lincoln.
You may remember that the fellow who ran against
Kennedy in 1960 quoted Lincoln on the proper role of
government. It went something like the following.

> *I believe the government should do only that which private
> citizens cannot do for themselves, or which they cannot do
> so well for themselves.*

One would think this is supposed to be saying something. Let us try it in its converse form.

I believe the private economy should be left alone to do those activities which, on balance after netting out all advantages and disadvantages, it can best do.

Obviously what I have stated is an empty tautology. It is no more helpful than the usual answer from Dorothy Dix to a perplexed suitor that merely says, "Look into your own heart to see whether you truly love the girl. And then after you have made up your mind, I am sure it will be the right decision."

But are these mere tautologies? Do the two Lincolnesque statements say exactly the same thing? There is a certain literal sense in which they can be interpreted to be saying the same thing. But we all bring to the words we hear certain preconceptions and attitudes.

I think Lincoln meant to imply in his formulation that there is needed a certain burden of proof that has to be established by anyone who proposes that the government do something. The balance of advantage in favor of the government must be something a little more than epsilon or you should stand with the *status quo* of private enterprise.[1]

Why? Lincoln does not say. But he takes it for granted that his listeners will understand that "personal liberty" is a value for its own sake and that some sacrifice of "efficiency" is worth making at the optimal point where activity is divided so as to maximize the total net advantage of "efficiency *cum* liberty" and vice versa.

The second statement that I have formulated also carries certain connotations. At a first hasty reading, it might suggest to some that the burden of proof is put on or against any proposal for *laissez faire* and individualism. And so it would be naturally construed in 1963 Soviet Russia.

After a second and more careful reading, it is seen to contain certain weasel words of qualification—such as "on balance," "netting" and "advantages" and "disadvantages." So interpreted, it can be made consistent with any desired emphasis on liberty as well as efficiency. And yet, even when almost completely emptied of its meaningful content, my formulation is left with a subtle connotation. It says, there are no absolutes here. The subject is an open one—open for debate and open to compromise. At some terms-of-trade, efficiency can be traded off against liberty. (Of course, Lincoln has already implied *this*, but not quite so strongly.)

Overture to the Program

So much for introduction. My Act I has prepared the way for what is to follow. In Act II, I want to examine the conditions under which efficiency is realizable by free enterprise or *laissez faire*. This is familiar ground, but too familiar and needs reexamination.

Then in Act III, I want to raise some questions about the notion that absence of government means increase in "freedom." Is "freedom" a simply quantifiable magnitude as much libertarian discussion seems to presume? Let me give you a hint of the kind of thing I have in mind: Traffic lights coerce me and limit my freedom, don't they? Yet in the midst of a traffic jam on the unopen road, was I really "free" before there were lights? And has the algebraic total of freedom, for me or the representative motorist or the group as a whole, been increased or decreased by the introduction of well-engineered Stop Lights? Stop Lights, you know, are also Go Lights.

Then I shall conclude on what may seem a *nihilistic* note, but which I hope is actually a *liberating* one.

Technical Requirements for Competitive Optimality

Consider a society with limited resources. Let certain facts about technology be "known" (in varying degrees). Let there be more than one person, so that we can speak of society. Let people have their tastes and values. And if you like, let there be one or more sets of ethical beliefs in terms of whose norms various

---

[1] Actually most people will in fact tend to give the benefit of the doubt to the *status quo*—any *status quo*. In our day the government does many things it did not do in Lincoln's time. When one of these activities is brought open to question, its being the *status quo* could shift the burden of proof on to the man who wants to bring the activity back into the private domain. I doubt that Lincoln would have agreed with this interpretation; in good nineteenth-century fashion, he thought of private activity as *natural* unless the contrary was demonstrated.

situations can be evaluated and ordered.

What I have now specified is so terribly general. Yet already I have been guilty of tremendous idealization and abstraction in comparison with any real life situation.

To some observers, none of the above admits of quantification. It is all quality, quality, quality. There is a possible utopia; there are a variety of actualities; one contemplates these as a whole, and reacts to them. And that's it. Such observers, patently, have little use for economics or economists.

Many observers, however, will note that one grain of sugar is much like another and rather different from grains of salt or Norwegian sweaters. Quantification is, so to speak, rearing its idealized head. Then one notes that five fingers and one nose tend to go together, and by a long chain of not-too-cogent arguments there emerges *Cogito, ergo sum* rather than *Cogitamus, ergo sumus*. Now individualism has reared its single head. And if I—or should it be said "we"?—can coin an Irish Bull, there is almost an anthropomorphic fallacy in considering that individuals exist in the sense that atoms exist.

Now, to save time, we plunge into heroic assumptions.

1. *Each person's tastes (and values) depend only upon his separable consumptions of goods. I.e., there must be no "consumption externalities."*
2. *Strict constant-returns-to-scale prevails.*
3. *Perfect competition, in senses too numerous to list here, prevails.*
4. *The interpersonal distribution of property (inclusive of personal attributes) is ethically correct initially or is to be made so by ideal lump-sum transfers of a perfectly nondistorting type.*

Then, and only then, has it been rigorously proved that perfect competitive equilibrium is indeed optimal. So strict are these conditions that one would have thought that the elementary consideration that a line is infinitely thinner than a plane would make it a miracle for these conditions to be met. Real life optimality, or an approach to it, would seem to cry out—not merely for departure from *laissez faire*—but for never having been remotely near to *laissez faire*. Yet, you might almost say by accident, our world is not galaxies away from this thin line.

Lawrence J. Henderson, a distinguished physiologist and philosopher at Harvard in my day, saw far beyond Darwinian evolution in which selection led to individuals that possessed fitness for the environment.

He wrote a charming book on *The Fitness of the Environment*. For example, life as we know it depends critically on the peculiar properties that water happens to have (with, I believe, only ammonia as a possible substitute). How remarkable that one planet should have the temperature in that special range where water is liquid! This planet got selected for its suitability to sustain life.

I say how miraculous that Victorian England came anywhere near the homogeneity-of-the-first-degree production conditions that perfect competition truly needs. If all production functions were homogeneous of degree 2 or 3.14156 . . . —and why shouldn't they be?—George Stigler would be out of work; he would be a brewer or a Nobel Prizeman in physics.

And note this. We each belong to many circles: the U.S.A., the Elks, the Samuelson family, the office pool, etc. In almost none of these relationships is the organizing principle that of decentralized competitive pricing. Let Abraham Lincoln ponder over that one.

The Nature of Freedom

But enough of these technicalities. . . . Adam Smith, our patron saint, was critical of state interference of the pre-Nineteenth-Century type. And make no mistake about it: Smith was right. Most of the interventions into economic life by the State were then harmful both to prosperity and freedom. What Smith said needed to be said. In fact, much of what Smith said still needs to be said: Good intentions by government are not enough; acts do have consequences that had better be taken into account if good is to follow. Thus, the idea of a decent real wage is an attractive one. So is the idea of a low interest rate at which the needy can borrow. None the less the attempt *by law* to set a minimum real wage at a level much above the going market rates, or to set a maximum interest rate for small loans at what seem like reasonable levels, inevitably does much harm to precisely the people whom the legislation is intended to help. Domestic and foreign experience—today, yesterday, and tomorrow—bears out the Smithian truth. Note that this is not an argument against *moderate* wage and interest fiats, which may improve the perfection of competition and make businessmen and workers more efficient.

Smith himself was what we today would call a pragmatist. He realized that monopoly elements ran through *laissez faire.* When he said that Masters never gather together even for social merriment without plotting to raise prices against the public interest, he anticipated the famous Judge Gary dinners at which the big steel companies used to be taught what every oligopolist should know. Knowing the caliber of George III's civil service, Smith believed the government would simply do more harm than good if it tried to cope with the evil of monopoly. Pragmatically, Smith might, if he were alive today, favor the Sherman Act and stronger antitrust legislation, or even public utility regulation generally.

The Invisible Hand Again

One hundred percent individualists skip these pragmatic lapses into good sense and concentrate on the purple passage in Adam Smith where he discerns an Invisible Hand that leads each selfish individual to contribute to the best public good. Smith had a point; but he could not have earned a passing mark in a Ph.D. oral examination in explaining just what that point was. Until this century, his followers—such as Bastiat—thought that the doctrine of the Invisible Hand meant one of two things: (a) that it produced maximum feasible total satisfaction, somehow defined; or (b) that it showed that anything which results from the voluntary agreements of uncoerced individuals must make them better (or best) off in some important sense.

Both of these interpretations, which are still held by many modern libertarians, are wrong. They neglect Assumption 4 of my earlier axioms for nongovernment. This is not the place for a technical discussion of economic principles, so I shall be very brief and cryptic in showing this.

First, suppose some ethical observer—such as Jesus, Buddha, or for that matter, John Dewey or Aldous Huxley—were to examine whether the total of social utility (as that ethical observer scores the deservingness of the poor and rich, saintly and sinning individuals) was actually maximized by 1860 or 1962 *laissez faire.* He might decide that a tax placed upon yachts whose proceeds go to cheapen the price of insulin to the needy might increase the total of utility. Could Adam Smith prove him wrong? Could Bastiat? I think not.

Of course, they might say that there is no point in trying to compare different individuals' utilities because they are incommensurable and can no more be added together than can apples and oranges. But if recourse is made to this argument, then the doctrine that the Invisible Hand maximizes total utility of the universe has already been thrown out the window. If they admit that the Invisible Hand will truly maximize total social utility *provided the state intervenes so as to make the initial distribution of dollar votes ethically proper,* then they have abandoned the libertarian's position that individuals are not to be coerced, even by taxation.

In connection with the second interpretation that anything which results from voluntary agreements is in some sense, *ipso facto,* optimal, we can reply by pointing out that when I make a purchase from a monopolistic octopus, that is a voluntary act: I can always go without alka-seltzer or aluminum or nylon or whatever product you think is produced by a monopolist. Mere voluntarism, therefore, is not the root merit of the doctrine of the Invisible Hand; what is important about it is the system of checks and balances that comes under perfect competition, and its measure of validity is at the technocratic level of efficiency, not at the ethical level of freedom and individualism. That this is so can be seen from the fact that such socialists as Oscar Lange and A.P. Lerner have advocated channeling the Invisible Hand to the task of organizing a socialistic society efficiently.

The Impersonality of Market Relations

Just as there is a sociology of family life and of politics, there is a sociology of individualistic competition. It need not be a rich one. Ask not your neighbor's name; enquire only for his numerical schedules of supply and demand. Under perfect competition, no buyer need face a seller. Haggling in a Levantine bazaar is a sign of less-than-perfect competition. The telephone is the perfect go-between to link buyers and sellers through the medium of an auction market, such as the New York Stock Exchange or the Chicago Board of Trade for grain transactions. Two men may talk hourly all their working lives and never meet.

These economic contacts between atomistic individuals may seem a little chilly or, to use the language of wine-tasting, "dry." This impersonality has its good side. Negroes in the South learned long ago that their money was welcome in local department stores.

Money can be liberating. It corrodes the cake of custom. Money does talk. Sociologists know that replacing the rule of status by the rule of contract loses something in warmth; it also gets rid of some of the bad fire of olden times.

Impersonality of market relations has another advantage, as was brought home to many "liberals" in the McCarthy era of American political life. Suppose it were efficient for the government to be the one big employer. Then if, for good or bad, a person becomes in bad odor with government, he is dropped from employment, and is put on a blacklist. He really then has no place to go. The thought of such a dire fate must in the course of time discourage that freedom of expression of opinion which individualists most favor.

Many of the people who were unjustly dropped by the federal government in that era were able to land jobs in small-scale private industry. I say small-scale industry because large corporations are likely to be chary of hiring names that appear on anybody's blacklist. What about people who were justly dropped as security risks or as members of political organizations now deemed to be criminally subversive? Many of them also found jobs in the anonymity of industry.

Wheat Growers Anonymous

Many conservative people, who think that such men should not remain in sensitive government work or in public employ at all, will still feel that they should not be hounded into starvation. Few want for this country the equivalent of Czarist Russia's Siberia, or Stalin Russia's Siberia either. It is hard to tell on the Chicago Board of Trade the difference between the wheat produced by Republican or Democratic farmers, by teetotalers or drunkards, Theosophists or Logical Positivists. I must confess that this is a feature of a competitive system that I find attractive.

We have seen how a perfect model of competitive equilibrium might behave if conditions for it were perfect. The modern world is not identical with that model. As mentioned before, there never was a time, even in good Queen Victoria's long reign, when such conditions prevailed.

Whatever may have been true on Turner's frontier,[2]

the modern city is crowded. Individualism and anarchy will lead to friction. We now have to coordinate and cooperate. Where cooperation is not fully forthcoming, we must introduce upon ourselves coercion. When we introduce the traffic light, we have by cooperation and coercion, although the arch individualist may not like the new order, created for ourselves greater freedom.

The principle of unbridled freedom has been abandoned; it is now just a question of haggling about the terms. On the one hand, few will deny that it is a bad thing for one man, or a few men, to impose their wills on the vast majority of mankind, particularly when that will involves terrible cruelty and terrible inefficiency. Yet where does one draw the line? At a 51 percent majority vote? Or, should there be no actions taken that cannot command unanimous agreement—a position which such modern exponents of libertarian liberalism as Professor Milton Friedman are slowly evolving toward. Unanimous agreement? Well, virtually unanimous agreement, whatever that will come to mean.

The principle of unanimity is, of course, completely impractical. My old friend Milton Friedman is extremely persuasive, but not even he can keep his own students in unanimous agreement all the time. Aside from its practical inapplicability, the principle of unanimity is theoretically faulty. It leads to contradictory and intransitive decisions. By itself, it argues that just as society should not move from *laissez faire* to planning because there will always be at least one objector—Friedman if necessary—so society should never move from planning to freedom because there will always be at least one objector. Like standing friction, it sticks you where you are. It favors the *status quo*. And the *status quo* is certainly not to the liking of arch individualists. When you have painted yourself into a corner, what can you do? You can redefine the situation, and I predicted some years ago that there would come to be defined a privileged *status quo*, a set of natural rights involving individual

pecuniary costs and social costs. They call for intervention: zoning, fiats, planning, regulation, taxing, and so forth.

But too much diluteness of the gas also calls for social interfering with *laissez faire* individualism. Thus, the frontier has always involved sparse populations in need of "social overhead capital." In terms of technical economics jargon this has the following meaning: when scale is so small as to lead to unexhausted increasing returns, free pricing cannot be optimal and there is a *prima facie* case for cooperative intervention.

---

[2]Density of population produces what economists recognize as external economies and diseconomies. These "neighborhood effects" are often dramatized by smoke and other nuisances that involve a discrepancy between private

freedoms, which alone requires unanimity before it can be departed from.

At this point the logical game is up. The case for "complete freedom" has been begged, not deduced. So long as full disclosure is made, it is no crime to assume your ethical case. But will your product sell? Can you persuade others to accept your axiom when it is in conflict with certain other desirable axioms?

Not by Reasoning Alone

The notion is repellant that a man should be able to tyrannize over others. Shall he be permitted to indoctrinate his children into any way of life whatsoever? Shall he be able to tyrannize over himself? Here, or elsewhere, the prudent-man doctrine of the good trustee must be invoked, and in the last analysis his peers must judge—i.e., a committee of prudent peers. And may they be peers tolerant as well as wise!

Complete freedom is not definable once two wills exist in the same interdependent universe. We can sometimes find two situations in which choice A is more free than choice B in apparently every respect and at least as good as B in every other relevant sense. In such singular cases I will certainly throw in my lot with the exponents of individualism. But few situations are really of this simple type; and these few are hardly worth talking about, because they will already have been disposed of so easily.

In most actual situations we come to a point at which choices between goals must be made: do you want this kind of freedom and this kind of hunger, or that kind of freedom and that kind of hunger? I use these terms in a quasi-algebraic sense, but actually what is called "freedom" is really a vector of almost infinite components rather than a one-dimensional thing that can be given a simple ordering.

Where more than one person is concerned the problem is thornier still. My privacy is your loneliness, my freedom to have privacy is your lack of freedom to have company. Your freedom to "discriminate" is the denial of my freedom to "participate." There is no possibility of unanimity to resolve such conflicts.

The notion, so nicely expounded in a book I earnestly recommend to you, Milton Friedman, *Capitalism and Freedom* (Chicago, 1962), that it is better for one who deplores racial discrimination to try to persuade people against it than to do nothing at all—but, failing to persuade, it is better to use no

democratic coercion in these matters—such a notion as a *general* precept is arbitrary and gratuitous. Its arbitrariness is perhaps concealed when it is put abstractly in the following form: If free men follow Practice X that you and some others regard as bad, it is wrong in principle to coerce them out of that Practice X; in principle, all you ought to do is to try to persuade them out of their ways by "free discussion." One counter-example suffices to invalidate a general principle. An exception does not prove the rule, it disproves it. As a counter-example I suggest we substitute for "Practice X" the "killing by gas of 5 million suitably-specified humans." Who will agree with the precept in this case?

Only two types would possible agree to it: (1) those so naïve as to think that persuasion can keep Hitlers from cremating millions; or (2) those who think the *status quo,* achievable by what can be persuaded, is a pretty comfortable one after all, even if not perfect. When we are very young we fall into the first category; when old and prosperous, into the second; perhaps there is a golden age in between. The notion that any form of coercion whatever is in itself so evil a thing as to outweigh all other evils is to set up freedom as a monstrous shibboleth. In the first place, absolute or even maximum freedom cannot even be defined unambiguously except in certain special models. Hence one is being burned at the stake for a cause that is only a slogan or name. In the second place, as I have shown, coercion can be defined only in terms of an infinite variety of arbitrary alternative *status quo.*

The precept "persuade-if-you-can-but-in-no-case-coerce" can be sold only to those who do not understand what it is they are buying. This doctrine sound a little like the "Resist-Not-Evil" precepts of Jesus or Gandhi. But there is absolutely no true similarity between the two doctrines, and one should not gain in palatability by being confused with the other.

Marketplace Coercion, or The Hegelian Freedom of Necessity

Libertarians fail to realize that the price system is, and ought to be, a method of coercion. Nature is not so bountiful as to give each of us all the goods he desires. We have to be coerced out of such a situation, by the nature of things. That is why we have policemen and courts. That is why we charge prices, which are high enough relative to limited money to limit consumption. The very term "rationing by the purse" illustrates the point. Economists defend such forms of rationing, but they have to do so primarily in terms of its efficiency and its fairness. Where it is not efficient—as in the case of monopoly, externality, and avoidable uncertainty—it comes under attack. Where it is deemed unfair by ethical observers, its evil is weighed pragmatically against its advantages and modifications of its structure are introduced.

Classical economists, like Malthus, always understood this coercion. They recognized that fate dealt a hand of cards to the worker's child that was a cruel one, and a favorable one to the "well-born." John Stuart Mill in a later decade realized that mankind, not Fate with a capital F, was involved. Private property is a concept created by and enforced by public law. Its attributes change in time and are man-made, not Mother-Nature-made.

Nor is the coercion a minor one. Future generations are condemned to starvation if certain supply-and-demand patterns rule in today's market. Under the freedom that is called *laissez faire,* some worthy men are exalted; and so are some unworthy ones. Some unworthy men are cast down; and so are some worthy ones. The Good Man gives the system its due, but reckons in his balance its liabilities that are overdue.

Anatole France said epigrammatically all that needs to be said about the coercion implicit in the libertarian economics of *laissez faire.* "How majestic is the equality of the Law, which permits both rich and poor alike, to sleep under the bridges at night." I believe no satisfactory answer has yet been given to this. It is certainly not enough to say, "We made our own beds and let us each lie in them."[3] For once Democracy

rears its pretty head, the voter will think: "There, but for the Grace of God and the Dow-Jones averages, go I." And he will act.

The whole matter of proper government policy involves issues of ethics, coercion, administration, incidence, and incentives that cannot begin to be resolved by semantic analysis of such terms as "freedom," "coercion," or "individualism."

A Final Law

At the end I must lay down one basic proposition.

There are no rules concerning the proper role of government that can be established by a priori reasoning.

This may seem odd to you: for to state the rule that there are no rules may sound like a self-contradiction, reminiscent of the breakfast cereal box that contains an exact picture of itself . . . of itself . . . of itself. . . . However, no Bertrand Russell theory of types is involved here. For, my proposition—call it Samuelson's Law if you like—does not claim to be established by Reason, but merely to be a uniformity of experience. Whose experience? My experience, and that of every (I mean, almost every) man of experience.

If I am wrong it will be easy to prove me wrong: namely, by stating one valid nontrivial proposition about the proper role of government derived by cogent *a priori* reasoning alone. After I have digested, it, I shall have no trouble in eating my own words.

---

[3]If one disagrees with Malthus and France and thinks that we all had equal opportunities and *have* made the beds we are to lie in, our judgment of *laissez faire* improves—as it should. But note it is because of its fine welfare results, and *not because the kind of freedom embodied in it is the end-all of ethics.*

PART TWO

Unemployment, National Output, and Fiscal Policy

Unemployment is one of the most frightening words in the English language, and for good reason. It results in terrible costs to the unemployed worker and his or her family, as well as substantial costs to society in the form of output forgone. In 1946, the Congress passed the Employment Act, which said that the government had the responsibility "to promote maximum employment, production, and purchasing power." The opening selection, by the Council of Economic Advisers, describes the events leading up to the passage of the Act, as well as the measures taken by the government to promote full employment during the 1950s and early 1960s The next selection, taken from a 1932 issue of *Fortune* magazine, describes what the Great Depression was like to those in the midst of it; later accounts, no matter how dramatically written, fail to give so vivid a feel for the plight of the unemployed, and of the nation as a whole.

In the decades since the Depression, economists (utilizing the ideas of John Maynard Keynes) have developed reasonably sophisticated theories of how the government's power to spend and to tax can be used to stabilize the economy at close to its full employment level. Joseph Pechman, in the following article, describes the impact of government spending and taxation, and discusses the use of the full-employment budget as a guide to fiscal policy. He concludes that: "When private demand is low and the economy is operating below capacity, taxes are too high relative to expenditures. In these circumstances, the ratio should be reduced—by cutting taxes, by raising expenditures, or by doing both. Conversely, when demand is too high, taxes should be raised or expenditures reduced, or both."

Milton Friedman is skeptical of this doctrine.

In his view, this theory has fostered an undesirable growth of government activities; and "far from being a balance wheel offsetting other forces making for fluctuations, the federal budget has if anything been itself a major source of disturbance and uncertainty." Moreover, according to Friedman, "the view, now so widely held, that an increase in government expenditures relative to tax-receipts is necessarily expansionary and a decrease contractionary . . . cannot be demonstrated . . . and is in fact inconsistent with the relevant empirical evidence." This is a point on which there is considerable controversy, with Friedman still in the minority.

In contrast to Pechman, Maurice Stans argues that "the federal government should have a balanced budget; its expenditures . . . should not exceed its income." Stans, more concerned than Pechman about the social costs of inflation, fears that budget deficits will lead to serious inflation. Most economists today would feel that, although reasonable price stability certainly is important, it also is important to utilize the federal budget, as Pechman describes, to promote high employment. James Tobin, in the next selection, tries to clarify the true nature of the federal debt, and points out that: "The federal government will not succeed in cutting its deficit by steps that depress the economy, perpetuate excess capacity, and deter business firms from using outside funds."

Economic models are used by decision-makers in both the public and private sectors of the economy to forecast short-term changes in gross national product. In the final selection in this part, Paul A. Samuelson discusses how well economists can do as forecasters, and concludes that, although they may not be as good as one would like, they "are better than anything else in heaven and earth at forecasting aggregate business trends—better than gypsy tea-leaf readers, Wall Street soothsayers and chartist technicians, hunch-playing heads of mail order chains, or all-powerful heads of state. This is a statement based on empirical experience." It is also a very important reason for studying economics.

9

The Employment Act of 1946: Background and Impact

COUNCIL OF
ECONOMIC ADVĪSERS

The following article comes from the 1966 Annual Report of the Council of Economic Advisers. It marked twenty years of experience with the Employment Act.

The Act and Its Background

The legislation of 1946 set forth the following declaration of policy:

> The Congress declares that it is the continuing policy and responsibility of the Federal Government to use all practicable means consistent with its needs and obligations and other essential considerations of national policy, with the assistance and cooperation of industry, agriculture, labor, and State and local governments, to coordinate and utilize all its plans, functions, and resources for the purpose of creating and maintaining, in a manner calculated to foster and promote free competitive enterprise and the general welfare, conditions under which there will be afforded useful employment opportunities, including self-employment, for those able, willing and seeking to work, and to promote maximum employment, production, and purchasing power.

In making this declaration, the Congress recognized that the billions of independent spending and saving decisions of a free economy could well result in levels of total demand either short of full employment or in excess of productive capacity. Furthermore, it took the view that Government policies could play a constructive role in improving the stability and balance of the economy.

The Act was a product of the experiences of the Great Depression and World War II. The Depression shook but did not destroy the faith in an automatic tendency of the economy to find its proper level of operation. In the early 1930s, public works and other antidepression programs were justified as temporary "pump priming," to help the private economy get back on its track after an unusual and catastrophic derailment. And the departure from orthodox fiscal principles was made with regret and without complete consistency. The Government expenditures explicitly designed to combat depression necessarily increased budget deficits; but this implication was veiled by financing these outlays through an "extraordinary" budget. Meanwhile, taxes were raised, and salaries and housekeeping expenditures cut in the regular budget, thereby reducing the overall stimulation of Government measures.

The relapse of the economy in 1937 into a sharp decline from a level still far below full employment gave rise to conflicting interpretations. To some, it proved that pump priming and Government deficits had undermined the confidence of the business community and thereby only worsened the situation. Others, however, concluded that it pointed to the need for larger and more sustained fiscal and monetary actions to revive the economy. In drawing this conclusion, economists were buttressed by the writings of J. M. Keynes, who offered a theoretical explanation of the disastrous depression. The Keynesian conclusions received additional support during World War II because they offered a satisfactory explanation of why the high deficit-financed defense expenditures of that period not only wiped out unemployment but went beyond to create inflationary pressures.

Memories of the disastrous 1930s were very much in the public mind as World War II was drawing to an end. Many active proponents of "full employment" legislation in 1945 and 1946 feared a relapse into depressed levels of economic activity like those of the 1930s, once military spending ended. They looked toward Federal public works spending as a peacetime replacement—at least, in part—for the wartime defense outlays.

The opponents of "full employment" legislation had several reservations and objections. Some feared that it would mean a statutory blessing for perpetual budgetary deficits, soaring public expenditures, and massive redistribution of income from upper to lower income groups. There were doubts that Government actions could and would on balance raise employment; and there were fears that these actions would lead to regimentation and would jeopardize the free enterprise system. The proponents of legislation, on the other hand, argued that the Act would merely provide a setting essential to the proper functioning of the free enterprise system because a depressed economy heightened social tensions, discouraged innovation and initiative, dulled competition, and undermined confidence.

The legislation which finally emerged from this discussion wisely abstained from diagnosing depression as the disease and public works as the cure, but instead concentrated on establishing the principle of continuing Government responsibility to review and appraise economic developments, diagnose problems, and prescribe approprate remedies. And it placed major responsibility squarely upon the President, who was asked to discuss his execution of that responsibility in an Economic Report to be transmitted to the Congress at the start of each year.

The Act also established two agencies—the Council of Economic Advisers in the Executive Branch and the Joint Committee on the Economic Report (later named the Joint Economic Committee) of the Congress—with interrelated but separate responsibilities. These institutions have each filled a vital and previously missing role in their respective branches of Government—they have provided a coordinated overview of the economic impact of the entire spectrum of Government tax, expenditure, monetary, and other acitvities. To maintain the emphasis on advice and coordination, the Joint Economic Committee was not given any substantive legislative responsibility nor the Council any policy-executing duties. Both agencies have participated actively in the counsels of Government; both have conscientiously striven for a thoroughly professional economic competence and approach in their respective reports and recommendations; and both have contributed to the public understanding of economic issues.

Today's economic policies reflect the continuing impact of the Employment Act in all the years since its inception. And our accumulating experience is certain to be reflected in the policies of the future. This paper reviews the development of policy during the 1950s and early 1960s and outlines the present relationship between economic analysis and economic policy.

Avoiding Depressions and Booms

The Congress proved wise in its decisions to state goals broadly and to concentrate on continuing review, analysis, and proposals, since the specific problems that actually arose were somewhat different from those which many supporters of the Employment Act had anticipated.

Although an important part of the impetus for the Employment Act derived from the prolonged depression of the 1930s and the resulting fear of stagnation in the American economy, this problem did not prove to be the primary challenge to economic policymaking under the Act. Indeed, immediately after World War II, excess-demand inflation proved to be the key problem. Subsequently, policy was focused on the age-old problem of limiting the size and duration of cyclical swings. Only much later and in a much different and milder form did stagnation arise as a live issue.

Thus, much of our experience under the Act

consisted of policy actions to combat recession—lest it turn into depression—and to contain excess demand pressure—lest it generate inflationary boom.

Combating Recessions

A series of relatively short and mild recessions required Government attention in the postwar period. The problem of cyclical declines was not unexpected by the framers of the Employment Act, nor was it new to the American economy. In the period between 1854 (the beginning of the business cycle annals of the National Bureau of Economic Research) and World War II, we had experienced twenty-one periods of recession or depression. Our postwar record is blemished by four additional periods of contracting economic activity—1948–49, 1953–54, 1957–58, and 1960–61.

Compared with the previous cyclical record, the postwar recessions have been far shorter, considerably milder, and substantially less frequent. Postwar recessions ranged in duration from eight to thirteen months; the average duration of previous declines had been twenty-one months, and only three had been shorter than thirteen months in length. Measured by the decline in industrial production from peak to trough, postwar recessions ranged in magnitude from 8 percent to 14 percent. By comparison, in the interwar period, the declines ranged from 6 to 52 percent; three of the five contractions exceeded 30 percent and only one was less than the 14 percent maximum of the postwar period. During the past twenty years, the economy has spent a total of forty-two months, or 18 percent of the time, in periods of recessions, far less than the 43 percent applicable to the 1854–1939 era.

This improvement in the postwar record of the economy was aided by the deliberate discretionary steps taken by the Government to modify the impact of business downturns and thereby to prevent cumulating declines into depression. The speed and force of these actions—in both the fiscal and monetary areas—varied among the recessions. Thus, in 1949 little new fiscal action was taken, partly because inflation was viewed as a key problem even during the decline, and partly because Government measures taken the previous year were expected to have a considerable impact on the economy: the tax reductions of 1948 were supplying large refunds, and large expenditure increases were forthcoming under the recently enacted Marshall Plan. The Federal Reserve did act to reduce reserve requirements in a series of steps during the spring and summer of 1949, reversing a two-year rise in short-term interest rates.

In 1953–54, as military outlays declined and aggregate activity retreated, the principal expansionary influence came from previously scheduled reductions of corporate and personal income taxes. But some new action was taken to reduce excise taxes and to speed up expenditures. All three major instruments of monetary policy—reserve requirements, the discount rate, and open market operations—were used to encourage the expansion of credit-financed expenditures. Meanwhile, the Administration planned larger fiscal steps that might be taken if the recession seemed likely to be prolonged. Significantly, in 1954, the bipartisan character of expansionary fiscal policies was established for the first time, as the Republican Administration of President Eisenhower adopted measures that had previously been linked to the New Deal and Keynesian economics.

In 1958, the recession was considerably deeper than its two postwar predecessors and both the Eisenhower Administration and the Congress were more vigorous in taking action. An important concern of earlier years—that business confidence might be disturbed by Government recognition of a recession—seemed insignificant since the sharp recession was obvious to all.

Several important measures were taken. The benefit period for unemployment compensation was temporarily extended. Grants to States under the Federal highway program were enlarged and accelerated, and other programs in the budget also were expanded or rescheduled to provide an earlier stimulative effect. The Government also acted to spur housing activity by financial operations in the mortgage market and by altering terms on Government-guaranteed home mortgages. The important measures were launched near, or after, the trough of the recession. Thus, in retrospect, policy helped most to strengthen the early recovery rather than to contain or shorten the recession. Nevertheless, in view of the general recognition that the Government would be running a substantial deficit in any case, these additions to Federal outlays were a significant reflection of changed attitudes toward the role of fiscal policy.

Monetary policy also played a constructive role in the 1957–58 recession, once the monetary authorities moved to ease credit three months after the peak in economic activity. Thereafter, Federal Reserve actions contributed to a revival in housing and other investment by promoting a sharp reduction in interest rates, both short- and long-term.

The first fiscal measures to deal with the 1960–61 recession were taken with the inauguration of President Kennedy in January 1961, when the recession had just about run its course. Nevertheless, improvements in the social insurance system, rescheduling of Federal expenditures, and expanded programs (including defense and space) were an important stimulus to the recovery during 1961. In contrast to the delay in taking fiscal measures, the Federal Reserve reversed a tight money policy early in 1960, prior to the downturn.

Not all discretionary changes in taxes or expenditures have contributed to economic stability. Indeed, some steps taken to pursue national security or social goals had destabilizing economic impacts, which were not always appropriately offset. Previously scheduled payroll tax increases took effect in 1954, 1959, and 1962, and drained off purchasing power in recession or in initial recovery. In 1953, defense outlays declined and triggered a recession before offsetting expansionary policies were adopted.

On the whole, discretionary fiscal and monetary actions made a distinct positive contribution in limiting declines. Even more important in this respect was the strengthened inherent stability of the postwar economy.

In large measure, this can be traced simply to the greater size of the Government relative to the total economy: that is, the increased importance of Government expenditures—both purchases of goods and services and transfer payments. Government outlays do not participate in the downward spiral of recession; because of its borrowing capacity, the Federal Government—unlike businesses and households—can maintain its spending in the face of declining income receipts. Although State and local governments do not have equal immunity from the need to tighten their belts, they have been able to maintain their growing spending programs relatively unaffected during the mild postwar recessions. Social insurance and national defense have added especially to the postwar totals of Federal outlays. State and local outlays have been rising rapidly in an effort to catch up with neglected needs and to keep up with the desires of a wealthier society for improved public services.

The contribution to the stability of the economy resulting from a high level of Government expenditures, insulated from revenue declines, has been augmented by the cushions to private purchasing power provided by the built-in fiscal stabilizers.

When private incomes and employment decline, purchasing power is automatically supported by both a decline of Federal revenues and an increase in unemployment compensation payments. Transmission of the virus of deflation is thus impeded. During postwar recessions, the progressive Federal personal income tax has not had to demonstrate its full stabilizing effectiveness because of the mildness of dips in personal earnings. There have, however, been sharp declines in corporate incomes; the Federal Treasury has shared about half of the drop in profits, thereby helping to bolster dividends and to cushion cash flow, and hence investment outlays.

A number of improvements in our financial structure were developed in the 1930s to assure that financial collapse and declines in economic activity would not generate a vicious downward spiral as they did after 1929. These important financial mechanisms include Federal insurance of private deposits; the separation of commercial and investment banking functions; the Federal Reserve's increased ability to provide banks with reserves in time of crisis; and the joint work of the Federal Reserve and the Securities and Exchange Commission to reduce harmful speculation in the stock market. The very existence of these structural changes has contributed to stability by improving confidence.

With the help of the more stable structure of the economy, recessions in the postwar era have been limited to declines in investment spending (and, in 1953–54, Federal outlays). Consumer incomes have not declined significantly, and hence households have maintained their spending in recession. With the nearly two-thirds of GNP represented by consumer expenditures insulated from decline and with a solid foundation of public outlays, declines in private investment have not cumulated. In contrast, the Great Depression generated a decline of consumer outlays of 40 percent from 1929 to 1933, and the shrinkage of consumer markets aggravated and reinforced the collapse in investment spending.

10

"The Great Depression"

FORTUNE

This article comes from the September 1932 issue of Fortune *magazine. Published at the bottom of the Great Depression, this is a vivid account of the nation's plight at that time.*

Dull mornings last winter the sheriff of Miami, Florida, used to fill a truck with homeless men and run them up to the county line. Where the sheriff of Fort Lauderdale used to meet them and load them into a second truck and run them up to *his* county line. Where the sheriff of Saint Lucie's would meet them and load them into a third truck and run them up to *his* county line. Where the sheriff of Brevard County would *not* meet them. And whence they would trickle back down the roads to Miami. To repeat.

It was a system. And it worked. The only trouble was that it worked too well. It kept the transients transient and it even increased the transient population in the process. But it got to be pretty expensive, one way or another, if you sat down and figured it all out—trucks and gas and time and a little coffee. . . .

That was last winter.

Next winter there will be no truck. And there will be no truck, not because the transients will have disappeared from Miami: if anything, there will be more blistered Fords with North Dakota licenses and more heel-worn shoes with the Boston trademark rubbed out next winter than there were last. But because the sheriff of Miami, like the President of the United States, will next winter think of transients and unemployed miners and jobless mill workers in completely different terms.

The difference will be made by the Emergency Relief Act. Or rather by the fact that the Emergency Relief Act exists. For the Act itself with its $300,000,000 for direct relief loans to the states is neither an adequate nor an impressive piece of legislation. But the passage of the Act, like the green branch which young Mr. Ringling used to lay across the forks of the Wisconsin roads for his circus to follow, marks a turning in American political history. And the beginning of a new chapter in American unemployment relief. It constitutes an open and legible acknowledgment of governmental responsibility for the welfare of the victims of industrial unemployment. And its ultimate effect must be the substitution of an ordered, realistic, and intelligent relief program for the wasteful and uneconomic methods (of which the Miami truck is an adequate symbol) employed during the first three years of the depression.

There can be no serious question of the failure of those methods. For the methods were never seriously capable of success. They were diffuse, unrelated, and unplanned. The theory was that private charitable organizations and semipublic welfare groups, established to care for the old and the sick and the indigent, were capable of caring for the casuals of a worldwide economic disaster. And the theory in application meant that social agencies manned for the service of a few hundred families, and city shelters set up to house and feed a handful of homeless men, were compelled by the brutal necessities of hunger to care for hundreds of thousands of families and whole armies of the displaced and the jobless. And to depend for their resources upon the contributions of communities no longer able to contribute, and upon the irresolution and vacillation of state legislatures and municipal assemblies long since in the red on their annual budgets. The result was the picture now presented in city after city and state after state—heterogeneous groups of official and semiofficial and unofficial relief agencies struggling under the earnest and untrained leadership of the local men of affairs against an inertia of misery and suffering and want they are powerless to overcome.

But the psychological consequence was even worse. Since the problem was never honestly attacked as a national problem, and since the facts were never frankly faced as facts, people came to believe that American unemployment was relatively unimportant. They saw little idleness and they therefore believed there was little idleness. It is possible to drive for blocks in the usual shopping and residential districts of New York and Chicago without seeing a breadline or a food station or a hungry mob or indeed anything else much more exciting than a few casuals asleep on a park bench. And for that reason, and because their newspapers played down the subject as an additional depressant in depressing times, and because they were bored with relief measures anyway, the great American public simply ignored the whole thing. They would still ignore it today were it not that the committee hearings and the Congressional debate and the Presidential veto of relief bills this last June attracted their attention. And that the final passage of the Emergency Relief and Construction Act of 1932 has committed their government and themselves to a policy of affirmative action which compels both it and them to know definitely and precisely what the existing situation is.

It should be remarked at this point that nothing the federal government has yet done or is likely to do in the near future constitutes a policy of *constructive* action. Unemployment basically is not a social disease but an industrial phenomenon. The natural and inevitable consequence of a machine civilization is a lessened demand for human labor. (An almost total elimination of human labor in plowing, for example, is now foreseeable.) And the natural and inevitable consequence of a lessened demand for human labor is an increase of idleness. Indeed the prophets of the machine age have always promised an increase of idleness, under the name of leisure, as one of the goals of industry. A constructive solution of unemployment therefore means an industrial solution—a restatement of industrialism which will treat technological displacement not as an illness to be cured but as a goal to be achieved—and achieved with the widest dispensation of benefits and the least incidental misery.

But the present relief problem as focused by the federal Act is not a problem of ultimate solutions but of immediate palliatives. One does not talk architecture while the house is on fire and the tenants are still inside. The question at this moment is the pure question of fact. Having decided at last to face reality and do something about it, what is reality? How many men are unemployed in the U. S.? How many are in want? *What are the facts?*

Twenty-five Millions

The following minimal statements may be accepted as true—with the certainty that they underestimate the real situation:

(1) Unemployment has steadily increased in the U.S. since the beginning of the depression and the rate of increase during the first part of 1932 was more rapid than in any other depression year.

(2) The number of persons totally unemployed is now at least 10,000,000.

(3) The number of persons totally unemployed next winter will, at the present rate of increase, be 11,000,000.

(4) Eleven millions unemployed means better than one man out of every four employable workers.

(5) This percentage is higher than the percentage of unemployed British workers registered under the compulsory insurance laws (17.1 percent in May, 1932, as against 17.3 percent in April and 18.4 percent in January) and higher than the French, the Italian,

and the Canadian percentages, but lower than the German (43.9 percent of trade unionists in April, 1932) and the Norwegian.

(6) Eleven millions unemployed means 27,500,000 whose regular source of livelihood has been cut off.

(7) Twenty-seven and a half millions without regular income includes the families of totally unemployed workers alone. Taking account of the numbers of workers on part time, the total of those without adequate income becomes 34,000,000 or better than a quarter of the entire population of the country.

(8) Thirty-four million persons without adequate income does not mean 34,000,000 in present want. Many families have savings. But savings are eventually dissipated and the number in actual want tends to approximate the number without adequate income. How nearly it approximates it now or will next winter no man can say. But it is conservative to estimate that the problem of next winter's relief is a problem of caring for approximately 25,000,000 souls.

These figures . . . are based upon estimates. For nothing but estimates exists. No heritage from the fumbling of the last three years is more discouraging than the complete lack of statistics. The Director of the President's Organization on Unemployment Relief, Walter S. Gifford of the American Telephone & Telegraph Co., was forced to acknowledge before a subcommittee of the Senate in January, 1932, that he did not know, nor did his organization know, how many persons were out of work and in need of assistance in the U.S. nor even how many persons were actually receiving aid at the time of his testimony. And more recently the Commissioner of Labor Statistics, Ethelbert Stewart, generally recognized as the government's foremost authority on unemployment, has been allowed to lose his office at the most critical period in American unemployment history because, according to press accounts, the Secretary of Labor, Mr. Doak, was irritated by the Commissioner's correction of one of his overoptimistic statements.

Fortunately, however, the more important estimators agree among themselves and the total of 25,000,000 may fairly be accepted.

But it is impossible to think or to act in units of 25,000,000 human beings. Like the casualty lists of the British War Office during the Battle of the Somme, they mean nothing. They are at once too large and too small. A handful of men and women and children digging for their rotten food in the St. Louis

dumps are more numerous, humanly speaking, than all the millions that ever found themselves in an actuary's column. The 25,000,000 only become human in their cities and their mill towns and their mining villages. And their situation only becomes comprehensible in terms of the relief they have already received.

That is to say that the general situation can only be judged by the situation in the particular localities. But certain generalizations are possible. Of which the chief is the broad conclusion that few if any of the industrial areas have been able to maintain a minimum decency level of life for their unemployed. Budgetary standards as set up by welfare organizations, public and private, after years of experiment have been discarded. Food only, in most cases, is provided and little enough of that. Rents are seldom paid. Shoes and clothing are given in rare instances only. Money for doctors and dentists is not to be had. And free clinics are filled to overflowing. Weekly allowances per family have fallen as low as $2.39 in New York with $3 and $4 the rule in most cities and $5 a high figure. And even on these terms funds budgeted for a twelve-month period have been exhausted in three or four. While city after city has been compelled to abandon a part of its dependent population. "We are merely trying to prevent hunger and exposure," reported a St. Paul welfare head last May. And the same sentence would be echoed by workers in other cities with such additions as were reported at the same time from Pittsburgh where a cut of 50 percent was regarded as "inevitable," from Dallas where Mexicans and Negroes were not given relief, from Alabama where discontinuance of relief in mining and agricultural sections was foreseen, from New Orleans where no new applicants were being received and 2,500 families in need of relief were receiving none, from Omaha where two-thirds of the cases receiving relief were to be discontinued, from Colorado where the counties had suspended relief for lack of funds . . . from Scranton . . . from Cleveland . . . from Syracuse. . . . But individual localities present their own picture.

New York City

About 1,000,000 out of the city's 3,200,000 working population are unemployed. Last April 410,000 were estimated to be in dire want. Seven hundred and fifty thousand in 150,000 families were receiving emergency aid while 160,000 more in 32,000 families were waiting to receive aid not then available. Of these latter families—families which normally earn an average of $141.50 a month—the average income from all sources was $8.20. Of families receiving relief, the allowance has been anything from a box of groceries up to $60 a month. In general, New York relief, in the phrase of Mr. William Hodson, executive director of the New York Welfare Council, has been on "a disaster basis." And the effects have been disaster effects. It is impossible to estimate the number of deaths in the last year in which starvation was a contributing cause. But ninety-five persons suffering directly from starvation were admitted to the city hospitals in 1931, of whom twenty died; and 143 suffering from malnutrition, of whom twenty-five died. While visiting nurses and welfare workers report a general increase in malnutrition, and the clinics and medical relief agencies are so overcrowded they can give adequate relief to no one, although 75 percent of persons applying to one relief agency had some form of illness. Housing is, of course, with the general lowering of standards and the doubling-up of families, worse even than it was during the boom. Relief expenditures for 1930 were something over $6,000,000; for 1931, more than $25,000,000; and for the first four months of 1932 over $20,000,000, or $5,000,000 per month. But large as this latter figure is it must be compared with the wage and salary loss by reason of unemployment, which is at least $100,000,000 per month. The need, even with static unemployment figures, is cumulative, and $75,000,000 for the next twelve months is a low estimate.

Philadelphia

The situation in Philadelphia was described by its Community Council in July, 1932, as one of "slow starvation and progressive disintegration of family life. . . ." "Normal" unemployment in Philadelphia is 40,000 to 50,000. In April 1931, 228,000 or 25.6 percent of the city's normally employed were unemployed, and 122,000 or 13.7 percent were on part time. Of the city's 445,000 families with employable workers, 210,000 had workers unemployed or on part time, about one in four had no worker employed on full time, and 12 percent had *no* worker employed.

Even the average person unemployed had been out of work for thirty-seven weeks and had had only a little over one week of casual or relief work during the period. By December, 1931, the number of unemployed had reached 238,000 with 43,000 families receiving relief and 56,000 families in which no one was at work. And by May, 1932, the total of unemployed was 298,000. In the following month the Governor of the state estimated that 250,000 persons in Philadelphia "faced actual starvation." Over the state at large the same conditions held. In June, 1931, 919,000 or 25 percent of the normally employed in the state were unemployed, according to the "secret" report then submitted to the Governor, and the number had risen to 1,000,000 by December and to 1,250,000 in August, 1932. One hundred and fifty thousand children were in need of charity. Malnutrition had increased in forty-eight counties—27 percent of school children being undernourished (216,000 out of a school population of 800,000). New patients in the tuberculosis clinics had doubled. And the general death rate and disease rate had risen. Only nine counties were well organized. Fifty-five gave cause for grave concern and nineteen were listed as distressed counties in dire need. Moreover, relief allowances have steadily dropped. Last December 43,000 of the 56,000 families in Philadelphia where no one was employed were receiving relief at the rate of $4.39 per week for families averaging 4.8 persons. By May the number of families receiving relief had risen to 55,000 and the amount of relief had dropped to $4.23, of which $3.93 was for food, being two-thirds of the minimum required for health. No provision is made for rents and the result is that the landlords of Philadelphia, like the landlords of the country at large, are compelled to choose between throwing their tenants into the streets or providing from their own pockets the shelter required. Outside of Philadelphia the weekly grant to a family is $3 or less in thirteen counties, and $3 to $4 in six more, while in some of the small steel towns it may be even lower. Funds in the counties are either exhausted or will be exhausted before November.

Detroit

Relief in Detroit was originally upon a boom-time, boom-extravagance basis with gross incompetence in the administration of funds, an embezzlement of

$207,000, and doles of silk stockings and cosmetics. The resultant imminent bankruptcy forced a contraction of expenditures, and relief in May, 1932, with a greatly increased need, was only $859,925 as against $2,088,850 in January, 1931. There were 223,000 unemployed last November in the city and 410,000 in the state. In January the city was caring for 48,000 distressed families. This number was cut to 22,000 in April and relief was given at the rate of fifteen cents per day per person. In July under pressure of further shortage a further cut of 5,000 families totaling 20,000 persons was determined. Aid was to be denied to ablebodied persons who had been public charges for a year or more whether work was available for them or not, and childless couples and small families with no definite ties in Detroit were to be forced to leave the city. The resultant relief roll was expected to be 17,757 families, of whom 7,000 were dependent because of age or illness. The great majority on relief are laborers but Detroit also carries or has carried forty-five ministers, thirty bank tellers, lawyers, dentists, musicians, and "two families after whom streets are named." Riots, chiefly employment riots, have been fairly common with bloodshed in at least one. And enormous breadlines and the like are daily sights. No adequate statistics on public health in Detroit exist but it may safely be assumed to be at least as low as New York's.

Chicago

Unemployed in Chicago number somewhere between 660,000 and 700,000 or 40 percent of its employable workers while the number for the state at large is about one in three of the gainfully employed. About 100,000 families have applied down to July for relief in Cook County. The minimum relief budget has been $2.40 per week for an adult and $1.50 per week for a child for food, with $22 to $23 per month to a family. But these figures have since been cut to $2.15 weekly for a man, $1.10 for a child. And persons demanding relief must be completely destitute to receive it. Rents are not paid by the relief agencies and housing is, in certain sections, unspeakably bad. While the situation of city employees is tragic. Teachers in May, 1932, had had only five months cash for the last thirteen months, 3,177 of them had lost $2,367,000 in bank failures, 2,278 of them had lost $7,800,000 in lapsed policies, 805 had borrowed $232,000 from loan sharks at rates adding up to 42 percent a year, and 759 had lost their homes. (The city at one time undertook to sell for tax default the houses of its employees unable to pay taxes because of its own default in wages.) It is estimated that $35,000,000 will be spent in 1932 for an inadequate job and that an adequate job would cost $50,000,000.

11

Fiscal Policy and Economic Stabilization

JOSEPH PECHMAN

Joseph Pechman is Director of Economic Studies at the Brookings Institution. The following article is taken from his book Federal Tax Policy, *published in 1971.*

During most of the nation's history, federal budget policy was based on the rule that tax receipts should be roughly equal to annual government expenditures. Declining receipts during a business contraction called for an increase in taxes or a reduction in expenditures, while surpluses that developed during periods of prosperity called for lowered tax rates or increased expenditures. This policy reduced private incomes when they were already falling and raised them when they were rising. By aggravating fluctuations in purchasing power, the policy of annually balanced budgets accentuated economic instability.

In the 1930s, new concepts of budget policy emerged that emphasized the relationship of the federal budget to the performance of the economy. Adjustments in federal expenditures and taxes were to be made to reduce unemployment or to check inflation. Budget surpluses were to be used to restrain private spending during prosperity, deficits to stimulate spending during recessions. But variations in government expenditures were expected to play a more active role than tax rate variations in counteracting fluctuations in private demand.

The view today is that private demand can be stimulated or restrained by tax as well as expenditure changes. Higher taxes and lower government expenditures help to fight inflation by restraining private demand; lower taxes and higher expenditures help to fight recession by stimulating private demand. Fiscal policy was actively used in the decade of the 1960s to promote economic stability, with results that exceeded expectations on some occasions (for example, when taxes were cut in 1964) and fell below expectations on others (for example, when the Vietnam war surtax was imposed in 1968).

Fiscal economics is based on national income analysis as it has developed over the past thirty-five years. The essence of this analysis is that the level of expenditures depends on total output or gross national product (GNP), which in turn depends on the total spending of consumers, business, and government. At any given time, there is a level of output that is consistent with full employment of the nation's supply of labor (except for seasonal, and a small amount of frictional, unemployment). This level is called *potential* or *full employment GNP* (Figure 1). The major objectives of fiscal policy are to stabilize the economy at full employment, maintain price stability, and promote economic growth and efficiency.

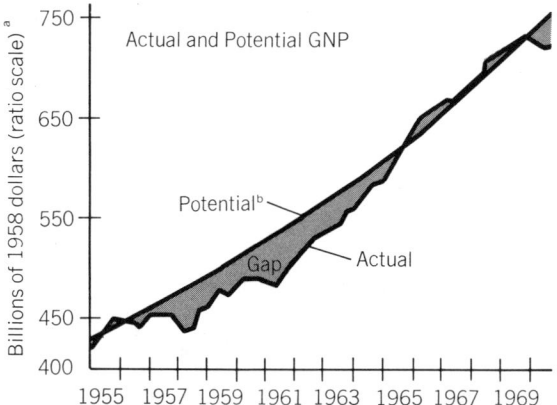

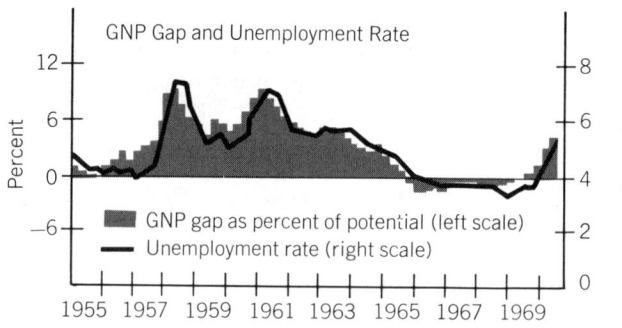

Sources U.S. Department of Commerce and Council of Economic Advisers.

[a]Seasonally adjusted annual rates.

[b]Trend line of 3-1/2 percent through middle of 1955 to 1962 IV, 3-3/4 percent from 1962 IV to 1965 IV, 4 percent from 1965 IV to 1969 IV, and 4.3 percent from 1969 IV to 1970 II.

Unemployment as percentage of civilian labor force; seasonally adjusted.

FIGURE 1.   Gross National Product, Actual and Potential, and Unemployment Rate, 1955–70

Stabilization Policy

The federal government exerts great influence on total spending, and hence on output, through its expenditure and tax policies. It alters total spending directly by varying its own spending, or indirectly by raising or lowering taxes. If expenditures are increased or taxes lowered, the spending of higher incomes by the recipients requires additional output, which in turn generates still more income and spending; and the cycle repeats itself. The cumulative increase in GNP is, therefore, a multiple of the initial increase in government expenditures or reduction in taxes. Correspondingly, reductions in expenditures or increases in taxes reduce GNP by a multiple of the initial action.

Impact of Expenditure and Tax Changes

The process of income and output creation through fiscal policy may be illustrated by the following hypothetical examples. Assume that out of each dollar of GNP, 25 cents is taken in federal taxes, and the remaining 75 cents goes to consumers and business. Assume also that consumers and business together spend 80 percent of any additional income they receive.

If the government increases its purchases by $10 billion, private income before tax will initially rise by the same amount. Tax revenues will be $2.5 billion higher, and private disposable income will rise by $7.5 billion, of which consumers and business will spend $6 billion. This additional spending will generate another increase in income, with $1.5 billion going to taxes and the remaining $4.5 billion to consumers and business. Of this latter amount, consumers and business will spend $3.6 billion, which will generate still another round of income and spending, and so on. The total increase in GNP (including the initial $10 billion of government purchases) will amount to $25 billion ($10+ $6+ $3.6+ . . .). This is a multiplier of 2.5 times the original increase in spending.

Consider what will happen if, instead of increasing expenditures, the government reduces taxes by $10 billion. Consumers and business will again spend 80 percent of the higher after-tax incomes, or $8 billion. This will generate the same amount of additional private income, of which consumers and business will receive $6 billion and spend $4.8 billion, and so on. The total increase in GNP will be $20 billion ($8+ $4.8+ . . .), or two times the original tax cut. The difference between the multipliers in the two illustrations reflects the differences in first-round effects of the expenditure and tax changes: in this round output is raised by the entire amount of the expenditure increase, but by only 80 percent of the tax reduction.

If expenditures and taxes are increased simultaneously by the same amount, the effects of these two actions will not cancel one another because, dollar for dollar, expenditures have a more potent effect on the economy than do tax changes. For example, given the assumptions in the previous illustrations, if a tax increase of $10 billion were enacted together with a $10 billion increase in government spending, the former would reduce GNP by $20 billion, while the latter would stimulate a $25 billion increase, leaving a net increase of $5 billion. In other words, an increase in expenditures that is fully financed by an increase in taxes will on balance increase the GNP. (This theorem assumes that the change in spending resulting from an increase or decrease in private disposable income will be the same regardless of the source of the income change and that investment and other economic behavior will not be influenced by the government's action. The multipliers used are illustrative only; estimates of the multipliers vary greatly.)

The effect of changes in government expenditures and taxes on the size of the government's deficit depends on the increase in GNP generated by the fiscal stimulus and on tax rates. In the previous examples, federal taxes were assumed to account for about 25 percent of an increment to GNP. Thus, the increase in GNP would raise tax receipts by $6.25 billion if expenditures were increased by $10 billion (0.25 × $25), causing an increase in deficit (or a reduction in surplus) of $3.75 billion. If taxes were reduced by $10 billion, the increase in GNP would raise tax receipts by $5 billion (0.25 × $20), causing a $5 billion increase in the deficit. If expenditures and taxes were raised simultaneously by $10 billion, the increase in GNP would raise tax receipts by $1.25 billion (0.25 × $5) and *reduce* the deficit (or increase the surplus) by that amount.

Monetary policy also plays an important role in stabilization policy. Suppose the federal government increases expenditures or reduces taxes. As GNP increases, individuals and business firms will need additional cash to conduct their business affairs. If the money supply fails to increase, the greater demand for cash will drive up interest rates. The higher interest rates will tend to reduce residential construction, business investment, and state-local construction, thus offsetting at least some of the effect of the initial increase in spending. Fiscal policy thus requires an accommodating monetary policy if it is to be fully effective, but the precise combination of monetary and fiscal measures necessary to obtain any desired response is not known.

Built-in Stabilizers

In addition to discretionary changes in taxes and expenditures (that is, deliberate government actions to vary taxes or the rate of expenditures), the fiscal system itself contributes to stabilization by generating automatic tax and expenditure adjustments that cushion the effect of changes in GNP. These *built-in stabilizers* moderate the fall in private income and spending when GNP declines and restrain private income and spending when GNP rises. They are automatic in the sense that they respond to changes in GNP without any action on the part of the government.

The two major groups of built-in fiscal stabilizers are: (1) taxes, in particular the federal individual income tax; and (2) transfers, such as unemployment compensation and welfare payments.

Among taxes, the federal individual income tax is the leading stabilizer. When incomes fall, many individuals who were formerly taxable drop below the taxable level; others are pushed down into lower tax brackets. Conversely, when incomes rise, individuals who were formerly not taxed become taxable, and others are pushed into higher tax brackets. Under the 1964 act rates, federal individual income tax receipts (excluding the Vietnam war surcharge) automatically increased or decreased by about 14 or 15 percent for every 10 percent increase or decrease in personal income. Since consumption depends on disposable personal income, automatic changes in receipts from the individual income tax tend to keep consumption more stable than it otherwise would be.

Variations in receipts from the corporation income tax are proportionately larger than variations in individual income tax receipts, because profits fluctuate widely over a business cycle. The variation in corporate profits is a major nonfiscal stabilizer in the economic system. When economic activity slows down, profits fall in absolute terms and as a percentage of GNP, thus absorbing much of the impact of the reduction in incomes. During a cyclical recovery, profits rise much faster than do other kinds of income. Corporation taxes vary almost directly with profits, and they assist corporations to absorb the impact of declining incomes during the downswing. During the upswing, rising tax liabilities tend to restrain the growth of corporation incomes. The effect of variations in corporation tax liabilities on dividends is relatively small because corporate managers try to keep dividends in line with long-term earnings.

Fluctuations in investment are probably reduced to some extent, but the precise effect is unknown.

On the expenditure side, the major built-in stabilizer is unemployment compensation. Insured workers who become unemployed are entitled to benefits for up to twenty-six weeks in most states. Benefits for an additional thirteen weeks are paid throughout the nation when the national unemployment rate is 4-1/2 percent for three consecutive months, and in any state when the state unemployment rate increases by 20 percent over the average of the two preceding years and is at least 4 percent. These payments help to maintain consumption as output and employment fall, even though the recipients are not participating in production. As incomes go up and employment increases, unemployment compensation declines. Other transfer payments (old-age insurance, public assistance, and the like) also tend to vary inversely with changes in GNP.

It is possible to calculate the effect of built-in stabilizers on the federal surplus, as distinct from the discretionary actions of the government. Because of the built-in stabilizers, the actual surplus or deficit reflects the prevailing levels of income and employment, as well as the government's fiscal policy. Figure 2 shows how the effect of the built-in stabilizers may be separated from the discretionary changes.

Each line in the figure shows the surplus or deficit

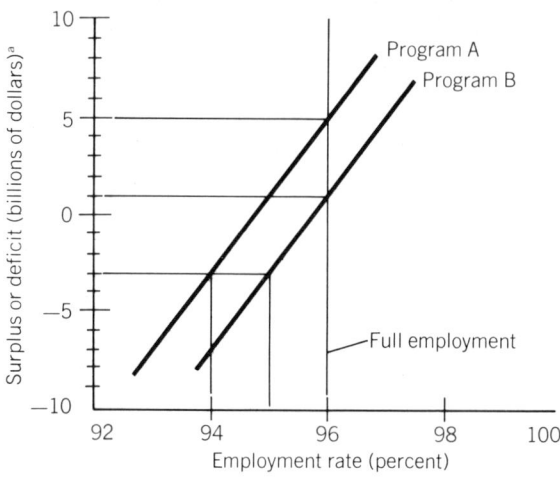

Source: Adapted from *Economic Report of the President, January 1962*, p. 79.
aNational income accounts basis.

FIGURE 2. Effect of Level of Activity on Federal Surplus or Deficit

that would be realized at various levels of employment under two different budget programs, A and B. For simplicity, it is assumed that the tax system is the same, but that expenditures are $4 billion higher under Program B. (The surplus is, therefore, $4 billion lower, or the deficit is $4 billion higher.) The lines slope upward, indicating that as employment and income increase, the deficits become smaller or the surpluses larger. The effect of the built-in stabilizers is given by the slope of each line: the greater the slope, the larger the impact of the built-in stabilizers on the surplus or deficit. As is shown in Figure 2, both programs have the same built-in stability features because the tax systems are identical. However, an actual deficit of $3 billion is realized when employment is at 94 percent of the labor force under Program A and 95 percent under Program B. Clearly, Program B is more expansionary than Program A. Differences between programs will also be due in practice to differences in tax rates; in such cases, the lines would not be parallel, but the slope of each line would still measure the built-in flexibility of each program.

The Full Employment Surplus

The degree of stimulation provided by fiscal policy is popularly regarded as a function of the *current* budget surplus or deficit (that is, the budget is considered to be restrictive when it is running a surplus and expansionary when it is in deficit). It should be clear from Figure 2 that actual surpluses or deficits are poor guides for evaluating fiscal policy because they include the effects of both automatic and discretionary fiscal actions.

The economic effects of two fiscal programs may be compared by examining the surplus or deficit at any given level of employment. By convention, the comparison is made at full employment, which is assumed to be when 96 percent of the labor force is employed. Defined in this way, the "full employment surplus" is $5 billion under Program A in Figure 2 and $1 billion under Program B. The difference of $4 billion reflects the assumed difference in expenditures. In practice, the differences are due to differences in taxes as well as expenditures.

There are two types of budget statements in current use—the official *unified budget* and the *national income accounts budget*. The full employment surplus is usually computed on a national income accounts basis, but it can be adjusted to the definitions in the unified budget.

The budget program that is appropriate at a given time depends upon the strength of private demand for consumption and investment goods. When private demand is high, a large full employment surplus is called for; when private demand is weak, a small full employment surplus, or even a full employment deficit, is required. Efforts to achieve a larger surplus or a lower deficit than is consistent with full employment would depress employment and incomes. If the budget called for too small a full employment surplus, total demand would be too high, and prices would rise.

Another characteristic of the full employment surplus is its tendency to increase with the passage of time and the growth of the economy. With the growth of the labor force, the stock of capital, and productivity, potential federal receipts also rise. At current tax rates and assuming full employment, federal receipts increase by about $18 billion a year. Thus, the full employment surplus will creep up by about $18 billion each year, or about 1.6 percent of potential GNP in 1971, unless the government takes steps to prevent it.

This upward creep in the full employment surplus has been called the *fiscal dividend* or the *fiscal drag*. It

THE TWO BUDGETS

The official budget statement of the federal government is the *unified budget*, which is an instrument of management and control of federal activities financed with federally owned funds. This budget includes cash flows to and from the public resulting from all federal fiscal activity, including the trust funds, and the net lending of government-owned enterprises. Thus, the unified budget provides a comprehensive picture of the financial impact of federal programs, but it does not measure their contribution to the current income and output of the nation. For this purpose, economists make use of the statement of receipts and expenditures in the official national income accounts, often called the *national income accounts budget*.

Like the unified budget, the national income accounts budget includes the activities of trust funds and excludes purely intragovernmental transactions (for example, interest on federal bonds owned by federal agencies) which do not affect the general public. However, there are significant differences between the two in timing and coverage. The national income accounts budget includes receipts and expenditures when they have their impact on private incomes, which is not necessarily when the federal government receives cash or pays it out. This adjustment involves putting receipts (except those from personal taxes) on an accrual basis and counting expenditures when goods are delivered rather than when payment is made. The adjustment for coverage excludes purely financial transactions because these represent an exchange of assets or claims and not a direct addition to income or production.

There are substantial differences in the size of surpluses or deficits between the two accounts, and even in their movements (Figure 3). In recent years, the national income accounts budget has shown the smaller deficit (or larger surpluses).

FIGURE 3.   **Federal Deficits and Surpluses, Two Budget Concepts, Fiscal Years 1954–70**

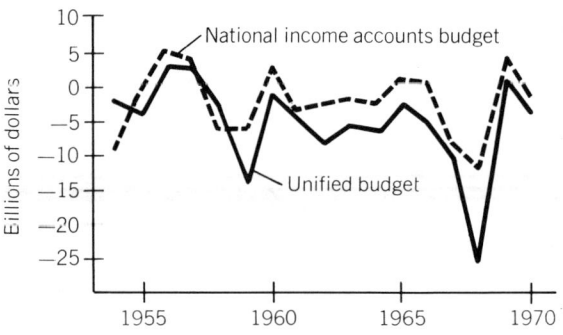

is identified as a *dividend* when used to describe the elbow room available in the federal budget to finance higher federal expenditures without raising tax rates. During the early 1960s, the fiscal dividend was large enough to finance tax rate reductions as well as expenditure increases. More recently, with continued high commitments for defense, the fiscal dividend has not been adequate to provide fully for urgently needed domestic social programs.

The automatic increase in federal receipts that accompanies economic growth is also called the *fiscal drag* because it acts as a retarding influence on the economy unless it is offset by rising expenditures or tax reductions. This terminology was in vogue in the early 1960s, when government expenditures were not rising fast enough to absorb the automatic growth in tax receipts.

According to current estimates, the federal budget would have been in surplus in every quarter between mid-1955 and mid-1965, had full employment been maintained (Figure 4). However, the actual budget showed a deficit during most of the period, reflecting the disappointing performance of the economy. It was only after the full employment surplus was sharply reduced in 1964 to stimulate the economy that employment began to move toward 96 percent of the

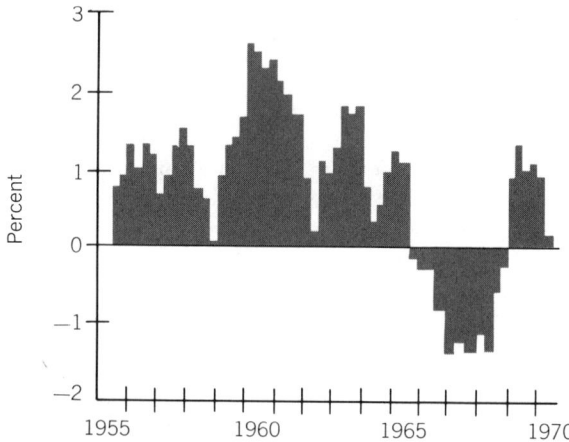

Sources: Arthur M. Okun and Nancy H. Teeters, "The Full Employment Surplus Revisited," in *Brookings Papers on Economic Activity* (1:1970), pp. 104–05; Teeters, "Budgetary Outlook at Mid-Year 1970," in *Brookings Papers on Economic Activity* (2:1970), p. 304 (adjusted to exclude the corporate financial adjustment).

FIGURE 4. Full Employment Surplus as a Percentage of Potential Gross National Product, National Income Accounts Basis, 1955–70

labor force, which is regarded by most people as the minimum acceptable level. This experience illustrates the principle that planning for a budget surplus, without regard to the strength of private demand, may produce unsatisfactory rates of employment and output and create budget deficits besides.

The rapid build-up of military expenditures for the Vietnam war quickly wiped out the full employment surplus beginning in mid-1965, the deficit on a full employment basis averaging 0.5 percent of potential GNP in 1966, 1.4 percent in 1967, and 0.9 percent in 1968. This was the period when prices rose at an unacceptably rapid rate. The full employment budget was restored to a surplus position in early 1969, reflecting the effect of the Vietnam war surtax and the strict limitations that were placed on domestic federal programs. The sharp increase in fiscal restraint, combined with an extremely tight monetary policy, helped to bring about a slowdown and then a decline in the real GNP beginning in the fourth quarter of 1969. Unfortunately, by this time the inflation had been converted to a "cost-push" type of inflation, and prices continued to rise at an excessive rate even in the face of the decline in real GNP.

Although it is the most convenient single measure of restrictiveness or ease in the federal budget, the full employment surplus must be used with considerable care. In the first place, the degree of fiscal restraint needed at any given time depends on the strength of private demand. The same full employment surplus that may be appropriate for one period may not be appropriate for another. Second, differences in the level and composition of expenditures and taxes have an important bearing on the significance of the full employment surplus. For example, an increase in the full employment surplus resulting from a reduction in government expenditures on goods and services would be more restrictive than would a tax increase of the same amount. Third, the restrictiveness of a given *amount* of surplus, say, $10 billion, would be much greater in a $750 billion economy than in a $1,000 billion economy. In making comparisons over time, the full employment surplus should be expressed as a percentage of potential GNP (see Figure 4). Finally, there is no simple way to adjust the full employment surplus for the effect of price increases. Most calculations of the full employment surplus remove the effect of the built-in response of the federal budget to a business recession, but do not remove the built-in response of the budget to inflation. For these reasons, the meaning of the full employment surplus is likely to be unambiguous only during relatively short periods when changes in expenditures and taxes, and in the rate of growth of prices, are relatively small. Analysis of the fiscal impact of the budget over long periods requires more detailed information than the full employment surplus provides by itself.

Expenditure versus Tax Adjustments to Promote Stability

Both expenditure and tax rate changes can be used for stabilization purposes. While it is true that expenditure changes have somewhat larger multiplier effects, they are not necessarily preferable to changes in tax rates. In the first place, government expenditures should be determined on the basis of long-run national needs and not of short-run cyclical considerations. The controlling principle is that government outlays should not exceed the level where the benefit to the nation's citizens of an additional dollar of expenditures would be the same in public and private use. It is hardly likely that this point would shift sharply in one direction or the other during such short periods as a business contraction or even during an inflation. Second, considerations of economic efficiency argue against large short-run variations in expenditures. For example, it would be wasteful to slow down construction of a road or hydroelectric facility, once construction has begun, in the interest of reducing aggregate spending. Third, there may be a long time lag between a decision to undertake an expenditure and its effect on output and employment. When recessions are relatively brief—as they have been since the end of World War II—the impact of a decision to make an expenditure change often is not felt until recovery is under way. However, during periods of rapidly rising defense expenditures, such as occurred during the Korean and Vietnam wars, a slowing down or deferment of some government programs usually becomes necessary to keep total demand from outstripping the productive potential of the economy.

Among the various taxes, the individual income tax is the best suited for stabilization purposes. Under the withholding system for wages and salaries, changes in tax rates can be made effective in a matter of days and can also be terminated quickly. In most cases, the effect of a tax change on a worker's take-home pay is indistinguishable from the effect of a change in his gross weekly wage. Corporation income tax changes are not likely to have significant effects on investment if it is known, or expected, that they will be of short

duration. Consumption tax changes may have a perverse effect in the short run; the expectation of a reduction may delay spending, and the expectation of an increase may accelerate spending. Nevertheless, once they become effective, consumption tax changes are at least as powerful as income tax changes in stimulating or restraining consumer demand.

Some economists believe that consumption depends on income that is expected to be received regularly and is not much affected by temporary or transitory changes in income. On this hypothesis, temporary income tax changes would have relatively little impact on consumption. Most economists believe that a temporary income tax change would have some effect on consumer spending, although they agree that it would be less powerful than a permanent tax change. Income tax changes also operate with a lag, because consumers do not alter their consumption immediately in response to changes in disposable income.

Tax changes are often assumed to have the largest effect on consumption if they are confined to the lower income classes. This view presupposes that poor people spend proportionately more out of any additional dollars they may receive than do the rich. There is no evidence, however, to confirm or deny this assumption. For policy purposes, it is probably satisfactory to assume that the incremental consumption rate is fairly high throughout most of the income distribution. This would suggest that, if the distribution of the tax burden is considered equitable by the large majority of taxpayers, tax rates could be moved up or down uniformly for stabilization purposes under a simple formula, such as an equal percentage change for all taxpayers.

Tax rate changes are sometimes criticized on the ground that they are too small to exert a significant economic effect. With sixty-five million taxpayers, a $13 billion individual income tax cut would be equivalent to an average increase in take-home pay of only $4 a week per taxpayer, a negligible amount in comparison with the total GNP of $1,000 billion. The comparison is erroneous, however, because it compares weekly and annual income flows. A $13 billion tax cut would amount to more than 1 percent of the GNP, whether expressed on a weekly, monthly, or annual basis, Because tax changes have a multiplier effect, a tax cut of this magnitude would provide a substantial stimulus to the economy. The deviation from full employment GNP, which tax cuts are intended to narrow, is usually less than 5 percent.

Tax adjustments can be used to restrain as well as to

stimulate demand and are therefore important policy instruments for counteracting inflation. It may be impractical, if not impossible, to cut back government expenditures when inflation threatens. About half of federal expenditures are for defense, foreign aid, education, and research and development, which should not be altered for short-run reasons. Much of the remainder of the federal budget provides assistance to low-income persons, who are particularly hard-pressed during an inflation. Moreover, the inflationary pressures may have been due to an increase in government spending for defense or war purposes. In these circumstances, tax increases must be used to withdraw excess purchasing power from the income stream.

The time required for the legislative process to be completed is the major obstacle to prompt use of tax changes for stabilization purposes. Congressional consideration of major tax legislation may take as long as eighteen months. Proposals have been made to give the President authority to make temporary changes in individual income tax rates, or to speed up congressional procedures for action on presidential recommendations. However, Congress has not seriously considered such plans.

Automatic Budget Rules

It is now widely understood that following a policy of annually balanced budgets would accentuate business fluctuations. But many people continue to believe that it is unwise to rely exclusively on discretion to guide budget decisions. Discretionary policy depends heavily on forecasting techniques that are still subject to error. There is also a fear that removing budgetary restraint would lead to excessive federal expenditures. To avoid these pitfalls, attempts have been made to formulate rules that would reduce the element of judgment in budget decisions without impairing economic growth and stability.

The best known plan is the *stabilizing budget policy* of the Committee for Economic Development (CED), a nonprofit organization of influential businessmen and educators. Under this policy, tax rates would be set to balance the budget or yield a small surplus at full employment. Tax rates would remain unchanged until there was a major change in the level of expenditures. Reliance would be placed on the built-in stabilizers to moderate fluctuations in private demand.

The CED plan would operate successfully, however, only if full employment could be achieved with a balance or a small surplus in the federal budget. Moreover, the CED plan does not offer a systematic method for raising additional revenues if federal expenditures should rise by more than the amount of the automatic growth in tax receipts, or of lowering taxes if federal expenditures should rise by less than the amount of the automatic growth in tax receipts. With federal expenditure needs rising rapidly and recession still a considerable threat to economic stability, it would be both hazardous and unwise to keep tax rates unchanged for long periods.

A second type of plan—which would aim at helping to solve the fiscal drag problem—would provide for individual income tax rates to be reduced each year by a given amount, say 1 percentage point (which would reduce income tax receipts by about $4 billion a year at 1971 income levels), with the $14 billion remaining from the fiscal dividend of approximately $18 billion to be used for increasing federal expenditures. Presumably, the plan would begin with a surplus or deficit consistent with full employment. The difficulty with this approach is that it would freeze the allocation of increased federal receipts between tax reduction and increased expenditures. Periods when it would have been desirable to cut tax rates by a fixed amount or a fixed percentage each year have been rare in the nation's history.

A third approach to an automatic budget policy would be to build into the budget a formula that would trigger upward or downward changes in tax rates when certain predetermined economic indices are reached. For example, legislation might provide for a 1 percentage point reduction in income tax rates for every increase of 0.5 percent in unemployment above 4.5 percent of the labor force, or an increase of 1 percentage point for every rise of 2 points in a general price index, such as the consumer or the wholesale price index. While this type of formula would add to the effectiveness of the built-in stabilizers if the changes were correctly timed, no one index or set of indices could be used with confidence to signal an economic movement justifying tax action.

It is evident that budget policy cannot be based on a rigid set of rules. Nevertheless, the search for budget rules has greatly improved public understanding of the elements of fiscal policy. Great emphasis is placed on the automatic stabilizers for their cushioning effect on private disposable incomes and spending. Recognition of the capacity of the federal tax system to generate rising revenues has alerted policy-makers to the need for making positive decisions to determine the relative social priorities of public and private expenditures, so that the appropriate amounts can be allocated to tax reduction and to higher government expenditures. Unfortunately, the political advantages of an immediate tax reduction tend to be more attractive than the long-run benefits of new or improved government programs. Thus, the Tax Reform Act of 1969 included net tax reductions, phased in over a period of years, which amount to $8 billion a year (at 1975 income levels), even though the remaining fiscal dividend was acknowledged to be inadequate to finance urgently needed federal programs.

Policies to Promote Economic Growth

Fiscal policies are useful in promoting long-run economic growth as well as short-run stability. The objective of growth policy is to provide relatively full employment for the labor force and industrial capacity, at stable prices. Growth may be disappointing for two reasons: the resources of the economy may not be employed up to their full potential because the economy is in recession or is being artificially held down to combat inflationary pressures, or the rate of growth of potential output at full employment may be too low. The policies required under these circumstances differ, although they are often confused.

Achieving Full Employment and Stable Prices

The major contribution that fiscal policy can make to economic growth is to help keep total demand roughly in line with the productive potential of the economy. An economy operating at less than full employment is one in which potential GNP is larger than the total of actual spending by consumers, business, and government. The remedy for this deficiency is to increase private or public spending through fiscal and monetary stimulation. Conversely, when total demand exceeds the capacity of the economy to produce goods and services, the remedy is to curtail private or public spending through fiscal and monetary restraint.

Although the basic principles of stabilization policy are clear, they have been difficult to apply in practice. Failure to absorb the normal growth in revenues will produce successively higher full employment surpluses, which may hold actual output below the economic potential of the economy. The high levels of unemployment and the large gap between potential and actual GNP in the late 1950s and early 1960s (see Figure 1) were caused largely by excessively restrictive fiscal policies that arose in this way. On the other hand, too large a growth in government expenditures relative to normal revenue growth may produce excess demand, which in turn leads to rising prices. The inflation that began in mid-1965 was triggered by the large rise in Vietnam war expenditures, which were superimposed on an economy already operating at close to full employment. A 10 percent surtax on individual and corporation income taxes was enacted in the summer of 1968, but this was about three years after the decision to escalate the war had been made.

It now seems clear that it will always be difficult to maintain full employment in a modern industrial economy and keep price increases within acceptable limits. Since the end of World War II, prices have shown a tendency to rise in the United States, even when total spending has been below potential GNP. Many economists believe that this dilemma can be resolved only by supplementing fiscal and monetary policies with some form of wage-price or "incomes" policy to keep wage increases roughly in line with the average growth in productivity of the economy as a whole, and to prevent price increases that are not justified by cost increases. Under such a policy, prices would decline in industries with above-average productivity increases and rise in industries with less-than-average productivity increases, but the average of all prices would be stable. These principles were established by the Council of Economic Advisers in 1962 as voluntary "guideposts" for wage and price behavior. The guideposts had the strong backing of Presidents Kennedy and Johnson and appeared to have some effect in restraining wage and price increases (a judgment that some professional economists dispute) until mid-1965, when the rapid build-up of military expenditures for the Vietnam war upset the balance between supply and demand. No country has yet devised a workable incomes policy under conditions of full employment, and the search continues.

Experience has shown that the major effect of inflation on growth is felt when the attempt is made to restore balance in the economy. Inflation distorts the distribution of the national income among different groups. Each group tries to protect itself against erosion of its share through wage or price increases or government transfer payments. Such pressures continue to be felt long after excess demand has been removed by fiscal and monetary restraint. Thus, without an effective incomes policy, it may be possible to halt inflation only at the cost of high unemployment and slow growth for relatively long periods. It is, of course, much less costly in social and economic terms to avoid inflation in the first place.

Raising the Growth Rate

If full employment is maintained, the rate of economic growth will depend on the ability of the economy to raise the rate of growth of potential output. The factors affecting potential output are the size of the labor force, the length of the average workweek and workyear, and productivity (output per man-hour). Productivity depends on the size of the capital stock, the quality of human resources, the attitudes and skills of management, the efficiency of resource use, and the amount of technological progress. Most of these factors are influenced to some extent by government expenditure and tax policy, but the influence is most direct and quantitatively most important with respect to the rate of national investment in both physical and human resources.

To increase the rate of growth, the rate of national investment must be raised to a permanently higher level and held there for a long period of time. The federal government can contribute toward increasing the investment rate through fiscal policy in three ways: (1) it can adopt a policy of budget surpluses when the economy is operating at full employment; (2) it can increase investment in physical and human capital directly through its own expenditures; and (3) it can adopt tax measures that provide incentives for private saving and investment.

SAVING THROUGH BUDGET SURPLUSES. The key to an understanding of growth policy is the relation between saving and investment. As measured statistically, national saving is the difference between national output and the amounts spent by consumers and government; private investment is also that part of the national product that is not consumed or used for government purposes. Thus, national saving is equal to private investment. In effect, through saving, the nation sets aside the resources needed for private investment purposes; otherwise the resources would be used to produce goods and services for consumers and government.

When the federal government runs a budget surplus, it adds its own saving to that generated by the private economy. When the budget is in deficit,

national saving is reduced. Since increased saving and investment are needed to raise the growth rate, the federal government can stimulate a higher growth rate by running budget surpluses at full employment. Moreover, the larger the surplus at full employment, the larger the potential contribution to growth.

This growth strategy can be implemented only if there is sufficient investment demand in the private economy to use up the saving generated in the federal budget. If private demand for investment is too low, the federal surplus will generate unemployment rather than more growth. In other words, the full employment surplus must be just large enough to offset the deficiency in private saving. If there is more than enough private saving for the existing investment demand, the budget should be in deficit even at full employment.

An important ingredient of any strategy to increase the rate of private investment is monetary policy. Easy money provides ready access to credit and lowers the cost of borrowing for investment purposes by reducing interest rates. Tight money restrains the growth of credit and raises interest rates. Therefore, the best policy to promote private investment would combine a budget surplus with easy money. In implementing such a policy, it is important to avoid taxes that impair investment incentives.

In practice, the extent of monetary ease that a nation can afford is limited by balance-of-payments considerations. If interest rates are driven down too far, private capital will leave the country to take advantage of higher interest rates abroad. In extreme cases, the outflow of funds may require devaluation of the nation's currency to restore international equilibrium. When interest rates must be kept up for balance-of-payments reasons, fiscal policy must be easier (that is, the surplus must be lower or the deficit higher) to prevent a drop in demand and employment.

INCREASING INVESTMENT DIRECTLY. It is not generally realized that investment is undertaken by government as well as by private firms. Outlays for education, training of manpower, health, research and development, roads, and other public facilities are essential elements of national investment. Such outlays are not substitutable for private investment, or vice versa. Education and research expenditures are perhaps the most important components of national investment, yet most of these expenditures are paid for by government (primarily state and local in the case of education, and primarily federal in the case of research). There is no basis for prejudging how total investment should be distributed between the public and private sectors, and it is important to avoid doctrinaire positions about one or the other. Both types of investment contribute to the nation's economic growth.

Public investment is financed directly by government through the tax system. If private demand is strong, the appropriate policy for growth would be to raise enough tax revenues to pay for needed government investment as well as to leave an additional margin of saving for private investment.

INCREASING SAVING AND INVESTMENT INCENTIVES. Given the aggregate level of taxation, the tax structure can be an important independent factor in determining the growth potential of the economy. The tax structure may encourage consumption or saving, help to raise or lower private investment in general or in particular industries, stimulate or restrain the outflow of investment funds to foreign countries, and subsidize or discourage particular expenditures by individuals and business firms. Most tax systems, including that of the United States, have numerous features specifically intended to promote saving and investment. For example, the federal income taxes provide liberal depreciation allowances, full offsets for business losses against other income over a period of nine years, averaging of individual income for tax purposes over a period of five years, and preferential treatment of capital gains. A 7 percent credit against corporation and individual income taxes was used to stimulate investment between 1962 and 1969. These and other provisions will be discussed in later chapters.

The "Debt Burden"

Effective use of fiscal policy to promote the full employment and growth objectives is hindered by public concern over a growth of the national debt. There is widespread fear that a long succession of annual deficits and a resulting rise in the national debt will impose dangerously heavy burdens on later generations. There is also concern about the economic burden of interest payments.

Growth of the national debt can impose a burden on future generations if it interferes with private capital formation. In this respect, there is a difference between debt created under conditions of excessive unemployment and debt created under conditions of full employment.

In a situation of substantial unemployment, an increase in the public debt can finance deficits that government uses to purchase goods and services directly or to provide transfer payments. Since there are unemployed resources, the goods and services acquired by government or by the recipients of transfer payments do not take the place of goods and services that might otherwise have been produced. If accompanied by the appropriate monetary policy, the debt increase can be absorbed without impeding the flow of funds into private capital formation. In fact, private investment will rise as a result of the stimulus that arises from a higher level of economic activity. The community is better off when the expenditures are made; and later generations will also benefit to the extent that the expenditures increase private and public investment in human or physical capital that will yield future services.

The situation is more complicated if the economy is at full employment. In this setting an increase in government expenditures that leads to a deficit (or reduces a surplus) in the federal budget cannot increase total output. This means either that prices will rise or that offsetting tax increases or monetary restraint will be required. If inflation is to be avoided, the necessary restraint must reduce consumption or investment. If the impact is on consumption, taxpayers will have in effect exchanged a collective good or service for current consumption. If the impact is on private or public investment, later generations will be worse off to the extent that the rate of growth of productive capacity has been reduced.

Since the federal government usually runs surpluses when the economy is at full employment (see Figure 4), there is little likelihood that the federal debt added in peacetime will be burdensome in an economic sense. Deficits incurred to restore or maintain full employment raise output and employment and actually increase the resources available to current and later generations.

The existence of the national debt does mean that interest must be paid to holders of the debt, and tax rates are therefore higher than they would be without the debt. The transfer of interest from general taxpayers to bondholders is a burden on the economy if the taxes levied to pay interest on the debt reduce saving or lower economic efficiency. (If the government debt is paid back by a per capita tax—which has no effect on economic incentives—and the market for bonds is competitive, the debt is exactly equivalent to the tax receipts and therefore does not impose a burden on future generations.) In any case, the debt burden in the United States must be small because net interest payments represent a relatively small proportion of federal expenditures (6 percent in 1969). Moreover, the ratio of net federal debt to the GNP has been declining since the end of World War II (Figure 5), and interest payments on the net debt, which fell markedly in the early postwar years, have amounted to only slightly more than 1 percent of GNP since the early 1950s. The growth of the economy over this period has kept the burden of the debt in relation to total production from rising, even though the interest rates at which debt can be issued have shown a rising trend over the entire period.

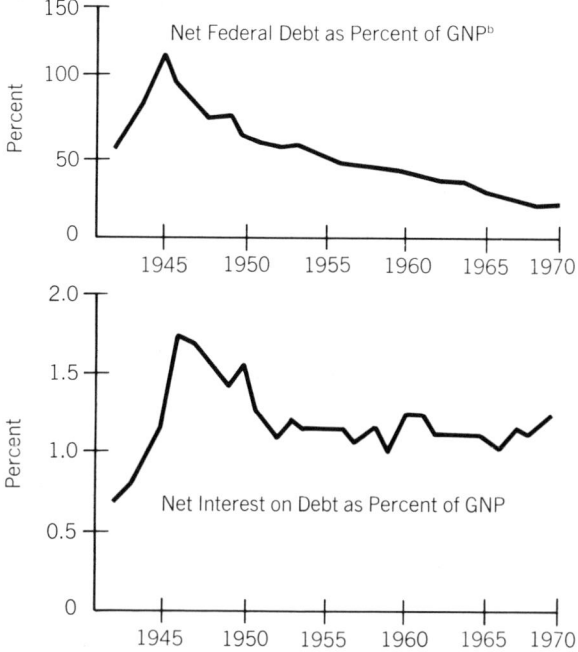

Sources: Net federal debt: *Economic Report of the President, February 1970*, p. 255. Net interest: 1946–69: Interest payments to the public shown in *The Budget of the United States Government*, various years, or supplied (for 1967–69) by the U.S. Bureau of the Budget, less Federal Reserve bank earnings on U.S. government securities by fiscal years (supplied by Board of Governors of the Federal Reserve System); 1942–45: Estimated from data in *Federal Reserve Bulletins*. Gross national product: *Survey of Current Business*, July 1970, pp. 8, 17; *The Budget of the United States Government, Fiscal Year 1971*, p. 593; and *The Budget of the United States Government, Fiscal Year 1969*, p. 544.

Net federal debt is debt held outside U.S. government investment account and Federal Reserve banks. Interest on net federal debt is total interest payments to the public less interest earned by Federal Reserve Banks.

Net federal debt at the end of calendar years divided by fiscal year gross national product.

FIGURE 5. Relation of Net Federal Debt and Net Interest on Debt to the Gross National Product, Fiscal Years 1942–69

12

Fiscal Policy: A Skeptical View

MILTON FRIEDMAN

Milton Friedman is Professor of Economics at the University of Chicago. This article is taken from his well-known book Capitalism and Freedom.

Ever since the New Deal, a primary excuse for the expansion of governmental activity at the federal level has been the supposed necessity for government spending to eliminate unemployment. The excuse has gone through several stages. At first, government spending was needed to "prime the pump." Temporary expenditures would set the economy going and the government could then step out of the picture.

When the initial expenditures failed to eliminate unemployment and were followed by a sharp economic contraction in 1937–38, the theory of "secular stagnation" developed to justify a permanently high level of government spending. The economy had become mature, it was argued. Opportunities for investment had been largely exploited and no substantial new opportunities were likely to arise. Yet individuals would still want to save. Hence, it was essential for government to spend and run a perpetual deficit. The securities issued to finance the deficit would provide individuals with a way to accumulate savings while the government expenditures provided employment. This view has been thoroughly discredited by theoretical analysis and even more by actual experience, including the emergence of wholly new lines for private investment not dreamed of by the secular stagnationists. Yet it has left its heritage. The idea may be accepted by none, but the government programs undertaken in its name, like some of those intended to prime the pump, are still with us and indeed account for ever-growing government expenditures.

More recently, the emphasis has been on government expenditures neither to prime the pump nor to hold in check the specter of secular stagnation but as a balance wheel. When private expenditures decline for any reason, it is said, governmental expenditures should rise to keep total expenditures stable; conversely, when private expenditures rise, governmental expenditures should decline. Unfortunately, the balance wheel is unbalanced. Each recession, however minor, sends a shudder through politically sensitive legislators and administrators with their ever present fear that perhaps it is the harbinger of another 1929–33. They hasten to enact federal spending programs of one kind or another. Many of the programs do not in fact come into effect until after the recession has passed. Hence, insofar as they do affect total expenditures, on which I shall have more to say later, they tend to exacerbate the succeeding expansion rather than to mitigate the recession. The haste with which spending programs are approved is not matched by an equal haste to repeal them or to eliminate others when the recession is passed and expansion is under way. On the contrary, it is then argued that a "healthy" expansion must not be "jeopardized" by cuts in governmental expenditures. The chief harm done by the balance-wheel theory is therefore not that it has failed to offset recessions, which it has, and not that it has introduced an inflationary bias into governmental policy, which it has done too, but that it has continuously fostered an expansion in the range of governmental activities at the federal level and prevented a reduction in the burden of federal taxes.

In view of the emphasis on using the federal budget as a balance wheel, it is ironic that the most unstable component of national income in the postwar period is federal expenditure, and the instability has not at all been in a direction to offset movements of other expenditure components. Far from being a balance wheel offsetting other forces making for fluctuations, the federal budget has if anything been itself a major source of disturbance and instability.

Because its expenditures are now so large a part of the total for the economy as a whole, the federal government cannot avoid having significant effects on the economy. The first requisite is therefore that the government mend its own fences, that it adopt procedures that will lead to reasonable stability in its own flow of expenditures. If it would do that, it would make a clear contribution to reducing the adjustments required in the rest of the economy.

Even if one were to accept the view that the federal budget should be and can be used as a balance wheel—a view I shall consider in more detail shortly—there is no necessity to use the expenditure side of the budget for this purpose. The tax side is equally available. A decline in national income automatically reduces the tax revenue of the federal government in greater proportion and thus shifts the budget in the direction of a deficit, and conversely during a boom. If it is desired to do more, taxes can be lowered during recessions and raised during expansions. Of course, politics might well enforce an asymmetry here too, making the declines politically more palatable than the rises.

If the balance-wheel theory has in practice been applied on the expenditure side, it has been because of the existence of other forces making for increased governmental expenditures; in particular, the widespread acceptance by intellectuals of the belief that government should play a larger role in economic and private affairs; the triumph, that is, of the philosophy of the welfare state. This philosophy has found a useful ally in the balance-wheel theory; it has enabled governmental intervention to proceed at a faster pace than would otherwise have been possible.

How different matters might now be if the balance-wheel theory had been applied on the tax side instead of the expenditure side. Suppose each recession had seen a cut in taxes and suppose the political unpopularity of raising taxes in the succeeding expansion had led to resistance to newly proposed governmental expenditure programs and to curtailment of existing ones. We might now be in a position where federal expenditures would be absorbing a good deal less of a national income that would be larger because of the reduction in the depressing and inhibiting effects of taxes.

I hasten to add that this dream is not intended to indicate support for the balance-wheel theory. In practice, even if the effects would be in the direction expected under the balance-wheel theory, they would be delayed in time and spread. To make them an effective offset to other forces making for fluctuations, we would have to be able to forecast those fluctuations a long time in advance. In fiscal policy as in monetary policy, all political considerations aside, we simply do not know enough to be able to use deliberate changes in taxation or expenditures as a sensitive stabilizing mechanism. In the process of trying to do so, we almost surely make matters worse. We make matters worse not by being consistently perverse—that would be easily cured by simply doing the opposite of what seemed at first the thing to do. We make matters worse by introducing a largely random disturbance that is simply added to other disturbances. That is what we seem in fact to have done in the past—in addition, of course to the major mistakes that have been seriously perverse. What I have written elsewhere in respect of monetary policy is equally applicable to fiscal policy: "What we need is not a skillful monetary driver of the economic vehicle continuously turning the steering wheel to adjust to the unexpected irregularities of the route, but some means of keeping the monetary passenger who is in the back seat as ballast from occasionally leaning over and giving the steering wheel a jerk that threatens to send the car off the road."

For fiscal policy, the appropriate counterpart to the monetary rule would be to plan expenditure programs entirely in terms of what the community wants to do through government rather than privately, and without any regard to problems of year-to-year economic stability; to plan tax rates so as to provide sufficient revenues to cover planned expenditures on the average of one year with another, again without regard to year-to-year changes in economic stability; and to avoid erratic changes in either governmental expenditures or taxes. Of course, some changes may be unavoidable. A sudden change in the international situation may dictate large increases in military expenditures or permit welcome decreases. Such changes account for some erratic shifts in federal expenditures in the postwar period. But they by no means account for all.

Before leaving the subject of fiscal policy, I should like to discuss the view, now so widely held, that an increase in governmental expenditures relative to tax-receipts is necessarily expansionary and a decrease contractionary. This view, which is at the heart of the belief that fiscal policy can serve as a balance wheel, is by now almost taken for granted by businessmen, professional economists, and laymen alike. Yet it cannot be demonstrated to be true by logical considerations alone, has never been documented by empirical evidence, and is in fact inconsistent with the relevant empirical evidence of which I know.

The belief has its origin in a crude Keynesian analysis. Suppose governmental expenditures are raised by $100 and taxes are kept unchanged. Then, goes the simple analysis, on the first round, the people who receive the extra hundred dollars will have that much more income. They will save some of it, say one-third, and spend the remaining two-thirds. But this means that on the second round, someone else receives an extra $66-2/3 of income. He in turn will save some and spend some, and so on and on in infinite sequence. If at every stage one-third is saved and two-thirds spent, then the extra $100 of government expenditures will ultimately, on this analysis, add $300 to income. This is the simple Keynesian multiplier analysis with a multiplier of three. Of course, if there is one injection, the effects will die off, the initial jump in income of $100 being succeeded by a gradual decline back to the earlier level. But if government expenditures are kept $100 higher per unit of time, say $100 a year higher, then, on this analysis, income will remain higher by $300 a year.

This simple analysis is extremely appealing. But the appeal is spurious and arises from neglecting other relevant effects of the change in question. When these are taken into account, the final result is much more dubious: it may be anything from no change in income at all, in which case private expenditures will go down by the $100 by which government expenditures go up, to the full increase specified. And even if money income increases, prices may rise, so real income will increase less or not at all. Let us examine some of the possible slips 'twixt cup and lip.

In the first place, nothing is said in the simple account about what the government spends the $100 on. Suppose, for example, it spends it on something that individuals were otherwise obtaining for themselves. They were, for example, spending $100 on paying fees to a park which paid the cost of attendants to keep it clean. Suppose the government now pays these costs and permits people to enter the park "free." The attendants still receive the same income, but the people who paid the fees have $100 available. The government spending does not, even in the initial stage, add $100 to anyone's income. What it does is to leave some people with $100 available to use for purposes other than the park, and presumably purposes they value less highly. They can be expected to spend less out of their total income for consumer goods than formerly, since they are receiving the park services free. How much less, it is not easy to say. Even if we accept, as in the simple analysis, that people save one-third of additional income, it does not follow that when they get one set of consumer goods "free," two-thirds of the released money will be spent on other consumer goods. One extreme possibility, of course, is that they will continue to buy the same collection of other consumer goods as they did before and add the released $100 to their savings. In this case even in the simple Keynesian analysis, the effect of the government expenditures is completely offset: government expenditures go up by $100, private down by $100. Or, to take another example, the $100 may be spent to build a road that a private enterprise would otherwise have built or the availability of which may make repairs to the company's trucks unnecessary. The firm then has funds released, but presumably will not spend them all on what are less attractive investments. In these cases, government expenditures simply divert private expenditures and only the net excess of government expenditures is even available at the outset for the multiplier to work on. From this point of view, it is paradoxical that the way to assure no diversion is to have the government spend the money for something utterly useless—this is the limited intellectual content to the "filling-holes" type of make-work. But of course this itself shows that there is something wrong with the analysis.

In the second place, nothing is said in the simple account about where the government gets the $100 to spend. So far as the analysis goes, the results are the same whether the government prints extra money or borrows from the public. But surely which it does will make a difference. To separate fiscal from monetary policy, let us suppose the government borrows the $100 so that the stock of money is the same as it would have been in the absence of the government expenditure. This is the proper assumption because the stock of money can be increased without extra government expenditure, if that is desired, simply by printing the money and buying outstanding government bonds with it. But we must now ask what the effect of borrowing is. To analyze this problem, let us assume that diversion does not occur, so in the first instance there is no direct offset to the $100 in the form of a compensating drop in private expenditures. Note that the government's borrowing to spend does not alter the amount of money in private hands. The government borrows $100 with its right hand from some individuals and hands the money with its left hand to those individuals to whom its expenditures go. Different people hold the money but the total amount of money held is unchanged.

The simple Keynesian analysis implicitly assumes that borrowing the money does not have any effects on other spending. There are two extreme circumstances under which this can occur. First, suppose people are utterly indifferent to whether they hold bonds or money, so that bonds to get the $100 can be sold without having to offer a higher return to the buyer than such bonds were yielding before. (Of course, $100 is so small an amount that it would in practice have a negligible effect on the required rate of return, but the issue is one of principle whose practical effect can be seen by letting the $100 stand for $100 million or $100 ten-million.) In Keynesian jargon, there is a "liquidity trap" so people buy the bonds with "idle money." If this is not the case, and clearly it cannot be indefinitely, then the government can sell the bonds only by offering a higher rate of return on it. A higher rate will then have to be paid also by other borrowers. This higher rate will in general discourage private spending on the part of would-be borrowers. Here comes the second extreme circumstance under which the simple Keynesian

analysis will hold: if potential borrowers are so stubborn about spending that no rise in interest rates however steep will cut down their expenditures, or, in Keynesian jargon, if the marginal efficiency schedule of investment is perfectly inelastic with respect to the interest rate.

I know of no established economist, no matter how much of a Keynesian he may regard himself as being, who would regard either of these extreme assumptions as holding currently, or as being capable of holding over any considerable range of borrowing or rise in interest rates, or as having held except under rather special circumstances in the past. Yet many an economist, let alone noneconomist, whether regarding himself as Keynesian or not, accepts as valid the belief that a rise in governmental expenditures relative to tax receipts, even when financed by borrowing, is *necessarily* expansionist, though as we have seen, this belief implicitly requires one of these extreme circumstances to hold.

If neither assumption holds, the rise in government expenditures will be offset by a decline in private expenditures on the part either of those who lend funds to the government, or of those who would otherwise have borrowed the funds. How much of the rise in expenditures will be offset? This depends on the holders of money. The extreme assumption, implicit in a rigid quantity theory of money, is that the amount of money people want to hold depends, on the average, only on their income and not on the rate of return that they can get on bonds and similar securities. In this case, since the total stock of money is the same before and after, the total money income will also have to be the same in order to make people just satisfied to hold that money stock. This means that interest rates will have to rise enough to choke off an amount of private spending exactly equal to the increased public expenditure. In this extreme case, there is no sense at all in which the government expenditures are expansionary. Not even money income goes up, let alone real income. All that happens is that government expenditures go up and private expenditures down.

I warn the reader that this is a highly simplified analysis. A full analysis would require a lengthy textbook. But even this simplified analysis is enough to demonstrate that any result is possible between a $300 rise in income and a zero rise. The more stubborn consumers are with respect to how much they will spend on consumption out of a given income, and the more stubborn purchasers of capital goods are with respect to how much they will spend on such goods regardless of cost, the nearer the result will be to the Keynesian extreme of a $300 rise. On the other side, the more stubborn money holders are with respect to the ratio they wish to maintain between their cash balances and their income, the closer the result will be to the rigid quantity theory extreme of no change in income. In which of these respects the public is more stubborn is an empirical question to be judged from the factual evidence, not something that can be 1930s by reason alone.

Before the Great Depression of the 1930s, the bulk of economists would unquestionably have concluded that the result would be nearer to no rise in income than to a $300 rise. Since then, the bulk of economists would unquestionably conclude the opposite. More recently, there has been a movement back toward the earlier position. Sad to say, none of these shifts can be said to be based on satisfactory evidence. They have been based rather on intuitive judgments from crude experience.

In cooperation with some of my students, I have done some fairly extensive empirical work, for the U.S. and other countries, to get some more satisfactory evidence. The results are striking. They strongly suggest that the actual outcome will be closer to the quantity theory extreme than to the Keynesian. The judgment that seems justified on the basis of this evidence is that the assumed $100 increase in government expenditures can on the average be expected to add just about $100 to income, sometimes less, sometimes more. This means that a rise in government expenditures relative to income is not expansionary in any relevant sense. It may add to money income but all of this addition is absorbed by government expenditures. Private expenditures are unchanged. Since prices are likely to rise in the process, or fall less than they otherwise would, the effect is to leave private expenditures smaller in real terms. Converse propositions hold for a decline in government expenditures.

These conclusions cannot of course be regarded as final. They are based on the broadest and most comprehensive body of evidence I know about, but that body of evidence still leaves much to be desired.

One thing is however clear. Whether the views so widely accepted about the effects of fiscal policy be right or wrong, they are contradicted by at least one extensive body of evidence. I know of no other coherent or organized body of evidence justifying them. They are part of economic mythology, not the demonstrated conclusions of economic analysis or quantitative studies. Yet they have wielded immense influence in securing widespread public backing for far-reaching governmental interference in economic life.

13

The Need for Federal Balanced Budgets

MAURICE H. STANS

Maurice H. Stans, later President Nixon's Secretary of Commerce, was director of the Bureau of the Budget when he presented this paper before the American Academy of Political and Social Science in 1959.

The federal government should have a balanced budget; its expenditures, especially in times like these, should not exceed its income. Of this I am deeply convinced.

As a matter of fact, I find it difficult to understand why there are still some people who do not seem to agree. Even though I have now been an official of the government almost four years and know by hard experience that there are at least two sides to all public questions, on this one the facts speak eloquently for themselves. And the arguments that are marshalled in opposition to show that a balanced budget is unimportant—or that it can be safely forsaken for lengthy periods of time—certainly seem unsound. It is true that we as a nation have been extremely fortunate in maintaining our fundamental strengths thus far despite the heavy deficit spending of the past thirty years. But we cannot count on being lucky forever, and more and more the consequences of past profligacy are now catching up with us.

Let us look at some of the facts;

1. It is a fact that in twenty-four of the last thirty years the federal government has spent more than it has received.

2. It is a fact that last fiscal year the federal government had a deficit (12.5 billion dollars) larger than ever before in time of peace.

3. It is a fact that the federal government debt is now 290 billion dollars and that the annual cost of carrying that debt is more than 10 percent of the budgeted income of the government—and has been going up.

4. It is a fact that our economy is operating at a higher rate of activity than it ever has before and that the standard of living it is producing for all America is far beyond that of any other country in the world.

5. It is a fact that in times of high economic activity there is competition among business, consumers, and government for the productive resources of the country; if government, by indulging in high levels of spending in such times, intensifies that competition, it openly invites inflation.

6. It is a fact that with an unbalanced budget, federal borrowings to raise the money to spend more than income tend to add to the money supply of the country and therefore are inflationary.

7. It is a fact that the purchasing power of the dollar has declined more than 50 percent in the last twenty years. Today we spend more than $2.00 to get what $1.00 would buy in 1939.

8. And finally, it is a fact that all too often in history inflation has been the undoing of nations, great and small.

True, there are many people who still feel that a bit of inflation is a tolerable, if not a good, thing. I think they fail to see that a bit of inflation is an installment on a lot of inflation—a condition in which nobody can hope to gain.

Those of our citizens who believe that inflation is not undesirable simply overlook the history of nations. Inflation is an insidious threat to the strength of the United States. Unless we succeed in exercising a tighter rein over it than we have been able to up to this point I am afraid that we will all lose—as individuals, as a nation, and as a people.

In my view, the facts that I have recited clearly demonstrate the need for:

1. Containing federal expenditures within federal income—which means balancing the budget—in fiscal years 1960 and 1961.

2. Establishing the principle of a balanced budget —including some surplus for reduction of the national debt—as a fiscal objective for the prosperous years ahead.

These are the standards on which fiscal integrity for the nation should rest. These are the standards by which the force of inflation induced by reckless fiscal policy can be averted. Yet in twenty-four of the last thirty years we have not been able to attain them.

Let us look at some of the circumstances which have caused heavy federal spending in the past and have, perhaps, made us insensitive to the dangers of deficits.

Looking Back

Over the last three decades the federal government has spent 264 billion dollars more than it has received. The six years in which there was an excess of income over expense produced negligible surpluses in relation to the deficits of the other years.

We need hardly be reminded of the cause of most of those deficits. In the earlier years it was depression; in the middle years it was war; in recent years it has been war again and then recession.

In the depression years it was not possible to balance the budget; while government services and costs were growing by popular demand, federal revenues declined as a result of economic inactivity. The efforts made to balance the budget by increasing tax rates in 1930 and 1932 and in 1936 to 1938 were apparently self-defeating.

As for the expenditure side of the budget, the decade of the 1930s produced a great deal of talk about "pump-priming" and "compensatory spending"—federal spending which would compensate in poor times for the decline in business and consumer demand and thus lend balance and stability to the economy. The theory was, of course, for the federal government to spend proportionately larger amounts during depression times and proportionately smaller amounts during good times—to suffer deficits in poor years and enjoy surpluses in prosperous years, with the objective of coming out even over the long pull.

Then, in the early 1940s came World War II. During the war years, the federal government's expenditures vastly exceeded its income, and huge further deficits were piled up. In retrospect, most students of wartime economic developments now agree that we did not tax ourselves nearly enough. We did not pay enough of the costs of war out of current income. We created a large debt while suppressing some of its inflationary consequences with direct economic controls, but the suppression was only temporary.

Depression and war, although major factors, were not the only reasons for increased federal expenditures and deficits during the past thirty years. It was more complex than that. In the 1930s the national philosophy of the responsibilities of the federal government underwent a major change. The country's needs for economic growth and social advancement were gradually given increased recognition at the federal level.

The aim of economic growth, of social advancement, and of "compensatory" economic stability became intertwined. Many federal activities of far-reaching implications were established in ways which affected federal expenditures for very long periods of time—if not permanently. Social security, greatly increased support for agriculture, rural electrification, aids to homeowners and mortgage institutions, public housing, public power developments like the Tennessee Valley Authority and other multipurpose water resource projects, and public assistance grants are just a few examples. All of them, however, remained as federal programs after World War II. And we were actually fighting in that war before federal spending for work relief could be stopped.

The immediate postwar period was marked by dramatic demobilization. Nevertheless, many of the major costs of war lingered on. The maintenance in the postwar period of even the reduced and relatively modest structure of our Armed Forces was far more costly than anything that existed in the way of the machinery of war prior to 1940. The war also left us with greatly increased expenditure commitments for interest on the public debt, for veterans, and for atomic energy. The Marshall Plan and the mutual security program followed in succession. It became obvious, next, that the cold war was going to be expensive. Then, with the Korean aggression, it became necessary to rearm and, even after the shooting stopped, the peacetime striking force and defensive machinery we had to maintain continued expenditures at levels that far exceeded in cost anything we had earlier imagined.

Thus, the postwar growth of the budget has been partly in the area of national security, partly deferred costs of World War II, and partly the inheritance of activities and ways of thinking that characterized the depression of the 1930s. We have now learned that many of the programs the federal government initiated in the 1930s were neither temporary nor "compensatory" in character. Moreover, we have not only retained many of them, but we have a so greatly expanded them in the postwar period. Since World War II we have seen large increases in federal expenditures for urban renewal, public health, federal aid for airports and highways, new categories and a higher federal share of public assistance grants, aid to schools in federally impacted areas, great liberalization in aid to agriculture, as well as new programs for science, education, and outer space.

The Present

What can we conclude from all of this?

It seems to me that in the first place we must recognize that the compensatory theory of federal spending has failed thus far and offers little hope for the future unless we exert a more forceful and courageous determination to control the growth of federal spending. The major spending programs which originated in the depression years have in most cases persisted in the following decades. A work relief project could be turned off when we started to fight a war, but most of the programs established in the 1930s developed characteristics of a far more permanent sort.

An example can be found in the program of the Rural Electrification Administration (REA). This program was started in 1936 when only a minority of farm families enjoyed the benefits of electricity. Today, 95 percent of our farms receive central station electric service. We have invested 4 billion dollars in this program, at 2 percent interest. Nonetheless, indications are that future demands for federal funds will be even greater as the REA cooperatives continue to grow.

The startling fact is that three out of four new users currently being added are nonfarm users. About one-half of REA electric power goes to industries, communities, or nonfarm families. The reasonable approach is that rural electric cooperatives should now be able to get some of their financing from other than government sources, especially for nonfarm purposes that compete with taxed private industry. Recognizing this, the President last year—and again this year—recommended that legislation be adopted to encourage cooperatives to switch from government to private financing, and his budget recommended a decrease in the funds for government loans. These proposals were not enacted by the Congress.

Inability to turn off expenditures is not all that is wrong with the compensatory theory of the prewar period. Initially, it dealt largely with the spending side of the fiscal equation whereas the income side now appears to be playing a more important part. Today—with corporate income tax rates at 52 percent—any substantial reduction of corporate earnings produces an immediate proportionate and large loss to the federal treasury. Personal income taxes also respond, though less sharply, to a fall in national production and employment. Thus, when times take a turn for the worse, federal revenues decline promptly and substantially.

Couple this with enlarged social obligations in times of recession or depression—employment compensation, public assistance, and so on—and you have substantial leverage of a more or less automatic character for the production of federal deficits in times of depressed economic activity. To do more than this—to deliberately step up expenditures still more, for public works and other construction, as was done last year—runs grave risks. There is, first, the risk that an antirecession expenditure program cannot be turned off after the recession, but instead represents a permanent increase in the public sphere at the expense of the private. Second, it is difficult to start programs quickly, so the major impact may come long after the need for the economic stimulation has passed. Both of these risks mean that antirecession actions can well represent an inflationary danger for the postrecession period. The danger is there even if, as some believe, positive governmental intervention is required to counter recessions. It is more grave, however, if—and I believe this was proved true in 1958–1959—the economy is vigorous and resilient enough to come out of a temporary recession and to go on through a revival period to new prosperous peaks without any direct financial federal interference.

I think we may conclude that it is inevitable that our nation will be faced with large budgets in the years ahead. This is particularly true for the defense obligations which our country has assumed, for its international undertakings to provide economic and military assistance to other free nations, and as a result of many programs which have been started over the years—major programs for water resource development, agriculture, veterans' benefits, low-cost housing, airways modernization, and space exploration—all these and many others have taken on a permanent quality which makes it clear that federal budgets will be large budgets in our lifetimes.

There is still another conclusion which springs from this short recitation of the history of the last thirty years. It is that the federal government has assumed more and more responsibility for activities which formerly were regarded as being under the jurisdiction of state and local governments. More and more the federal government has assumed responsibility for public assistance, housing, urban renewal, educational aid to areas with federal installations, and many other programs that are now supported by federal grants-in-aid to the states. All this, of course, contributes to the conclusion that these federal programs are not only large at the present time, but have a built-in durability—a staying power with which we must reckon as a fact of life.

I think these thoughts are well summarized in the words of Mr. Allen Sproul, former President of the New York Federal Reserve Bank, who recently said:

Government, in our day, touches upon the economic life of the community in an almost bewildering variety of ways, but its overall influence comes into focus in the consolidated cash budget and, in a subsidiary way, in the management of the public debt. When we abandoned the idea of taxation for revenue only and admitted, as we must, a more important role of Government in economic affairs, we thought up a tidy little scheme called the compensatory budget. This envisaged a cash budget balanced in times of real prosperity, in deficit in times of economic recession, and in surplus in times of inflationary boom. What we have got is a budget that may throw up a shaky surplus in times of boom, but that will surely show substantial deficits in times of recession. The bias, over time, is toward deficits, with only wobbly contracyclical tendencies.

Looking Ahead

It seems to me that as we move into another decade it will be essential to recognize that unless we have a more positive program for operating our federal government within its income, the forces that have gained such tremendous momentum in the past will perpetuate the tradition of deficits—to the great disadvantage of the country as a whole.

Assuming a continuous, but not uninterrupted, economic growth for the country, accompanied by ever-increasing, but not uninterrupted, growth of federal revenues, we should nevertheless expect that the growth of programs started in the past will have a strong tendency to absorb the expected additional revenues—unless aggressive controls are exercised by an alert administration and a statesmanlike Congress during those years.

On those occasions when the economy recedes from its way of growth, we must expect great leverage to be exerted toward the building up of additional deficits. We must learn to live with recession-induced deficits as a matter of necessity, but we should not take unneeded actions which mortgage our nation's future with both more debt and an inflationary potential.

Conclusions

It seems to me to follow from these facts and analyses that it should be the policy of the federal government to strive determinedly for a balanced budget at all times, for, clearly, if it does not, the forces at work to upset financial stability will surely prevail as a matter of momentum.

As we move into the next decade we have the lessons of the three past decades to guide us:

1. Federal programs persist and in most cases grow. As demand expands, the programs expand. It is extremely difficult to curtail them. Their growing costs—and a growing economy—must be reckoned with realistically. This means that actions should be taken to reduce or to end them as they accomplish the purposes for which they were initiated (eighteen such proposals were made in the President's budget message for the fiscal year 1960).

2. In times of recession, it is important to avoid doing things as temporary expedients which will become longer range programs and create major problems later on. We have plenty of these as carry-overs from earlier days; we should avoid creating new ones for the years ahead.

3. We must, of course, learn to live with deficits when major national emergencies threaten or exist in our country. But we should resolve to create equivalent surpluses later on to offset such deficits.

The lesson is clear. We should pay as we go, and if we are to look for debt reduction or tax reduction on a sound footing—as we should—we must do more than this. We must plan for substantial budgetary surpluses in good years—or we will surely contribute to further dangerous inflation in the years ahead.

14

Deficit, Deficit, Who's Got the Deficit?

JAMES TOBIN

James Tobin is Sterling Professor of Economics at Yale University. This article was first published in The New Republic *in 1963.*

For every buyer there must be a seller, and for every lender a borrower. One man's expenditure is another's receipt. My debts are your assets, my deficit your surplus.

If each of us was consistently "neither borrower nor lender," as Polonius advised, no one would ever need to violate the revered wisdom of Mr. Micawber. But if the prudent among us insist on running and lending surpluses, some of the rest of us are willy-nilly going to borrow to finance budget deficits.

In the United States today one budget that is usually left holding a deficit is that of the federal government. When no one else borrows the surpluses of the thrifty, the Treasury ends up doing so. Since the role of debtor and borrower is thought to be particularly unbecoming to the federal government, the nation feels frustrated and guilty.

Unhappily, crucial decisions of economic policy too often reflect blind reactions to these feelings. The truisms that borrowing is the counterpart of lending and deficits the counterpart of surpluses are over-looked in popular and Congressional discussions of government budgets and taxes. Both guilt feelings and policy are based on serious misunderstanding of the origins of federal budget deficits and surpluses.

American *households* and *financial institutions* consistently run financial surpluses. They have money to lend, beyond their own needs to borrow. Figure 1 shows the growth in their combined surpluses since the war; it also shows some tendency for these surpluses to rise in periods of recession and slack business activity. Of course, many private households have financial deficits. They pay out more than their incomes for food, clothing, cars, appliances, houses, taxes, and so on. They draw on savings accounts, redeem savings bonds, sell securities, mortgage houses, or incur installment debt. But deficit households are far outweighed by surplus households. As a group American *households* and *nonprofit institutions* have in recent years shown a net financial surplus averaging about $15 billion a year—that is, households are ready to lend, or to put into equity investments, about $15 billion a year more than they are prepared to borrow. In addition, *financial institutions* regularly generate a lendable surplus, now of the order of $5 billion a year. For the most part these institutions—banks, savings and loan associations, insurance companies, pension funds, and the like—are simply intermediaries which borrow and relend the public's money. Their surpluses result from

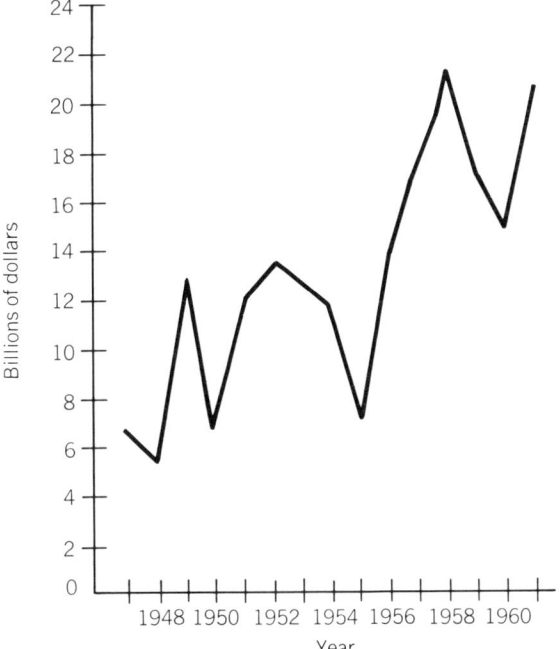

Source: Board of Governors of the Federal Reserve System

FIGURE 1. Financial Surpluses of Consumers, Nonprofit Institutions, and Financial Institutions, 1947–61.

the fact that they earn more from their lending operations than they distribute or credit to their depositors, shareowners, and policyholders.

Who is to use the $20 billion of surplus funds available from households and financial institutions? *State and local governments* as a group have been averaging $3–4 billion a year of net borrowing. Pressures of the expanding populations of children, adults, houses, and automobiles, plus the difficulties of increasing tax revenues, force these governments to borrow in spite of strictures against government debt. *Unincorporated businesses,* including farms, absorb another $3–4 billion. To the rest of the world we can lend perhaps $2 billion a year. We cannot lend abroad—net—more than the surplus of our exports over our imports of goods and services, and some of that surplus we give away in foreign aid. We have to earn the lendable surplus in tough international competition. Recent experience shows clearly that when we try to lend and invest too much money abroad, we either have to borrow it back or else pay in gold.

These borrowers account for $8–10 billion. The remainder—some $10–12 billion—must be used either by *nonfinancial corporate business* or by the *federal government.* Only if corporations as a group take $10–12 billion of external funds, by borrowing or issuing new equities, can the federal government

expect to break even. This is, moreover, an understatement of what is required to keep the federal debt from rising, for the federal government itself provides annually $3 to $4 billion of new lending; the Treasury would have to borrow to finance these federal lending programs even if the government absorbed no *net* funds from the economy. It is *gross* federal borrowing that offends the conservative fiscal conscience, whether or not the proceeds are used to acquire other financial assets.

The moral is inescapable, if startling. If you would like the federal deficit to be smaller, the deficits of business must be bigger. Would you like the federal government to run a surplus and reduce its debt? Then business deficits must be big enough to absorb that surplus as well as the funds available from households and financial institutions.

That does not mean that business must run at a loss—quite the contrary. Sometimes, it is true, unprofitable businesses are forced to borrow or to spend financial reserves just to stay afloat; this was a major reason for business deficits in the depths of the Great Depression. But normally it is businesses with good profits and good prospects that borrow or sell new shares of stock, in order to finance expansion and modernization. As the President of American Telephone and Telegraph can testify, heavy reliance on outside funds, far from being a distress symptom, is an index and instrument of growth in the profitability and worth of the corporation. The incurring of financial deficits by business firms—or by households and governments for that matter—does not usually mean that such institutions are living beyond their means and consuming their capital. Financial deficits are typically the means of accumulating nonfinancial assets—real property in the form of inventories, buildings, and equipment.

When does business run big deficits? When do corporations draw heavily on the capital markets? The record is clear: when business is very good, when sales are pressing hard on capacity, when businessmen see further expansion ahead. Though corporations' internal funds—depreciation allowances and plowed-back profits—are large during boom times, their investment programs are even larger.

Figure 2 shows the financial deficits or surpluses of corporate business and of the federal government since the war. Three facts stand out. First, the federal government has big deficits when corporations run surpluses or small deficits and vice versa. Second, government surpluses and business deficits reach their peaks in periods of economic expansion, when industrial capacity is heavily utilized, as in 1947–48, 1951–52, and 1956–57. Third, the combined deficit of corporate business and the federal government is greater now than in the early postwar years; this is the counterpart of the upward trend in available surpluses shown in Figure 1.

Recession, idle capacity, unemployment, economic slack—these are the enemies of the balanced government budget. When the economy is faltering, households have more surpluses available to lend, and business firms are less inclined to borrow them.

The federal government will not succeed in cutting its deficit by steps that depress the economy, perpetuate excess capacity, and deter business firms from using outside funds. Raising taxes and cutting expenses seem like obvious ways to balance the budget. But because of their effects on private spending, lending, and borrowing, they may have exactly the contrary result. Likewise, lowering taxes and raising government expenditures may so stimulate private business activity and private borrowing that the federal deficit is in the end actually reduced.

This may seem paradoxical, and perhaps it is. Why is it that the homely analogy between family finance and government finance, on which our decisive national attitudes toward federal fiscal policy are so largely based, misleads us? If John Jones on Maple Street is spending $8,700 a year but taking in only $8,000, the remedy is clear. All Mr. Jones need do to balance the family budget is to live resolutely within his income, either spending some $700 less or working harder to increase his earnings. Jones can safely ignore the impact of either action on the incomes and expenditures of others and the possible ultimate feedback on his own job and income. The situation of the President on Pennsylvania Avenue, spending $87 billion a year against tax revenues of $80 billion is quite different. Suppose that he spends $7 billion less, or tries through higher tax rates to boost federal revenues by $7 billion. He cannot ignore the inevitable boomerang effect on federal finances. These measures will lower taxpayers' receipts, expenditures, and taxable incomes. The federal deficit will be reduced by much less than $7 billion; perhaps it will even be increased.

Incidentally, many of the very critics who are most vocal in chiding the government for fiscal sin advocate policies that would make fiscal virtue even more elusive. They want to keep private borrowing in check by the use of tight credit policies and high interest rates. They want to increase corporations' *internal*

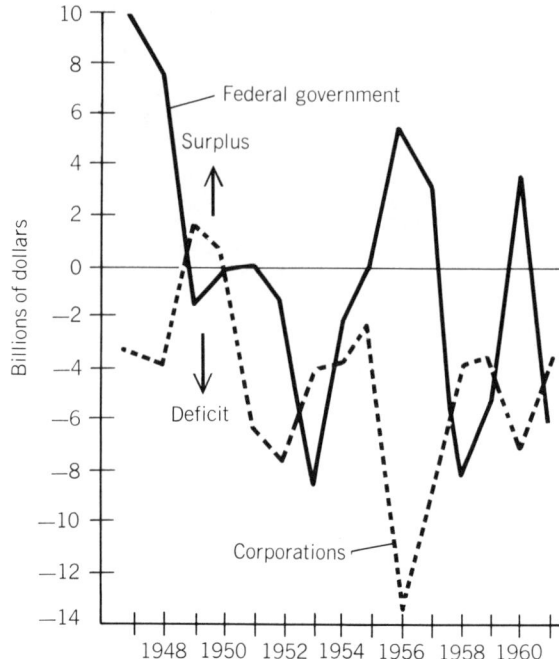

Source: Board of Governors of the Federal Reserve System

FIGURE 2. Net Financial Surpluses and Deficits of the Federal Government and of Nonfinancial Corporations, 1947–61

flow of funds by bigger depreciation allowances and higher profit margins, making business still less dependent on external funds to finance investment, even in boom times. When these apostles of sound finance also tell the government to shun external finance, have they done their arithmetic? If everyone is self-financing, who will borrow the surpluses?

The nation is paying a high price for the misapplied homely wisdom that guides federal fiscal policy. The real toll is measured by unemployment, idle capacity, lost production, and sluggish economic growth. But fiscal conservatism is also self-defeating. It does not even achieve its own aim, the avoidance of government deficits. Federal fiscal and monetary policies consciously and unashamedly designed to stimulate the economy would have sufficient justification in economic expansion itself. But they might well "improve" the federal budget too—by inducing business to use the private surpluses that now have no destination other than a rising federal debt.

15

Economic Forecasting and Science

PAUL A. SAMUELSON

Paul A. Samuelson is Institute Professor at Massachusetts Institute of Technology. This paper appeared in the Michigan Quarterly Review *in 1965.*

If prediction is the ultimate aim of all science, then we forecasters ought to award ourselves the palm for accomplishment, bravery, or rashness. We are the end-product of Darwinian evolution and the payoff for all scientific study of economics. Around the country, students are grinding out doctoral theses by the use of history, statistics, and theory—merely to enable us to reduce the error in our next year's forecast of GNP from $10 billion down to $9 billion.

Just as ancient kings had their soothsayers and astrologers, modern tycoons and prime ministers have their economic forecasters. Eastern sorcerers wore that peaked hat which in modern times we regard as a dunce's cap; and I suppose if the head fits, we can put it in.

Actually, though, I am not sure that the ultimate end of science is prediction—at least in the sense of unconditional prediction about what is likely to happen at a specified future date. Students are always asking of professors, "If you are so smart, how come you ain't rich?" Some of our best economic scientists seem to be fairly poor forecasters of the future. One of our very best economists, in fact, couldn't even correctly foresee the results of the last election. Is it legitimate to ask of a scholar: "If you are so scientific and learned, how come you are so stupid at predicting next year's GNP?"

I think not, and for several different reasons. In the first place, a man might be a brilliant mathematician in devising methods for the use of physicists and still be a very poor physicist. Or he might be a genius in devising statistical methods while still being rather poor at conducting statistical investigations. Let us grant then at the beginning, that a person might be poor himself at *any* predictions within a field, and still be a useful citizen. Only we would then call him a mathematician—rather than simply a physicist, statistician, or economist.

The late Sir Ronald Fisher, for instance, was a genius, as we all gladly acknowledge. And perhaps he did good empirical work in the field of agronomy and applied fertilizer. But I must say that his work on genetics—in which he blithely infers the decline of Roman and of all civilizations from the dastardly habit infertile heiresses have of snatching off the ablest young men for mates, thereby making them infertile—seems awfully casual statistical inference to me. And I can't think Fisher covered himself with immortal glory at the end of his life when he doubted that cigarette smoking and inhaling has anything to do with reducing longevity.

Yet even a good economist or physicist may be a bad predictor—if we want simply an ability to forecast the future. My old teacher, Joseph Schumpeter, was by anyone's admission a pretty good economist. But I would certainly not have trusted him to predict next year's income or tomorrow's stock market. His vision was focussed to a different distance. He could tell you what was going to happen to capitalism in the next fifty years, even though he often had to ask his wife twice for the time of day. Of course, the *inability* to predict well does not thereby make a man a better economist. Schumpeter would not have been soiled if he had been able to make shrewd guesses about the near future.

A good scientist should be good at *some* kind of prediction. But it need not be flat prediction about future events. Thus, a physicist may be bad at telling you what the radioactivity count in the air will be next year, but be very good at predicting for you what will be the likely effects on air pollution of a given controlled experiment involving fissionable materials. If he is a master scientist, his hunches about experiments never yet performed may be very good ones.

Similarly, a good economist has good judgment about economic reality. To have good judgment means you are able to make good judgments—good predictions about what will happen under *certain specified conditions*. This is different from having a model that is pretty good at doing mechanical extrapolation of this year's trends of GNP to arrive at respectable guesses of next year's GNP. Time and again your naive model may win bets from me in office pools on next year's outcome. But neither of us would ever dream of using such a naive model to answer the question, "What will happen to GNP, compared to what it would otherwise have been, when the Kennedy-Johnson massive tax cut is put into effect?" The mechanical, naive model does not have in it, explicitly, the parameter tax rates. And if we insist upon differentiating the result with respect to such a parameter, we will end up with a zero partial derivative and with the dubious conclusion that massive tax cuts cannot have any effect on GNP. The model that I use, which is perhaps very nonmechani-

cal and perhaps even non-naive, may be bad at predicting unconditionally next year's GNP, and still be very good at answering the other-things-equal question of the effect of a change in tax rates or in some other structural parameter of the system.

What I have been saying here can be put in technical language: to make good year-to-year predictions, you need not necessarily have accomplished good "identification" of the various structural relations of a model. And conversely, to be a scientist skilled in making predictions about various hypothetical structural changes in a system, you do need to have what Haavelmo, Koopmans, and others call "identification," of the type that is by no means necessarily contained in models that perform well in ordinary predictions.

Is it possible to have everything good?—to be able to make good annual predictions as well as good predictions of identified structural relationships? The best economists I have known, in the best years of their lives, were pretty good at making just such predictions. And that is what I call good judgment in economics.

Obviously, they have to be men of much experience. In the last analysis, empirical predictions can be made only on the basis of empirical evidence. But it is an equal empirical truth that the facts do not tell their own story to scientists or historical observers, and that the men who develop top-notch judgment have an analytical framework within which they try to fit the facts. I should say that such men are constantly using the evidence of economic time series; the evidence of cross-sectional data; the evidence of case studies and anecdotes, but with some kind of judgment concerning the frequency and importance of the cases and instances. And they are even using conjectures of the form, "What if I were no smarter than these businessmen and unionists? What would I be likely to do?"

We all know the great statistical problems involved in the small samples economic statisticians must work with. We have few years of data relevant to the problem at hand. Maybe the data can be found by months or by quarters; but since there is much serial correlation between adjacent monthly data, we can by no means blithely assume that we have increased our degrees of freedom twelvefold or more by using monthly data. Nature has simply not performed the controlled experiments that enable us to predict as we should wish.

This means that the master economist must piece together, from all the experience he has ever had, hunches relevant to the question at hand.

If science becomes a private art, it loses its characteristic of reproducibility. Here is an example. Sumner Slichter, from 1930 to his death in the late 1950s, was a good forecaster. Dr. Robert Adams of Standard Oil (New Jersey), comparing different methods of forecasting, found that "being Sumner Slichter" was then about the best. But how did Slichter do it? I could never make this out. And neither, I believe, could he. One year he talked about Federal Reserve policy, another year about technical innovation. Somehow the whole came out better than the sum of its parts. Now what I should like to emphasize is that the private art of Sumner Slichter died with him. No less-gifted research assistant could have had transferred to him even a fraction of the Master's skill. And thus one of the principal aims of science was not achieved—namely, reproducibility by any patient person of modest ability of the empirical regularities discerned by luck or by the transcendental efforts of eminent scholars.

The models of Klein, Goldberger, Tinbergen, and Suits have at least this property. Take away Frankenstein and you still have a mechanical monster that will function for awhile. But unlike the solar system, which had to be wound up by Divine Providence only once, any economic model will soon run down if the breath of intelligent life is not pumped into it. When you see a 7094 perform well in a good year, never forget that it is only a Charlie McCarthy; without an Edgar Bergen in the background it is only a thing of paint and wood, of inert transistors and obsolescing matrices.

How well can economists forecast? The question is an indefinite one, and reminds us of the man who was asked what he thought about his wife, and had to reply, "Compared to what?"

When I say that as an economist I am not very good at making economic forecasts, that sounds like modesty. But actually, it represents the height of arrogance. For I know that bad as we economists are, we are better than anything else in heaven and earth at forecasting aggregate business trends—better than gypsy tea-leaf readers, Wall Street soothsayers and chartist technicians, hunch-playing heads of mail order chains, or all-powerful heads of state. This is a statement based on empirical experience. Over the years I have tried to keep track of various methods of forecasting, writing down in my little black book what people seemed to be saying before the event, and then comparing their prediction with what happened. The result has been a vindication of the hypothesis that there is no efficacious substitute for economic analysis in business forecasting. Some maverick may hit a home run on occasion; but over the long season, batting averages tend to settle down to a sorry level when the more esoteric methods of soothsaying are relied upon.

What constitutes a good batting average? That depends on the contest. In baseball these days, .300, or 300-out-of-1,000, is very good. In economic forecasting of the direction of change, we ought to be able to do at least .500 just by tossing a coin. And taking advantage of the undoubted upward trend in all modern economies, we can bat .750 or better just by parrotlike repeating, "Up, Up." The difference between the men and the boys, then, comes between an .850 performance and an .800 performance. Put in other terms, the good forecaster, who must in November make a point-estimate of GNP for the calendar year ahead, will, over a decade, have an average error of perhaps one percent. And a rather poor forecaster may, over the same period, average an error of 1-1/2 percent. When we average the yearly results for a decade, it may be found that in the worst year the error was over 2 percent, compensated by rather small errors in many of the years not expected to represent turning points.

In a sense this is a modest claim. But again I must insist on the arrogance underlying these appraisals. For I doubt that it is possible, on the basis of the evidence now knowable a year in advance, to do much better than this. It is as if Nature does not even begin to toss the dice upon which next year's fate will depend by November of this year. There is then nothing that the clever analyst can peek at to improve his batting average beyond some critical level.

I do not mean to imply that this critical level is fixed for all time. Once our prefession got new surveys of businessmen's intentions to invest, of their decisions as to capital appropriations, and of consumers' responses to random polling, the critical level of imprecision was reduced. In all likelihood, the critical level of uncertainty is a secularly declining one. But is its asymptote (for forecasting a year ahead, remember) literally zero? I do not know how to answer this question. Although it may seem pessimistic to give a negative answer, I am tempted to do so. For remember, you cannot find what is in a person's mind by interrogation, before there is anything in his mind. That is why preliminary surveys of the McGraw-Hill type, taken in October before many corporations have made their capital-budgeting decisions, are necessarily of limited accuracy—which does not deny that they are of some value to us.

The imprecision inherent in forecasting raises some questions about the propriety of making simple point-estimates. If you twist my arm, you can make me give a single number as a guess about next year's GNP. But you will have to twist hard. My scientific conscience would feel more comfortable giving you my subjective probability distribution for all the values of GNP. Actually, it is a pain in the neck to have to work out the whole probability distribution rather than to give a single point-estimate. But satisfying one's scientific conscience is never a very easy task. And there is some payoff for the extra work involved.

For one thing, just what does a point-estimate purport to mean? That is often not clear even to the man issuing it. Do I give the number at which I should just be indifferent to make a bet *on either side,* is forced to risk a large sum of money on a bet whose side can be determined by an opponent or by a referee using chance devices? If that is what I mean in issuing a point-estimate, I am really revealing the *median* of my subjective probability distribution. Other times estimators have in the back of their minds that over the years they will be judged by their mean-square-error, and hence it is best for them to reveal the *arithmetic mean* of their subjective distribution.

I have known still others who aimed, consciously or unconsciously, at the mode of their distribution—sometimes perhaps using the modal value of forecasts among all their friends and acquaintances as the way of arriving at their own mode. Warning: the distribution of all point-estimates issued from a hundred different banks, insurance companies, corporations, government agencies, and academic experts is usually more bunched than the defensible *ex ante* subjective probability distribution any one of them should use in November. This is illustrated by a story I heard Roy Blough once tell at a Treasury meeting. He said: "Economic forecasters are like six eskimos in one bed; the only thing you can be sure of is that they are all going to turn over together." Blough is right. In a few weeks time one often sees all the forecasts revised together upward or downward.

The difference between median, mean, and mode is not very significant if our expected distributions are reasonably symmetrical. But often they are not: often it will be easier to be off by $15 billion through being too pessimistic rather than too optimistic. Making your soothsayer provide you with a probability range may seem to be asking him to be more pretentiously accurate than he can be. But that is not my interpretation: using the language of arithmetical probability is my way of introducing and emphasizing the degree of uncertainty in the procedure, not its degree of finicky accuracy. There is a further advantage of using probability spreads rather than single point-estimates. One of the whizziest of the Whiz Kids in the Pentagon told me that they get better point estimates from Generals and Admirals if they make them always give high and low estimates. Before, you could never be sure whether some conservative bias or discount was not already being applied to data. Henri Theil of Rotterdam has studied how well forecasters perform and has found a similar tendency toward conservative bias in economic forecasters.

Suppose we think that GNP is likely to rise, say by $30 billion. If we issue the forecast of a rise of $20 billion, we shall certainly have been in the right direction. And we shall be in the ball park with respect to general magnitude. Why be hoggish and try for better? Particularly since GNP might go down, and then you would be standing all alone out there in right field, more than $30 billion off the mark. "Better be wrong in good company, than run the risk of being wrong all alone" is a slogan that every Trustee knows to represent wisdom for his actions.

But here I am talking about science, not about gamesmanship for the forecaster. Gamesmanship introduces a whole new set of considerations. Many forecasters, particularly amateurs, don't really care whether they turn out to be wrong or by how much they turn out to be wrong. They want to tell a good story. To amateurs it usually does not matter by how much you are wrong. The only prize is to be at the top. In science and in real economic life, it is terribly important not to be wrong by much. To be second-best year after year in a stock-portfolio competition would be marvelous for a mutual fund manager, and especially where the first-place winners are a shifting group of crapshooters who stake all on one whim or another.

As an economic scientist, I take economic forecasting with deadly seriousness. I hate to be far wrong. Every residual is a wound on my body. And I'd rather make two small errors, than be right once at the cost of being wrong a second time by the sum of the two errors. The reason is not vanity—because forecasting serves a purpose: each dollar of error costs something in terms of corporate or national policy: and if the "loss function" or "social welfare function" is a smooth one in the neighborhood of its optimum, it will be the square of the error of forecast that gives a rough measure of local error.

If we use mean-square-error as our criterion of fit, I think it will be found that forecasters have another persistent bias, namely a tendency to be too pessimistic. This is different from the conservatism that makes forecasters shade both their upward and downward forecasts below the true magnitude. Why is there this downward bias? First, because it is never easy to know where next year's dollar is going to come from, and many forecasters try to build up their total by adding up the elements that they can see. There is a second, perhaps more defensible, reason for erring on the downward or pessimistic side in making a forecast. The social consequences of unemployment and underproduction may be deemed more serious than those of over-full-employment and (mild) demand inflation. I once shocked the late John Maurice Clark at a meeting in Washington by saying, "Although the chance of a recession next year is only one-third, for policy purposes we should treat it as if it were two-thirds." He thought that a contradiction in terms. But in terms of his colleague Wald's loss-function concept, I could make sense of my statement by postulating that each dollar of deflationary gap had social consequences more serious than each dollar of inflationary gap.

Often a forecaster is forced to give a single point-estimate because his boss or consumers cannot handle a more complicated concept. Then he must figure out for himself which point-estimate will do them the most good, or the least harm. Years ago one of the publishing companies used to have every staff member make a prediction of the sales each textbook would enjoy. If people tried to play safe and guess low figures, the President of the company would penalize them for having too little faith in the company's sales staff and authors. (Incidentally, the sales manager used to come up with the least inaccurate predictions, odd as that may sound.)

A good speech should tell the audience something that it already knows to be true. Then having gained their good approval for soundness, it should tell them something they didn't previously know to be true. I don't know whether I have been able to complete the second part of this recipe, but I want to add a third requirement for a good speech. It should call attention to some problem whose true answer is not yet known. Let me conclude, therefore, by raising an unanswered question.

Naive models based upon persistence, momentum, or positive serial correlation do rather well in economics as judged by least-square-error of predictions. An extreme case is one which merely projects the current level or the current direction of change. Yet such models do badly in "calling turning points." Indeed, as described above, such naive models are like the Dow System of predicting stockmarket prices, which never even tries to call a turning point in advance and is content to learn, not too long after the fact, that one has actually taken place.

Forecasters regard models which merely say, "Up and up," or "more of the same," as rather dull affairs. When I once explained to editors of a financial magazine that one disregarded this continuity only at one's risk, they said: "Professor, that may be good economic science, but it's darn dull journalism." But are we forecasters here to have a good time? Dullness may be part of the price we must pay for good performance. More than that? Are we here to cater to our own vanity? One hates to be wrong; but if one's average error could be reduced at the cost of being more often wrong in direction, is that not a fair bargain?

I don't pretend to know the answer to these questions. But they do have a bearing on the following issue. Often an economist presents a model which he admits does worse than some more naive model, but which he justifies for its better fit at the turning points. Is this emphasis legitimate? That question I leave open.

Is policy action most important at the turning points? Is policy action most potent at the turning points? Is a correct guess about turning points likely to lead to correct guesses for the next several quarters? And if so, why doesn't this importance of accuracy of the turning points already get duly registered in the minimum-squared-error criterion? The whole notion of a turning point would be changed in its timing if we shifted, as many dynamic economies in Europe have to do, to changes in direction of trend-deviations rather than changes in absolute direction as insisted on by the National Bureau. Does this lack of invariance cast doubt on the significance of turning points?

Finally, is it possible that public preoccupation with

economics is greatest at the turning point and that we are essentially catering to our own vanity and desire for publicity when we stress accuracy at such times?

I promised to end up with a question, and I find by count that I have ended up with seven. I guess that is what practical men must expect when they invite an academic theorist to give a lecture.

But for all that, to the scientific forecaster I say, "Always study your residuals." Charles Darwin, who lived before the age of Freud, made it a habit to write down immediately any arguments *against* his theory of evolution, for he found that he invariably tended to forget those arguments. When I have steeled myself to look back over my past economic forecasts in the London *Financial Times*, they have appeared to be a little less prescient than I had remembered them to be. Janus-like, we must look at the past to learn how to look into the future.

After I had made some innocent remarks like this in my 1961 Stamp Memorial Lecture at the University of London, I ran into Professor Frank Paish, himself one of England's best economic forecasters.

"Great mistake ever to look back," he quipped, "you'll lose your nerve."

This is almost precisely what the great Satchel Paige of baseball said. "Never look backward. Somebody may be gaining on you."

Like Sir Winston, I bring you blood, sweat, and tears. The way of the scientific forecaster is hard. Let Lot's wife, who did look back, be your mascot and guide. What Satchel Paige didn't mention is that "they may be gaining on you anyway." Know the truth—and while it may not make you free—it will help rid you of your amateur standing.

PART THREE

Money, Monetary Policy, and Incomes Policy

Changes in the quantity of money have an important effect on total spending and the price level. The resurgence of interest in monetary policy in recent years is due in no small measure to the work of Milton Friedman. In the opening selection, Friedman describes the evidence that, in his opinion, supports his views concerning the way in which money influences the economy. He draws on his own studies of monetary history as well as recent empirical findings by the Federal Reserve Bank of St. Louis. Concluding that one cannot predict economic events well enough to adopt a discretionary monetary policy, Friedman argues in favor of a rule specifying that the money supply should increase at a fixed rate.

Walter W. Heller is skeptical of many of Friedman's conclusions. In the next selection, he begins by saying that he and other Keynesians agree that money matters, but that they do not accept Friedman's postulate that money alone matters; consequently, they would supplement monetary policy with fiscal policy. Heller asks questions like: "Which money-supply indicator do you believe? . . . Don't observed variations in monetary time lags and velocity cast serious doubt on any simple relation between money supply and GNP? Can a rigid monetary rule find happiness in a world beset with rigidities and rather limited adjustment capabilities? That is, is the rigid Friedman rule perhaps a formula made in heaven, which will work only in heaven?"

Arthur M. Okun takes an eclectic view. He begins by saying that "When economists write textbooks or teach introductory students or lecture to laymen, they happily extol the virtues of two lovely handmaidens of aggregate economic stabilization—fiscal policy and monetary policy. But when they write for learned journals or assemble for professional meetings, they often insist on staging a beauty contest between the two. And each judge feels somehow obliged to decide that one of the two entries is just an ugly beast. My remarks here are in the spirit of bigamous devotion rather than invidious comparison. Fiscal policy and monetary policy are both beautiful; we need them both and we should treat them both lovingly."

Carl Christ agrees with those who feel that the money supply should increase at a "slow, steady rate of 3 or 4 percent per year, come what may." Henry C. Wallich, in the next paper, opposes a rule for a stable increase in the money supply, on the grounds that the Federal Reserve's control over the money supply is less than complete, that the rule would require flexible exchange rates, that the definition of the money supply is not clear-cut, and that the relationship between money and income (and the relevant lags) are imperfectly understood.

No matter where one stands on the money-supply issue, the role of the Federal Reserve in money matters must be understood. The article by Sherman Maisel, a recent governor of the Federal Reserve Board, gives an insider's account of decision-making there. Maisel describes the relative influence of various groups and individuals on the formulation of monetary policy, and contrasts the styles and approaches of the last two chairmen of the Federal Reserve System: William M. Martin and Arthur F. Burns. These vignettes are both informative and interesting. The next paper, published by the Federal Reserve Bank of New York, is an interesting case study of how open market operations are actually carried out by the Fed. David P. Eastburn, in the following article, discusses the political pressures on the Fed and concludes that: "If there were times when officials could sit in their marble halls and mysteriously pull strings that affect the economy without anyone questioning their actions, those times are gone."

Inflation has been a serious problem in recent years. Robert M. Solow describes the various price indexes that are used to measure the rate of inflation and discusses the effects of inflation as well as its causes. He is less fearful of inflation than Arthur F. Burns, the author of the next article. According to Burns, "our long-run problem of inflation has its roots in the structure of our economic institutions and the financial policies of our government." He believes that some form of incomes policy might be useful. In the short run, the unemployment rate seems to be inversely related to the rate of inflation. This relationship is of great importance, as Henry and Mable Wallich point out in the next piece. But another important question concerns the permanence of this relationship. In the long run, increases in inflation may buy little or nothing in the way of reductions in unemployment, as the Wallichs emphasize.

According to some economists, efforts to influence wages and prices directly can play a constructive role when cost-push inflation reaches serious proportions. Milton Friedman, in the following selection, argues strongly against such guidelines. He concludes that: "Inflation being always and everywhere a monetary phenomenon, the responsibility for controlling it is governmental. Legally enforced price and wage ceilings do not eliminate inflationary pressure. At most they suppress it and suppressed inflation is vastly more harmful than open inflation." In contrast, Robert M. Solow, while being careful to emphasize that wage-price guideposts "are not the sort of policy you would invent if you were inventing policies from scratch," argues in the final paper that they may "offer a little help at even less cost."

16

Monetary vs. Fiscal Policy

MILTON FRIEDMAN

Milton Friedman is Professor of Economics at the University of Chicago. This article comes from his dialogue with Walter W. Heller, Monetary vs. Fiscal Policy, *published in 1969.*

The key source of misunderstanding about the issue of monetary policy, in my opinion, has been the failure to distinguish clearly what it is that money matters for. What I and those who share my views have emphasized is that the quantity of money is extremely important for nominal magnitudes, for nominal income, for the level of income in dollars—important for what happens to prices. It is not important at all, or, if that's perhaps an exaggeration, not very important, for what happens to real output over the long period.

I have been increasingly impressed that much of the disagreement about this issue stems from the fact that an important element in the Keynesian revolution in economics was the notion that prices are an institutional datum determined outside the system. Once you take that view, once you say that prices are somehow determined elsewhere, then the distinction between nominal magnitudes and real magnitudes disappears. The distinction between magnitudes in dollars and magnitudes in terms of goods and services is no longer important.

That is why the qualifications we have always attached to our statements about the importance of money tend to be overlooked. We have always stressed that money matters a great deal for the development of nominal magnitudes, but not over the long run for real magnitudes. That qualification has tended to be dropped and a straw man has been set up to the effect that we say that money is the only thing that matters for the development of the economy. That's an absurd position, of course, and one that I have never held. The real wealth of a society depends much more on the kind of institutional structure it has, on the abilities, initiative, driving force of its people, on investment potentialities, on technology—on all of those things. That's what really matters from the point of view of the level of output. But, how many dollars will that be valued at? When you ask that question, that's where money matters.

Let me turn more directly to the questions: Is fiscal policy being oversold? Is monetary policy being oversold? I want to stress that my answer is yes to both of those questions. I believe monetary policy is being oversold; I believe fiscal policy is being oversold. What I believe is that fine tuning has been oversold. And this is not a new conclusion. It so happens that the facts haven't been inconsistent with them, and, therefore, we haven't had to change them over time.

Just this past week I came across a paper I gave to

the Joint Economic Committee in 1958. I would like to quote from that paper some sentences which expressed my view at that time, and which still express my view today, on the issue of fine tuning, rather than on the separate issues of monetary and fiscal policy.

I said: "A steady rate of growth in the money supply will not mean perfect stability even though it would prevent the kind of wide fluctuations that we have experienced from time to time in the past. It is tempting to try to go farther and to use monetary changes to offset other factors making for expansion and contraction. . . . The available evidence . . . casts grave doubts on the possibility of producing any fine adjustments in economic activity by fine adjustments in monetary policy—at least in the present state of knowledge. . . . There are thus serious limitations to the possibility of a discretionary monetary policy and much danger that such a policy may make matters worse rather than better."

I went on: "To avoid misunderstanding, it should be emphasized that the problems just discussed are in no way peculiar to monetary policy. . . . The basic difficulties and limitations of monetary policy apply with equal force to fiscal policy."

And then I went on: "Political pressures to 'do something' in the face of either relatively mild price rises or relatively mild price and employment declines are clearly very strong indeed in the existing state of public attitudes. The main moral to be drawn from the two preceding points is that yielding to these pressures may frequently do more harm than good. There is a saying that the best is often the enemy of the good, which seems highly relevant. The goal of an extremely high degree of economic stability is certainly a splendid one. Our ability to attain it, however, is limited; we can surely avoid extreme fluctuations; we do not know enough to avoid minor fluctuations; the attempt to do more than we can will itself be a disturbance that may increase rather than reduce instability. But like all such injunctions, this one too must be taken in moderation. It is a plea for a sense of perspective and balance, not for irresponsibility in the face of major problems or for failure to correct past mistakes."

That was a view that I expressed ten years ago, and I do not believe that the evidence of the past ten years gives the lie to that view. I think that the evidence of the past ten years rather reinforces it, rather shows the difficulties of trying to engage in a very fine tuning of economic policy. I would emphasize today even more than I did then my qualifications with respect to monetary policy because thanks fundamentally, I think, to the difficulties that have been experienced with fiscal policy and to the experience of other countries, there has been an enormous shift in opinion.

Walter Heller says we all know that money matters; it's only a question of whether it matters very much. His saying that is, in itself, evidence of the shift in opinion. Before coming up here today I reread the reports of the Council of Economic Advisers that were published when he was chairman of the Council. I do not believe that anybody can read those reports and come out with the conclusion that they say that money matters significantly. While there was some attention paid to money in those reports, it was very limited.

There has been a tremendous change in opinion on this subject since then. And I am afraid that change may go too far. I share very much the doubts that Mr. Heller expressed about the closeness of the monetary relations. There is a very good relation on the average. But the relation is not close enough, it is not precise enough, so that you can, with enormous confidence, predict from the changes in the money supply in one quarter precisely what's going to happen in the next quarter or two quarters later.

Indeed, that's the major reason why I'm in favor of a rule. If I thought I could predict precisely, well then, to go back to the statement I quoted from, I would be prepared to make fine adjustments to offset other forces making for change. It's precisely because we don't know how to predict precisely that you cannot in fact use monetary policy effectively for this purpose. So I emphasize that my basic view is that what has been oversold is the notion of fine tuning.

Yet, fiscal policy has, in my view, been oversold in a very different and more basic sense than monetary policy. I believe that the rate of change of the money supply by itself—and I'm going to come back to those two words "by itself"—has a very important effect on nominal income and prices in the long run. It has a very important effect on fluctuations in nominal and real income in the short run. That's my basic conclusion about changes in the stock of money.

Now let's turn to fiscal policy. I believe that the state of the government budget matters; matters a great deal—for some things. The state of the government budget determines what fraction of the nation's income is spent through the government and what fraction is spent by individuals privately. The state of the government budget determines what the level of our taxes is, how much of our income we turn over to the government. The state of the government budget has a considerable effect on interest rates. If the federal government runs a large deficit, that means the government has to borrow in the market, which raises the demand for loanable funds and so tends to raise interest rates.

If the government budget shifts to a surplus, that adds to the supply of loanable funds, which tends to lower interest rates. It was no surprise to those of us who stress money that enactment of the surtax was followed by a decline in interest rates. That's precisely what we had predicted and what our analysis leads us to predict. But—and I come to the main point—in my opinion, the state of the budget by itself has no significant effect on the course of nominal income, on inflation, on deflation, or on cyclical fluctuations. . . .

I'd like to call your attention to some [evidence] relevant to the particular issue of the potency of fiscal and monetary policy. Some sixteen years ago, I wrote an article that compared the Civil War to World War I and World War II. The particular question I asked was, "Do you get a better understanding of what happened to prices during those three wars by looking at what was happening to monetary magnitudes, or by looking at what was happening to fiscal magnitudes?" The answer was completely unambiguous. And nobody has since produced any evidence contradicting that analysis. It turns out that you get a very clear, straightforward interpretation of price behavior in those three wars by looking at monetary magnitudes; you do not get an explanation by looking at fiscal magnitudes.

Anna Schwartz and I have studied the relation between monetary magnitude and economic magnitudes over the course of a hundred years, roughly a century. During that period, fiscal policy changed enormously. At the beginning of that period, the government budget was negligible. In the period since World War II, the government budget has been mammoth. And yet we found roughly the same kind of a relationship between monetary and economic magnitudes over the whole of that one-hundred-year period.

If fiscal policy were playing a dominant influence, it should have introduced more variability . . . into the relation between money and income in the later part than in the earlier; but as far as we can see, it's a homogeneous universe.

Third, some years back David Meiselman and I published a study directed specifically at the question, "Do monetary magnitudes or autonomous expenditure magnitudes give you a better interpretation of the movements in nominal income over short periods of time?" That article produced a great controversy and a large number of replies and counterreplies. It's a matter of biblical exegesis to trace through the thrusts and counterthrusts of that controversy though I am sure it would be good for all your souls to do so. But one thing that came out of that controversy is that everybody agreed that the monetary magnitudes did have an important and systematic influence. The complaint that was made against us was that we had gone too far in denying that the autonomous magnitudes exerted an influence.

The most recent study is one by the Federal Reserve Bank of St. Louis in which they have related quarter-to-quarter changes in GNP to changes in monetary totals over prior quarters and also to changes in governmental expenditures and taxes. They have been very thorough. Anything that anybody suggested to them which might be wrong with what they initially did, they have tried out. As a result, they have tried out many of the possible permutations and combinations. They have tried the high-employment budget and they have tried other budget concepts. But I'll refer to their findings about the high-employment budget.

What they have done is to try to see whether the monetary or the fiscal magnitudes play a more consistent and systematic role in explaining the course of GNP change over the period 1952 to 1968.

Let me quote their summary conclusion. They say: "This section tested the propositions that the response of economic activity to fiscal actions relative to monetary actions is (I) larger, (II) more predictable, and (III) faster."

Let me repeat this more explicitly. The proposition they tested was that the response of economic activity to fiscal action was larger, more predictable, and faster than the response of the economy to monetary action. "The results of the tests," they say, "were not consistent with any of these propositions. Consequently, either the commonly used measures of fiscal influence do not correctly indicate the degree and the direction of such influence, or there was no measurable net fiscal influence on total spending in the test period." To put it in simpler terms, what they found—far from there being a proven efficiency of fiscal policy—was that, as a statistical matter, the regression coefficients of the high-employment budget surplus or deficit, if the monetary variables are held constant, were not statistically significant.

17

Is Monetary Policy Being Oversold?

WALTER W. HELLER

Walter W. Heller is Regents' Professor of Economics at the University of Minnesota. During 1961–64, he was Chairman of the Council of Economic Advisers. This article comes from his dialogue with Milton Friedman, Monetary vs. Fiscal Policy, *published in 1969.*

My intent today is neither to praise nor to bury that towering iconoclast Milton Friedman, for to praise him and his works would absorb far too much of my limited time, and to bury him is, in a word, impossible.

At the outset, let's clarify what is and what isn't at issue in this discussion of fiscal-monetary policy. When we do this, I'm afraid that the lines may not be drawn quite as sharply as the journalists, who love a fight and drama, would have us believe with their headlines like "Is Keynes Defunct?"

The issue is *not* whether money matters—we all grant that—but whether *only* money matters, as some Friedmanites, or perhaps I should say Friedmanics, would put it. Or really, whether only money matters *much,* which is what I understand Milton Friedman to say—he is more reasonable than many of the Friedmanites.

It's important in this connection, too, to make clear that the economic policy of the 1960s, the "new economics" if you will, assigns an important role to *both* fiscal and monetary policy. Indeed, the appropriate mix of policies has often been the cornerstone of the argument. It was, for example, early in the 60s,

when we feared that tight money might stunt recovery, might thwart the expansionary impact of the 1962–64 income tax cuts. It was again, in 1966, when in strongly urging a tax increase, we put heavy emphasis on avoiding the ill effects of imposing too much of the burden of restraint on Federal Reserve policy. It was once again, in 1967–68, when we sought the surtax in considerable part to insure against a repetition of the monetary crunch of 1966. And it will be in the future, when full employment surpluses in the federal budget may be the only defensible way to buy the monetary ease that commitment to rapid economic growth implies. In short, to anyone who might fear that the "new economics" is all fiscal policy, the record offers evidence, and the new economists offer assurance, that money *does* matter.

With that straw man removed, we can identify the real monetary issues with which the monetarists confront us: First, should money supply be the sole or primary guide to Federal Reserve policy? Should it, at the very least, be ranged side by side with interest rates and credit availability in the Fed's affections? Second, should we rely on the Federal Reserve authorities to adapt monetary policy flexibly to changing economic events and to shifts in fiscal policy, or should we instead not only enthrone money supply but encase it in a rigid formula specifying a fixed increase of 3, 4, or 5 percent a year?

Again, in the fiscal field, the issue is not *whether* fiscal policy matters—even some monetarists, perhaps in unguarded moments, have urged budget cuts or tax changes for stabilization reasons. The issues are *how much* it matters, and how heavily we can lean on discretionary changes in taxes and budgets to maintain steady economic growth in a dynamic economy: Is the close correlation of activist fiscal policy and strong expansion—which has brought our economy into the narrow band around full employment—a matter of accident or causation?

Pervading these operational issues is a basic question of targets, as yet not answered in any conclusive way by either analysis or evidence. Should the target be, as the Phillips Curve analysis suggests, somewhat less unemployment in exchange for somewhat more price creep? Or is this trade-off illusory, as the adherents of the classical real-wage doctrine are now reasserting? To hark back to words and men of the past—is a little inflation like a little pregnancy? Or was Sumner Slichter prophetic when he said that if we wanted to live with steady full employment and brisk growth, we also had to—and could—live with a little chronic inflation, with a price creep of 2 percent or so a year?

Summing up the key operational issues, they are: Should money be king? Is fiscal policy worth its salt? Should flexible man yield to rigid rules? You will note that I purposely cast these issues in a show-me form to put both the monetarists and the new economists on their mettle.

Let me review with you the factors that say "stop, look, and listen" before embracing the triple doctrine that only money matters much; that control of the money supply is the key to economic stability; and that a rigid fixed-throttle expansion of 4 or 5 percent a year is the only safe policy prescription in a world of alleged economic ignorance and human weakness and folly.

Turning to doubts, unresolved questions, and unconvincing evidence, I group these into eight conditions that must be satisfied—if not completely, at least more convincingly than they have been to date—before we can even consider giving money supply sovereignty, or dominance, or greater prominence in economic policy. These conditions center on such questions as: Which money-supply indicator do you believe? Can one read enough from money supply without weighing also shifts in demand and interest rates—that is, don't both quantity *and* price of money count? Don't observed variations in monetary time lags and velocity cast serious doubt on any simple relation between money supply and GNP? Can a rigid monetary rule find happiness in a world beset with rigidities and rather limited adjustment capabilities? That is, is the rigid Friedman rule perhaps a formula made in heaven, that will work only in heaven?

The first condition is this: the monetarists must make up their minds which money-supply variable they want us to accept as our guiding star—M_1, the narrow money supply, just currency and bank deposits; M_2, adding time deposits; or perhaps some other measure like the "monetary base?" And when will the monetarists decide? Perhaps Milton Friedman has decided; but if he has, his disciples do not seem to have gotten the word.

Let me give you an example. M_1 (the money stock) was all the rage. It spurted for four months in a row, from April through July. But when that slowed down, most of the alarmists switched horses to M_2 (money plus time deposits), which quite conveniently began rising sharply in July. And listen to the latest release from the St. Louis Federal Reserve Bank—the unofficial statistical arm of the Chicago School—which very carefully throws a sop to all sides: "Monetary expansion since July has decelerated as measured by the money stock, accelerated as measured by money plus time deposits, and remained at about an unchanged rate as measured by the monetary base. As a result, questions arise as to which monetary aggregate may be currently most meaningful in indicating monetary influence on economic activity." Precisely.

It doesn't seem too much to ask that this confusion be resolved in some satisfactory way before putting great faith in money supply as our key policy variable.

Second, I would feel more sympathetic to the money-supply doctrine if it were not so one-track-minded about money stock—measured any way you wish—as the *only* financial variable with any informational content for policy purposes.

If we look at 1967 *only* in terms of the money stock, it would appear as the easiest-money year since World War II. M_1 was up 6 percent, M_2 was up 12 percent. Yet there was a very sharp rise in interest rates. Why? Probably because of a big shift in liquidity preference as corporations strove to build up their protective liquidity cushions after their harrowing experience the previous year—their monetary dehydration in the credit crunch of 1966. Again, the behavior of interest rates is vital to proper interpretation of monetary developments and guidance of monetary policy. Interest rates are endogenous variables and cannot be used alone—but neither can money stock. Either interest rates or money stock, used alone, could seriously mislead us.

The point is that a change in the demand for money relative to the supply, or a change in the supply relative to demand, results generally in a change in interest rates. To insist that the behavior of the price of money (interest rates) conveys no information about its scarcity is, as Tobin has noted, an "odd heresy."

Third, given the fluctuations in money velocity, that supposedly inexorable link between money and economic activity has yet to be established. We should not forget this, however sweet the siren song of the monetarists may sound. We should not forget the revealing passage from that monumental Friedman-Schwartz volume, *A Monetary History of the United States,* that makes my point:

> . . . the observed year-to-year change in velocity was less than 10 percent in 78 out of 91 year-to-year changes from 1869, when our velocity figures start, to 1960. Of the 13 larger changes, more than half came during either the Great Contraction or the two world wars, and the largest change was 17 percent. Expressed as a percentage of a secular trend, velocity was within the range of 90 to 110 in 53 years, 85 to 115 in 66 years. Of the remaining 26 years, 12 were during the first 15 years, for which the income figures are seriously defective, and 17 during the Great Contraction and the two wars.

Clearly, velocity has varied over time—some might say "greatly," others "moderately." Let me sidestep a bit and say, for purposes of this discussion, "significantly."

What Friedman and Schwartz report about the behavior of velocity suggests that there are other factors—strangely, such fiscal actions as tax cuts or budget changes come to mind—that influence the level of economic activity. Velocity has changed, as it were, to accommodate these other influences and will go on doing so, I have no doubt, in the future.

The observed changes in velocity underscore the broader point I was hinting at a moment ago: The Friedman-Schwartz study did not find anything like a near-perfect correlation—a rigid link—between money and economic activity. And such correlation as

they did find was based on complex and often quite arbitrary adjustments of their raw data.

Fourth, it would help us if the monetarists could narrow the range on *when* money matters. How long *are* the lags that have to be taken into account in managing monetary policy? Here, I quote from Professor Friedman's tour de force, *A Program for Monetary Stability:*

> In the National Bureau study on which I have been collaborating with Mrs. Schwartz we found that, on the average of 18 cycles, peaks in the rate of change in the stock of money tend to precede peaks in general business by about 16 months and troughs in the rate of change in the stock of money to precede troughs in general business by about 12 months. . . . For individual cycles, the recorded lag has varied between 6 and 29 months at peaks and between 4 and 22 months at troughs.

So the Friedman-Schwartz study found a long average lag, and just as important it would seem, a highly variable lag. But why this considerable variance? No doubt there are several possible answers. But again, the most natural one is that the level of economic activity, or total demand for the nation's output, is influenced by variables other than the stock of money—possibly even by tax rates and federal spending and transfer payments!

Suppose I told you that I had checked and found that in repeated trials, it required from 100 to 300 feet for a car going so and so many miles an hour to stop. That is quite a range. But would you be surprised? I think not. You would simply remind me that the distance it takes a car to stop depends, among other things, on the condition of the road surface. If I had allowed for the condition of the road surface, I would not have ended up with such a wide range of stopping distances.

Just so. If Professor Friedman and Mrs. Schwartz had taken account of other variables that influence total demand, or if they had estimated the lag of monetary policy using a complete model of the U.S. economy, they would not have found the lag of monetary policy to be quite so variable. Again, then, one correctly infers that their findings are quite consistent with fiscal policy mattering, and mattering a great deal.

Professor Friedman has also used this finding of (a) a long average lag, and (b) a highly variable lag in support of his plea for steady growth of the money supply. With so long an average lag, the argument goes, forecasters are helpless; they cannot see twelve or fifteen months into the future with any accuracy. And even if they could, they would be at a loss to know how far ahead to appraise the economic outlook. But I doubt that he can properly draw this inference from his finding of a long and highly variable lag.

It seems to me misleading to estimate a discreet lag as the Friedman-Schwartz team did. It's reasonable to suppose, given the research findings of other investigators, that the effect of a change in monetary policy cumulates through time. To begin, there's a slight effect; and as time passes, the effect becomes more pronounced. But insofar as the feasibility of discretionary monetary policy is at issue, what matters *most* is whether there is some near-term effect. If there is, then the Federal Reserve can influence the economy one quarter or two quarters from now. That there are subsequent, more pronounced, effects is not the key question. These subsequent effects get caught, as it were, in subsequent forecasts of the economic outlook, and current policy is adjusted accordingly. At least this is what happens in a non-Friedmanic world where one enjoys the benefits of discretionary policy changes.

Lest I leave any doubt about what I infer from this: if there is a near-immediate effect from a change in policy, then discretionary monetary policy does not impose an unbearable burden on forecasters. For six or nine months ahead, they can do reasonably well. But given the too-discreet way Friedman-Schwartz went about estimating the lag of monetary policy, I see no way of determining the shape of the monetary policy lag. Until they know more about the shape of this lag, I don't see how they can insist on a monetary rule.

Fifth, I'd be happier if only I knew which of the two Friedmans to believe. Should it be the Friedman we have had in focus here—the Friedman of the close causal relationship between money supply and income, who sees changes in money balances worked off gradually, with long lags before interest rates, prices of financial and physical assets, and, eventually, investment and consumption spending are affected? Or should it be the Friedman of the "permanent-income hypothesis," who sees the demand for money as quite unresponsive to changes in current income (since current income has only a fractional weight in permanent income), with the implied result that the monetary multiplier is very large in the short run, that there is an immediate and strong response to a change in the money stock?

Sixth, if Milton's policy prescription were made in a

frictionless Friedmanesque world without price, wage, and exchange rigidities—a world of his own making—it would be more admissible. But in the imperfect world in which we actually operate, beset by all sorts of rigidities, the introduction of his fixed-throttle money-supply rule might, in fact, be destabilizing. Or it could condemn us to long periods of economic slack or inflation as the slow adjustment processes in wages and prices, given strong market power, delayed the economy's reaction to the monetary rule while policy makers stood helplessly by.

A seventh and closely related concern is that locking the money supply into a rigid rule would jeopardize the U.S. international position. It's quite clear that capital flows are interest-rate sensitive. Indeed, capital flows induced by interest-rate changes can increase alarmingly when speculators take over. Under the Friedman rule, market interest rates would be whatever they turned out to be. It would be beyond the pale for the Fed to adjust interest rates for balance-of-payments adjustment purposes. Milton has heard all of this before, and he always has an answer—flexible exchange rates. Parenthetically, I fully understand that it's much easier to debate Milton in absentia than in person! Yet, suffice it to note that however vital they are to the workings of his money-supply peg, floating exchange rates are not just around the corner.

Eighth, and finally, if the monetarists showed some small willingness to recognize the impact of fiscal policy—which has played such a large role in the policy thinking and action underlying the great expansion of the 1960s—one might be a little more sympathetic to their views. This point is, I must admit, not so much a condition as a plea for symmetry. The "new economists," having already given important and increasing weight to monetary factors in their policy models, are still waiting for signs that the monetarists will admit fiscal factors to theirs.

The 1964 tax cut pointedly illustrates what I mean. While the "new economists" fully recognize the important role monetary policy played in facilitating the success of the tax cut, the monetarists go to elaborate lengths to "prove" that the tax cut—which came close to removing a $13 billion full-employment surplus that was overburdening and retarding the economy—had nothing to do with the 1964–65 expansion. Money-supply growth did it all. Apparently, we were just playing fiscal tiddlywinks in Washington.

It seems to me that the cause of balanced analysis

and rational policy would be served by redirecting some of the brilliance of Friedman and his followers from (a) single-minded devotion to the money-supply thesis and unceasing efforts to discredit fiscal policy and indeed all discretionary policy to (b) joint efforts to develop a more complete and satisfactory model of how the real world works; ascertain why it is working far better today than it did before active and conscious fiscal-monetary policy came into play; and determine how such policy can be improved to make it work even better in the future.

In a related asymmetry, as I've already suggested in passing, some Friedmanites fail to recognize that if fiscal policy actions like the 1964 tax cut can do no good, then fiscal policy actions like the big budget increases and deficits associated with Vietnam can also do no harm. Again, they should recognize that they can't have it both ways.

Now, one could lengthen and elaborate this list. But enough—let's just round it off this way: if Milton Friedman were saying that (as part of an active discretionary policy) we had better keep a closer eye on that important variable, money supply, in one or more of its several incarnations—I would say well and good, by all means. If the manifold doubts can be reasonably resolved, let's remedy any neglect or underemphasis of money supply as a policy indicator relative to interest rates, free reserves, and the like. But let's not lock the steering gear into place, knowing full well of the twists and turns in the road ahead. That's an invitation to chaos.

18

Fiscal and Monetary Policy: An Eclectic Analysis

ARTHUR M. OKUN

Arthur M. Okun is a senior staff member at the Brookings Institution. He was Chairman of the Council of Economic Advisers under President Johnson. This article is taken from his paper in Issues in Fiscal and Monetary Policy, *published in 1971.*

When economists write textbooks or teach introductory students or lecture to laymen, they happily extol the virtues of two lovely handmaidens of aggregate economic stabilization—fiscal policy and monetary policy. But when they write for learned journals or assemble for professional meetings, they often insist on staging a beauty contest between the two. And each judge feels somehow obliged to decide that one of the two entries is just an ugly beast. My remarks here are in the spirit of bigamous devotion rather than invidious comparison. Fiscal policy and monetary policy are both beautiful; we need them both and we should treat them both lovingly.

The General Eclectic Case

In particular, both fiscal and monetary policy are capable of providing some extra push upward or downward on GNP. In fact, if aggregate stimulus or restraint were all that mattered, either one of the two tools could generally do the job, and the second— whichever one chose to be second—would be redundant. The basic general eclectic principle that ought to guide us, as a first approximation, is that either fiscal or monetary policy can administer a required sedative or stimulus to economic activity. As every introductory student knows, however, fiscal and monetary tools operate in very different ways. Monetary policy initially makes people more liquid without adding directly to their incomes or wealth; fiscal policy enhances their incomes and wealth without increasing their liquidity.

In a stimulative monetary action, the people who initially acquire money are not simply given the money; they must part with government securities to get it. But once their portfolios become more liquid, they presumably use the cash proceeds to acquire alternative earning assets, and in so doing they bid up the prices of those assets, or equivalently, reduce the yields. Thus prospective borrowers find it easier and less expensive to issue securities and to get loans; and investors who would otherwise be acquiring securities may be induced instead to purchase real assets such as capital goods. Also, because market values of securities are raised, people become wealthier, if in an indirect way, and may hence increase their purchases of goods and services. Thus many channels run from the easing of financial markets to the quickening of real economic activity.

A stimulative fiscal action is appropriately undertaken when resources are unemployed; in that situation, an action such as expanded government purchases, whether for good things like hospitals or less good things like military weapons, puts resources to work and rewards them with income. The additional cash received by some people is matched by reduced cash holdings of those who bought government securities to finance the outlay. But the securities buyers have no income loss to make them tighten their belts; they voluntarily traded money for near money. In contrast, the income recipients become willing to spend more, and thus trigger a multiplier process on production and income. So, while fiscal and monetary routes differ, the ultimate destination—the effect on national product—is the same, in principle.

Indeed, the conditions under which either fiscal tools or monetary tools, taken separately, have zero effect on GNP are merely textbook curiosities rather than meaningful possibilities in the modern U.S. economic environment. For stimulative monetary policy to be nothing more than a push on a string, either interest rates would have to be just as low as they could possibly go, or investment and consumption would have to show zero response to any further reduction in interest rates. The former possibility is the famous Keynesian liquidity trap, which made lots of sense in describing 1936, but has no relevance to 1971. With prime corporations paying 8 percent on long-term bonds, interest rates are still higher than at any time in my lifetime prior to 1969. There is plenty of room for them to decline, and, in turn, for states and localities, home-buyers and consumer installment credit users, as well as business investors, to be encouraged to spend more by lower costs of credit.

The opposite extreme, impotent fiscal policy, is equally remote. Fiscal policy must exert some stimulative effect on economic activity (even when the monetary policy makers do not accommodate the fiscal action at all) unless the velocity of money is completely inflexible so that no economizing on cash balances occurs. Though the money supply does not rise in a pure fiscal action, spending will tend to rise unless people are totally unable or unwilling to speed up the turnover of cash. And money holders do economize on cash to a varying degree—they do so

seasonally and cyclically, and they do so dependably in response to changes in the opportunity cost of holding money. The holder of zero-yielding cash is sacrificing the opportunity to receive the going interest rates of earning assets. The higher interest rates are, the more he sacrifices; and hence, economic theory tells us, the more he will economize on his holdings of cash.

And the facts confirm the theory. The negative relationship between the demand for money and the rate of interest is one of the most firmly established empirical propositions in macroeconomics. So a pure fiscal stimulus produces a speedup in the turnover of money and higher interest rates, and more GNP.

The fact that people do economize on cash balances in response to rises in interest rates demonstrates the efficacy of fiscal policy. Anybody who reports that he can't find a trace of fiscal impact in the aggregate data is unreasonably claiming an absolutely inflexible velocity of money—a vertical liquidity preference function—or else he is revealing the limitations of his research techniques rather than those of fiscal policy.

A few other artful dodges, I submit, make even less sense. Try to defend fiscal impotence on grounds of a horizontal marginal efficiency schedule—that means investment is so sensitive to return that even the slightest interest variation will unleash unlimited changes in investment demand. Or make the case that people subjectively assume the public debt as personal debt and feel commensurately worse off whenever the budget is in deficit. Or contend that businessmen are so frightened by fiscal stimulation that their increased demand for cash and reduced investment spoils its influence. Or use the argument that Say's law operates even when the unemployment rate is 6 percent. It's a battle between ingenuity and credulity!

The eclectic principle is terribly important, not because it answers any questions, but because it rules out nonsense questions and points to sensible ones. It warns us not to get bogged down in such metaphysical issues as whether it is really the Fed that creates inflation during wartime. Every wartime period has been marked by enormous fiscal stimulus, and yet that fiscal fuel-injection could have been neutralized by some huge amount of pressure on the monetary brakes. In that sense, the Fed could have been sufficiently restrictive to offset the stimulus of military expenditures. Anyone who chooses to blame the resulting inflation on not slamming on the monetary brakes, rather than on pumping the fiscal accelerator, can feel free to exercise that curious preference. Take another example: Did the expansion following the tax cut in 1964–65 result from monetary policy? Of course it did, the eclectic principle tells us. If the Fed had wished to nullify the expansionary influence of the tax cut, surely some monetary policy would have been sufficiently restrictive to do so. There is no unique way of allocating credit or blame in a world where both tools can do the stabilization job.

Side Effects as the Central Issue

So long as both tools are capable of speeding up or slowing down demand, the decisions on how to use them and how to combine them must be made on the basis of criteria other than their simple ability to stimulate or restrain. Nor do we typically get any help by considering *how much* work monetary or fiscal tools do, because usually the right answer is, "as much as needed," providing the shift in policy is large enough. In more formal terms, two instruments and one target produce an indeterminate system.

Of course, there are two basic targets of stabilization policy: price stability and maximum production. But the two tools will not serve to implement those two goals simultaneously. A pen and a pencil are one more tool than is needed to write a letter, but the second tool can't be used to mow the lawn. In the same way, fiscal and monetary policy can both push up aggregate demand or push down aggregate demand, but neither can solve the Phillips curve problem. Subject to minor qualifications, the fiscal route to a given unemployment rate is neither less nor more inflationary than the monetary route to that same unemployment rate.

We can have the GNP path we want equally well with a tight fiscal policy and an easier monetary policy, or the reverse, within fairly broad limits. The real basis for choice lies in the many subsidiary economic targets, beside real GNP and inflation, that are differentially affected by fiscal and monetary policies. Sometimes these are labeled "side effects." I submit that they are the main issue in determining the fiscal-monetary mix, and they belong in the center ring.

Composition of output. One of the subsidiary targets involves the composition of output among sectors. General monetary policy tools, as they are actually employed, bear down very unevenly on the various sectors of the economy. Homebuilding and state and local capital projects are principal victims of monetary restraint. Although the evidence isn't entirely conclusive, it suggests that monetary restraint discriminates particularly against small business. In the field of taxation, we agonize about incidence and equity. The same intense concern is appropriate in the case of monetary restraint and, in fact, increasing concern is being registered in the political arena. In the 1969–70 period of tight money, many efforts were made to insulate housing from the brunt of the attack. But the impact on homebuilding was still heavy. Moreover, there is considerable basis for suspicion that these actions defused—as well as diffused—the impact of monetary restraint. A more restrictive monetary policy, as measured in terms of either monetary aggregates or interest rates, is required to accomplish the same dampening effect on GNP if the sectors most vulnerable to credit restraint are shielded from its blows.

The concern about uneven impact may be accentuated because, in 1966 and again in 1969–70, monetary restraint hit sectors that rated particularly high social priorities. But that is not the whole story. Any unusual departure of monetary policy from a "middle-of-the-road" position may lead to allocations that do not accord with the nation's sense of equity and efficiency. For example, in the early sixties, it was feared that a very easy monetary policy might encourage speculative excesses in building because some financial institutions would be pressured to find mortgage loans in order to earn a return on their assets.

In the last few years, some economists—most notably, Franco Modigliani—have argued that monetary policy may have a significant impact on consumption through its influence on the market value of equity securities and bonds in addition to its more direct impact through the cost and availability of installment credit. In my view, the jury is still out on this issue. On the one hand, it's easy to believe that a huge change, say, $100 billion, in the net worth of the American public, such as stock market fluctuations can generate, could alter consumer spending in relation to income by a significant amount like $3 billion, even though that change in wealth, is concentrated in a small group at the very top of the income and wealth distribution. On the other hand, previous empirical work on this issue came up with a nearly unanimous negative verdict. In 1966 and 1969, however, the timing of stock market declines and the sluggishness in consumer demand seemed to fit fairly well with the hypothesis. One would like to believe the wealth hypothesis because it would suggest that monetary policy has broad and sizable effects on consumption, especially on that of high-income consumers; monetary restraint would then be revealed as less uneven and less inequitable. But before embracing that judgment, one should wait for more decisive evidence.

Interest rates and asset values. Another major consideration in monetary policy is its effects on interest rates and balance sheets. Some economists may argue that the only function of interest rates is to clear the market and the only sense in which rates can be too high or too low is in failing to establish that equilibrium. Every Congressman knows better! Interest rates are a social target. That is the revealed preference of the American public, reflected in the letters it writes to Washington and the answers it gives to opinion polls. And this is no optical illusion on the part of the citizenry. They have the same good reasons to dislike rising interest rates that apply to rising prices—the haphazard, redistributive effects. And they are concerned about *nominal* interest rates just as they are concerned about prices. It is not clear that such major groups as businessmen or workers are particularly hurt or particularly helped by tight money (or by inflation), but the impacts are quite haphazard in both cases. The resulting lottery in real incomes strikes most Americans as unjust.

The largest redistributive effect of tight money, like that of inflation, falls on balance sheets rather than income statements. People care about their paper wealth and feel worse off when bond and equity prices nose dive. Even though society is not deprived of real resources when security prices drop, it is hard to find gainers to match the losers. Although Alvin Hansen stressed the social costs of distorted, fluctuating balance sheets in the 1950s, this issue gets little attention from economists. But it never escapes the broader and keener vision of the American public.

Financial dislocation. A restrictive monetary policy may also have important, dislocating effects on the financial system. The key function of a financial system is to offer people opportunities to invest without saving and to save without investing. If people want risky assets, they can acquire them beyond the extent of their net worth; if they wish to avoid risk, they can earn a moderate return and stay liquid. The trade of funds between lovers of liquidity and lovers of real assets produces gains to all. "Crunch" and "liquidity crisis" are names for a breakdown in the functioning of the financial system. Such a breakdown deprives people of important options and may

permanently impair their willingness to take risks and to hold certain types of assets. To the extent that very tight money curbs an inflationary boom by putting boulders in the financial stream, a considerable price is paid. And to the extent that extremely easy money stimulates a weak economy by opening the flood gates of speculation, that too may be costly.

Balance of payments. The pursuit of a monetary policy focused single-mindedly on stabilization goals would have further "side effects" on the balance of payments, to the extent that it changes international interest rate differentials and hence influences capital flows. There are strong arguments for fundamental reforms of the international monetary system—especially more flexible exchange rates—that would greatly reduce this concern. But those reforms are not on the immediate horizon; nor is the United States prepared to be consistently passive about international payments. Meanwhile, the external deficit casts a shadow that cannot be ignored in the formulation of fiscal-monetary policies.

Growth. A final consideration in the mix of stabilization tools is the long-run influence of monetary policy on the rate of growth of our supply capabilities. An average posture of relatively easy money (and low interest rates) combined with tight fiscal policy (designed especially to put a damper on private consumption) is most likely to produce high investment and rapid growth of potential. That becomes relevant in the short run because the long-run posture of monetary policy is an average of its short run swings. If, for example, the nation relies most heavily on monetary policy for restraint and on fiscal policy for stimulus, it will unintentionally slip to a lower growth path. The contribution of extra investment to growth and the value of the extra growth to a society that is already affluent in the aggregate are further vital issues. Recently, enthusiasm for growth-oriented policies has been dampened by the concern about the social fallout of rapid growth and by the shame of poverty, which calls for higher current consumption at the low end of the income scale. Nonetheless, the growth implications of decisions about the fiscal-monetary mix should be recognized.

In the light of these considerations, there are good reasons to avoid extreme tightness or extreme ease in monetary policy—even if it produces an ideal path of real output. Tight money can be bad medicine for a boom even if it cures the disease, just as amputation of the hand is a bad remedy for eczema. The experience of 1966 provides an object lesson. Judged by its performance in getting GNP on track, the Federal Reserve in 1966 put on *the* virtuoso performance in the history of stabilization policy. It was the greatest tight-rope walking and balancing act ever performed by either fiscal or monetary policy. Single-handedly the Fed curbed a boom generated by a vastly stimulative fiscal policy that was paralyzed by politics and distorted by war. And, in stopping the boom, it avoided a recession. To be sure, real GNP dipped for a single quarter, but the unemployment rate did not rise significantly above 4 percent; the 1967 pause was as different from the five postwar recessions, including 1970, as a cold is different from pneumonia. Moreover, inflation slowed markedly in the closing months of 1966 and the first half of 1967. What more could anyone want? Yet, you won't find the 1966 Fed team in the hall of fame for stabilization policy. In the view of most Americans, the collapse of homebuilding, the disruption of financial markets, and the escalation of interest rates were evils that outweighed the benefits of the nonrecessionary halting of inflation. The Fed itself reacted by refusing to give an encore in 1967–68, accepting renewed inflation as a lesser evil than renewed tight money.

19

A Critique of U.S. Monetary Policies

CARL CHRIST

Carl Christ is Professor of Economics at Johns Hopkins University. This article comes from his testimony before the Senate Banking Committee in 1975.

The Fed's Short-Run Policies

The Federal Reserve's short-run monetary policy behavior has not changed fundamentally in 30 years. Federal Reserve action has been too much and too late, with respect to the money stock and business cycle fluctuations. In recession after recession, the Federal Reserve has allowed the growth rate of money stock to decline, and in every major recession, including this one, the actual level of the money stock has been allowed to decline. This aggravates recession at the very best.

In recovery after recovery, the Federal Reserve has allowed the growth rate of the money stock to become substantially greater than it was in the previous recession and substantially greater than the 3 or 4 percent a year that would be consistent with price-level stability in the long run. This accelerates the recovery, but it makes it necessary to choose at the completion of the recovery between increased inflation on the one hand and a subsequent recession on the other hand.

The size of the decline allowed by the Federal Reserve in the growth rate of the money stock from a re-covery period to the subsequent recession is typically between 3 and 6 percentage points on the annual growth rate.

For example, from early 1972 to mid-1974, the Federal Reserve allowed the money stock to grow at an annual rate of 7.4 percent. Then from June 1974 to January 1975, as the recession grew, the Federal Reserve allowed an average growth rate in the money stock of only 1.4 percent, which is 6 percentage points less than during the previous recovery.

We know that an increase in the rate of growth of money stock stimulates the economy and that a decrease in the rate of growth of the money stock depresses the economy, with a lag of about six to eighteen months. Since presently available methods cannot accurately and reliably predict the timing and severity of a recession six to eighteen months ahead, the Federal Reserve cannot use monetary policy effectively to prevent recessions that arise from nonmonetary causes.

If the Federal Reserve waits to increase the growth of the money stock until it is clear there is recession, as in February 1975, there is a grave risk that by the time the effects of that increase come to fruition there will be no further need to combat recession, and indeed by that time the problem is likely to be inflation.

That is why so many economists have urged that the Federal Reserve increase the money stock at a slow, steady rate of 3 or 4 percent a year, come what may. It would avoid the "too much, too late" kind of mistake that the Federal Reserve has been making for thirty years and more, and it would avoid inflation too.

The Fed's Long-Run Policies

The Federal Reserve's long-run policy, unlike its short-run policy, has changed substantially over the last thirty years, and the change has been for the worse, toward inflation.

From the end of World War II until 1962 the Federal Reserve kept the growth rate of the money stock at about 2 percent a year, and prices rose at about that same rate. From 1962 to 1966, the Federal Reserve allowed the money stock to grow more rapidly, and the price level began to increase more rapidly in 1966.

From the end of 1966 to mid-1974 the Federal Reserve allowed the money stock to grow at a much more rapid rate, at an average of about 7 percent a year from 1972 to 1974. The price level responded by continuing to increase more rapidly too.

The inflation we have had since 1966 is the direct result of the more rapid increase in the money stock that the Federal Reserve has allowed to take place since 1962. The sad truth about the past is that the inflation was totally unnecessary. The happy truth about the future is that we need not continue it. What is required is that the Federal Reserve return to a long-run average growth rate of the money stock in the neighborhood of 3 to 4 percent a year.

Now, the short-run stabilization problem and the long-run inflation problem are independent of each other except in periods of transition from one long-run rate of inflation to another. The Federal Reserve can choose whatever long-run average rate of inflation it wants, positive, negative, as from 1864 to 1896, or zero, by choosing the appropriate long-run growth rate for the money stock.

The cyclical behavior of real output and employment will be essentially unaffected by the choice as to a long-run inflation rate once the economy has adjusted to that choice.

The Federal Reserve could improve its short-run and long-run policy in the absence of ability to predict the timing and severity of cycles six to eighteen months ahead, by maintaining a growth rate of the money stock nearly constant, at something like 3 or 4 percent a year.

There is an interaction problem between the stabilization problem and the inflation problem if the long-run inflation rate is being changed from one rate to another. An increase in the rate of growth of the money stock will increase the average rate of inflation, and in the two or three years that are required for people to adjust their expectations to the new rate of inflation there will be a temporary increase in real output and employment, but that will disappear when the new inflation rate is built into people's expectations. The experience of 1966–1975 confirms this.

Therefore, in order to maintain a permanently higher level of real output and employment by means of monetary policy, an ever-increasing rate of inflation, without limit, would be needed. We do not want to go the way of those countries that generated hyperinflation. Recognizing that the pattern of unemployment we experience will be about the same at any constant rate of inflation as at any other, I believe we should choose a zero average inflation rate for the long run.

20

Standards for Guiding Monetary Action

HENRY C. WALLICH

Henry C. Wallich, a member of the Federal Reserve Board, was formerly at Yale University and a member of the Council of Economic Advisers from 1959 to 1961. This selection comes from his testimony before the Joint Economic Committee in 1968.

Among the numerous standards of monetary policy that have been suggested, such as money supply, credit, interest rates, and bank reserves, one has attracted particular attention: a rule for a stable increase in the money supply. This proposal is associated principally with the name of Professor Milton Friedman of the University of Chicago.

Rationale of the Rule

The rule rests upon the theoretical and statistical finding, not universally accepted, that the *rate of growth* of money supply and the *level* of economic activity are closely related. A downturn in the rate of money growth, even when it does not lead to a positive shrinkage of the money supply, tends to be followed by a decline in the level, rather than the rate of growth, of economic activity. The same applies to troughs in the two series. It is argued that the behavior of money, because it precedes movements in the economy, causes the latter. The effect takes place with

a long and variable lag, however. Hence, while those controlling the money supply have a great power over the economy, the long and unstable lag makes it difficult to apply monetary policy on a discretionary basis for stabilization purposes. Monetary policy has so often been wrong that it seems preferable to deprive it of discretion and subject it to a fixed rule. It is not claimed that the fixed rule will produce perfect policy. But it will produce better policy than discretion is likely to do.

The main burden of my argument will be that this reasoning is fallacious. Before proceeding with the argument, I would like to point out, however, that while the rule at times is likely to have very bad results, it will probably have better results than alternative fixed rules that have sometimes been proposed. For instance, a rule that fixes the rate of growth of money supply is vastly superior to a rule fixing the interest rate. The fixed-money growth rule may at times lead to wrong action. It may also have bad side effects through instability in the capital markets and in the balance of payments. But so long as the money supply is kept growing at a stable rate, roughly commensurate with the growth rate of the economy, cumulative instability is unlikely to develop. Short-run fluctuations may be wider than under a competent discretionary policy. But in the long run money and income will move broadly hand in hand, with at most a moderate rate of inflation or deflation, and moderate changes in the foreign exchange value of the dollar.

A rule pegging the interest rate, on the other hand, for which some time ago there was widespread support, would be cumulatively destabilizing. If, for instance, interest rates were pegged below their equilibrium values, i.e., below the level consistent with stable prices or a stable rate of inflation, the open market purchases required to keep rates at the pegged level will sharply increase the money supply. Inflation would start or accelerate. This would raise the equilibrium rate of interest, which must be higher, in nominal terms, the faster the rate of inflation. This in turn would widen the gap between the equilibrium rate and pegged rates. The scale of open market operations, and the growth in the money supply, would then have to be stepped up. The process would lead to accelerating inflation. In the unlikely case that the pegged rates should be above equilibrium rates, an accelerating deflation would follow.

The same is true with respect to a rule that would try to peg the level of unemployment. In the long run, there is only one level of unemployment consistent with stable prices: the unemployment at which real wage increases are equal to nationwide productivity gains. At a lower level of unemployment, labor demands, and business is willing to grant, higher money wage increases than are consistent with productivity gains. This leads to price increases. These reduce nominal wage increases to less than what labor and business had anticipated. In the following bargaining round, therefore, the existing rate of inflation will be taken into account; nominal wage increases will be higher. Then the process repeats itself, the bargaining parties always vainly trying, by higher nominal settlements, to achieve a rate of real wage increase that, because it is in excess of productivity gains, the economy cannot provide. A policy rule seeking to peg the level of unemployment above or, more likely, below its equilibrium value will lead to increasing deflation or inflation. In this it resembles a fixed interest rate policy, both contrasting with a fixed money growth rule. This, however, does not show that a fixed money growth rule is superior to discretionary monetary policy. I shall argue the case by pointing to the difficulties that a fixed money growth rule is likely to encounter. Obviously this does not prove that discretionary policy is bound to be better. Discretionary policy *can* be worse. All that can be done is to compare the probable defects of the two systems.

Can the Money Supply Be Controlled?

The fixed money growth rule takes for granted that the central bank can make the money supply anything it pleases. That assumption is made also, of course, by all those who argue for a discretionary money supply target. The process of money creation encounters leakages, however. These may slow down attainment of the desired money volume. In the extreme case, they may prevent it altogether. At the level of the banking system, changes in excess reserves and in rediscounts can temporarily prevent the central bank from achieving its objective. The tendency of banks, after a period of great stringency, to rebuild liquidity by paying off rediscounts rather than purchasing assets is familiar. The central bank can overcome these obstacles, by operating on a scale sufficiently large to make its objective prevail. This involves some danger, of course, of overshooting if the banking system later makes fuller use of the reserves supplied.

At the level of the money holding public, shifts from demand deposits into time deposits may frustrate the central bank's effort to increase the money supply. Again, operations on a sufficiently large scale will overcome the resistance of the public, again with some danger of overshooting later. Because the relative expansiveness of an added dollar of demand deposits and of time deposits, respectively, is not known, the ultimate effects of a monetary expansion that increases time deposits along with demand deposits are difficult to estimate. The same applies in the case of relative or absolute contraction.

In the longer run, however, the most serious leakage is that via the balance of payments. A monetary policy that generates either interest rates much below foreign rates, or prices much above foreign prices, will produce a deficit on capital or current account, or both. This deficit reduces the money supply. If the central bank increases the scales of its expansive operations to compensate, it will increase the leakage. In the United States, the desired money supply may prove attainable most of the time despite this leakage. In a smaller economy, where the balance of payments leakage is proportionately larger, it is quite obvious that the central bank cannot put the money supply at any level it pleases so long as the currency is to be kept stable and convertible.

For all these reasons, control over the money supply on the part of the central bank is less than complete.

A Fixed Rule Requires Flexible Exchange Rates

Let us assume that the Federal Reserve achieves its money supply objective. This may, however, lead to large international reserve losses if the money supply objective leads to outflows on current or capital account. In time the outflows will exhaust exchange reserves. Thereafter, unless payments controls are introduced, the dollar would be on a floating exchange rate. If the money growth rule continues to be overly expansive, this would result, not in a deficit, but in a continuously declining exchange rate for the dollar. Academic discussions of a money growth rule generally recognize that floating exchange rates are its logical and necessary counterpart. This has not been the case, so far as I know, in congressional discussions. If a flexible exchange rate is not acceptable, then the money growth rule will have to be modified from time to time to prevent reserves from being exhausted. Related considerations apply to the case where a fixed money growth rule would produce a continuing balance of payments surplus. To avoid draining the world of its reserves, the dollar would have to be allowed to appreciate, or the fixed rule would have to be abandoned.

Balance-of-Payments Objectives

If an internationally stable dollar and an equilibrated balance of payments are desired, any money supply target, whether based on a rule or on discretion, is inferior to a monetary policy using interest rates as a target. An important part of the balance of payments is determined by flows of short and long term capital, so long as these are not subject to controls. These flows reflect interest rate differentials between the United States and abroad. They can best be controlled, therefore, by a monetary policy using an interest rate target.

That an interest rate target, pursued without regard to domestic equilibrium, can be much more disruptive than a money supply target, whether based on rule or discretion, has already been pointed out. Nevertheless, monetary policy, in one form or another, is the appropriate weapon for balance of payments management. It is superior, in this regard, to fiscal policy. If the objectives of domestic and external stability should conflict, as they sometimes do, it is best to pursue domestic stability by means of fiscal policy, balance of payments equilibrium by means of monetary policy. The reason for this is that while both fiscal and monetary policy affect domestic activity and thereby also the level of imports, monetary policy additionally affects the balance of payments via capital movements. Thus, monetary policy has a "comparative advantage" in dealing with the balance of payments. To implement this advantage, an interest rate target is superior to a money supply target or rule.

Stable Money Growth—Unstable Interest Rates

If the volume of money were rigidly fixed from day to day, interest rates probably would jump about within a wide range. The exact amount of money demanded by the economy varies from day to day. It depends on the payments that firms and households have to make, subject to weekly, monthly, quarterly, and annual "seasonals," and also to purely random fluctuations. The normal policy of central banks is to stabilize interest rates in the short run by allowing bank reserves and the money supply to vary. The Federal Reserve's policy of maintaining "net free reserves" roughly constant over short periods has the same effect. Any change in the economy's demand for money is thus validated by a change in the supply of reserves and of money. Without this flexibility in the money supply, those in need of money would have to sell short term securities, thereby unsettling interest rates.

A fixed money growth rule would put an end to this accommodating central bank behavior. The ensuing instability of interest rates would probably be moderated, in the course of time, by the market itself. Speculators and arbitragers would buy short term securities when they seemed depressed by transitory factors and sell them when they have risen because of temporary excess liquidity. This smoothing activity of the market would not be perfect, however, nor costless.

Unstable interest rates are not an intolerable calamity. They are painful mainly to participants in the financial markets. They would damage the real sector of the economy only if instability was transmitted to it, or if uncertainty in financial markets leads to a reduction in the flow and an increase in the cost of capital for investment. Some cost increase probably would result, since market participants would have to protect themselves against interest instability by charging higher risk premia.

Unstable interest rates might destabilize international capital flows. It is true that these international flows would help to limit the amplitude of domestic interest rate fluctuations. They would also, however, destabilize foreign capital and exchange markets. Foreign countries might reasonably complain about an American monetary policy that interfered with their own stability.

What Definition of Money?

Reference was made above to the leakage from the money supply through the creation of time deposits. The problem goes deeper, however. All near-monies are substitutes for money in some degree. The exact equivalents are unknown. No doubt they vary from time to time and from holder to holder. The historical evidence seems to say that it does not matter greatly whether a fixed money growth rule is based upon money supply narrowly or broadly defined, i.e., including or excluding time deposits. For the broad definition, a higher rate of growth would be needed than for the narrower, since time deposits have grown more rapidly. But recent gyrations of time deposits and other near-monies make clear this much: either the conditions that in the past made the two types of rules equivalent have changed, or else that equivalence and hence the precision of the monetary growth rule itself was of a very rough sort. The rules specified by Representative Reuss have tried to take unstable behavior of near-monies into account but they do not provide for quantitatively precise adjustment. In the present state of knowledge, not even a discretionary policy can take erratic behavior of near-monies adequately into account. To allow for it accurately in a fixed money growth rule would be even more difficult.

The Relation of Money to Income

Less than twenty years ago, it was fashionable to argue that money had no influence on income. Monetary policy was considered powerless by a great majority of economists in and out of government. Today we are in danger of overshooting in the opposite direction. The existence of an effect running from money to economic activity seems well documented. Its mechanics and its timing are only imperfectly understood.

That the relationship should be between the rate of money *growth* and the *level* of economic activity, for one thing, is not intuitively obvious. One would expect more likely a relationship between the *level* of money supply and the *level* of economic activity, or else between their respective rates of growth. The principal reason why some investigators have chosen the rate of growth rather than the level of money supply seems to be that historically the money supply has declined much less frequently than the level of economic activity. Thus, the level of money and the level of activity have at times moved in opposite directions, casting doubt on the relationship. On the other hand, a relationship between a rate of growth and a level may well be meaningless. It is true of any time series moving in a cyclical, i.e. wavelike pattern, that its rate of growth must decline before the absolute value of the series can decline. Thus, to the extent that money and economic activity are in fact correlated, the rate of money growth is bound to decline before the level of activity, without this implying any causal relationship.

Furthermore, while there is good reason to think that money influences activity, it is obvious also that activity can influence money. It does so by stimulating the demand for bank credit. The banks can meet this demand by using their excess reserves and by borrowing from the central bank. Moreover if the central bank is interested in maintaining reasonably stable interest rates, it will supply the banks with reserves needed to meet a strong loan demand. Alternatively, if the central bank is determined to curb an expansion, the appearance of incremental loan demand may cause it to tighten the financial markets even more than the incremental demand itself would. Thus, an incipient change in the level of economic activity may very well cast its shadow ahead, in the form of a prior change in the demand for credit and in the rate of growth of money.

To the extent that money does determine income, the mechanics of this influence remain only partly resolved. There is wide agreement that interest rates play a key role. But if interest rates are the mechanism that transmits impulses from money to the real economy, why look at money instead of at interest rates?

One possible answer to this question is that there is a "direct effect," running from money to income and bypassing interest rates. An increase in money may raise aggregate demand, not because money holders buy securities and drive down interest rates, but because they use their excess money holdings to buy goods directly. This is the manner in which the "quantity theory" often is explained: "when people have more money than they want, they spend it and drive up prices."

But the "direct effect" is less plausible than appears. Households presumably make a decision how much to consume and how much to save. If they accumulate cash, it is by virtue of a prior saving decision. It seems unlikely that, having just decided to save this money, they should then turn around and spend it on consumer goods. The most likely use of excess money saved would seem to be for financial assets, for residential housing, and conceivably for durable consumer goods, if these are regarded as assets. In the case of households, therefore, a "direct effect" seems to be precluded except in the narrow areas of housing and durables.

For firms, saving means to retain profits. The resulting cash balances can be spent on any of the assets that firms acquire—receivables, inventories, fixed assets—or for debt repayment. Here the range for a "direct effect" is wider.

Any demand for physical assets—plant and equipment, inventories, homes—will stimulate economic activity. This demand may be influenced by the liquidity of households and firms. Very importantly, this demand will depend, however, on the rate of return that the assets yield, and on the rate of return that potential asset holders want to obtain. Anything that raises the return on assets, e.g., technological improvements, or reduces the return that asset holders expect, e.g., a fall in rates of return on financial assets—will increase the demand for physical assets and stimulate economic activity. The rate of money growth will affect economic activity insofar as, directly or indirectly, it affects these key elements. This is considerably more complex a process than one described by the statement "more money means more demand."

For the setting of a precise rule it is important to know whether money tends to grow faster, as fast, or more slowly than real income. This decisive question unfortunately remains unsolved. According to one theory, money is a luxury good. It follows that the demand for it should expand more rapidly than per capita income, i.e., the velocity of circulation tends to fall. According to a second theory, there are economies of scale in the use of money that allow larger transactors to operate with relatively smaller balance, i.e., velocity tends to rise. The historical

evidence shows that there have been long periods of declining velocity of money, which would seem to confirm the "luxury good" theory. Since World War II, however, velocity of money has greatly increased. This change has been accompanied by a rise in interest rates, by a growing expectation that inflation will be a permanent condition, and by various technological improvements that permit economies in the holding of balances.

Another factor that may possibly influence the velocity of money is the proportion of the money supply based upon government debt and international assets ("outside money"). According to some findings which must be considered highly tentative, a decline in this proportion tends to increase velocity. In the United States, this proportion has in fact declined substantially in the postwar period.

Some progress has been made in estimating the quantitative impact upon velocity of these various determinants. But even if we were prepared to rely on such calculations in setting a money growth rule, which is premature, it would remain necessary to estimate future levels of the determinants. It would be necessary, that is to say, to forecast such factors as interest rates and inflationary expectation as would prevail given any proposed rate of money growth. Only then would we know what the appropriate rate of money growth should be. To set a fixed rate of money growth without knowing these determinants is hazardous in the extreme. In the postwar period, for instance, a rule based on money growth during the interwar period would have been highly inflationary.

The manner in which money is created may also count, especially in the short run. Money created through bank loans and therefore spent immediately may have a more stimulating effect than money created through banks' purchase from investors of highly liquid short-term assets.

Likewise, the phase of the business cycle may affect the apppropriate rate of money growth. Historically, velocity has increased during periods of cyclical expansion, even during epochs when the long run trend of velocity was downwards. The same money growth rule may not, therefore, be equally appropriate for all cyclical phases, assuming that even under a fixed money growth rule some cyclical fluctuations will remain.

Finally, it is necessary to point out that all these relationships are highly aggregative. Households with different income levels and firms with different kinds of cash flows have different individual velocities.

National velocity is an average. Changes in the mix of households and firms almost certainly would alter average velocity and hence the appropriate growth rate of money.

Lags

Research performed by Professor Milton Friedman and Mrs. Anna Schwartz has shown that the lag between peaks in money growth and in economic activity has ranged from 6 to 29 months. The lag from the trough in money growth to the trough in economic activity has ranged from 3 to 22 months. This great variability has been interpreted as demonstrating the uncertainty of monetary policy. It is argued that an action taken, say, to curb an expansion may achieve its main effects only in the succeeding recession.

This reasoning seems unconvincing. The peak rates of monetary growth rarely can be interpreted as indicating a deliberate stance of monetary policy. Monetary policy has not been guided by money growth. Certainly one cannot assume that the start of a decline in money growth marks the moment when the monetary authority decided to put on the brakes. Accordingly, the lag from the peak in money growth to the peak in economic activity is not indicative of the lag of monetary policy. The same applies to the troughs of money growth and economic activity.

A better test of the lag in monetary policy can be derived from observing its effect on the occasion of drastic shifts in policy. Such a shift occurred in 1966. It took only four months to move from reasonable liquidity in the financial markets in April to a serious crunch in August. It took little time to convert a crunch into expectations of recession, and only another four months to move from the crunch to a positive halt in the growth of industrial production in November. Mild monetary measures are another thing—their effect may well be long delayed, since they are not intended to produce abrupt changes in economic activity.

At a more theoretical level, the lead-lag relationships exhibited by money growth and the level of income, respectively, have been examined, as well as some properties of models embodying a fixed money rule. These analyses show that the nature of the leads and lags depends heavily on what factor is assumed to be "driving" a cyclical fluctuation, and what causal relationships are assumed to exist among the various factors. It is even possible to show that money growth

may lead income in a model where, by assumption, money has no influence on income at all. Under different assumptions, the rate of money growth, or the level of money supply, may lag changes in income, yet by assumption have a causal effect upon income. The length of time over which a system, once thrown out of balance, returns to equilibrium tends to be, in general, longer under a fixed rule than under a reasonable discretionary policy. While these models cannot form a basis for policy, they serve to show that observed relationships, such as the lead of money growth over income levels, do not unambiguously point to any particular causal mechanism. They also show that a fixed rule may be a costly substitute for sensible discretionary policy. To use a simple analogy, a fall in the barometer usually—not always—precedes rain. No conclusions as to causality can be drawn.

Comparison of Results of a Fixed Rule and of Actual Policy Measures

Studies have been made seeking to compare the performance of variously specified money growth rules with actual performance. Usually this involves specifying what policy would have been optimal at any given time, and examining the degree to which the rule and actual policy, respectively, have conformed to this optimum. The cyclical behavior of the economy makes specification of optimum policy rather uncertain. For instance, it depends entirely on the lags with which monetary policy is assumed to work, how soon during a cyclical expansion monetary policy should shift from stimulation to restraint, and whether it should shift back again from restraint to stimulation ahead of the upper turning point. Analogous problems arise on the downside. Again, the relative weight given to full employment, price stability and the balance of payments, respectively, will influence what is considered optimal policy. There is also the question of defining "policy." Policy may not look the same in terms of a money supply standard, a credit expansion standard, or an interest rate standard. Thus the attempt to compare policy by rule and by discretion against an optimal policy is in any event questionable.

The comparison becomes virtually invalid, however, when another circumstance is taken into account. The cyclical and other conditions of the economy, in terms of which optimal policy is defined, are those brought about, at least in part, by the actual policies pursued. They are never the conditions that would have prevailed had policy been guided by a fixed money growth rule. But if the money growth rule, under certain circumstances, destabilizes the economy, then the proper test for it would be how it performs in correcting a disequilibrium of its own making. To such a disequilibrium, a discretionary policy could react flexibly. The fixed rule can respond only by doing more of the same. For a while, at least, that may increase the disequilibrium.

For example, if a fixed rule should lead to inadequate growth of the money supply, as it might have in 1967, and cause or contribute to a recession, nothing can be done under the rule to turn the economy around quickly. The same would be true in case of an inflation, or of a balance-of-payments deficit. Conceivably, very extreme conditions might develop before the economy returns to equilibrium. Discretionary policy, whatever its defects, usually has succeeded in preventing the occurrence of such extreme conditions, with a few lamentable exceptions. Thus a comparison of a rule and an actual policy, employing the actual historical record, gives the rule the wholly unjustified advantage of always starting from a situation that discretionary policy has kept from going to an extreme. Put in simplest terms, a rule could get us into a big mess, yet the tests rarely confront the rule with such a mess.

Will the Rule Be Sustained?

No Congress, no President can bind a successor. Short of being anchored in the Constitution, any money growth rule can be altered or dropped. What are the chances that a rule, whether simple or complex, whether enacted into law or adopted voluntarily by the Federal Reserve, will be broken?

I believe the chances are excellent the first time the rule deviates substantially from what discretionary policy would counsel. In a recession, when the Federal Reserve would be inclined to generate liquidity rapidly, would the Congress, the public, and the Federal Reserve itself be satisfied with money being pumped out slowly? In an inflation, when money growth should be slowed sharply, would we be satisfied to see the Federal Reserve continuing to feed the process? In a balance-of-payments crisis, would we sacrifice a large volume of reserves instead of adopting the monetary policy that would stop the drain? In simplest terms, if the car is going off the road and one wheel is over the ditch, will we keep turning slowly because we have made a rule never to jerk the wheel?

In addition to the prospect of major breaches, there is the probability that minor adjustments in the rule will be demanded from time to time, unless the rule is very broadly defined. Evolving circumstances will show that any single percentage growth rate, or narrow range, is not the right one. If the range is wide, and if full discretion is given to the Federal Reserve within that range, the policy will not differ greatly from a discretionary one. In the end, therefore, even if a rule were adopted, discretion probably would be reestablished soon in one way or another. I would regard that outcome as fortunate.

21

Makers of Monetary Policy

SHERMAN J. MAISEL

Sherman J. Maisel is Professor of Business Administration at the University of California at Berkeley. Until 1973, he was a member of the Federal Reserve Board. This article comes from his book Managing the Dollar, *published in 1973.*

A distinguished group gathered in the East Room of the White House the morning of January 31, 1970. Headed by the President and his family, the cabinet, and the senior White House staff, it also included some who had been on the White House staff under President Eisenhower, the entire Federal Reserve Board, and many of the country's most prominent bankers. The working White House press and national television were there in full force. The occasion was the swearing-in of Dr. Arthur F. Burns as the tenth Chairman of the Board of Governors of the Federal Reserve System.

No one was quite certain how to act. It was nearly nineteen years since a new Chairman had been sworn in. At that time, William McChesney Martin had taken over what was then a far less prominent post. For the past month the financial press had been filled with praise of Martin, both as an individual and as Chairman. (The Federal Reserve Act precluded his reappointment.) Some, however, expressed reservations about what they considered to be his conservatism and penchant for tight money. As the end of his term approached, some feeling of coolness and

dissatisfaction toward him had emanated from the inner White House staff. Now all wondered what would happen as the result of the change.

The President made it clear that he expected a new Chairman would mean a new Federal Reserve policy. In a news conference the preceding night, the President had indicated that he thought an immediate easing of monetary policy was necessary. At the swearing-in ceremony, President Nixon publicly greeted the new Chairman with some pointed, joking-in-earnest comments about easing credit and lowering interest rates: "I respect his independence," said Mr. Nixon. "However, I hope that independently he will conclude that my views are the ones that should be followed." After a burst of applause, the President added, "You see, Dr. Burns, that is a standing vote of appreciation in advance for lower interest rates and more money."

It did not take a very close observer to see that both the incoming and the outgoing Chairmen were extremely uncomfortable with the President's jokes. Both knew that the Fed had acted to ease credit and lower interest rates several weeks earlier. When it would become obvious in future weeks that easing had occurred, the President's words on this occasion might cause the press to raise questions as to the reasons for the change. Was it due to the change in Chairmen?

Much of the public's awareness of the Federal Reserve System comes through the Chairman and his public statements. He personifies the System, and monetary policy is seen as a reflection of his ideas and personality. His role in monetary decisions is paramount. Since 1934 the Federal Reserve had had two strong Chairmen: Marriner Eccles and William McChesney Martin, with only a brief interval between their terms. Their dominance is illustrated by the remark current in Washington during much of Eccles's and Martin's tenures that the Federal Reserve Board consisted of the Chairman and six nonentities.

With a new man taking over, what effect would the change have on the economy? Would the influence of the White House be increased at the Fed? Obviously, the fact of a new Chairman was important to estimates of future financial conditions. Monetary policy does not merely reflect monetary doctrine; it is strongly influenced by the personalities in the Federal Reserve System and by their interaction, as well as by their responses to external suggestions and pressures.

The Interactions of Influence

Many pundits agree that "the Supreme Court follows the election returns." But they wonder what drum sets the pace of monetary expansion at the Federal Reserve. The power of semiautonomous agencies has long been a subject of fascination to political scientists. Many, fearing that the political process may overrespond to popular pressure, believe it useful to have nine or seven "wise men" who can take a longer, more dispassionate view of the national welfare, immune to special interest groups or large contributors. But the problem then arises, Who will guard the guardians?

Hard as it tries, the Federal Reserve cannot make monetary policy in a completely unbiased manner, free from all background influences and generalized business and professional pressures on the individual Board Members. Each time a new governor is appointed and confirmed, the stance of the Board shifts to some degree. The critical question is how much freedom and independence from the political process should be granted any small group, given the existence of these biases and special influences.

The question of the Fed's power and its use was vividly illustrated in January 1971 when members of the Federal Reserve, both as individuals and as a Board, were publicly explaining the dangers of expanded prices and reduced output the economy could incur if no price-wage or incomes policy were adopted. In articles and speeches, the press and prominent economists began to predict a new confrontation between the Federal Reserve and the Administration, suggesting that, unless the Administration adopted a price-wage policy, the Fed might slow the creation of money, with the result that output would not rise in accordance with the Administration's plans.

I became concerned that the public was getting a false picture of the Fed's power. When Hobart Rowen, financial editor of the Washington *Post*, wrote in his nationally syndicated column that the Fed was wielding a big stick in threatening to hold monetary policy hostage if the Administration failed to act, I called him to say that I believed he was leaving an incorrect impression of what the Fed could or would do. He expressed surprise at my statement, pointing out that his columns reflected the views of many informed observers, including his own experience of over fifteen years. I said perhaps the situation had changed gradually, but enough so that the past experience no longer applied. We agreed that he ought not to take my word for this change, but ought to investigate the best possible opinions from different sources as to the real situation, which he did. Shortly thereafter his column reported what I considered to be a correct evaluation of the situation, "The internal view at the Fed of its own proper role does not call for it to veto the official stance of the Government in any significant way. . . . The Fed cannot and will not hold its ability to be 'liberal' as hostage for White House acquiescence to a wage-price restraint program." Although this statement accurately expresses the predominant attitude within the Fed, the opposite view continues to be widely held. Again in 1973 stories almost identical to those of 1971 were current, to the effect that the Fed would tighten unless the government reduced its deficit.

In short, both individuals and the structure of the Federal Reserve System influence the monetary process. In answer to the question of what drum is heard where policy is made, I have drawn up Chart 1. It illustrates my estimate of the relative monetary power of various groups, both within and without the Federal Reserve System, during the time I served on

Chart 1. Degree of Monetary Power 1965–1973

THE FEDERAL RESERVE SYSTEM

The Chairman	45%
The staff of the Board and FOMC	25%
The other governors	20%
Federal Reserve Banks	10%

OUTSIDE INFLUENCES

The Administration	
The President	
The Treasury	35%
The Council of Economic Advisers	
The Office of Management and Budget	
All other nonfinancial	
The Congress	
House and Senate	
Committees on Banking	25%
Joint Economic Committee	
Senate Finance Committee	
House Ways and Means Committee	
The public directly	
Unorganized	
The press	20%
Economists	
Lobbyists	
The financial interests	
Banks	
S and Ls	10%
Stockbrokers	
Etc.	
Foreign interests	5%
Other regulatory agencies	
FDIC	
Comptroller	5%
FHLBB	
SEC	

the Board. The length of the line after a group's name indicates its impact on policy in relation to the others in the same section.

One cannot estimate the relative importance of internal as opposed to external pressures. The comparative impact on monetary policy of the President of the United States, the chairman of the House Banking and Currency Committee, the Secretary of the Treasury, or the Chairman of the Federal Reserve Board varies widely from one situation and one period to another.

The first section of the chart shows the power relationships within the Federal Reserve System. It is here that individual perceptions might show the largest divergence in the weights assigned. Other knowledgeable persons would certainly draw charts with different weights; in fact, if I were to chart another period, it would not be the same. No one would question that the Chairman of the Board of Governors holds the most monetary power. The second most important group is the staff of both the Board of Governors and the Federal Open Market Committee, including the two managers of the Open Market Desk in New York and their assistants. The third group is made up of the six other members of the Board of Governors. Finally come the Federal Reserve regional banks, within each of which the power is divided, depending upon personal and historical relationships, among the president, the staff, and the board of directors.

The second chart section is "Outside Influences." These are the groups whose speeches, phone calls, letters, memoranda, articles, and so forth are likely to be heard in monetary policy decisions. The most significant influence on the Federal Reserve comes from the President and other members of the Administration. Within this group the greatest force emanates from the White House staff and the other three Quadriad members, the Treasury, the Council of Economic Advisers (CEA), and the Office of Management and Budget (OMB). The remaining nonfinancial agencies in Washington have only a minor impact.

The relative power within the Administration has varied greatly depending upon the President, how he organizes his advice, and who occupies the various chairs. At times the weight of the Treasury has been greater than all the others. In other periods, either the CEA or OMB has been most significant. In recent years the White House staff has dominated.

The next most important influence is the United States Congress. While some pressure emanates from individual congressmen, most of the actual influence is wielded by the committees with oversight in the banking and economic fields: that is the Committees on Banking, the Joint Economic Committee, the Senate Finance Committee, and the House Ways and Means Committee. Within a committee, power tends to be concentrated in the hands of the chairman, the staff, and a few members who have either seniority or the personalities and abilities to use the press to publicize their economic views. Novices on the Washington scene often assume that congressional power is somewhat evenly divided among the 100 members of the Senate and the 435 members of the House. In fact, the Federal Reserve sees almost all of the oversight concentrated in the 10 to 20 members of Congress on the committees; their effective power far surpasses that of all the other congressmen together.

Another group is labeled "The Public Directly." Both the public and financial interests carry a great deal of indirect as well as direct weight, through their influence on the Administration and Congress. I divide the public into four primary groups, each with a roughly similar impact. They include the unorganized voters who write and speak out; the press; economists who criticize, evaluate, and suggest new or better policies; and finally, organized interests, including business, labor, and consumers, whose impact varies with the effectiveness of their Washington lobbies. The Federal Reserve listens carefully to the public, since each governor is primarily a public representative. How well messages are received, however, varies with the ability of a group to be heard above the general clamor, and with the understanding and clarity with which positions are presented.

The fourth category includes the financial interests recognized as having a special concern with monetary policy. It comprises the commercial banks, the government security dealers, other financial institutions such as savings and loans and insurance companies, and stockbrokers. All of these groups constantly make their presence felt in Washington through official committees, individual calls, letters, and publications aimed specifically at the Federal Reserve. They are important as a source of information on what is happening in the financial spheres and as the medium through which monetary policy influences the economy. On the other hand, they are recognized as special interest groups; their views and statements are carefully analyzed in that light.

The fifth line shows "Foreign Interests," which are foreign governments and central banks. They influence international monetary reserves and the exchange rate of the dollar. Again, their influence varies greatly, depending upon the importance attached to international reserves by the President and upon the strength or weakness of the dollar in international exchanges.

The final category shows the other financial regulatory agencies, which include the FDIC, the Comptroller of the Currency, the Federal Home Loan Bank Board, and the Securities and Exchange Commission. All of these agencies have certain coordinate powers with the Federal Reserve.

Two Chairmen: Contrasts in Style and Approach

The reaction to the change in the Chairmanship illustrates two conflicting views on how to predict Federal Reserve action. One assumes continuity. What the Federal Reserve will do tomorrow can be predicted by referring to actions taken ten, twenty, or thirty years ago. The other holds that tomorrow's acts depend on the views and personality of the current Chairman. Clearly both views are extreme. The Chairmen both affect and are affected by the System itself. If the Federal Reserve primarily reflected its Chairman, each change in the Chairmanship would bring major shifts in policy. Policies and operations in the past ten years would have shifted more than they actually did.

Both Chairmen, Martin and Burns, have been dominant public figures. For nearly nineteen years, Bill Martin *was* the Federal Reserve to most of the public. After he took over, Burns also moved from backstage at the White House to the center of news interest. A comparison of the two men gives some idea as to how individual ideas, beliefs, and personalities create changes in monetary policy and doctrine.

Were Federal Reserve policy closely correlated with the physical characteristics of its Chairman, the replacement of Martin by Burns would have caused a complete about face in the Federal Reserve's actions. Outwardly the two men are opposites. Martin is slight of build, quick in speech and attitudes, athletic, an ex-champion tennis player who still plays an excellent game of tennis or squash almost daily. Burns is larger, stolid, stocky, giving the appearance of a determined man; he is slow in speech and movement. Martin is a nonsmoker. Burns is rarely seen without a pipe in the corner of his mouth. He appears always to be in the process of preparing his pipe or lighting it, actions which give more time for careful preparation of his thoughts, allowing ideas to emerge in a logical, constant flow, although spoken so quietly as to be almost inaudible.

Martin likes people and has the ability to put others at ease. His interest in individuals he felt to be a significant part of his job. He enjoyed talking to people in depth, trying to obtain a better feel for the economy and an understanding of the problems faced by people in every walk of life. In addition, he believed his job required interpretation of the Federal Reserve to others. One can truly say, in a slight alteration of Will Rogers's statement, that no man who really knew Bill Martin disliked him. Whenever I traveled throughout the world, people would make a point of meeting me in order to be remembered to Bill Martin. They wanted to express their great fondness for him.

Contrasting Views of the Function of Economics

While physical differences are interesting, they do not, of course, play a major role in monetary policy. However, the sharply contrasting views of two consecutive chairmen as to how the Federal Reserve should function are important in understanding the development of monetary doctrines and operations.

In many of his public statements, Chairman Martin made clear his view that the primary function of the Federal Reserve Board was to determine what was necessary to maintain a sound currency. This required, primarily, judgment as to whether the economy was in danger of inflation or deflation. The press frequently reported Martin's dismay over the number of economists appointed to the Board. He felt that the economy was too complex to explain in detail; intuition would be lost and false leads followed if too much stress were put on measurement. It was stated that he had opposed the nomination of Burns as Chairman on the ground that he would bring to the job too much of an economist's viewpoint instead of the necessary broad vision of a generalist.

Burns's view was almost diametrically opposed to that of Martin. He sees the Federal Reserve as primarily an economic agency which cannot function without a clear view of where the economy is and of what economic policy is necessary to move it closer to the best possible track. While he does not underestimate the difficulties of measurement and analysis of the current and future situation, he still makes it clear that good monetary policy requires good economic knowledge and judgment.

William McChesney Martin

Bill Martin has aptly been described as a fun-loving Puritan. He has a high sense of personal integrity. He is convinced of the need and advantages for both individuals and the country to maintain high eco-

nomic standards. Among the many attempts to characterize the position of Chairman Martin, I think most apt is that which describes him as a "money moralist." Through speeches and writings over many years, his doctrine on money has become widely known. Money as Martin sees it is a basic moral force. Throughout history it has been misused by governments creating too much of it and depreciating its value. This is an immoral act. It is as immoral for a country today to allow the value of its currency to fall as it was for kings of old to clip coinage.

Martin has been almost universally described as the "symbol of monetary integrity." The Federal Reserve has the critical function of seeing that there is not too much money. The dollar must be protected from constant attacks, either from the government or from corporations or promoters seeking a free ride in financial markets. Martin's experience on Wall Street left many scars. He made it clear in speeches that he was concerned when elevator girls or shoeshine boys began to buy stock, fearing that this signaled irresponsibility and a possible return to the 1929 situation of uninformed speculation.

Martin's Federal Reserve was inward-looking in its relationship to the Administration and other groups in the economy. The importance of monetary policy made it vital that the Fed avoid entanglements with other groups which might, at critical times, restrain it from making its necessary moves. The fact that the Fed was governed by a board of seven members with terms spread over a long period enabled it to make independent judgments as to the cost of inflation for the future. It was given political independence so that it would be able, when necessary, to point out that the public interest required a halt to inflationary pressures.

Martin felt it vital to build up sufficient strength, particularly among those with power and the interest to use it, to insure that the Federal Reserve would be free of domination by the President or Congress. He wanted it known that the Federal Reserve stood for the public interest and that it was one of the few bodies that did so. Thus, when unpopular positions had to be taken, there would be a base for popular support, or at least support among those in the Establishment with the ability to make themselves heard. Consequently one of Martin's major efforts as Chairman was to promote the image of the Federal Reserve throughout the country. He did this by direct example, by speeches, and by the use of the Regional Banks and their boards of directors.

In line with this posture, Martin avoided taking stands or expressing views in areas outside the monetary field. He was concerned that if the Federal Reserve offered advice, advice would be thrust upon it in return, causing it to lose some of its freedom of action in the critical monetary field.

In the same way, the Federal Reserve had to be sensitive to the political pressures on Congress and the Administration. It had to remain as free of politics as possible so that when it acted it would not embarrass those who had to act for political reasons. As a matter of policy, the Federal Reserve avoids attacking individual politicians and their ideas; even when under bitter attack from particular congressmen or segments of the Administration, the Federal Reserve has attempted to answer in a restrained, factual manner.

As another example of its nonpartisanship, Federal Reserve policy has always been to avoid, if possible, taking any major monetary actions as elections approach. This follows from the view that the Fed can better perform its long-run functions if it does not become the focal point of political battles.

Since Martin's philosophy played such an important role in the development of Federal Reserve doctrine during his tenure, it is significant to discussions of the Federal Reserve's approach to monetary policy and operations. Martin often characterized himself as a man skilled in the interpretation of financial markets. He pointed out again and again the inability of everyone, including himself, to explain movements in the money supply—a fact which led him to put his faith in the tone and feel of financial markets as opposed to specific measurements.

Believing in the importance of psychological reactions, Chairman Martin had very little faith in the value of attempting to quantify Federal Reserve policy. In his opinion, measurement was dangerous, if not impossible: Numbers obtained would not accurately reflect real conditions and the Fed could do best by carefully evaluating events in the financial markets. He consequently spent a great deal of his own time in this pursuit. Through a wide network of friends and meetings with bankers, he was always extremely well informed as to what was occurring in financial circles. The Federal Reserve had to be concerned with the impact of its operations on market psychology. Its moves, even if made gradually, would create announcement effects. Dealers and others intimately involved would recognize that Fed policy had changed and would adjust their operations accordingly. Market psychology would spread to the banks, whose loans and loan commitments would be affected.

On the basis of its knowledge of the markets, the Federal Reserve acted to adjust the degree of ease with which money could be obtained. One might picture the Federal Reserve as operating like a giant rubberband: As the markets became too ebullient or expansionary, they would have to push harder and harder against the restraining action of Federal Reserve policy. If the markets or the economy were becoming too deflationary, the Federal Reserve would attempt to ease the pressure.

Banks could also be influenced directly through moral suasion. It was assumed that the major banks recognized the importance of their roles in fighting inflation and would, therefore, operate in accordance with the public interest. One of the principal functions of the Chairman of the Federal Reserve was to make clear to the banks, through speeches and private meetings, what the public interest consisted of and how they could cooperate in protecting the dollar.

In 1969, the largest banks were expanding credit rapidly, contrary to general monetary policy, by borrowing dollars in Europe and relending them in the United States. These funds, in so-called Euro-dollars, were not subject to reserve requirements. In fact, through a subterfuge, some of the largest banks were using these transactions to reduce sharply their normal reserve requirements. As a result, each Euro-dollar transaction caused a double increase in credit. This appeared to be a case in which moral suasion might work. The primary activity in the Euro-dollar market was concentrated in less than a dozen banks. The Federal Reserve could issue regulations covering these transactions; but, if banks cooperated voluntarily instead, they could retain a good deal of flexibility. They would have a safety valve which they could use in emergencies. Consequently, Chairman Martin asked them to restrain voluntarily their importation of Euro-dollars. However, the voluntary program collapsed rapidly. As individual banks came under pressure, they ceased to cooperate and, instead, met their desired credit expansion by continuing to borrow funds abroad. Banks which were cooperating complained bitterly that they were being unfair to their stockholders; they could not continue unless their competitors did. As a result, the Federal Reserve had to issue a rather complex regulation. Its effect and policing caused constant problems for both the banks and the Fed.

While the public view of Chairman Martin was certainly that of a deflationist, one who, on the whole, sought tighter money throughout his chairmanship, I do not think that this is a correct reading of the record.

In the spectrum of the Board and the Open Market Committee, during most of the 1960s he was either on the expansionist side or in the middle. His own personal views of the economy favored maximum possible growth and a financial structure that made this possible.

He was, however, probably less expansionist than the Administration. His belief that most currencies lost value because of budget deficits made it difficult for Martin to accept the new economic view that fiscal policy was based on a relative rather than an absolute standard. It was hard to believe that whether budgets should be in surplus or deficit depended on whether or not aggregate demand in the economy was excessive, and not on some arbitrary concept of balance. As a result, Martin occasionally issued strong statements on the need for a balanced budget. However, the Federal Reserve did not operate so as to attempt to offset budgetary deficits.

On the whole, Martin believed that the Federal Reserve ought to accommodate normal growth. However, the amount of attention paid to financial markets meant that too little account was devoted to how the overall economy was performing in relation to its potential. This led, at times, to a tendency to tighten credit too soon.

Arthur F. Burns

Chairman Burns approaches monetary policy as a trained economist who is also one of the country's foremost experts on the business cycle. In contrast to Martin, in policy making he has sought more and more information and better and better measurement.

Burns started out with the reputation of a semi-monetarist, placing considerable emphasis on the money supply. For the year prior to becoming Chairman, he had been a special counselor to President Nixon in the White House. During that period, numerous monetarist statements issued from both the White House staff and the President himself. However, experience with the problems of operating the Federal Reserve has deepened Burns's understanding of monetary policy. Never doctrinaire, his views have become increasingly eclectic. Policy is made in the real world, not the abstract world of theory.

Burns has been more involved than Martin with the political process in Washington. He has devoted more effort to relations with Congress. His concerns have encompassed the entire scope of the Administration's economic programs, while Martin primarily consid-

ered their impact on the Federal Reserve. In their relationships to the President, Burns has been a general economic adviser; Martin's role was more largely limited to monetary developments. While attempting to be nonpolitical as Chairman of the Federal Reserve, he could not fully suppress either his ideology or his personal relationships: His strong belief in President Nixon's policies was frequently visible. While Chairman Martin hesitated to intervene in Administration plans, this has not been the case with Chairman Burns. As a former head of the Council of Economic Advisers and White House adviser, his concern has been with overall macroeconomic policy. Monetary policy is only a part of the total picture. Because its success or failure depends on the budget and other governmental activities, monetary policy must be coordinated with other government programs.

In addition to his awareness of his own value as an economic adviser, Burns recognized the excellence of the Federal Reserve's economic staff. Given these two factors, he saw the Fed's role as one of innovator, supporter, and public pleader for good macropolicy. The Federal Reserve, if successful in this role, could influence economic policy as much as or even more than through its direct actions in the monetary field.

Burns spends much time on general economic policies not necessarily related to those of the Federal Reserve. In addition to being an adviser to the Cost of Living Council and a frequent adviser to the President, Burns was appointed chairman of the Committee on Interest Rates and Dividends in 1971. He played an active role in convincing Congress to pass legislation allowing the government to guarantee loans to major corporations such as Lockheed.

An illustration of the new activist role of the Fed Chairman is evident in the events attendant on the birth of the new economic policy in August 1971. Had Martin still been Chairman, he probably would have participated in some of the planning of the new economic program, or at least would have been called in to help obtain agreement on the international aspects, but Burns was present from the beginning as a personal adviser to the President. He played a major role in planning the program, helped to determine its initial shape, and then, as a member of the Cost of Living Council, monitored new programs as they developed. Only a few of these functions could be considered responsibilities of the Federal Reserve.

Another interesting contrast between Martin and Burns appears in their attitude toward Wall Street. Martin, coming from the stock market, was well aware of its problems. He was concerned that the market not become a speculative danger to the country. He feared a repetition of 1929 and was always on guard lest too rapid a rise in stock prices lead to a future sharp fall and deflation. Burns, on the other hand, shares the view that the stock market is a critical determinant of the country's economic future. It is necessary to treat the market delicately and to feed its concerns and ego. Success in this effort will increase confidence and improve the level of spending and output in the country.

Burns remains at heart a National Bureau of Economic Research business cycle economist. He supplements the Fed staff work with his own sources of information and a personal evaluation of the current status of the economy and of optimum macroeconomic policy. He increased the emphasis of the Federal Reserve on the problems of recession and stressed its functions as a lender of last resort. He was one of the strongest advocates in Washington of attempting to keep the Penn Central from going bankrupt and, failing that, to minimize the secondary reactions of the financial markets to the bankruptcy. His approach is pragmatic. More importantly, however, he knows from history that monetary policy has to prevent the secondary credit liquidation that caused severe depressions in the past, even though furnishing

the liquidity to avoid such crunches reduces the impact of monetary policy on inflationary expectations.

Most of those who experienced the change of chairmen were extremely thankful that Burns was a trained economist. 1970 and 1971 were successful years for the Federal Reserve because Burns assumed the Chairmanship with an understanding of the economy and a knowledge of past recessions, depressions, and crises. Learning to understand the operations of the Federal Reserve System alone is an immense and time-consuming task. If, in addition, an incoming Chairman had to bone up on fiscal policy, monetary policy, and the role of the Fed therein, a disastrous hiatus or impasse in monetary policy could occur.

Watching this transition, I was repeatedly struck by the thought of how dangerous it would be for the economy if, in the future, a new Chairman of the Federal Reserve was not well trained in economics. A *sine qua non* for the position is a thorough understanding of the economy in general and of the role government economic policy plays in its functioning. The need for this knowledge is so great that it probably could not be acquired quickly enough and completely enough by anyone who has not spent as least part of his career as a professional economist.

22

Open-Market Operations: A Case Study

FEDERAL RESERVE BANK OF NEW YORK

This article is taken from Open Market Operations, *published by the Federal Reserve Bank of New York in 1973. It is by Paul Meek, Monetary Adviser of the Bank.*

The Manager of the Federal Reserve System Open Market Account has made his decision. He will buy about $250 million in United States Treasury bills, which mature within the next twelve months. The time is just before noon on the Tuesday before Thanksgiving Day. In a room on the eighth floor of the Federal Reserve Bank of New York, eight securities traders gather around an officer of the securities department to receive instructions.

Each of the eight returns to his seat around a U-shaped trading desk. Each presses a button on a telephone console with wires linked to the nation's 20 or so primary dealers in United States Government securities. The trader's ring sounds a buzzer in the trading room of one of the two to four Government securities dealers he has been assigned to call.

"Jack," says the Reserve Bank's trader, "what can you offer in bills for cash delivery?"

Taking a quick look at the list of Treasury bills which the dealer firm owns, Jack replies, "Bill, I can offer you for cash $5 million of January 4 bills to yield 5.45 percent, $10 million of January 25 bills at

5.50—$10 million of March 22 bills at 5.50—and $8 million of May 17 bills at 6.12."

Bill says, "Can I have those offerings firm for a few minutes?"

"Sure."

Within a few minutes the "go-around" of the Government securities market is completed. Each of the eight Reserve Bank traders has recorded the results of his calls on special forms. The officer-in-charge attaches each to a board until the full array of individual dealer offerings is before him. Addition quickly shows that dealers have offered $753 million in Treasury bills for sale for cash—that is, with delivery and payment that very day.

A glance at a list of the Federal Reserve System's current holdings enables the experienced Reserve Bank officer to choose the issues likely to be most useful for future System operations. Seeking the best— that is the highest—yield on each issue, the officer checks a large quotation board across the open end of the U-shaped trading desk. This shows yields to maturity as they were in the market just before the "go-around" began. After selecting the specific offers he will accept, the officer informs the traders and they return to their telephone consoles to tell the dealers.

"Jack, we'll take the $5 million of January 4 bills at 5.45 and the $10 million of January 25 bills at 5.50 both for cash; no, thanks, on the others."

Within thirty minutes from the time the initial decision was made, all the calls have been completed. The Manager has selected and purchased $242 million in Treasury bills for cash. The paper work remains. On the same day, the clearing bank that handles each dealer's paper work will instruct the Federal Reserve Bank of New York, usually by wire, to deliver the specific Treasury bills purchased to the System's account. The Federal Reserve will credit its payments for the securities to the reserve account of the bank concerned. The bank, in turn, will credit the dealer's account with the proceeds of the sale. The transfer of these bills takes place through the Government Securities Clearing Arrangement in which changes in the Treasury securities holdings of the System and of the dealers are reflected as bookkeeping entries. This arrangement considerably reduces the physical transfer of such securities.

The day's open market purchases will not retain their separate identities in the Federal Reserve System's weekly report on the monetary system. They will be merged with all other operations conducted during the week that ends on Wednesday, the next day. The figures, normally released to the press at 4 P.M. on Thursday in New York and Washington, will be released this week on Friday afternoon because of the holiday.

The next morning many officers of banks, financial corporations and business concerns will turn automatically to the weekly Federal Reserve statement appearing in leading newspapers to see if there have been any significant shifts in the reserve positions of the nation's banks. All who are charged with raising money or investing funds for their firms know that changes in bank reserves normally have a major impact on the cost and availability of borrowed money in the national market for credit. They will spot the Federal Reserve's large open market purchases in the pre-Thanksgiving week and ask themselves: "Is the Federal Reserve only moving to make it possible for the banks to meet the public's seasonal demands for cash and credit, or is it moving to increase, or reduce (after allowance for seasonal factors), the ability of banks to extend credit?" Such questions can rarely be answered on the basis of a single week's figures. Only over a peri-

od of several weeks will financial men be able to sort out any gradual shift in Federal Reserve policy from transitory fluctuations in bank reserves.

All Part of a Day's Work

Each day presents a new challenge to the Manager of the Open Market Account. Yet each day has much in common with every other day. Let us consider that Tuesday before Thanksgiving Day and follow the developments which led to the purchase of $242 million in Government securities. On such a day, as on all days, the Manager must bear in mind the current directive and the consensus of the last FOMC [Federal Open Market Committee] meeting. Let us suppose that the directive calls for fostering growth in the money and credit aggregates conducive to sustainable economic expansion and that these broad objectives are to be pursued by keeping reserves generally in line with the paths developed by the FOMC's staff.

The main outlines of the task which lies ahead are at least roughly visible to the Manager early on Tuesday morning. He has before him the preceding day's projections of the behavior expected of nonborrowed reserves over the coming three weeks. Tuesday's projections will be available a bit later at about 10:45 A.M. The projections are based upon the behavior of reserve factors over the same calendar period during the past several years. They also take into account any special factors such as a Treasury financing.

Yesterday's projections indicated that the Manager will have to supply reserves in substantial amounts to offset reserve drains and provide for the seasonal rise in required reserves. Indeed the day before, Monday, the Manager provided $280 million in reserves by making $65 million in repurchase agreements with dealers early in the afternoon, after buying $215 million in Treasury bills outright for cash in the morning.

Useful as they are as a rough yardstick, the projections cannot be used as a precise guide to operations. Each year, for all its similarities to the past, produces a pattern of financial flows that is all its own. The Manager and his experienced officers must look to the Federal funds market itself for signals of the timing and magnitude of the reserve pressures actually at work on this particular day.

The new business day begins a few minutes after 9 A.M. in the trading room of the Federal Reserve Bank of New York. The news tickers are pounding out the financial news that has accumulated since it closed down the night before. The securities traders scan the closing quotations recorded on the board across the open end of the U-shaped trading desk to reorient themselves before the new day begins. The traders concerned with the routine flow of Treasury, member bank and foreign transactions begin to check on the day's orders.

Dealer Conference

By 9:15 A.M., two officers of the securities department hurry to a tenth-floor conference room to meet with one or two representatives of a Government securities dealer firm. Dealers confer every business day on a rotating schedule with the Reserve Bank officers directly responsible for the conduct of open market operations. At these conferences, the dealers comment on market developments and on any matter of interest to the firm. The Reserve Bank officers listen and ask questions.

This morning, representatives of three dealers are scheduled to appear, one after the other. At the first conference, a senior partner of a dealer firm observes that the market has been rather quiet during the last few days, and that he has been rather disappointed by the lack of corporate demand for Treasury bills. He finds that insurance companies and pension funds are holding off on bond purchases until the $100-million bond issue of the XYZ Corporation due to be offered on Wednesday hits the market. The dealer gives his views on whether the Treasury should issue short-term or long-term securities, or both, in meeting its cash needs, and indicates the kind of reception he thinks the market would give the new issues. After answering questions asked by one of the Reserve Bank officers, the dealer departs at 9:30 A.M.

Two representatives of a second dealer firm enter the conference room. Among other things, they indicate that while the market as a whole has been quiet, their firm has handled some sizable transactions in the last few days. They feel that many investors have large cash positions and are merely waiting for more attractive yields. One also feels that conditions in the money market were a little tight yesterday afternoon even after the System's intervention; his firm had to pay a relatively high interest rate to obtain financing for its position through loans and repurchase agreements negotiated with banks and others. The second firm's representatives leave at 9:45 A.M., and the vice president in charge of the dealer operations of a New York

City bank enters. The third conference covers much the same ground. The last dealer departs at 10 A.M., and the Reserve Bank officers return to their offices to prepare for the daily call from the U.S. Treasury.

The Treasury Call

Each morning shortly after 10 A.M., the Fiscal Assistant Secretary of the Treasury uses a direct telephone line to compare notes with the Manager or his deputy on the outlook for the Treasury's cash balance at the Reserve Banks. Their objective is to coordinate changes in the Treasury's balance at the Reserve Banks with the System's management of bank reserves. They estimate the amount of funds that need to be transferred from the Treasury's Tax and Loan accounts at commercial banks to the Reserve Banks in order to maintain a working balance in the face of checks they expect to be presented for payment at the Reserve Banks. (The Treasury channels a large part of its receipts from taxes and from sales of its securities through Tax and Loan accounts to reduce the sudden impact of these large flows on bank reserves.)

Today, the Assistant Secretary tells the Reserve Bank officer that his projections of daily Government receipts and expenditures indicate that the Treasury will need to transfer $500 million from Treasury Tax and Loan accounts at about 275 large commercial banks across the country (the Class C banks) to its account at the Federal Reserve Banks. This will be in addition to calls previously scheduled on Tax and Loan accounts at other commercial banks. The Reserve Bank official notes that projections of the New York Bank's staff point to a need to call about $300 million to maintain the Treasury balance at about the desired level. However, since bank reserve positions are expected to be under pressure from seasonal factors, the Reserve Bank officer and Assistant Secretary agree that the call be limited to 30 percent of the previous night's Treasury balances at the "C" banks—about $350 million.

The conversation over, the Reserve officer dials another officer in the Bank to inform him that the Treasury has decided to make a special call today on the "C" banks. By 11 P.M., the large banks will have been informed that they must transfer 30 percent of the Treasury's deposits with them at Monday's close to their district Reserve Banks. These transfers out of their reserve accounts are intended only to offset the bulk of the increase in member bank reserves expected to flow from the deposit of Treasury checks drawn on the Treasury's accounts at the Federal Reserve Banks. In practice, these checks are likely to be deposited widely over the country so that the big-city banks may find that the transfer of Treasury deposits from them to the Reserve Banks exceeds the amount of Treasury checks deposited with them. Typically, these banks will need to step up their overnight borrowing in the Federal funds market.

Getting the "Feel" of the Market

In the meantime, the Government securities market has become active. At the trading desk, opening quotations are beginning to come in. Several of the traders around the desk are talking to dealers to learn if any trend is developing. Other traders have a pretty good fix on orders to be executed for foreign accounts or for Treasury trust accounts. Reports have arrived from the research and statistics departments on dealer positions and on the previous day's reserve positions and Federal funds transactions of eight major banks in New York City and 38 banks in other cities. On hand also is a complete nationwide picture of the reserve positions of member banks as of Monday's close, including information on the distribution of reserves among money market banks and other reserve city and country banks.

Shortly after 10 A.M., two clerks bring the quotation board up to date with "runs" of price and yield quotations obtained from telephone calls to securities dealers. The Federal Reserve's traders already know from their conversations with dealers what the board shows—that the market is steady with few changes either up or down. They also know that there has been little trading except for the professional activity of the dealers who are testing each other's markets by occasionally "hitting a bid"—selling securities at the price bid by another dealer. About 10:45 A.M., the desk receives the first tentative quotation on Federal funds. The quote is 6 percent, a shade higher than yesterday's rate of $5^3/4$ percent, which exceeded the $5^1/2$-percent discount rate at which member banks can borrow from their Reserve Banks.

One member of the staff calls each of the nonbank dealers to find out the volume of funds needed to replace loans maturing today or to finance securities for which payment must be made today. A few minutes before 11 A.M., his tabulation shows that the dealers

need loans of about $950 million to finance their present securities holdings. Money was available at yesterday's close at 6 percent, but the dealers are not too sure about today. Several think money may be harder to get and more expensive.

The officer in charge of the desk, who has just been joined by the Account Manager and another officer, summarizes for them the early morning market developments. Together they review the newest projection of the factors affecting bank reserves over the next three weeks—a report received only moments before from the research department. A last-minute check with the traders reveals that banks and others are beginning to sell Treasury bills to the dealers in greater volume than buyers are coming to the dealers for bills. Treasury bill yields are beginning to rise—that is, prices are beginning to decline.

Meanwhile, a preliminary call is made to the Board of Governors in Washington and to the office of one of the Reserve Bank presidents currently on the FOMC. Information is provided on the full range of data available on bank reserves and the money and Government securities markets. Thus, the Reserve Bank president will have before him the data on which the desk's plan of action is based. The officers hurry to an adjoining office to participate in a very important telephone conversation—the conference call, which takes place at about 11:10 A.M.

The Conference Call

"Washington and Minneapolis are standing by" announces the telephone operator, completing the three-way telephone hookup that each morning enables the Account Manager to review developments with the staff of the Board of Governors in Washington and one of the Reserve Bank presidents currently serving on the FOMC. Sitting in on the conversation in New York today are the President of the Bank, the Manager of the System Account, and the officers of the securities department. One of the officers seated directly behind a telephone microphone speaks:

"Conditions have changed somewhat since we spoke yesterday. The Government securities market opened steady this morning with very few changes in prices and rates, and with little activity. But Treasury bills now seem to be in increasing supply so that yields are rising. There are some indications that long-term investors are holding off to see how the market will take the $100-million bond issue of the XYZ Corporation tomorrow. Our first tentative information on Federal funds showed a bid of 6 percent, $1/4$ percentage point above yesterday's closing rate, and word just received from the trading room indicates that funds have now begun to trade at $6^1/4$ percent. Dealer financing needs this morning are about $950 million. The banks have raised their call loan rates on dealer loans from $6^1/4$ percent to $6^1/2$ percent.

"Yesterday, nonborrowed reserves dipped slightly despite our action to supply reserves. The outlook is for a sharp decline in reserves today and tomorrow. New York City and Chicago banks are under pressure and have been heavy buyers of Federal funds on each of the last three business days. Banks in several other major cities show reserve deficiencies. Today's call on the 'C' banks will withdraw $350 million and will probably add to pressure on the money market banks."

The officer then reads the Manager's proposed plan for the day:

"In view of the expected stringency in reserves, the Account plans to purchase securities for cash. If the market continues to tighten, we may buy as much as $300 million of Treasury bills. Repurchase agreements with the dealers can be used to supply additional reserves if needed."

The conversation is, of course, more detailed than the above colloquy, and conclusions are supported by a marshalling of facts. Prospective developments in the next couple of days and weeks are discussed. Participants in Washington and Minneapolis may report additional information. They express views as to appropriateness of the proposed action.

By 11:30 A.M., the call is usually completed. A member of the Board's staff who participated promptly summarizes the call in a memorandum sent to each member of the Board of Governors. A telegram from the Board provides each Reserve Bank president with a summary of the telephone discussion, within an hour or two after the call is concluded.

The Decision

Shortly before noon conditions in the market begin to jell rapidly, indicating a sharp increase in reserve pressures. Federal funds are heavily bid for at $6^1/4$ per-

cent and dealers, New York City banks, and other participants in the funds market report that funds are hard to find. Dealers report they have not been able to make any progress in meeting their financing needs by borrowing from their out-of-town contacts even though they have been offering to pay $6^1/8$ percent for money.

The Manager reviews the evidence: "The market has really started tightening up. We had better move in right away in size to prevent this from getting out of hand. Let's go in and buy about $250 million in treasury bills for cash today."

The Manager of the System Open Market Account has made his decision. Eight securities traders gather around an officer of the securities department to receive instruction. As we have seen, within thirty minutes the Reserve Bank's traders purchase $242 million in Treasury bills for cash in a "go-around" of the market. A summary report from the New York Reserve Bank of the day's developments and System action will be on the desks of the Board members and all Reserve bank presidents on the following morning.

The officers continue to watch the situation after the "go-around" is completed at around 12:20 P.M. The Federal funds rate eases back to 6-percent bid for a time, but then the brokers report that the bid appears to be building while the supply available remains limited. Given the persistence of tightness, the Manager approves the recommendation of the desk officers that the System purchase about $300 million of Treasury and Federal agency securities under overnight repurchase agreements. By 1 P.M. the additional injection of reserves has been made—bringing the day's total to $542 million. A better balance returns to the Federal funds market.

The market may debate whether the day's action was designed simply to head off the developing strain in the market or whether it had broad policy significance. The market may not be able to be sure on that score until it can look back on several weeks of action and see if a cumulative easing of bank reserves overlays the weekly fluctuations not ironed out by System operations. But for today it is sufficient that the reserve strains which threatened to become acute have disappeared.

Tomorrow is another day . . .

23

The Fed in a Political World

DAVID P. EASTBURN

David P. Eastburn is President of the Federal Reserve Bank of Philadelphia. This article appeared in the Business Review *of the Federal Reserve Bank of Philadelphia in 1975.*

Anyone following the banking press at all closely will notice questions like these appearing frequently:

- *Whether the Fed in the eyes of Congress is putting enough money into the economy to assure recovery.*
- *Whether it is proper for a Federal Reserve Bank to spend nearly $80 for cigars.*
- *Whether the Fed should be audited by the General Accounting Office.*
- *Whether appointments of Federal Reserve Bank Presidents should be confirmed by the Senate.*
- *Whether the Fed will push up the money supply in order to help reelect President Ford in 1976 as some people allege it did for President Nixon in 1972.*

There is a strong *political* overtone to each of these questions. Yet, it is frequently said that the Fed is *nonpolitical.* Which is it? Are we political, or aren't we? A simple "yes" or "no" answer, I'm afraid, is just that—too simple. A more realistic way to phrase the question is: *how* political is the Fed and *in what sense?*

In a broad sense the Fed must be part of the political process. Politics is the art of government—in our system, representative government. Government must do what the people want; politics is the process of discovering what they want and how to get it for them.

Accordingly, the Fed must be responsive to the public. To say that it is nonpolitical—at least in this broad sense—implies that the Fed knows better than the people themselves what they should have. This is an elitist view inconsistent with our form of government.

Yet, there is something special about the Federal Reserve. It manages the money supply. A lesson in history is that sovereigns frequently have abused their power to manage money. Some years ago we published an analysis of this history which pointed out how Henry VIII at one time became known as Old Copper Nose.[1] The reason was that once he needed money and called in all the silver coins, and melted and recoined them with a copper base. As the new coins became worn and blotched, the most prominent part of Henry's features, his nose, protruded through the thin silver coating in a dull relief of copper—hence, Old Copper Nose. Even our own George

[1]"Henry VIII Revisited: The Problems and Temptations of Money Creation," *Business Review* of the Federal Reserve Bank of Philadelphia, January 1960, pp. 3–18.

Washington was saddled with the problem of paying his troops with paper money that declined so precipitously in value that the Continental dollar cost more to print than it was worth as money.

Given this long history of abuse, the founders of the Federal Reserve System had good reason for insulating the Fed from narrow political pressures. The Fed is nonpolitical in this sense. Its fortunes are not tied to the reelection of any Government official. It is for this reason that any official in the Fed properly resents allegations that policy has at any time been slanted to influence elections. Having either observed or participated in meetings of the Open Market Committee for a decade and a half, I can recall not a single instance when this motivation was present either explicitly or implicitly.

There is constant tension between these two concepts—being responsive to the public in the broad sense and being insulated from narrow, short-run politics. This tension characterizes much of what happens in the Fed. It is seen in what we do and how we do it.

What the Fed Does

This is *the* biggest political issue because it is *the* most fundamental. It has to do with the kind of economy the people want. Let me make a generalization that is oversimplified but nevertheless says a lot about the environment in which the Fed operates: political liberals tend to advocate full-employment policies, conservatives a stable dollar. The emphasis given to these objectives shifts over time. Last year public opinion polls indicated that inflation was the number one problem. Now it is unemployment. The Fed finds itself constantly in the middle, trying to reconcile these two views. For example, in recent Congressional hearings some experts argued for increasing money at the rate of 10 percent a year in order to reduce unemployment. Others argued that money growth should be kept considerably below this rate because of the fear of resumption of double-digit inflation.

The official Fed position is that unemployment is the short-run problem, and that we should try to facilitate recovery and bring down unemployment. Inflation, though, is the long-run problem and we must be careful not to rekindle it. Overstimulating the economy now to achieve greater success on the unemployment front is likely to produce another round of double-digit inflation later. The Fed must keep an eye on both the short and long run when making policy. I

agree with this position but would feel better about it if there were stronger Government programs to deal with unemployment by other means. These include liberalized unemployment compensation and more vigorous commitments to public service jobs, more effective training, and a more enterprising minimum-income program.

The pushing and pulling between the objectives of stable prices and full employment, whatever the outcome today, will be a political struggle which will be with us for a long time. It involves value judgments on which people have strong differences.

How the Fed Does It

Dispersion of Power through Organization

Political considerations strongly influence the ways in which the Fed goes about accomplishing its objectives. They are reflected first of all in its *organization*. The Federal Reserve Act was very much the result of a political process and the founders of the System had political considerations in mind when they hammered out the organizational framework.

Internally, the organization emphasizes dispersion of power. In this sense, the organization of the Fed parallels that of government. Heading the System is the Board of Governors—seven Governors, not one as in most other central banks—appointed by the President and confirmed by the Senate. As a further dispersion of power, the Fed has 12 semi-autonomous Banks. Each Bank has a Board of nine Directors. Three come from banking, three from the ranks of borrowers, and three (those appointed by the Board of Governors) from the public at large. The Federal Open Market Committee (which has the major responsibility for monetary policy formation) is a combination of the Board of Governors and Presidents of Federal Reserve Banks. The Federal Advisory Council is a group of bankers which advises the Board of Governors. This is a complicated mixture of different groups designed to avoid concentration of power in one person or place.

Authority over policy tools is also distributed. The Board of Governors determines reserve requirements and sets many regulations, such as Regulation Q and margin requirements. Open Market operations are governed by the Federal Open Market Committee. The discount rate is set by each Board of Directors subject to review and determination by the Board of Governors.[2]

In all these arrangements the Board of Governors has most of the power and this is as it should be, but the decentralized nature of the organization and the decision-making process provides an internal balance to this power. Although it is inevitable that power relationships will change in this kind of an administrative situation, the "dispersion principle" is so fundamental to the Fed and the national interest that power shifts over time should be back and forth rather than in one direction—offsetting instead of reinforcing.

Externally, the organization provides insulation from certain kinds of political pressure. The 14-year terms of the Governors are designed to protect them against short-term swings of partisan politics. This arrangement enables the Governors to give appropriate weight to the long-run consequences of policy decisions. Without these long terms, Governors would be subjected to political pressures to achieve short-run changes in the economy, possibly at the expense of what is best for the economy over the long haul.

In my view, this complex organization provides adequate insulation against political pressures. However, some minor modifications could be made. First, as has been proposed by several commissions in the past, the term of the Chairman of the Board of Governors could be made to coincide with that of the President of the United States. Second, shorter terms for Governors, say ten years, could be provided without much risk.

Fed Philosophy: Free Markets versus Credit Allocation and Fine Tuning.

A second way in which political considerations influence how the Fed does its job is in the *philosophy of operation*. Let me make another generalization that is somewhat oversimplified but nevertheless goes far to explain many conflicts: the Fed tends to emphasize the free market; many politicians tend to emphasize intervention in the free market and fine tuning.

This difference is seen first of all in the allocation of

credit. In emphasizing the free market the Fed traditionally argues that the economy works best with least detailed intervention. The economy does need overall regulation in the sense that, as Walter Bagehot[3] said, money will not manage itself. But the Fed has considered its job simply to be one of regulating the overall supply of money and credit and leaving it to the market to allocate that credit. However, there are those who believe that the market doesn't do the job well. It allocates credit in a manner that is incompatible with their view of social priorities. For example, during periods of tight money the market allocates credit in a way that severely affects housing and small business. Yet, many individuals rank these sectors of the economy high on their lists of social priorities and seek methods of shielding them when credit is tight.

This is a matter that greatly concerns many people and it is not going to go away. It is also one for which I happen to have a good deal of sympathy. Undoubtedly, one approach is to do what we can to improve financial markets. Ceilings on interest rates, for example, limit the free flow of funds, often to the detriment of "high priority" sectors of the economy. The Hunt Commission (President's Commission on Financial Structure and Regulation) tried to get to the heart of this problem by its recommendations for sweeping changes among financial intermediaries. Improving markets is all to the good, but it is likely to happen slowly and with difficulty. Another approach is for the Federal Government to intervene in markets through fiscal action. In recent years, the formation of a number of Government mortgage agencies has been effective in helping the housing sector. Such actions are a more direct method of providing funds. The problem with them is that Government may become involved in credit markets to a greater extent than desired.

Finally, this leaves us with selective credit controls. This is a possibility that has always had a great deal of appeal to me. Unfortunately, there is a real question as to whether such controls work. Representative Reuss's proposal to place differential reserve requirements on different kinds of assets, for example, is an intriguing possibility. Our analysis of this, however, raises practical problems. If the Fed were to try to encourage banks to make mortgage loans by putting a

[2]Reserve requirements set the amount of reserves that member banks are to hold. Regulation Q places a ceiling on all interest rates paid by member banks on time and savings deposits. Margin requirements set the cash down payment required when purchasing stock on credit. Open Market operations—the buying and selling of securities by the Fed—affect bank reserves, interest rates, and the growth of the money supply. The discount rate is the interest rate which the Fed charges member commercial banks that borrow from it.

[3]This nineteenth-century English economist, political analyst, and editor was a practically trained theorist on banking and financial matters. His *Lombard Street* (1873), written to explain the necessity of keeping a greater reserve in the hands of the Bank of England, helped formulate the modern theory of central banking.

low reserve requirement against them and discourage banks from making business loans by putting a high reserve requirement against them, other lenders would more likely begin to fill the gap left by commercial banks. If controls were applied to these other lenders, the open market could move in to close the gap. We could find ourselves in a costly strait jacket of credit controls.

In my view, no one has *the* answer to the question of credit allocation. I'm certain only of one thing: the Fed cannot afford to ignore it and despite practical and philosophical problems should continue to study all possibilities.

In addition to those focusing on the allocation of credit, there are others who advocate fine tuning the money supply and interest rates. We are, of course, familiar with the longstanding dispute between the monetarists and the fiscalists with respect to fine tuning the economy. What's not always appreciated, however, is that both schools have their fine tuners.

Traditional monetarists are mostly anti–fine tuning. They argue that if the Fed tries to vary the rate of growth of money it will do more harm than good. Consequently, it should simply aim for constant growth of money regardless of what happens to interest rates. A new breed of monetarist—one who pores over weekly money supply figures in great detail—has been developing. He puts great stress on very short-run movements in the money supply. Financial houses, for example, put out letters which make mountainous interpretations out of molehill changes in the money supply.

Most of us in the Fed take an eclectic view of the money supply and interest rates. Both are important. On fine tuning, we believe that money growth should not be constant but know from experience that it cannot be controlled precisely. At the same time, to be honest, there is often in the Fed a tendency to pay undue attention to small fluctuations in interest rates. Hopefully, we're getting over that syndrome.

I hope also we can avoid the syndrome of fine tuning the money supply, but it is clear to me that as attention paid to the money supply has grown there has been a tendency to expect too much precision in controlling it. I believe we should try to smooth out extreme movements without yielding to the temptation of trying to *eliminate* all unwanted movements in money. To do even this much smoothing of the money supply will mean we will have to permit more flexibility in money-market rates.

There are a few modifications that would be helpful in this regard. The first has to do with making information about monetary policy decisions more readily available. The Fed now announces its Open Market decision 45 days after the fact. This departure from secrecy has done much to dispel the belief that financial markets would be unduly disturbed or that large financial firms would gain an unfair advantage in money markets. In my view, the next step is to move to a 30-day delayed announcement. If this action has no damaging impact, the immediate announcement of policy decisions should be considered. More information of this nature would promote better understanding of the Fed and its decision-making process.

The second modification has to do with improving money-stock control by the Fed. Member banks have been leaving the System primarily because they must forego earnings on the reserves they are required to hold while their nonmember counterparts often are permitted to earn interest on a portion of their reserves. Declining membership means a smaller portion of the nation's stock of money is directly influenced by the Fed. To give the Fed greater control over the money supply, I support legislation that would establish uniform reserve requirements for *all* commercial banks. An alternative that would also resolve the problem is Congressional action to permit the Fed to pay interest on member bank reserves. While either change would not be a cure-all, it would enhance the Fed's chances of achieving its monetary policy goals.

In sum, it is clear to me that all this pressure for fine tuning and improved credit allocation reflects something basic in our society—the rising standards expected of public officials. It reflects the fact that people are not content to watch the market exert what they consider adverse effects on sectors they are concerned about. It reflects increasing pressure for intervention in markets and demand for greater precision in controlling them. But it is also clear that the state of the art is not up to these demands and that this conflict between rising expectations and limitations of performance will continue to be a source of political dispute. As the conflict continues, I believe the Fed should stand by its free-market philosophy but it cannot ignore these pressures or take an extreme *laissez-faire* view in dealing with them.

Intragovernmental Relations: A Delicate Balance

A third way in which political considerations are reflected in how we do our job is in the *relation to the executive and legislative branches of Government*. The Fed reports to Congress, not to the President. The reason for this is the history of the abuse of money by the Executive. The Secretary of the Treasury was once an ex-officio member of the Federal Reserve Board. He was removed because he has to borrow money to pay the bills and might have a tendency to want the lowest possible interest rates.

Yet, the relationship between the Fed and the Executive branch is a very delicate arrangement. Obviously, monetary policy cannot go completely off on its own without some coordination with the Government's economic organization. Much consultation and coordination goes on—say 99.99 percent of the time. The important thing is to preserve a degree of independence needed for that .01 percent of the time—that rare and extreme situation in which the Fed disagrees fundamentally with the President. This is the meaning of "independence."

A special case in the Fed's relationship with the Executive branch has to do with Treasury financing. The Federal Reserve System has a great responsibility to see that a new issue of the Treasury does not fail. At stake is the credibility of the Government's credit. There is a danger, of course, in going too far in this direction as we learned during and immediately after World War II. At that time, the Fed supported prices of Government securities to the point where it had become "an engine of inflation." This problem was solved in 1951 when the Fed and the Treasury reached an *Accord* by which the Fed gave up its support of the Government securities market. In return the Fed ever since has pursued an "even keel" policy during periods of Treasury financing. This policy in effect pledges the Fed to a position of neutrality while the Treasury is raising money.

In times when the Treasury is almost constantly in the market, even keel could seriously erode the Fed's flexibility in changing policy. However, in recent years, particularly as the Treasury has evolved new methods of financing, even keel has gradually been getting more flexible. This is no longer a crucial problem in the relationship between the Fed and the Executive.

A more difficult question currently has to do with the Fed's relationship with the Legislative branch. The Federal Reserve is a creature of Congress. Congress can take any action it wishes with respect to the Fed, including abolishing it. The immediate question is how much should Congress be involved in the details of monetary policy? The Constitution gives Congress the power to coin money and to regulate the value thereof. But this leaves open the question of how

much authority it should retain and how much it should delegate to the Fed. I believe it is clear that Congress should retain general oversight but should allow the Fed enough room to make unpopular decisions in the short run that will prove wise in the long run. Also, Congress should not involve itself in the details of monetary policy. For one reason, Congress can be just as susceptible to temporary political pressure as the President. For another, Congress lacks the necessary expertise in monetary policy formation and in its implementation to be calling the day-to-day or even month-to-month monetary signals.

Earlier this year both houses passed a resolution which provided for more direct control over monetary policy.[4] This was a proper step and promises to help focus policy on longer-run objectives. It remains to be seen, however, if Congress uses the tool effectively. As the Fed and Congress proceed to feel their way under the concurrent resolution, a great deal of cooperation and good faith will be necessary on both sides.

A final aspect of Fed-Congressional relationships has to do with the proposal to have the General Accounting Office audit the Federal Reserve System. I can speak from personal experience that the Fed is thoroughly audited now. I can understand that in a post-Watergate environment there would be a desire to provide for the assurance that the billions of dollars of assets are all there. As has been pointed out many times, however, the danger in the proposal is GAO involvement in monetary policy. The Fed already reports all policy actions to Congress and the concurrent resolution further strengthens that reporting relationship. The GAO is not well-equipped to interpose itself between the Fed and Congress on the matter of monetary policy.

Conclusions

Politics is an art. Central banking is an art. This means that there are no absolutes and that political influences are constantly fluid. For example, recently the emphasis on consumerism has involved the Fed in Truth in Lending, Fair Credit Billing, and Equal Opportunity in Credit. This additional responsibility promises to involve the Fed even further in political considerations. An irony of this is that the Fed tends

[4]U.S., Congress, Senate, *Referring to the Conduct of Monetary Policy: Report to Accompany H. Con. Res. 133,* 94th Cong., 1st sess., 17 March 1975.

to get these jobs because it is regarded as nonpolitical.

Thus, pressures toward greater political involvement for the Fed are increasing. Awareness on the part of the public of the Fed is greater than ever. Opinions about what the Fed should do are more pronounced than ever. Pressures on Federal Reserve officials to perform better are greater than ever. Demand for information about what they are doing is stronger than ever. If there were times when officials could sit in their marble halls and mysteriously pull strings that affect the economy without anyone questioning their actions, those times are gone. We must be increasingly open, responsive, and flexible. The challenge will be to accomplish this and yet be as firm and far-seeing as necessary to do our job of securing a healthy economy.

24

The Intelligent Citizen's Guide to Inflation

ROBERT M. SOLOW

Robert M. Solow is Professor of Economics at Massachusetts Institute of Technology. This paper appeared in The Public Interest *in 1975.*

Two broadly opposite frames of mind seem to dominate the current discussion of inflation. One says that we are beset by some utterly mysterious plague of unknown origin. If it is not stopped soon, it will cause unimaginable, or at least unspecified, disasters. The only hope is that some Pasteur or Jenner or Ehrlich will discover The Cure. The other view is that it is all quite simple. There is some one thing we have failed to do: control the money supply or balance the budget or legislate price controls or abolish the unions. As soon as we do it, the problem will then go away.

This essay is written in the belief that both these currents of opinion are wrong. I do not, however, have an alternative solution to offer. Indeed, I rather doubt that there is a Solution, in the sense of some policy that your average mixed capitalist economy can reasonably be expected to pursue which will drastically reduce the tendency to inflation, without substituting some equally damaging and intractable problem instead.

What I can hope to do is to explain the vocabulary and intellectual framework evolved by economists for discussing and analyzing inflation. By itself, this will

contribute to clarity of thought—much, perhaps most, of current popular discussion is hopelessly confused. I hope to be able to go further than that, however. There are some positive statements one can reasonably make about the behavior of modern mixed economies. We know less than we would like to know, but much more than nothing. Where I verge on speculation, or where there are real differences of opinion within the economics profession, I will try to be honest about it.

What Is Inflation?

Inflation is *a substantial, sustained increase in the general level of prices.* The intrinsic vagueness of "substantial" is harmless. One would not want to use a heavyweight word to describe a trivial rise in the price level; granted, it will never be perfectly clear where to draw the line, but neither can it be important since only a word is at stake. "Sustained" is a little trickier. One would not want to label as inflationary a momentary (six-month? one-year?) upward twitch of the price level, especially if it is soon reversed. There is no point in being forced to describe mere short-term fluctuations in prices as alternating bouts of inflation and deflation. "Sustained" also carries some connotation of "self-perpetuating" and that raises broader questions. It is obviously important to know whether each step in an inflationary process tends to generate further inflation unless some "outside" force intervenes, or whether the inflationary process is eventually self-limiting. The answer need not be the same for all inflations, and it certainly depends on what you mean by "outside." So it is probably best not to incorporate this aspect as a part of the definition.

It is the notion of the "general price level" that will lead us somewhere. Economists make a sharp and important distinction between the system of relative prices and the general price level. Relative prices describe the terms on which different goods and services exchange for *one another;* the general price level describes the terms on which some representative bundle of goods and services exchanges for *money.* Imagine an economy in which the only goods produced are meat and vegetables, and first suppose that all exchange is barter; some people trade meat for vegetables with other people who want to trade vegetables for meat. If one pound of meat exchanges for three pounds of vegetables, then the relative price is established. But since there is no money, there is no such thing as the general price level. Notice that inflation is inconceivable in a barter economy. It would be logically contradictory for "all prices" to rise at the same time. Suppose that, because of a change in tastes or a natural catastrophe, one pound of meat should come to exchange for six pounds of vegetables. One could say that the price of meat (in terms of vegetables!) had doubled. But that is exactly the same thing as saying that the price of vegetables (in terms of meat!) had halved. A carnivorous farmer would find himself worse off; but a vegetarian rancher would be sitting pretty.

So inflation has intrinsically to do with money. Now let us introduce some greenbacks to serve as money in our meat-and-vegetables economy. Suppose meat goes for $1.50 a pound and vegetables for 50 cents a pound—i.e., one pound of meat for three of vegetables, as before. Now suppose that at a later time meat goes to $3.00 a pound and vegetables to $1.00. The relative price is unchanged. From most points of view the meat-and-vegetables economy goes along as if nothing has happened, and from most points of view nothing has. (Not quite nothing: A tradesman or a

miser who happened to be sitting on a load of greenbacks at the time will have taken quite a beating.)

We can go a step further. Suppose the average daily diet consists of one pound of meat and one pound of vegetables (though very few individuals may actually consume exactly the average diet). We could agree to measure the general price level by the money cost of the average consumption bundle. In that case, we would say that the price level was 200 in the initial situation, and 400 after the price increases. (It is the custom to choose some year as "base year" and set its price level arbitrarily at 100. If the initial year is the base year, then the later price level would be 200.) In any case, we would certainly want to say that the general price level had doubled, and if it had doubled in exactly 12 months, we would say that the rate of inflation had been 100 per cent a year.

Since the prices of all goods and services had exactly doubled, it is no trick to say that the general price level had doubled. But we now have a routine that will take care of less obvious situations. Suppose meat goes from $1.50 to $2.40 a pound and vegetables from 50 cents to 60 cents. The price of meat has risen by 60 per cent, that of vegetables by 20 per cent. But the cost of the average consumption bundle rises from $2.00 to $3.00 (or the price index from 100 to 150). So we could say that the price level had gone up by 50 per cent. Notice also that this time relative prices have also changed: A pound of meat exchanges for four pounds of vegetables at the new prices. The vegetarian rancher gains at the expense of the carnivorous farmer, but *that is because of the change in relative prices.* In the case of "pure inflation," when *all* prices change *in the same proportion,* nobody loses (except owners of money) and nobody gains (except owers of money).[1]

Perhaps the simplest way to define inflation is as a loss in the purchasing power of money. That has the merit of emphasizing the fact that inflation is essentially a monetary phenomenon. But there is a possible semantic trap here. Some economists believe that the whole inflationary mechanism is primarily or exclusively monetary, in particular that the main or only cause of inflation is too rapid a growth in the supply of money. They may be right or they may be wrong. (I happen to think that doctrine is too simple by half.)

[1] The smart kids in the class will now ask: If meat gets more expensive relative to vegetables, won't consumers buy less meat and more vegetables, and won't that change the make-up of the average consumption bundle, and what will that do to the price index? They can go on to the course in Index-Number Theory, but they will find it dull.

But the mere fact that you can have inflation only in a monetary economy is neither here nor there, just as the fact that you can't have a drowning without water doesn't prove that the way to understand drowning is to study water, I will come back to this analytical question later.

Measuring Inflation

In the real world there are thousands of goods and services, whose relative prices are changing all the time in complicated ways. The measurement of the general price level thus becomes a major statistical enterprise. But it is done, and generally according to the principles just described. In fact, the American reader is confronted with at least three separate indexes of the general price level: the Consumer Price Index (CPI), the Wholesale Price Index (WPI), and the GNP Deflator. Since there are some conceptual differences among them, and since they may occasionally say different things, it is worthwhile to understand exactly what each of them means.

The CPI (what is sometimes called the cost-of-living index) is produced and published monthly; it is closest in principle to the kind of price index described earlier. At intervals of a decade or more, the Bureau of Labor Statistics (BLS) conducts an expensive survey of the spending habits of families of different size, income, and other characteristics. From this survey it calculates the typical budget of a middle-income, urban wage-earner or clerical worker with a family of four. Then each month it actually prices out that budget in a number of cities around the country. If the cost of that bundle goes up or down by 1 per cent, the CPI goes up or down by 1 per cent.

That is certainly a reasonable and meaningful price index, but it does have some drawbacks. (Of course, any method of reducing all those thousands of price changes to a single number will have drawbacks.) It relates only to consumers; the prices of industrial machinery and raw materials could go sky-high, and the CPI would register that fact only later, when cost increases filtered down to retail prices. Moreover, the CPI relates only to some consumers—those middle-income, urban, wage-earning families of four. Old people, or poor people, or oil millionaires, who buy different bundles, may have different experiences. Finally, economists have a technical reservation. The CPI covers, as its concept dictates it should, everything consumers spend money on, including sales taxes, monthly mortgage payments, used cars, and so on. It reflects changes in state and local taxes, interest rates, used-car prices, etc. For some purposes, economists would prefer a price index confined to currently produced goods and services. Certainly it matters whether a rise in the CPI reflects mainly higher sales taxes and interest rates or higher prices for food and clothing.

The WPI, also available monthly, is based on prices collected at the wholesale level. Its coverage is wide but rather peculiar, for several reasons. For one thing, it omits all services, medical care, house rents, etc. For another, it counts some prices over and over again, and thus gives them more weight than they deserve. For example, a change in the price of raw cotton will appear first as a crude material, then again as it is reflected in the price of cloth, then again as it is reflected in the price of clothing. This pyramiding overemphasizes crude material prices and can cause the WPI to behave quite erratically, especially when the prices of materials are changing. Its main utility is that, just because of its coverage of the early stages of fabrication, it often catches price developments early. The WPI, like the other indexes, is broken down into sub-indexes (in the case of the WPI, farm products, processed foods, industrial materials, various categories of finished manufactures, etc.), and these may be very informative.[2]

The GNP Deflator

The GNP Deflator is by and large the economists' favorite. Unlike the CPI, it covers only currently produced goods and services, and unlike the WPI, it avoids all double-counting. But it is constructed in a more complicated way. The Department of Commerce calculates every quarter the country's Gross National Product. This is essentially the value at current market prices of the current flow of newly produced final goods and services. (The force of "final" is that one omits goods and services which are immediately used up in the production of something else, because their value will be included in the value of the final product.) At the same time, Commerce also calculates the GNP "in constant prices." That is, it takes

[2]For more on the WPI, and for a very informative and interesting article complementary to this one, I recommend "Inflation 1973: The Year of Infamy" by William Nordhaus and John Shoven in the May/June 1974 issue of *Challenge* magazine.

the current flow of final goods and services, but instead of valuing them at this quarter's prices, it values them at the prices of some fixed year, currently 1958. For instance, in 1973 the GNP in current prices was $1,295 billion, but the GNP in 1958 prices was $839 billion, because 1958 prices were lower than 1973 prices.

How much had prices risen between 1958 and 1973? The natural computation is $1,295/$839 = 1.54, for an increase of 54 per cent. If the 1973 flow of output valued in 1973 prices is 54 per cent higher than the *same* flow of output valued in 1958 prices, then the obvious inference is that the general level of prices must have risen by 54 per cent since 1958. So the general formula for the GNP Deflator in year X is: GNP in year X in current prices/GNP in year X in base-year prices. (Exercise: Convince yourself that the GNP Deflator for the base year itself is automatically 1.00 or 100, because in the base year GNP in current prices and GNP in base-year prices are the same quantity.)

Economists like this price index for the analysis of inflation not because it is obscure, but for the reasons I mentioned before: It eliminates double-counting, and it focuses on the pricing of currently produced goods, not existing assets. For that very reason, of course, it may not reflect exactly the experience of consumers. Another disadvantage is that the GNP Deflator is available only at quarterly intervals.[3]

All price indexes suffer from a common difficulty. Commodities change in character and quality. How can the BLS price the same consumer-bundle in 1955 and 1975 when many of the things consumers buy in 1975 did not exist, and so had no prices, in 1955? How can the Commerce statisticians value 1975 GNP in 1958 prices, when there were no 1958 prices for some of the items entering the 1975 GNP? If the price of an ordinary shirt rises 10 per cent in the course of a year, but simultaneously the wrinkle-resisting properties of the shirt are improved, how is one to decide how much of the 10 per cent represents the greater value of an improved product and how much represents pure price increase? The agencies do the best they can, but it is hardly a job that can ever be done perfectly. It used to be thought that there was systematic underallowance for quality improvements to such an

extent that an annual rise of 1 or 2 per cent in the measured price level could be ignored as not being a true price increase; but no one knows for sure. Perhaps the best conclusion is that one ought not to attach great significance to small changes in price indexes.

This discussion of price indexes has given us another concept of absolutely fundamental importance for rational discussion. GNP in constant prices is in an important sense a "physical" concept. It is an attempt to measure the size of the flow of actual production in a way that is independent of inflationary and deflationary aberrations. When GNP in constant prices changes, it is because the production of goods and services has changed, not because prices have changed. In terms of my earlier example, the difference between the 1968 GNP of $707 billion in 1958 prices and the 1973 GNP of $839 billion in 1958 prices permits us to say that "aggregate output" rose by 18.7 per cent between those years. In the jargon, GNP in constant prices is called "real GNP" or "real aggregate output." We will be coming back to it.

The Last One Hundred Years

Figures 1 and 2 show what has happened to the general price level since 1867. The price index used is the GNP Deflator.[4] Figure 1 shows the price index itself on what is called a logarithmic scale, to draw attention to the proportional changes that really matter. The base year is 1929 = 100. The fact that the price level in 1973 (291.5) is almost four times that in 1867 (78.0) is not to be taken as utterly precise, in view of the vast difference between the commodities making up the GNP in 1867 and those actually produced in 1973. But for orders of magnitude, the figures will do. Steep portions of the curve represent periods of more severe inflation; when the curve points downward, the price level was actually falling.

Figure 2 converts the price index into percentage rates of inflation and deflation; prices are rising when this curve is above the zero line, and falling when it is below.

---

[3]There is another minor problem. The basis for putting a price on the output of governments—education, police services, "plumbers'" services, etc.—is pretty tenuous, though these are all part of the GNP. It is possible to produce a price index for privately produced GNP, nearly all of which is actually sold on a market.

[4]I owe the figures to Professor Benjamin Klein of the University of California at Los Angeles, who pieced them together from estimates made by Robert Gallman for 1874–1909 and Simon Kuznets for 1910–1946, and the official Commerce Department figures for 1947–1973. The earlier figures are based on very sketchy data.

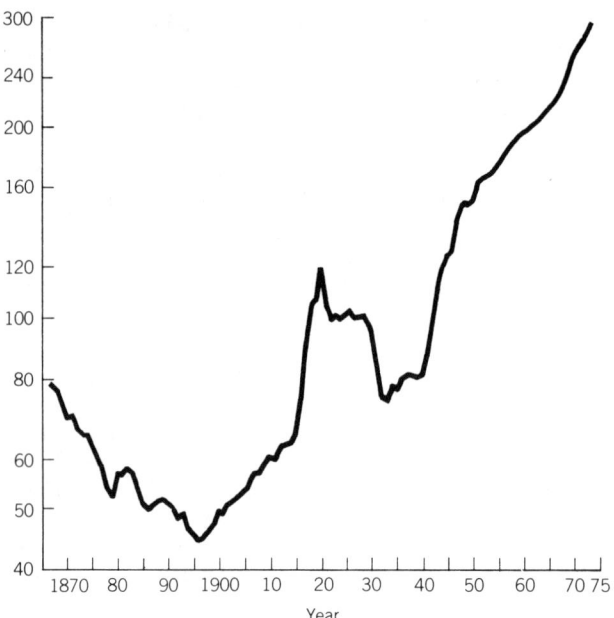

FIGURE 1.   **The Price Index, 1867–1973 (1929 Base)**

The broad outlines of the history of the price level are easily read from the charts. From the end of the Civil War to the end of the 19th century, the predominant trend was deflationary. The GNP Deflator fell by more than 40 per cent between 1867 and 1896. Although the curve turned upward about then, by the eve of the First World War the price index had gone back up only to the level of 1873.

Really big inflationary bursts are associated with major wars, and their aftermath. Between 1914 and 1920, prices almost doubled. Between 1940 and 1948, prices almost doubled. The Korean War added only about 10 per cent to the price level. In the case of the Vietnamese War it is hard to know where to start; between 1966 and 1972, the index rose about 30 per cent.

But that is only half of it, and in some ways the less interesting half. There were at least two years of deflation after the First World War; by 1922 the index was back to the 1917–1918 level. The depression of the 1930's, like those of the 1870's and 1890's, pushed the price level down. The index, pegged at 100 in 1929, fell to 73.3 in 1933, rose to 80.3 in 1936, and stayed there until the eve of the Second World War in 1940. But the last minus-sign on Figure 2 appears briefly in

1949 when the first of the mild postwar recessions lowered the price index by a point. (On a quarterly basis one could find a somewhat bigger decline.) From 1950 on we have had a quarter-century without a dip in the general price level. The best one can find is the period beginning with the recession of 1958, running through the milder recession of 1960, and continuing during the slow return to approximate full employment at the end of 1965. During that interval, the Deflator rose at an average annual rate of about 1.5 percent. It is simply not possible to know with any confidence what would have happened if the escalation of the war either had not occurred or had not been allowed to overheat the economy in the last years of the Johnson Administration.

Why Is Pure Inflation a Bad Thing?

There seems to be universal agreement that rising prices are a cause for alarm and perhaps fear. Candidates for office accuse incumbents of having fostered inflation or failed to prevent it, and promise to eliminate it themselves. Incumbents announce that they are working on the problem. And surveys of public opinion show that very many ordinary people regard inflation of the price level as one of the most serious problems they face, or at least as an important background worry. Yet it is fair to say that public discussion offers no insight at all into the precise way in which a rising price level damages the current or prospective welfare of the representative citizen. Occasionally, the implied mechanism in the background makes no sense at all. Such a peculiar situation clearly deserves the most thorough investigation.

For the sake of clarity, let us first make an abstraction and think about a "pure" inflation, during which all prices rise at the same proportional rate—so many per cent per year—so that relative prices are unchanged throughout. Real inflations don't happen that way; but if we are to understand how and why inflation is a burden on society, we had better be able to understand the hypothetical special case of a pure inflation. After all, relative prices can change without any change in the general price level; we ought not to confuse the effects of the one with those of the other.

Well, then, who gets hurt in a pure inflation? If you think back to our meat-and-vegetables economy, it is hard to see how producers, including workers, suffer at all. So long as the prices of meat and vegetables, and wage rates in both industries, go up at the same

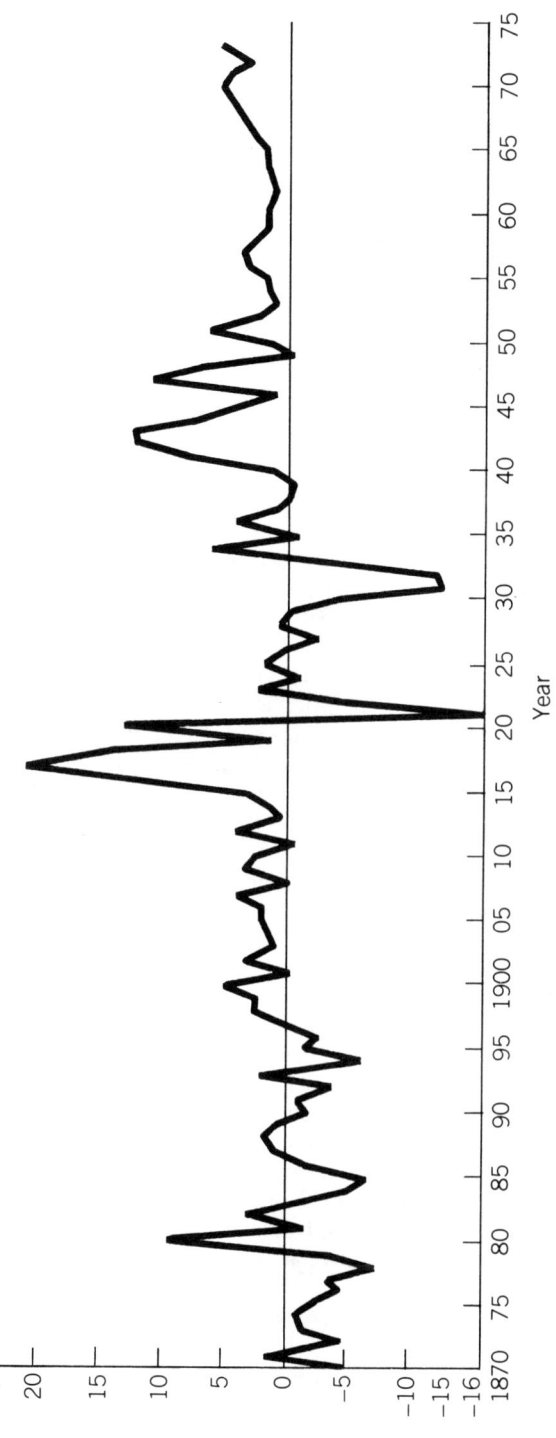

FIGURE 2. Percentage Rates of Inflation and Deflation, 1870–1973

percentage rate, every participant in the economy continues to have the same purchasing power over all goods and services as before. The inflation appears to have no "real" effects. The general point is that a person's economic welfare depends on the prices of the things he or she buys and sells, including labor and the services of property; if the prices of all those things go up or down in the same proportion, then economic welfare stays the same.

Now there is an optical illusion that clearly plays some role in popular discussions of inflation. Many people see no connection between the prices of the things they buy and the prices of the things they sell. The ordinary person works hard and feels that each year's wage increase is deserved. When it turns out that prices have also increased, so that all or part of the wage increase is illusory, the ordinary person regards that price rise—inflation—as a form of theft, a hand in his or her pocket. But of course, wages could not have increased had prices not increased. I cannot estimate how widespread this illusion may be, but there can hardly be any doubt that such an illusion does exist.[5]

If you want to know how the country as a whole is doing, then the course of the price level will not tell you. In narrowly economic terms, the proper measure of success is the flow of goods and services produced and made available to the society for consumption and other uses. The closest thing we have to look at is the real GNP, which we have already met. GNP in constant prices is the most comprehensive available measure of the performance of the economy in doing what it is supposed to do—the generation of want-satisfying commodities. It is far from perfect for reasons that involve the treatment of depreciation, environmental effects of economic activity, the organization of work, the "quality of life," governmental activity, and other things, but none of them has to do with inflation. So if inflation is a net burden to society, that ought to show up in a reduction of real GNP, or at least a slowing-down of its normal upward trend. But that is not what happens; in fact the opposite is more nearly true. Peri-

---

[5]No one could make that mistake in the simple meat-and-vegetables economy. But the real world is more complicated. For instance, the timing of price and wage increases is irregular, with some temporary advantage from getting in early, and some loss from getting in late. Moreover, the normal experience is that standards of living rise as productivity improves. Then only part of a wage increase is eroded away by price increases, but even the loss of that part is felt as robbery.

ods of prosperity are somewhat more likely to coincide with periods of inflation and periods of recession are somewhat more likely to coincide with intervals of stable or more slowly rising prices.[6]

Is the social cost of inflation a mirage? There is one earlier hint that needs to be followed up. In a monetary economy—the only kind that can have inflation—holders of cash see their real wealth eroded by a rising price level, even in a pure inflation. So do creditors who hold claims for payment fixed in money terms. Offsetting at least some of these losses are the gains of debtors, who can pay back in dollars of smaller purchasing power what they had borrowed and spent in dollars of higher real value. Perhaps the true social costs of inflation are to be found among the holders of money, or among cash creditors more generally.

Anticipated Inflation

Another distinction—this time between anticipated and unanticipated inflation—is required for this analysis. So let us take the strongest case first: a pure inflation which is confidently and accurately expected by everyone in the economy. Suppose you lend me a dollar today and I agree to pay back $1.05 a year from today. Then we have agreed on an interest rate of 5 per cent annually. (You laugh, somewhat bitterly. But it's just an example.) If we both correctly expect the general price level to be quite steady during the next year, then that is all there is to it. You as lender and I as borrower are both willing to make the transaction at an interest rate of 5 per cent a year. Now imagine instead that we both confidently expect the general level of prices (which means each individual price and wage, since we are talking about a pure inflation) to be 4 percent higher a year from now. I would be delighted to take your dollar today and pay you $1.05 in a year. Why not? If meat is a dollar a pound today and will be $1.04 a pound in a year, then in effect you would be lending me a pound of meat today, and I would be obliged to pay you only 1.05/1.04 or about 1.01

[6]There is an exception to all this, but it need not concern us. Imagine a country which must import a large fraction of its basic necessities, like food and oil, and pay for them with exports of other commodities. Such a country may experience steady or rising real production, but if world food and oil prices are rising faster than the prices of its exports, its own standard of living could deteriorate. The United States is not in that position because it is so nearly self-sufficient; but of course it is hardly a hypothetical possibility for Japan and some European countries.

pounds of meat next year. In *real* terms, you would be getting interest at 1 per cent a year, not 5 per cent. Of course for the same reasons that I would be pleased at the transaction, you would not be. In fact, if we were both prepared to make the deal at 5 per cent with stable prices, we ought both to be prepared to make the deal at 9 per cent when we both confidently expect the price level to rise at 4 per cent a year; in the real purchasing-power terms that matter, you will then be collecting interest at 5 per cent per year. In the professional jargon, the *real* rate of interest (5 per cent) is the *nominal* or *money* rate of interest (9 per cent) less the expected rate of inflation (4 per cent). Thus the very high interest rates of early 1974 have to be read against the substantial inflation of the same period. Real rates are not as high as nominal rates; in fact, they are lower by about the expected future rate of inflation—about which we can only guess. Of course, anyone who borrows long and is locked in at high interest rates is left holding the bag if the inflation should unexpectedly slow down or stop.

What follows? *If* the inflation is fully anticipated by everyone, *if* everyone has complete access to the capital markets, and *if* all interest rates are free to adjust to expectations about the price level, and do so quickly and smoothly, then borrowers and lenders will be able to protect themselves against inflation. Once again, the inflation would seem to have no real effects.

Well, not quite. Those qualifications are pretty strong. Obviously, we will have to consider the case of unanticipated inflation; but even before we get to that there are some important things to say. First of all, some assets bear no interest at all: the important ones are currency and balances in ordinary checking accounts. They constitute the money supply. It would be mechanically difficult for the Treasury to pay interest on currency. Commercial banks are restrained by law from paying interest on checking accounts. (They do the next best thing by providing financial services free of charge, or at a fee that diminishes with the size of balance; but that is hardly the same thing and cannot in any case serve the same purpose as a nominal interest rate in adjusting to expectations about rising prices.) So, even if the inflation is correctly anticipated, holders of currency and checking accounts will suffer (as they would symmetrically gain if deflation should ever come back into style). These losses to holders of money are not, so to speak, net losses to society, because there are corresponding gains to others. In the case of checking accounts, the gainer is the bank and its stockholders, who earn the higher nominal interest rates on their own assets and pay no interest—except for those free financial services—on deposit liabilities. In the case of currency, the U.S. Government, in the person of the Federal Reserve, is the issuer of the paper, but it is rather special paper, and a special kind of liability, and in any case not very important.

The "Deadweight Loss"

Since anticipated inflation redistributes to others part of the wealth of holders of money, it is natural that businesses and people should try to reduce their holdings of money when they expect prices to be rising. One can hardly do without any cash in the modern world, but nevertheless it is usually possible to substitute effort for liquidity. Corporations can buy relatively liquid short-term securities and try correspondingly harder to synchronize inflows and outflows of cash. Individuals can rely more on savings banks as a repository of funds, making correspondingly more frequent trips downtown to deposit and withdraw cash, and to transfer funds to a checking account just before large payments have to be made. Indeed they can, and the figures suggest that they do. It is true that this minimization of cash holdings costs time, trouble, and shoe leather. Clever comptrollers are thinking about cash management when they could be worrying about higher things. Moreover, and this is the point, these expenditures of time and effort are a real net burden to society, not merely a transfer to others. They are sometimes described as a "deadweight loss" to emphasize this. They are a true cost of inflation in the same sense that the maintenance of expensive police forces is a cost of crime. Some economists seem to regard these losses as the main social cost of pure inflation. But in that case, something very peculiar is afoot, because one finds it hard to believe that they amount to much. For *this* governments tremble and people cry on the pollster's shoulder? Even if you add in the computational difficulties of planning with changing prices, the discomfort that comes from not knowing whether your anticipations about future price levels are approximately right or dangerously wrong, it is hard to get excited.[7]

There is one other important "real" effect of anticipated pure inflation; it works through the tax system. Think of any progressive tax, a tax that takes a higher fraction of a higher income than of a lower income. Now let all prices, and thus all before-tax incomes, rise in the same proportion. Nobody's purchasing power has changed. But the general rise in nominal incomes will drive everyone into a higher tax bracket. If the general rise in prices amounted to X per cent, incomes after tax will rise by less than X per cent, because of the higher effective tax rate, and the government's revenues will rise by more than X per cent, for the same reason. So taxpayers suffer a loss in purchasing power after taxes, and their loss is the Treasury's gain. Our tax system is not as progressive in action as it is on paper, but nevertheless this effect is quite real. The sharpest case is that of someone whose income is low enough not to be taxable at all; pure inflation can push such a person into the taxable range and thus impose a loss of real income.

In summary, a perfectly anticipated pure inflation imposes a small deadweight loss on society, mostly through a waste of effort directed toward economizing on the holding of money; in addition, it redistributes wealth, from holders of cash and checking accounts to banks, and from everyone to the Treasury. Not good, one is tempted to say, but no worse than a bad cold. Real GNP, for all its faults, is the best measure we have of the current production of valued goods and services; that's the number to watch.

Unanticipated Inflation

Now real-life inflations are not perfectly anticipated. Neither do they come as a complete surprise. But different people have different opinions about the future of the price level; not all of them can be right, and most of them can be wrong. The consequences of this fact are important, but still special. Interest rates cannot adjust to cushion both debtors and creditors from the effects of pure inflation. Some people will be caught with their pants down: those creditors who

---

[7] In very rapid inflations—what are usually called "hyperinflations"—the losses from holding money are so great that one observes a genuine flight from the currency, whence come the stories from Germany in the 1920's of children meeting their fathers at the factory gate to bicycle madly into town and spend the day's pay before it has had a chance to depreciate further. In such cases there may be a return to barter. This kind of disorganization of the economy and society can be very costly, but it is not what we have to talk about. Even at relatively small rates of inflation, a little ingenuity can sometimes invent substitutes for the non-interest-bearing checking account—e.g., the *NOW account*.

have locked themselves into long-term loans at interest rates that do not fully reflect the particular rate of inflation that happens, and borrowers who have agreed to pay high nominal interest rates in the expectation of faster inflation than actually materializes. Of course, for each of these unlucky lenders and borrowers, there is a lucky borrower or lender. Needless to say, when the losers include the broad class of pensioners whose expectations of a viable old age are dashed, it is not a trivial matter.

These gains and losses are not restricted to loans. *Anyone* who has concluded a long-term contract of any kind, stipulated in money terms, stands to gain or lose, depending on which side of the contract we are talking about and whether the rate of inflation turns out in fact to be higher or lower than had been expected when the terms of the contract were agreed. (If rapid inflation continues, we can expect to see more long-term contracts with renegotiation clauses, or with rates of payment explicitly tied to some index of prices. These are a form of insurance against windfall gains and losses from unexpectedly fast or slow inflation.)

Finally, it should be realized that many people, especially non-rich people, are more or less excluded from the benefits of higher nominal interest rates in an inflationary period. Small savers lack either the knowledge or the minimal stake needed to gain access to the sorts of assets whose yields will provide protection against inflation. The small saver is limited in practice to savings accounts and Series E government bonds. The rate on Series E bonds is not set by a market but is managed by the Treasury, and usually kept low enough to constitute a swindle on the non-rich. (One wonders what would happen if Secretaries of the Treasury were required by law to keep all their private wealth in Series E bonds.) The maximum deposit rate payable by savings banks is also limited by law, and by the peculiar role of those institutions as essentially nothing but mortgage lenders. Heaven does not protect the working girl.

The net result of all this is that imperfectly anticipated inflation—the only kind we have—generates massive redistribution of wealth between some borrowers and some lenders, some buyers and some sellers. From a very lofty point of view, these are still transfers, not a net burden on society as a whole. But that doesn't make them good. Moreover, in the public mind these transfers come to look like a net loss: The gainers attribute their gains to their own perspicacity,

energy, and virtue; the losers attribute their losses to inflation.

"Impure" Inflation

Pure inflation is an abstraction, though a necessary and useful one. If you can't understand the workings of pure inflation, you will never be able to understand what is actually happening. What is actually happening, of course, is a mixture: The general price level is rising, and at the same time relative prices are changing, sometimes drastically. The price indexes I described earlier are supposed to measure the pure inflationary component of the complicated set of price changes we experience. When I tell you that in the 12 months between June 1973 and June 1974 the CPI rose by 11.1 per cent, the WPI by 14.5 per cent, and the GNP Deflator by 9.7 per cent, I am saying something like: It is approximately as if there were a pure inflation of about 10 per cent, accompanied by a "pure" change in relative prices around a stationary level. In fact, I can add such information as this: The price of food went up by 14.7 per cent during the year, while rents went up by 4.7 per cent, so there was clearly a rise in the price of food relative to rental housing.

This is conceptually clear (though not quite as clear as I am pretending). The trouble is that what you observe and feel in the course of the year is the Total Experience, and it is by no means easy to sort out in one's mind the causes and consequences of a rising general level of prices and the causes and consequences of simultaneous changes in relative prices. This difficulty is complicated further by the fact that price movements are not synchronized. Even if, when all is said and done, the price of A and the price of B are both going to rise by X per cent, A may take off first and B only later. You would think that these timing differences would all come out in the wash, but they may actually have important independent consequences of their own.

The important thing to say about an inflation in which some prices and some incomes rise faster than others is that the *redistribution* of income can become both quite drastic and quite haphazard. It may be that real GNP is high and rising, so that the country as a whole is not being deprived of goods and services and the satisfactions they bring. But definable groups in the population may find their own standards of living deteriorating, either because the prices of the things they buy are rising faster than the average, or because the prices of the things they sell—including their labor—are rising slower than the average of all prices. And often enough it will appear to them that the inflation is the cause of their troubles, when in fact the real thief is the accompanying change in relative prices. Some economically and socially pointless or harmful redistributions can happen just because certain prices and incomes are less flexible than others and adapt sluggishly to a generally inflationary climate.

There are fewer valid universal generalizations about these redistributions than one might think. The rhetorical commonplaces are not always true. If is often said that inflation is especially hard on the poor. One careful study by Robinson G. Hollister and John G. Palmer found that this was not the case in the inflationary episodes of the 1950's, and until 1967, if by "the poor" you mean those below the official poverty line (that is, pretty damn poor). Their figures show that a cost-of-living index weighted the way the poor spend their incomes rose no faster than, perhaps slightly less fast than, the official middle-income CPI. The sources of income that matter for the poor—mainly wages and salaries, Social Security benefits, and various forms of social assistance—just about kept pace with other forms of income in purchasing-power terms. And the poor have little wealth exposed to the risk of erosion. Hollister and Palmer conclude: " . . . because the relative position of the poor seems to improve during inflationary periods and overall real income gains per capita occur during such periods, the poor as a whole must be gaining both absolutely and relatively in economic well-being during periods in which inflationary processes operate."

But not all inflations are alike. Between 1947 and 1967, food prices rose a little more slowly than the CPI as a whole. In 1973, I hardly need tell you, food prices went up about three times as fast as the rest of the CPI. Poor people spend a larger fraction of their incomes on food than richer people do. Moreover, as it happens, food costs at home went up faster than restaurant prices in 1973, and hamburger faster than steak. It would not be surprising to find that the inflation of 1973 did contribute to a redistribution of income away from poor people.[8]

Are We in a Whole New Ball Game?

In trying to understand the accelerated inflation of the last few years, it is worth remembering that the same thing has been happening everywhere. Here, for instance, are the percentage rates of increase of the CPI for a number of advanced countries between January/February 1973 and January/February 1974:

Country	Percentage rate of inflation of CPI
Japan	24.1
Denmark	14.6
United Kingdom	13.2
Italy	12.6
France	10.9
Switzerland	10.8
United States	9.7
Canada	9.3
Norway	8.7
Sweden	8.4
Austria	8.3
Netherlands	8.2
Belgium	7.9
West Germany	7.5

You will notice that the United States is somewhere around the middle of this league. A similar table compiled for 1970-71, say, would show rates of inflation centered around 5 per cent rather than 10 per cent.

By itself, the universality of inflation tells us very little. It could come about because all countries are exposed to the same forces, characteristic of modern advanced economies or because the international trading and monetary system works to spread the impact of forces originating anywhere in the system, or because different countries happen to be inflating for different reasons, and find it easier to do so when others are doing the same. Or the explanation could involve elements of all these possibilities. I am going to concentrate on the first line of explanation, but I believe each of the other two has something to say. My main reason for insisting on the importance of these comparative figures is to warn that no entirely parochial account of the causes of inflation will do.

---

[8]Poor people spend a larger fraction of their income on housing than rich people do, and a smaller fraction on transportation, especially automobile transportation. So the run-up in oil prices has more complicated effects: The rise in fuel oil prices hits the poor worse than the rich, but the rise in gasoline prices affects the rich more than the poor. Of course, all this is apart from the fact that any reduction in purchasing power is harder to take when you're poor.

Modern mixed-capitalist economies seem to have an inflationary bias near full employment. That is a description, not an explanation, but it seems to summarize the situation. An economy that is running along moderately prosperously, but hardly straining its capacity to produce, will see its price level drift upward. In the good old days, the demands of war or the stimulus of excessively expansionary policy might bring an economy to flat-out operation and consequent inflation, but a return to more normal levels of demand would stabilize prices, and a touch of recession might bring on actual deflation. The trouble is that nowadays economies begin to inflate while they are showing no signs of excess pressure, and to reverse the price rise would appear to require longer and deeper recessions than seems reasonable or natural. The question is: Why should that be? Why, for instance, do so few prices ever actually fall?

Let me answer a question with a question. Is it possible that the price level was *more* stable on the average in the good old days because the economy was *less* stable on the average? More particularly, until very recently it was reasonable to fear that any momentary weakness in the economy might be the prelude to substantial and prolonged recession. Under those circumstances, businesses might see the wisdom of cutting prices early and often, to protect markets and market shares against competitors in their own and neighboring industries who would also be feeling the pinch of widespread market softness. The same fear might be expected to stiffen the resistance of employers to wage demands; a longish period of reduced sales and lowered prices is no time to bear the burden of higher wage costs, and discontent in the work-place is easier to handle when production has to be cut back anyway. To complete the circle, the danger of prolonged unemployment would induce workers to accept wage reductions, or at least reductions relative to long-term productivity gains. It is not hard to believe that the reality of major recessions and depressions would account for greater flexibility of prices and wages in the downward direction.[9]

If the threat of prolonged recession is absent, the situation is quite otherwise. There is less pressure to reduce prices when markets soften, if it is expected that they will soon improve. Similarly, there is less incentive to resist wage increases if prices are being maintained or even raised themselves; and if production will soon need to be increased, one is less likely to tempt strikes, ill will, and the reputation of being a lousy employer. Finally, when mass unemployment is unlikely workers are able more confidently to keep up the pressure for higher wages.

[9] The same argument would work in reverse. Prices and wages would respond more quickly and amply upward when markets tighten. In fact, the knowledge that prices could easily rise or fall later would make it easier to let them fall or rise now. All that I need from this argument is an explanation of the fact that prices used sometimes to fall. If prices never fall, there is no way the price trend can ever be horizontal.

25

The Inflationary Bias in Our Economy

ARTHUR F. BURNS

Arthur F. Burns is Chairman of the Board of Governors of the Federal Reserve System. This article is taken from a speech he gave at the University of Georgia in 1975.

Our country is now engaged in a fateful debate. There are many who declare that unemployment is a far more serious problem than inflation, and that monetary and fiscal policies must become more stimulative during the coming year even if inflation quickens in the process. I embrace the goal of full employment, and I shall suggest ways to achieve it. But I totally reject the argument of those who keep urging faster creation of money and still larger governmental deficits. Such policies would only bring us additional trouble; they cannot take us to the desired goal.

The American economy has recently begun to emerge from the deepest decline of business activity in the postwar period. During the course of the recession, which began in late 1973, the physical volume of our total output of goods and services declined by 8 per cent. The production of factories, mines, and power plants fell even more—by 14 per cent. As the overall level of economic activity receded, the demand for labor rapidly diminished and unemployment doubled, reaching an intolerable 9 per cent of the labor force this May.

The basic cause of the recession was our nation's failure to deal effectively with the inflation that got under way in the mid-sixties and soon became a dominant feature of our economic life. As wage and price increases quickened, seeds of trouble were sown across the economy. With abundant credit readily available, the consruction of new homes, condominiums, and office buildings proceeded on a scale that exceeded the underlying demand. Rapidly rising prices eroded the purchasing power of workers' incomes and savings. Managerial practices of business enterprises became lax and productivity languished, while corporate profits—properly reckoned—kept falling. Inventories of raw materials and other supplies piled up as businessmen reacted to fears of shortages and still higher prices. Credit demands, both public and private, soared and interest rates rose to unprecedented heights. The banking system became overextended, the quality of loans tended to deteriorate, and the capital position of many banks was weakened.

During the past year many of these basic maladjustments have been worked out of the economic system by a painful process that could have been avoided if inflation had not gotten out of control. As the demand for goods and services slackened last winter, business managers began to focus more attention on efficiency and cost controls. Prices of industrial materials fell substantially, price increases at later stages of processing became less extensive, and in many instances business firms offered price concessions to clear their shelves. With the rate of inflation moderating, confidence of the general public was bolstered and consumer spending strengthened. Business firms were thus able to liquidate a good part of their excess inventories in a rather brief period. Meanwhile, as the demand for credit diminished, tensions in financial markets were relieved, and the liquidity position of both banks and business firms generally improved.

These self-corrective forces internal to the business cycle were aided by fiscal and monetary policies that sought to cushion the effects of economic adversity and to provide some stimulus to economic recovery. On the fiscal side, public employment programs were expanded, unemployment insurance was liberalized, and both personal and corporate income taxes were reduced. On the monetary side, easier credit conditions were fostered, resulting in lower interest rates and a rebuilding of liquidity across the economy.

With the base for economic recovery thus established, business activity has recently begun to improve. Production of goods and services turned up during the second quarter and is continuing to advance. The demand for labor has also improved. Both the number of individuals at work and the length of the work week are rising again, and unemployment has declined three months in a row. Retails sales have risen further, and of late residential construction has joined the recovery process.

Along with these favorable developments, however, some ominous signs have emerged. Despite an occasional pause, inflation once again may be accelerating. By the second quarter of this year, the annual rate of increase in the general price level was down to 5.5 per cent—about half the rate of inflation registered in the same period a year earlier. But over the summer, prices began to rise more briskly.

This behavior of prices is particularly worrisome in view of the large degree of slack that now exists in most of our nation's industries. Price increases in various depressed industries—aluminum, steel, auto, industrial chemicals, among others—are a clear warning that our long-range problem of inflation is unsolved and, therefore, remains a threat to sustained economic recovery.

History suggests that at this early stage of a business

upturn, confidence in the economic future should be strengthening steadily. A significant revival of confidence is indeed underway, but it is being hampered by widespread concern that a fresh outburst of double-digit inflation may before long bring on another recession. By now, thoughtful Americans are well aware of the profoundly disruptive consequences of inflation for our economy. They also recognize that these consequences are not solely of an economic character. Inflation has capricious effects on the income and wealth of a nation's families, and this inevitably causes disillusionment and discontent. Social and political frictions tend to multiply, and the very foundations of a society may be endangered. This has become evident in other nations around the world, where governments have toppled as a result of the social havoc wrought by inflation.

If we in the United States wish to enjoy the fruits of a prosperous economy and to preserve our democratic institutions, we must come to grips squarely with the inflation that has been troubling our nation throughout much of the postwar period, and most grievously during the past decade.

A first step in this process is to recognize the true character of the problem. Our long-run problem of inflation has its roots in the structure of our economic institutions and in the financial policies of our government. All too frequently, this basic fact is clouded by external events that influence the rate of inflation—such as a crop shortfall that results in higher farm prices, or the action of a foreign cartel that raises oil prices. The truth is that, for many years now, the economies of the United States and many other countries have developed a serious underlying bias toward inflation. This tendency has simply been magnified by the special influences that occasionally arise.

A major cause of this inflationary bias is the relative success that modern industrial nations have had in moderating the swings of the business cycle. Before World War II, cyclical declines of business activity in our country were typically longer and more severe than they have been during the past thirty years. In the environment then prevailing, the price level typically declined in the course of a business recession, and many months or years elapsed before prices returned to their previous peak.

In recent decades, a new pattern of wage and price behavior has emerged. Prices of many individual commodities still demonstrate a tendency to decline when demand weakens. The average level of prices, however, hardly ever declines. Wage rates have become even more inflexible. Wage reductions are nowadays rare even in severely depressed industries and the average level of wage rates continues to rise inexorably in the face of widespread unemployment.

These developments have profoundly altered the economic environment. When prices are pulled up by expanding demand in a time of prosperity, and are also pushed up by rising costs during a slack period, the decisions of the economic community are sure to be influenced, and may in fact be dominated, by expectations of continuing inflation.

Thus, many businessmen have come to believe that the trend of production costs will be inevitably upward, and their resistance to higher prices—whether of labor, or materials, or equipment—has, therefore, diminished. Labor leaders and workers now tend to reason that in order to achieve a gain in real income, they must bargain for wage increases that allow for advances in the price level as well as for such improvements as may occur in productivity. Lenders in their turn expect to be paid back in cheaper dollars and, therefore, tend to hold out for higher interest rates. They are able to do so because the resistance of borrowers to high interest rates is weakened by their anticipation of rising prices.

These patterns of thought are closely linked to the emphasis that governments everywhere have placed on rapid economic growth throughout the postwar period. Western democracies, including our own, have tended to move promptly to check economic recession, but they have moved hesitantly in checking inflation. Western governments have also become more diligent in seeking ways to relieve the burdens of adversity facing their peoples. In the process they have all moved a considerable distance toward the welfare state.

In the United States, for example, the unemployment insurance system has been greatly liberalized. Benefits now run to as many as sixty-five weeks, and in some cases provide individuals with after-tax incomes almost as large as their earnings from prior employment. Social security benefits, too, have been expanded materially, thus facilitating retirement or easing the burden of job loss for older workers. Welfare programs have been established for a large part of the population, and now include food stamps, school lunches, medicare and medicaid, public housing, and many other forms of assistance.

Protection from economic hardship has been extended by our government to business firms as well. The rigors of competitive enterprise are nowadays eased by import quotas, tariffs, price-maintenance laws, and other forms of governmental regulation. Farmers, home builders, small businesses, and other groups are provided special credit facilities and other assistance. And even large firms of national reputation look to the federal government for sustenance when they get into trouble.

Many, perhaps most, of these governmental programs have highly commendable objectives, but they have been pursued without adequte regard for their cost or method of financing. Governmental budgets—at the federal, state, and local level—have mounted and at times, as in the case of New York City, have gotten out of control. In the past ten years, federal expenditures have increased by 175 per cent. Over that interval, the fiscal deficit of the federal government, including government-sponsored enterprises, has totaled over $200 billion. In the current fiscal year alone, we are likely to add another $80 billion or more to that total. In financing these large and continuing deficits, pressure has been placed on our credit mechanisms, and the supply of money has frequently grown at a rate inconsistent wihh general price stability.

Changes in market behavior have contributed to the inflationary bias of our economy. In many businesses, price competition has given way to other forms of rivalry—advertising, changes in product design, and "hard sell" salesmanship. In labor markets, when an excessive wage increase occurs, it is apt to spread faster and more widely than before, partly because workmen have become more sensitive to wage developments elsewhere, partly also because many employers have found that a stable work force can be best maintained by emulating wage settlements in unionized industries. For their part, trade unions at times seem to attach higher priority to wage increases than to the jobs of their members. Moreover, the spread of trade unions to the rapidly expanding public sector has fostered during recent years numerous strikes, some of them clearly illegal, and they have often resulted in acceptance of union demands—however extreme. Needless to say, the apparent helplessness of governments to deal with this problem has encouraged other trade unions to exercise their latent market power more boldly.

The growth of our foreign trade and of capital movements to and from the United States has also increased the susceptibility of the American economy to inflationary trends. National economies around the world are now more closely interrelated, so that inflationary developments in one country are quickly communicated to others and become mutually reinforcing. Moreover, the adoption of a flexible exchange rate system—though beneficial in dealing with large-scale adjustments of international payments, such as those arising from the sharp rise in oil prices—may have made the Western world more prone to inflation by weakening the discipline of the balance of payments. Furthermore, since prices nowadays are more flexible upward than downward, any sizable decline in the foreign exchange value of the dollar is apt to have larger and more lasting effects on our price level than any offsetting appreciation of the dollar.

The long-run upward trend of prices in this country thus stems fundamentally from the financial policies of our government and the changing character of our economic institutions. This trend has been accentuated by new cultural values and standards, as is evidenced by pressures for wage increases every year, more holidays, longer vacations, and more liberal coffee breaks. The upward trend of prices has also been accentuated by the failure of business firms to invest sufficiently in the modernization and improvement of industrial plant. In recent years, the United States has been devoting a smaller part of its economic resources to business capital expenditures than any other major industrial nation in the world. All things considered, we should not be surprised that the rate of improvement in output per manhour has weakened over the past fifteen years, or that rapidly rising money wages have overwhelmed productivity gains and boosted unit labor costs of production.

Whatever may have been true in the past, there is no longer a meaningful trade-off between unemployment and inflation. In the current environment a rapidly rising level of consumer prices will not lead to the creation of new jobs. On the contrary, it will lead to hesitation and sluggish buying, as the increase of the personal savings rate in practically every industrial nation during these recent years of rapid inflation indicates. In general, stimulative financial policies have considerable merit when unemployment is extensive and inflation weak or absent; but such policies do not work well once inflation has come to dominate the thinking of a nation's consumers and businessmen. To be sure, highly expansionary monetary and fiscal policies might, for a short time, provide some additional thrust to economic activity. But inflation would inevitably accelerate—a development that would create even more difficult economic problems than we have encountered over the past year.

Conventional thinking about stabilization policies is inadequate and out of date. We must now seek ways of bringing unemployment down without becoming engulfed by a new wave of inflation. The areas that need to be explored are many and difficult, and we may not find quickly the answers we seek. But if we are to have any chance of ridding our economy of its inflationary bias, we must at least be willing to reopen our economic minds. I shall briefly sketch several broad lines of attack on the dual problem of unemployment and inflation that seem promising to me.

First, governmental efforts are long overdue to encourage improvements in productivity through larger investment in modern plant and equipment. This objective would be promoted by overhauling the structure of federal taxation so as to increase incentives for business capital spending and for equity investments in American enterprises.

Second, we must face up to the fact that environmental and safety regulations have in recent years played a troublesome role in escalating costs and prices and in holding up industrial construction across our land. I am concerned, as are all thoughtful citizens, with the need to protect the environment and to improve in other ways the quality of life. I am also concerned, however, about the dampening effect of excessive governmental regulations on business activity. Progress toward full employment and price stability would be measurably improved, I believe, by stretching out the timetables for achieving our environmental and safety goals.

Third, a vigorous search should be made for ways to enhance price competition among our nation's business enterprises. We need to gather the courage to reassess laws directed against restraint of trade by business firms and to improve the enforcement of these laws. We also need to reassess the highly complex governmental regulations affecting transportation, the effects on consumer prices of remaining fair trade laws, the monopoly of first-class mail by the Postal Service, and the many other laws and practices that impede the competitive process.

Fourth, in any serious search for noninflationary measures to reduce unemployment, governmental policies that affect labor markets have to be reviewed. For example, the federal minimum wage law is still pricing many teenagers out of the job market. The Davis-Bacon Act continues to escalate construction costs and damage the depressed construction industry. Programs for unemployment compensation now provide benefits on such a generous scale that they may be blunting incentives to work. Even in today's environment, with about 8 per cent of the labor force unemployed, there are numerous job vacancies—perhaps because job seekers are unaware of the opportunities, or because the skills of the unemployed are not suitable, or for other reasons. Surely, better results could be achieved with more effective job banks, more realistic training programs, and other labor market policies.

I believe that the ultimate objective of labor market policies should be to eliminate all involuntary unemployment. This is not a radical or impractical goal. It rests on the simple but often neglected fact that work is far better than the dole, both for the jobless individual and for the nation. A wise government will always strive to create an environment that is conducive to high employment in the private sector. Nevertheless, there may be no way to reach the goal of full employment short of making the government an employer of last resort. This could be done by offering public employment—for example, in hospitals, schools, public parks, or the like—to anyone who is willing to work at a rate of pay somewhat below the federal minimum wage.

With proper administration, these public service workers would be engaged in productive labor, not leaf-raking or other make-work. To be sure, such a program would not reach those who are voluntarily unemployed, but there is also no compelling reason why it should do so. What it would do is to make jobs available for those who need to earn some money.

It is highly important, of course, that such a program should not become a vehicle for expanding public jobs at the expense of private industry. Those employed at the special public jobs will need to be encouraged to seek more remunerative and more attractive work. This could be accomplished by building into the program certain safeguards—perhaps through a constitutional amendment—that would limit upward adjustment in the rate of pay for these special public jobs. With such safeguards, the budgetary cost of eliminating unemployment need not be burdensome. I say this, first, because the number of individu-

als accepting the public service jobs would be much smaller than the number now counted as unemployed; second, because the availability of public jobs would permit sharp reduction in the scope of unemployment insurance and other governmental programs to alleviate income loss. To permit active searching for a regular job, however, unemployment insurance for a brief period—perhaps 13 weeks or so—would still serve a useful function.

Finally, we also need to rethink the appropriate role of an incomes policy in the present environment. Lasting benefits cannot be expected from a mandatory wage and price control program, as recent experience indicates. It might actually be helpful if the Congress renounced any intention to return to mandatory controls, so that businesses and trade unions could look forward with confidence to the continuance of free markets. I still believe, however, that a modest form of incomes policy, in some cases relying on quiet governmental intervention, in others on public hearings and the mobilization of public opinion, may yet be of significant benefit in reducing abuses of private economic power and moving our nation toward the goal of full employment and a stable price level.

Structural reforms of our economy, along some such lines as I have sketched, deserve more attention this critical year from members of the Congress and from academic students of public policy than they are receiving. Economists in particular have tended to concentrate excessively on overall fiscal and monetary policies of economic stimulation. These traditional tools remain useful and even essential; but once inflationary expectations have become widespread, they must be used with great care and moderation.

Our nation cannot now achieve the goal of full employment by pursuing fiscal and monetary policies that rekindle inflationary expectations. Inflation has weakened our economy; it is also endangering our economic and political system based on freedom. America has become enmeshed in an inflationary web, and we need to gather our moral strength and intellectual courage to extricate ourselves from it.

26

What Have We Learned about Inflation?

HENRY C. WALLICH and
MABLE I. WALLICH

Henry C. Wallich is a member of the Federal Reserve Board. Mable I. Wallich has been an economist at the Federal Reserve Bank of New York. This article appeared in Challenge *in 1973.*

Over the last three years, the annual rise in prices has come down from a rate of 6 percent to 3–3.5 percent. This progress in reducing the rate of inflation has been accomplished by a sequence of the "orthodox" method of tight budgets and money and, subsequently, an "incomes policy" in the form of controls over wages, prices, and profit margins. It has been a partial success at best, although better than many other countries have been able to do. The standard forecast for 1973 points to a renewed rise in the rate of inflation. We can learn something about our chances of avoiding the inflations of the future by looking at the inflations of the past.

Some Lessons of the Past

Our knowledge, such as it is, has not been derived exclusively from the inflation that began in 1965. The United States has been through other big price movements, down as well as up. An econometric finding that even today sends chills down the backs of portfolio managers was made as early as 1896 by Professor Irving Fisher at Yale. He concluded that prolonged increases in interest rates and declines in the bond market were the results of past inflation, and he interpreted this as an effort on the part of investors to compensate for the erosion of their principal. Fisher's finding remains valid today, but with a vital difference. Whereas in the nineteenth century it took savers and borrowers many years to diagnose inflation and adjust interest rates accordingly, current studies have found that nowadays this reaction happens very quickly. Today one can predict with some assurance that another substantial upsurge of inflation would drive interest rates up and push the bond market, and possibly also the stock market, down sharply with very little lag. This is the natural result of the expected drop in the purchasing power of money, which induces investors to demand compensation in the form of higher interest rates.

Since our biggest inflations have been associated with wars, the lessons of experience in dealing with them focus mainly on wage and price controls. World Wars I and II have shown that, under wartime conditions, these controls have to be very comprehensive if they are to work. Even then they constitute a delaying action at best. Rationing and black markets are inevitable accompaniments, and compliance diminishes as time drags on. This experience was one reason for abstaining so long from direct controls in the present case. Meanwhile it has become obvious, however, that the problems created by a violent demand-pull inflation, such as occurred during two World Wars, cannot serve as a guide to dealing with a cost-push inflation, accompanied by an easy supply situation, such as has characterized the present inflation.

Demand-pull and Cost-push

The distinction between demand-pull and cost-push inflation—or, better perhaps, its widespread acceptance—dates back to the inflation of the middle 1950s. That was the first real peacetime inflation of this century. It began with a boom that engendered excess demand in the economy. But when the boom collapsed and was succeeded by rising unemployment, prices nevertheless continued rising. This was contrary to the textbooks, as textbooks were then written. Most economists had firmly believed that prices were governed by demand, not by cost. But the evidence of prices rising as costs went up while demand was falling made numerous converts.

Since that time, a number of econometric studies have shown that manufacturing prices are indeed very importantly governed by costs, which for the economy as a whole are mainly labor costs. The costs that manufacturers use in their pricing, however, usually are not the costs incurred at their current level of operations, which may be high or low relative to their capacity, but costs computed on some "standard volume."

Demand-pull and cost-push are not only economic concepts but belong also to the vocabulary of political economy. Labor, particularly, is sensitive to the allegation of cost-push, since wages represent much the largest part of costs. To refute the view that cost-push really means wage-push, the doctrine of "administered prices" has been developed. This says that price increases are really due to the arbitrary use of market power by large corporations. If these corporations were to hold prices constant or even lower them, as would be appropriate in recessions, wage increases would not raise prices.

There is little doubt that large corporations have market power and can, within reason, set their prices in a way that wheat farmers cannot. Profits, however, are a rather thin layer on top of "compensation of employees," which makes up the bulk of national income. Profit margins, moreover, typically have declined in recessions even when prices were rising. There is merit in the idea of reducing market power. But the contribution that administered pricing makes to inflation is probably too small to allow this to become an effective means of combating inflation. Relatively little has been heard about administered price-push in the current inflation.

The Phillips Curve

As so often happens in scientific work, the most fruitful discovery about inflation was made quite independently of current problems. The Phillips Curve, named after a British economist who described his findings in an article in 1958, hypothesizes that unemployment and inflation are functionally related. Phillips found that, over many decades reaching far back into the nineteenth century, wage increases in Britain had been high when unemployment was low, and vice versa. Given that wages and prices are closely related, this points to a similar relationship between unemployment and prices. Phillips's work has proved to be perhaps the most fruitful piece of economic research since the war. Its policy implications were recognized quickly, and have been influential in the thinking of probably the dominant group of economists ever since.

If inflation and unemployment are inversely related, the Phillips Curve theorists argue, unemployment can be reduced by pushing the economy to a higher rate of inflation. This means a gain in output, as well as the benefits of a lower level of unemployment. Among the latter are gains for minority groups, who historically have made breakthroughs against discrimination during periods of very tight labor markets. Minimum unemployment thus becomes the source of some very major gains.

Against these, many Phillips Curve theorists argue, the cost of inflation does not weigh heavily. Output, real goods, determines welfare. Prices, which are tickets attached to the real goods, do not. What difference does it make whether bread costs ten cents or a quarter or a dollar, whether its price is rising at 5 percent or 15 percent, so long as everything else goes up in proportion?

Defenders of price stability were put on the defensive by this doctrine. They seemed to find themselves in the morally untenable position of arguing in favor of more unemployment. They were arguing for the interests of bankers and bondholders, and against those of debtors and minorities. The ramparts defending price stability were not crowded.

The defenders of stability could argue, of course, that inflation was not really costless. Everything did not go up together. In the words of a Yale student whose father teaches at Yale, "Inflation is when Yale raises tuition 10 percent every year and freezes Daddy's salary." Some people get ahead of the game, some fall behind. Debtors gain, creditors lose. Adjustments to inflation, through bigger wage increases, or higher interest rates, are always imperfect because the future rate of inflation is itself uncertain. Uncertainty, moreover, is a cost; and this uncertainty mounts with the rate of inflation.

Even so, it would be difficult to assign a high value to price stability if the gains from tolerating inflation were at all substantial. The real battle between the inflationists and the stability advocates has been over the size and permanence of the gain.

The gain, in the short run, is indicated by the trade-off inherent in the Phillips Curve. What reduction in unemployment does one additional percentage point of inflation buy? A reduction by one percentage point would be a very substantial gain, and almost impossible to reject. A reduction of unemployment by one-tenth of a percentage point could be considered not worth the cost. Numerous econometric estimates have been made, showing, as one might expect, that the trade-off varies with the levels of unemployment and inflation.

Money Illusion

The principal argument has been, however, not over the rate of the trade-off, but over its permanence. Moving from Phillips' empirical finding to a policy prescription involves an assumption that may be illegitimate. The British inflations examined by Phillips were unpredictable. The best that a contemporary observer might have been able to conclude would have been that whenever inflation became pronounced, the Bank of England's credit policy or, in

its default, the normal forces of the gold standard would bring it to a halt. The assumption that must be made in turning the Phillips Curve into a policy instrument is that business and labor will behave just the same in an inflation that is the announced policy of the government as in one that is predictable or even likely to disappear. In technical terms, the assumption requires that business and labor have "money illusion," i.e., are unaware of inflation or ignore it, at least in part.

Suppose that at some low level of unemployment, labor demands and business will grant a 5 percent wage increase. Suppose, however, that productivity, i.e., output per man-hour, is rising at only 3 percent, which has been the long-run average rate of gain. In that case, costs will go up 2 percent. If business bases prices on costs, so as to keep profit margins constant, prices will have to go up by 2 percent. This inflation will reduce the 5 percent nominal wage increase to a 3 percent increase in real terms, i.e., in constant purchasing power. Labor cannot get more than that, assuming the share of profits in the national income remains constant, because that is the increment in production available for distribution. The economy has no more to give; and if business promises in excess, inflation takes the excess away. If business and labor have money illusion, things will settle down in this way, with annual wage increases of 5 percent in nominal terms, inflation of 2 percent reducing them to a real 3 percent, and unemployment remaining at its low level as promised by the Phillips Curve analysis.

Suppose, however, that labor becomes aware of the inflation. It is disappointed at getting a real increase of only 3 percent when it had bargained for 5 percent. Expecting a continued inflation of 2 percent, in the next bargaining round labor settles for 7 percent. Costs and prices now go up faster, and labor is again disappointed. In this way, inflation can spiral upward, while real wage gains never exceed 3 percent.

This suggests a very simple conclusion. Inflation will continue to accelerate so long as the level of unemployment is low enough to cause labor to demand, and business to grant, wage increases that labor expects to be larger in real terms, i.e., after deducting the expected inflation, than productivity gains. Inflation will cease to accelerate when unemployment is at a level at which labor's wage demands in real terms are just equal to productivity gains. Inflation will diminish, and eventually prices will begin to fall, if unemployment is larger than the level at which real wage demands equal productivity gains.

The simple notion that price stability depends on wage increases' being equal to productivity gains, these being interpreted as a long-run average for the whole economy, is not particularly controversial. It was the basis of appeals made to labor and business by President Eisenhower; it was spelled out with greater sophistication by President Kennedy's Council of Economic Advisers in the "Guideposts on Prices and Wages"; and it forms the basis for the price and wage standards applied today by the Nixon Administration.

Acceleration

The controversy has been over the tendency of inflation to accelerate, a view which the proponents of the Phillips Curve refer to as the "accelerationist" position. The accelerationists maintain that the Phillips Curve is not stable. If the government tries to reduce unemployment by moving to some particular rate of inflation, the curve will shift upward. The government will find that in order to hold to the chosen level of unemployment, higher and higher rates of inflation must be tolerated. In the long run, these successive points on a curve that is shifting upward will trace out a vertical line. Hence the accelerationists claim that the Phillips Curve in the long run tends toward the vertical.

There is only one set of circumstances in which inflation neither accelerates nor decelerates. That occurs when labor's wage demands in real terms equal productivity gains, as noted before. This equilibrium rate of unemployment has been called by Milton Friedman the "natural rate" of unemployment. Unemployment at this rate does not imply zero inflation. Inflation can be at any level. But whatever it is, it will not change. Labor is getting, in real terms, exactly what it wants. It has no reason to change its demands in nominal terms, which of course include allowance for the expected rate of inflation. Hence inflation stays at whatever level it happens to find itself.

The implication of the accelerationist doctrine, if true, is very damaging to the Phillips Curve philosophy. In the long run, there is no way of reducing unemployment by means of inflation. All rates of inflation produce the same equilibrium unemployment. Only two seemingly minor factors speak for the inflationist case: (1) once a high rate of inflation has been reached, it may be preferable to stick with it

rather than go through a period of high unemployment to bring it down to zero, and (2) if the "long run" is very long, it may still pay to work the short-run trade-off between unemployment and inflation, especially from the time perspective of an elected politician.

No Return to Full Stability

The first of these two options confronts the United States at this time. Are we going to make a great effort to get inflation down to zero? It is a fair guess that the decision will be on the side of the Phillips Curve supporters. That is to say, the United States, after making a costly effort to halt an accelerating inflation and then to bring it down from a rate of 6 percent to one of 3.5 percent, is probably not willing to go through the additional agony of bringing inflation down to zero. In order to achieve this, we would have to use wage and price controls in a manner apparently more drastic than the nation is willing to tolerate, or else maintain unemployment above the equilibrium rate in order to obtain deceleration even without controls.

We do not know with precision what the equilibrium rate of unemployment is in the American economy. All we do know is that changes in the composition of the labor force have pushed it higher in recent years. Probably it is now somewhere near 5 percent rather than 4 percent. The widespread expectation that inflation will be rising in 1973 implies that unemployment will be below its equilibrium rate, although the speed of the boom also may push inflation up. In that sense, one may say that we are now practicing the Phillips Curve philosophy.

Lags in Acceleration

There remains the question of how soon and how quickly the Phillips Curve is likely to shift upward. If the lag is long, we could trade low unemployment now against more inflation later. The length of the lag has been much debated, and there is evidence from a number of sources. The kind of explosive inflation that occurred in various European countries after World Wars I and II is not a relevant precedent for the United States. Anyone whose opposition to inflation is based on fear of that kind of development in the United States is not putting up a very strong case. Again, there have been inflations at annual rates of 50 percent and more in various Latin American countries. Obviously, inflation had to accelerate in order to get to those levels. But although some countries, for instance, Chile and Brazil, have long lived with inflations fluctuating over wide ranges, an ultimate explosion has always been avoided. What the Latin American inflations seem to demonstrate is that inflation tends to be unstable and therefore unpredictable, because stabilization efforts, usually associated with high unemployment, tend to be made from time to time.

Why Models Underpredicted

Our own experience of the last few years, however, seems to point in an accelerationist direction. In the late 1960s, the econometric models and equations that are used to predict the course of the economy began to exhibit peculiar miscarriages. Based on the principle of the Phillips Curve, the models predicted a moderate rate of inflation reflecting low but by no means minimal unemployment. Actual inflation increasingly exceeded the forecasts, and the errors became more alarming as unemployment began to rise while inflation also was speeding up. The model builders, their faith in the Phillips Curve unshaken, went to work to revise the models. They built in the fact that, during the early 1960s, the economy had experienced what could be called hidden unemployment—discouraged workers who had withdrawn from the labor force and no longer were counted as unemployed. This hidden unemployment could be made to explain why inflation was so low during the early 1960s, and its disappearance during the subsequent boom then explained the acceleration. The model builders also discovered and built in the fact that the dispersion of unemployment, i.e., the range of unemployment rate in different parts of the economy, had increased. This meant that some labor markets were tight long before average unemployment had come down much, which could also be used to explain high rates of inflation. Finally, it was observed that the structure of the labor force had shifted toward a higher proportion of women and teenagers. Their unemployment, typically above the national average, pulled that average up. The unemployment of the core of the labor force, the heads of households, on the other hand, was lower relative to the national average than before.

With these various adjustments, it remained possible, for a couple of years, to defend the proposition that the Phillips Curve was not shifting upward. But as new data became available year after year, the case became harder and harder to maintain. Increasingly the models and equations began to show that as prices increased by some additional percentage, labor in its wage settlements was not prepared to ignore the increase, nor to settle for some fraction of it, but insisted on raising its demands by the full amount. That, of course, is precisely what the accelerationists had maintained.

Finally, another ingenious piece of econometrics showed that one could do without all the refinements of the unemployment data and explain the course of inflation quite adequately if one were prepared to make one plausible assumption. This was to assume that below some moderate level of inflation, which the equations showed to be about 2.5 percent, people tended to ignore what was happening to prices. Above that flashpoint, however, money illusion vanished and wage demands began to take expected inflation into account fully and quickly. The presumed long lag in the response to inflation, upon which earlier Phillips Curve findings may have rested, had been telescoped.

Changing Responses of Workers and Investors

What had happened to the Phillips Curve theorists was precisely what happened to old Irving Fisher and his finding that interest rates demanded by investors and conceded by borrowers tended to adjust to inflation with a very long lag. This was reasonable so long as governments aimed at price stability and nobody knew whether the long-term trend of prices was up or down. The Phillips Curve theorists could assume the same of the wage demands of labor, which had no grounds for escalating so long as inflation was not expected to continue. Once that premise was changed, investors and workers acted rationally to protect themselves immediately. Inflation began to enter into wages and interest rates fully and with little lag. In other words, it began to escalate.

In real time economics, of course, the last word is

never spoken. New facts may appear, new explanations may be devised. Meanwhile, however, the refinements produced by the model builders in their efforts to reconcile the behavior of unemployment with that of prices have supplied some valuable pointers in another direction.

A New Measure of Labor Market Tightness

They have drawn attention to the fact that the overall unemployment rate is a composite of widely divergent rates for particular sectors of the economy and of the labor force. A rate of 5.5 percent, as prevailed in late 1972, is an average of 3.4 percent for heads of households, 5.5 percent for women, 15 percent for teenagers, and 34 percent for black teenagers—in other words, an average of apples and nuts. Simulations with econometric models have shown that even if the average unemployment rate were reduced to some low level, the problems of teenagers and others would remain in large part unsolved. Overheating the economy, aside from the disproportionate costs that it imposes on many people, is an inefficient and inadequate way of curing minority unemployment. Direct action, such as the emergency employment program and training programs, is needed.

The examination of the structure of unemployment has also made clear that the overall unemployment rate, which at 4 percent supposedly signals "full employment," is in fact a poor indicator of inflationary pressure. If the men and women who are strongly unionized, who hold the core jobs in the economy, experience an unemployment rate of 1.8 percent, as they did in 1969, the presence of large numbers of women and teenagers who are only loosely attached to the labor force will not keep wages from rising rapidly. The "heads of households" unemployment rate is a much better signal. To gauge labor market pressure even more accurately, one should eliminate from the unemployment of heads of households that part lasting less than five weeks, which contributes little to labor market balance. In 1969, this would have left 0.9 percent of males in the age bracket 25–64 unemployed for more than five weeks, while the overall unemployment rate was 3.5 percent. Here we have the explanation why inflationary pressures recently have begun to be felt at seemingly high rates of average unemployment.

More evidence keeps coming in, and definitive conclusions are out of place. But the nature of that evidence certainly will be of a sort to tell us that what we call "unemployment" is a very varied and complex phenomenon. The more this is the case, the more we shall be driven to search for varied and complex solutions, and the less we shall probably be able to resolve the problem by the simple method of pushing the economy to the point of inflation.

27

What Price Guideposts?

MILTON FRIEDMAN

Milton Friedman is Professor of Economics at the University of Chicago. This article first appeared in Guidelines: Informal Controls in the Market Place, *edited by George Shultz and Robert Aliber, 1966.*

The student of inflation is tempted to rejoin, "I've heard that one before," to exhortations now emanating from Washington. Since the time of Diocletian, and very probably long before, the sovereign has repeatedly responded to generally rising prices in precisely the same way: by berating the "profiteers," calling on private persons to show social responsibility by holding down the prices at which they sell their products or their services, and trying, through legal prohibitions or other devices, to prevent individual prices from rising. The result of such measures has always been the same: complete failure. Inflation has been stopped when and only when the quantity of money has been kept from rising too fast, and that cure has been effective whether or not the other measures were taken. . . .

Why Direct Control of Prices and Wages Does Not Eliminate Inflationary Pressure

An analogy is often drawn between direct control of wages and prices as a reaction to inflation and the breaking of a thermometer as a reaction to, say, an overheated room. This analogy has an element of validity. Prices are partly like thermometers in that they register heat but do not produce it; in both cases, preventing a measuring instrument from recording what is occurring does not prevent the occurrence. But the analogy is also misleading. Breaking the thermometer need have no further effect on the phenomenon being recorded; it simply adds to our ignorance. Controlling prices, insofar as it is successful, has very important effects. Prices are not only measuring instruments, they also play a vital role in the economic process itself.

A much closer analogy is a steam-heating furnace

running full blast. Controlling the heat in one room by closing the radiators in that room simply makes other rooms still more overheated. Closing all radiators lets the pressure build up in the boiler and increases the danger that it will explode. Closing or opening individual radiators is a good way to adjust the relative amount of heat in different rooms; it is not a good way to correct for overfueling the furnace. Similarly, changes in individual prices are a good way to adjust to changes in the supply or demand of individual products; preventing individual prices from rising is not a good way to correct for a general tendency of prices to rise.

Suppose that there is such a general tendency, and suppose that some specific price (or set of prices), say, the price of steel, is prevented from rising. Holding down the price of steel does not make more steel available; on the contrary, given that other prices and costs are rising, it reduces the amount that producers can afford to spend in producing steel and is therefore likely to reduce the amount available from current production. Holding down the price of steel does not discourage buyers; on the contrary, it encourages consumption. If the suppressed price is effectively enforced and not evaded by any of the many channels that are available to ingenious sellers and buyers, some potential buyers of steel must be frustrated —there is a rationing problem. Chance, favoritism, or bribery will have to decide which buyers succeed in getting the steel. Those who succeed pay less than they are willing to pay. They, instead of the steel producers, have the remainder to spend elsewhere. Those who fail will try to substitue other metals or products and so will divert their demand elsewhere; the excess pressure is shifted, not eliminated.

The situation is precisely the same on the labor market. If wages are tending to rise, suppressing a specific wage rise will mean that fewer workers are available for that type of employment and more are demanded. Again rationing is necessary. The workers employed have less income to spend, but this is just balanced by their employers having larger incomes. And the unsatisfied excess demand for labor is diverted to other workers.

But, it will be said, I have begged the question by *starting* with a general tendency for prices to rise. Can it not be that this general tendency is itself produced by rises in a limited number of prices and wages which in turn produce sympathetic rises in other prices and wages? In such a case, may not preventing the initial

price and wage rises nip a wage-price or price-price spiral in the bud?

Despite its popularity, this cost-push theory of inflation has very limited applicability. Unless the cost-push produces a monetary expansion that would otherwise not have occurred, its effect will be limited to at most a temporary general price rise, accompanied by unemployment, and followed by a tendency toward declining prices elsewhere.

Suppose, for example, a strong (or stronger) cartel were formed in steel, and that it decided to raise the price well above the level that otherwise would have prevailed. The price rise would reduce the amount of steel people want to buy. Potential purchasers of steel would shift to substitute products, and no doubt the prices of such substitutes would tend to rise in sympathy. But there is now another effect. Steel producers would hire fewer workers and other resources. These would seek employment elsewhere, tending to drive down wages and prices in other industries. True, wages and prices might be sticky and decline only slowly, but that would only delay the downward adjustments and only at the expense of unemployment.

A textbook example is provided by John L. Lewis and the United Mine Workers. Coal mining hourly earnings rose by "163 percent from 1945 to 1960. Bituminous coal mining employment dropped from 284,000 to 168,000. By way of comparison, in the same period, manufacturing production hourly earnings rose . . . 122 percent and manufacturing employment rose." High coal prices undoubtedly put upward pressure on the prices of oil and gas; but the high unemployment put downward pressure on other prices.

The only example I know of in United States history when such a cost-push was important even temporarily for any substantial part of the economy was from 1933 to 1937, when the NIRA, AAA, Wagner Labor Act, and associated growth of union strength unquestionably led to *increasing* market power of both industry and labor and thereby produced upward pressure on a wide range of wages and prices. This cost-push did not account for the concomitant rapid growth in nominal income at the average rate of 14 percent a year from 1933 to 1937. That reflected rather a rise in the quantity of money at the rate of 11 percent a year. And the wage and cost-push had nothing to do with the rapid rise in the quantity of money. That reflected rather the flood of gold, initiated by the change in the United States price of gold in 1933 and 1934 and sustained by the reaction to Hitler's assumption of power in Germany.

The cost-push does explain why so large a part of the growth in nominal income was absorbed by prices. Despite unprecedented levels of unemployed resources, wholesale prices rose nearly 50 percent from 1933 to 1937, and the cost of living rose by 13 percent. Similarly, the wage cost-push helps to explain why unemployment was still so high in 1937, when monetary restriction was followed by another severe contraction.

The popularity of the cost-push theory of inflation, despite its limited applicability, stems I believe from two sources: first, the deceptiveness of appearances; second, the desire of governmental authorities to shift the blame for inflation.

One of the fascinating features of economic relations is the frequent contrast between what is true for the individual and what is true for the community. Time and again the one is precisely the opposite of the other. Each individual takes for granted the prices of the things he buys and regards himself as having no effect on them; yet, consumers as a whole greatly affect those prices by the combined effects of their separate actions. Each individual can determine the amount of currency he carries around in his pocket; yet, all individuals together may have nothing to say about the total amount of currency to be carried around; that may be determined by monetary authorities, the individuals being free only to shuffle it around and transfer it from one to the other. Indeed, it is precisely this contrast between what is true for the individual and for the community that underlies many, perhaps most, common economic fallacies. They arise from invalid generalization from the individual to the community.

The widespread belief in the cost-push theory of inflation is a striking example. To each businessman separately, inflation tends to come in the form of increasing costs, and, typically, he correctly regards himself as having to raise the price at which he sells because his costs have risen. Yet, those cost rises may themselves reflect an increase in demand elsewhere and simply be part of the process whereby the demand increase is transmitted; and his ability to raise his price without a drastic decline in sales reflects the existence of excess demand. The monetary expansion and the associated increase in money demand take place through mysterious, widely dispersed, and largely invisible channels. The cost and price increases are their visible tracks. . . .

Inflation Is a Monetary Phenomenon

Yet, the central fact is that inflation is always and everywhere a monetary phenomenon. Historically, substantial changes in prices have always occurred together with substantial changes in the quantity of money relative to output. I know of no exception to this generalization, no occasion in the United States or elsewhere when prices have risen substantially without a substantial rise in the quantity of money relative to output or when the quantity of money has risen substantially relative to output without a substantial rise in prices. And there are numerous confirming examples. Indeed, I doubt that there is any other empirical generalization in economics for which there is as much organized evidence covering so wide a range of space and time.

Some confirming examples are extremely dramatic and illustrate vividly how important the quantity of money is by comparison with everything else. After the Russian Revolution of 1917, there was a hyperinflation in Russia when a new currency was introduced and printed in large quantities. Ultimately, it became almost valueless. All the time, some currency was circulating which had been issued by the prerevolutionary Czarist government. The Czarist government was out of power. Nobody expected it to return to power. Yet, the value of the Czarist currency remained roughly constant in terms of goods and rose sharply in terms of the Bolshevik currency. Why? Because there was nobody to print any more of it. It was fixed in quantity and therefore it retained its value. Another story has to do with the United States Civil War. Toward the end of the war, the Union troops overran the place where the Confederates had been printing paper money to finance the war. In the course of moving to a new location, there was a temporary cessation of the printing of money. As a result, there was also a temporary interruption in the price rise that had been proceeding merrily.

The fact that inflation results from changes in the quantity of money relative to output does not mean that there is a precise, rigid, mechanical relationship between the quantity of money and prices, which is why the weasel-word "substantial" was sprinkled in my initial statement of the proposition. First, over short periods, the rate of change in the quantity of money can differ and sometimes by appreciable amounts from the rate of change in nominal income or prices because of other factors, including fiscal policy. Second, and more important, changes in the quantity of money do not make their effects felt immediately. It may be six months, or a year or a year and a half before a change in the quantity of money appreciably affects nominal income or prices. Failure to allow for this difference in timing is a major reason for the misinterpretation of monetary experience. Third, and most important of all, there is a systematic and regular difference between changes in money and in prices in the course of an inflationary episode that is itself part of the very process by which monetary changes produce changes in prices.

The typical life history of an inflation is that the quantity of money per unit of output initially increases more rapidly than prices. During this period, the public does not anticipate price rises, interprets any price rise that occurs as temporary, and hence is willing to hold money balances of increased "real" value (i.e., corresponding to a larger volume of goods and services) in the belief that prices will be lower in the future. If the quantity of money continues to increase faster than output, however, prices will continue to rise, and sooner or later the public will come to anticipate further price rises. It then wishes to reduce its money balances not only to their former real value but to an even smaller level. Cash has now become a costly way to hold assets, since its purchasing power is decreasing. People therefore try to reduce their cash balances. They cannot, as a whole, do so in nominal terms (i.e., in terms of dollars), because someone or other must hold the amount in existence. But the *attempt* to do so bids up prices, wages, and nominal incomes. The result is to reduce "real" balances. During this stage, therefore, prices rise more rapidly than the quantity of money, and sometimes much more rapidly. If the rate of rise of the quantity of money stabilizes, no matter at how high a level, the rate of price rise will ultimately settle down also. The total price rise may bear very different relations to the rise in the quantity of money per unit of output depending on the size of the monetary expansion. In moderate inflations, as for example the rise in prices in the United States by a third from 1896 to 1913, prices and money may rise by about the same percentage. In really substantial inflations, such as have occurred in recent decades in many South American countries, the price rise will generally be

several times the monetary rise; in hyperinflations, the price rise will be many times the monetary rise.

The United States today is in the early stages of such an episode. From 1961 to 1965, the quantity of money per unit of output rose more rapidly than prices—the typical initial reaction. From early 1965 to early this year, the monetary rise has been accelerated, and the price rise accelerated accelerated even more rapidly as anticipations of inflation have become widespread. As of now, if the rate of monetary growth were stabilized at the high level attained in 1965, the rate of price rise would continue to accelerate for a time. Even if the rate of monetary growth were sharply reduced, prices would continue to rise for a time under the combined influence of earlier monetary growth and changing anticipation.

Why should money be so critical a factor in price level behavior? Why should it occupy such a central role in the process? The key to an answer is the difference, already referred to, between the *nominal* quantity of money, the quantity of money expressed in terms of dollars, and the *real* quantity of money, the quantity of money expressed in terms of the goods and services it will buy or the number of weeks of income it is equal to.

People seem to be extraordinarily stubborn about the real amount of money that they want to hold and are unwilling to hold a different amount, unless there is a strong incentive to do so. This is true over both time and space.

Let me illustrate with currency in circulation alone, which is more comparable among countries and over time than a broader definition of money, including deposits. In the United States, the amount of currency held by the nonbanking public amounts to roughly four weeks' income. I know that this result seems surprising. When I ask people separately whether they have as much as four weeks' income in the form of currency, I have rarely had anyone say yes. Part of the explanation is that about one-fifth of the currency is held by businesses such as retail stores. The main explanation, I am sure, is that there are a small number of people who hold very large sums in this form while the rest of us hold more moderate amounts. In any event, that is what the figures show. The fascinating thing is that the corresponding number was not very different a century ago. In 1867 people on the average held about five weeks' income in the form of currency, compared to today's four weeks' income. In the interim this number has gone as low as 2-1/4 weeks' income in 1929, as high as 8-1/2 weeks' in 1946. That is a substantial range, it is true, but those are long periods spanning major changes in circumstance.

This range, moreover, contains the figures for most countries in the world. In Israel, the amount held is about the same as in the United States, a little over four weeks' income; in Japan and Turkey, about five weeks' income; in Greece and Yugoslavia, about six weeks' income; in India, about seven weeks' income. Again, these are not negligible differences; yet, they are small compared to the differences among the countries in wealth, economic structure, political forms, and cultural characteristics.

Even these relatively small differences over time and space can be largely explained by a few major factors, of which the prevalence of deposit banking is perhaps the single most important.

Given that people are so stubborn about the amount they hold in the form of money, let us suppose that, for whatever reasons, the amount of money in a community is higher than people want to hold at the level of prices then prevailing. It does not for our purposes matter why, whether because the government has printed money to finance expenditures or because somebody has discovered a new gold mine or because banks have discovered how to create deposits. For whatever reason, people find that although on the average they would like to hold, let us say, the four weeks' income that they hold in the United States, they are actually holding, say, five weeks' income. What will happen? Here again it is essential to distinguish between the individual and the community. Each individual separately thinks he can get rid of his money and he is right. He can go out and spend it and thereby reduce his cash balances. But for the community as a whole the belief that cash balances can be reduced is an optical illusion. The only way I can reduce my cash balances in nominal terms is to induce somebody else to increase his. One man's expenditures are another man's receipts. People as a whole cannot spend more than they as a whole receive. In consequence, if everybody in the community tries to reduce the nominal amount of his cash balances, on the average nobody will do so. The amount of nominal balances is fixed by the nominal quantity of money in existence and no game of musical chairs can change it.

But people can and will try to reduce their cash balances and the process of trying has important effects. In the process of trying to spend more than they are receiving, people bid up the prices of all sorts of goods and services. Nominal incomes rise and real cash balances are indeed reduced, even though nominal balances, the number of dollars, are not affected. The rise in prices and incomes will bring cash balances from five weeks' income to four weeks' income. People will succeed in achieving their objective, but by raising prices and incomes rather than by reducing nominal balances. In the process, prices will have risen by about a fifth. This in a nutshell and somewhat oversimplified is the process whereby changes in the stock of money exert their influence on the price level. It is oversimplified because there is a tendency to overshoot, followed by successive readjustments converging on the final position, but this complication does not affect the essence of the adjustment process.

Emphasis on the key role of the quantity of money leaves open the question of what produced the changes in the quantity of money. Hence, if an analysis of inflation is to deal not only with the change in the quantity of money but with what brought it about, it will be a very pluralistic theory. Historically, the actual sources of monetary expansion have been very different at different times and in different places.

In United States history, the most dramatic inflations have been wartime inflations—those associated with the Revolution, when prices skyrocketed and the declining value of the money produced the phrase "not worth a continental," and with the War of 1812, the Civil War, and the two world wars, in all of which prices roughly doubled. In these episodes, the increase in the quantity of money was produced mainly by the printing of money to pay for governmental wartime expenses.

But even these episodes are not wholly to be explained in that fashion. In the final year of the World War I inflation (1919–20), when prices rose at their most rapid pace, the government budget was in surplus, and the rapid increase in the quantity of money was being produced for private, not governmental, purposes.

The two main periods of peacetime inflation in the United States were in the 1850s and from 1896 to 1913. Both were parts of worldwide movements. The first resulted from the gold discoveries in California, the second from the development of a commercially feasible cyanide process for extracting gold from low-grade ore plus gold discoveries.

There is a widespread belief that inflation is somehow related to government deficits. This belief has a sound basis. The existence of deficits tempts governments to finance them by printing money (or the equivalent, creating deposits), hence deficits have often been the source of monetary expansion. But deficits per se are not necessarily a source of inflation. As already noted, the federal budget ran a surplus during 1919–20 when prices rose rapidly; similarly, there were extremely large surpluses immediately after World War II, when prices also rose rapidly. On the other side, the budget was in deficit during 1931–33, when prices fell sharply. Deficits can contribute to inflation by raising interest rates and so velocity; for the rest they are a source of inflation if and only if they are financed by printing money.

The same considerations apply to other alleged sources of inflation. Increasingly strong trade unions can be a source of inflation if by their actions they produce unemployment and if a government committed to full employment expands the quantity of money as part of a policy of eliminating unemployment. This particular chain of events has often been alleged but, as already noted, seldom observed in the United States. More generally, a full employment policy can be a source of inflation if it produces undue monetary expansion.

Suppressed Inflation Is Worse Than Open Inflation

The distinction between inflation and deflation, important as it is, is less important than the distinction between open inflation, one in which prices are free to rise without governmental price controls, and suppressed inflation, one in which the government attempts to suppress the manifestations of the inflationary pressure by controlling prices, including prices not only of products but also of factor services (i.e., wage rates, rents, interest rates) and of foreign currencies (i.e., exchange rates).

Open inflation is harmful. It generally produces undesirable transfers of income and wealth, weakens the social fabric, and may distort the pattern of output. But if moderate, and especially if steady, it tends to become anticipated and its worst effects on the distribution of income are offset. It still does harm, but, *so long as prices are free to move,* the extremely flexible private enterprise system will adapt to it, take it in stride, and continue to operate efficiently. The main dangers from open inflation are twofold: first, the temptation to step up the rate of inflation as the economy adapts itself; second, and even more serious, the temptation to attempt cures, especially suppression, that are worse than the disease.

Suppressed inflation is a very different thing. Even a moderate inflation, if effectively suppressed over a wide range, can do untold damage to the economic system, require widespread government intervention into the details of economic activity, destroy a free enterprise system, and along with it, political freedom. The reason is that suppression prevents the price system from working. The government is driven to try to provide a substitute that is extremely inefficient. The usual outcome, pending a complete monetary reform, is an uneasy compromise between official tolerance of evasion of price controls and a collectivist economy. The greater the ingenuity of private individuals in evading the price controls and the greater the tolerance of officials in blinking at such evasions, the less the harm that is done; the more law-abiding the citizens, and the more rigid and effective the governmental enforcement machinery, the greater the harm.

A dramatic illustration of the difference between open and suppressed inflation is the contrast between the experience of Germany after World War I and after World War II. This happens to be one of those beautiful examples that history turns up for us from time to time in which experience is almost in the nature of a controlled experiment, because the difference in the character of the monetary phenomena is so great compared to differences in other relevant respects. After World War I, Germany had an open inflation of extremely large magnitude. It is difficult for us to contemplate the kind of inflation Germany experienced at that time because it is so extreme. A student of mine, Phillip Cagan, wrote a doctoral dissertation on hyperinflation in different countries, which has become something of a classic. He had the problem of how to define hyperinflation. He defined it as beginning when prices started to rise at the rate of more than 50 percent a month. In the German hyperinflation after World War I, there were periods when prices rose not 50 percent a month but doubled every week and some occasions on which they were doubling every day. Indeed, it got to the point that firms started to pay their employees their wages three times a day—after breakfast, lunch, and dinner, so that they could go out and spend them before they lost their value. That was really a whopping inflation, yet it went on for something like three years.

The inflation did untold harm to Germany. The

impoverishment of the middle classes, the arbitrary redistribution of income, and the frantic instability unquestionably helped to lay the groundwork for Hitler's emergence later. Looked at, however, from the purely technical point of view of its effect on production, the astounding thing is that until the last six months of the inflation, total output in Germany never declined. Indeed, Germany was one of the few countries in the world that did not experience a great depression in 1920–21, when prices in the gold standard part of the world dropped by 50 percent. Total output remained up. Why? Because the inflation was open. Prices were allowed to rise freely and hence the price system could still be used to allocate resources. Of course, after a time people started to use all sorts of escalation devices to link their contracts to the value of the mark in the foreign exchange market, which was also a free market price, and so on. The price system, however, could work even under those handicaps.

After World War II, Germany was under inflationary pressure as a result of an increase in the quantity of money during the war and the fixation of prices. By our usual standards, the pressure was substantial. If prices had been allowed to rise freely immediately after the war, the price level would probably have quadrupled. That is a large price rise. But it is negligible by comparison with the price rise after World War I which has to be described in terms of factors like 10^{10}. The price rise after World War II, however, was suppressed. Ordinarily, it is extremely difficult to suppress a price rise of that magnitude, to enforce price control when the market price would be four times the controlled price. But there were certain especially favorable circumstances from the point of view of enforcing price control in Germany at that time. Germany was occupied by the armed forces of Britain, France, and the United States, and the occupation forces enforced price control.

The result of suppressing inflation was that output in Germany was cut in half. The price system was not allowed to function. People were forced to revert to barter. Walter Eucken in an article describing this period tells the story of people who worked in a factory making pots and pans. They would work there for two or three days and then they would be given their pay in the form of aluminum saucepans. They would take the saucepans and spend the rest of the week scouring the countryside trying to find some farmer who would be willing to trade a few potatoes or other produce for the saucepans. That is not a very efficient way to

organize resources. It was so inefficient that something had to be done and something was done. People developed their own forms of money. Cigarettes came into use as money for small transactions and cognac for large transactions—the most liquid money I have ever come across. But even with these expedients, suppressed inflation cut output in half from the level at the immediate end of the war.

In 1948 as you know, the so-called German miracle began. It was not a very complicated thing. It amounted to introducing a monetary reform, eliminating price control, and allowing the price system to function. The extraordinary rise in German output in the few years following this reform was not owing to any miracle of German ingenuity or ability or anything like that. It was the simple, natural result of allowing the most efficient technique people have ever found for organizing resources to work instead of preventing it from working by trying to fix prices here, there, and everywhere.

Although this is the most dramatic example, numerous other examples can be cited of a less extreme kind. In the immediate postwar period, I visited Europe and spent some time in Britain and France. Both countries at that time had widespread price controls. But there was an important difference. The people of Britain were relatively law-abiding, the people of France were not. The result was that Britain was being strangled by the law obedience of her people and France was being saved by the black market.

The reason suppressed inflation is so disastrous, as these examples suggest, is that the price system is the only technique that has so far been discovered or invented for efficiently allocating resources. If that is prevented from operating, something else must be substituted. What do we substitute? It is always some kind of clumsy physical control.

What Harm Will Be Done by the Guideposts?

Even granted that legally imposed and vigorously enforced wage and price ceilings covering a wide range of the economy would do enormous harm, some may argue that the enunciation of guideposts, their approval by businessmen and labor leaders, and voluntary compliance with them, or even lip service to them, is a palliative that can do no harm and can temporarily help until more effective measures are taken. At the very least, it may be said, it will enable businessmen and labor leaders to display their sense of social responsibility.

This view seems to me mistaken. The guideposts do harm even when only lip service is paid to them, and the more extensive the compliance, the greater the harm.

In the first place, the guideposts confuse the issue and make correct policy less likely. If there is inflation or inflationary pressure, the governmental monetary (or, some would say, fiscal) authorities are responsible. It is they who must take corrective measures if the inflation is to be stopped. Naturally, the authorities want to shift the blame, so they castigate the rapacious businessman and the selfish labor leader. By approving guidelines, the businessman and the labor leader implicitly whitewash the government for its role and plead guilty to the charge. They thereby encourage the government to postpone taking the corrective measures that alone can succeed.

In the second place, whatever measure of actual compliance there is introduces just that much distortion into the allocation of resources and the distribution of output. To whatever extent the price system is displaced, some other system of organizing resources and rationing output must be adopted. As in the example of the controls on foreign loans by banks, one adverse effect is to foster private collusive arrangements, so that a measure undertaken to keep prices down leads to government support and encouragement of private monopolistic arrangements.

In the third place, "voluntary" controls invite the use of extralegal powers to produce compliance. And, in the modern world, such powers are ample. There is hardly a business concern that could not have great costs imposed on it by antitrust investigations, tax inquiries, government boycott, or rigid enforcement of any of a myriad of laws, or on the other side of the ledger, that can see no potential benefits from government orders, guarantees of loans, or similar measures. Which of us as an individual could not be, at the very least, seriously inconvenienced by investigation of his income tax returns, no matter how faithfully and carefully prepared, or by the enforcement to the letter of laws we may not even know about? This threat casts a shadow well beyond any particular instance. In a dissenting opinion in a recent court case involving a "stand-in" in a public library, Justice Black wrote, "It should be remembered that if one group can take over libraries for one cause, other groups will assert the right to do it for causes which, while wholly legal, may not be so appealing to this court." Precisely the same point applies here. If legal powers granted for other purposes can today be used for the "good" purpose of holding down prices, tomorrow they can be used for other purposes that will seem equally "good" to the men in power—such as simply keeping themselves in power. It is notable how sharp has been the decline in the number of businessmen willing to be quoted by name when they make adverse comments on government.

In the fourth place, compliance with voluntary controls imposes a severe conflict of responsibilities on businessmen and labor leaders. The corporate official is an agent of his stockholders; the labor leader, of the members of his union. He has a responsibility to promote their interests. He is now told that he must sacrifice their interests to some supposedly higher social responsibility. Even supposing that he can know what "social responsibility" demands—say by simply accepting on that question the gospel according to the Council of Economic Advisers—to what extent is it proper for him to do so? If he is to become a civil servant in fact, will he long remain an employee of the stockholders or an agent of the workers in name? Will they not discharge him? Or, alternatively, will not the government exert authority over him in name as in fact?

Conclusion

Inflation being always and everywhere a monetary phenomenon, the responsibility for controlling it is governmental. Legally enforced price and wage ceilings do not eliminate inflationary pressure. At most they suppress it. And suppressed inflation is vastly more harmful than open inflation.

Guideposts and pleas for voluntary compliance are a halfway house whose only merit is that they can more readily be abandoned than legally imposed controls. They are not an alternative to other effective measures to such inflation, but at most a smokescreen to conceal the lack of action. Even if not complied with they do harm, and the more faithfully they are complied with, the more harm they do.

Nonetheless, we should not exaggerate either the problem or the harm that will be done by false cures. Prices will almost surely rise in coming months. We shall probably continue to experience inflationary pressure on the average over the coming years. The price rise, however, will be moderate. A major war aside, I cannot conceive that the monetary authorities will permit the quantity of money to rise at a rate that would produce inflation of more than, say, 3 to 10 percent a year. Such inflation will be unfortunate, but if permitted to occur reasonably openly and freely, not disastrous. And, despite all the talk, prices and wages will be permitted to rise in one way or another. The guideposts will be more talked about than they will be voluntarily complied with or enforced by extralegal pressure. Hypocrisy will enable effective evasion to be combined with self-congratulation. Debasing the coin of public and private morality is unfortunate, but in moderate doses not disastrous. The greatest harm will continue to be done by the measures taken to peg exchange rates. It is well to keep in mind Adam Smith's famous comment, "There is much ruin in a nation," but only to avoid overstating a good case, not to condone bad policy.

28

The Case against the Case against the Guideposts

ROBERT M. SOLOW

Robert M. Solow is Professor of Economics at Massachusetts Institute of Technology. This article first appeared in Guidelines: Informal Controls in the Market Place, *edited by George Shultz and Robert Aliber, in 1966.*

I choose this defensive-sounding title because it points to an important truth. The wage-price guideposts, to the extent that they can be said to constitute a policy, are not the sort of policy you would invent if you were inventing policies from scratch. They are the type of policy you back into as you search for ways to protect an imperfect economy from the worst consequences of its imperfect behavior. For this reason, it seems to me that the best way to start an evaluation of the wage-price guideposts is with recognition of the dilemma to which they are a response.

The Problem of Premature Inflation: Some Obvious Remedies

The problem is that modern mixed capitalist economies tend to generate unacceptably fast increases in money wages and prices while there is not general excess demand. No particular view of the economic process or of the determinants of demand need be implied by this observation. It is a fact, however, or at least it is widely believed to be a fact, that wages and prices begin to rise too rapidly for comfort while there is still quite a bit of unemployed labor and idle productive capacity and no important bottlenecks. This tendency creates a dilemma for public policy. Governments generally do not wish to acquiesce in an inflationary spiral; indeed, in our rather international trading world, governments may not be able to do so. On the other hand, governments value employment and output, for the very good reason that people value employment and output, so governments generally do not wish to choke off economic expansion while there is room for more.

This dilemma is not confined to the United States. Most of the advanced capitalist economies of the world have faced it, despite the differences in their wage- and price-making institutions. So far as I know, none of them has found a very satisfactory solution; and most of them have been driven to some form of "incomes policy," to something very like the wage-price guideposts. These policies have not been entirely successful either, but that may be too much to expect anyway.

It is no accident that the Council of Economic Advisers launched the local version of incomes policy in the January 1962 Economic Report, despite the fact that the unemployment rate was then near 6 percent and manufacturing capacity only 83 percent utilized, according to the McGraw-Hill survey. Wholesale prices were not then rising, nor did they begin to rise until 1965. But still the Council felt—with good reason—that it had to protect its flank against those who argued, even then, that an expansionary fiscal and monetary policy would dissipate itself almost immediately in inflationary wage and price behavior. The argument proved wrong; but that it could be seriously made suggests the nature and the seriousness of the problem of premature inflation.

Given the character of the problem, it is natural for an economist to turn elsewhere before he settles for anything so weak, so uncertain, and so uneven in its effects as exhortation. In particular, two possible policy lines present themselves as straightforward and natural. The first is simply to accept the universe: The appropriate remedy is either to restrict demand enough through fiscal and monetary means to keep the price level reasonably stable, or else to accept some inflation. The second approach is to recognize that the threat of premature inflation reflects significant departures from perfect competition in labor and product markets: The appropriate remedy is to create or restore competition by breaking up all concentrations of market power, whether in the hands of trade unions or large firms, and by eliminating all or most legal protections against domestic and foreign competition.

Both these suggestions have attractive aspects. The first promises that economic policy can be more or less confined to the impersonal tools of the fiscal and monetary policy that we know something about. The second caters to the economist's prejudice in favor of the mechanism of the competitive market. If there is a case against the case against the guideposts, part of it has to be that the first obvious remedy may be very costly, and the second obvious remedy is more than a little unrealistic.

The experience of the years 1958–64 certainly indicates that the economy can be run with quite a lot of slack, but not a catastrophic amount, so that the price level will more or less police itself. That is a possible policy. But it is not a costless policy. In the first place, one of the necessary concomitants of this policy is a pretty substantial unemployment rate. Since the incidence of unemployment is typically uneven, and the unevenness has no claim to equity, common decency requires that this policy be accompanied by a major reform and improvement of the unemployment compensation system, and possibly of other transfer payment systems as well. This is a budgetary cost, but not a real burden on the economy as a whole. In the second place, however, the maintenance of slack does represent a real burden to the economy as a whole in the form of unproduced output. It is not easy to make any estimate of that cost. The usual rule of thumb is that one-half point on the unemployment rate corresponds to something between 1 and 2 percent of real GNP. In that case, the amount of relief from inflation that could be had by keeping the unemployment rate one-half point higher than otherwise desirable would have an annual cost of about $10 billion at 1965 prices and GNP. Just because that is a large number does not mean that the price is not worth paying. Everyone must choose for himself. But it does mean that an alternative policy capable of having the same restraining effect as a half point of unemployment is a preferable policy unless it imposes social costs of about that order of magnitude.

The policy of heading off premature inflation by strengthening competition is in many ways the opposite of costly. Most economists, at least, have a preference for competition, free trade, mobility, and the like, on the ground that they promote economic efficiency, while any inequities that may result can be offset by other means. Most economists, therefore, would argue in favor of strengthening competition, free trade, and mobility even if there were no problem of premature inflation; all the more so, since there might be beneficial effects on the inflation front as well. But realism suggests that significant steps in this direction will be very slow in coming, if they come at all. In the meanwhile, the problem of premature inflation remains, and the unattainable best should not be allowed to become the enemy of the second best. To anyone who argues against guideposts that competition is the best policy, I reply: Yes indeed, and go to it, but meanwhile, . . .

The logic of a guidepost policy is, I suppose, something like this. In our imperfect world, there are important areas where market power is sufficiently concentrated that price and wage decisions are made with a significant amount of discretion. When times are reasonably good, that discretion may be exercised in ways that contribute to premature inflation. (Institutions with market power may actually succeed in exploiting the rest of the economy temporarily or permanently, or they may see their decisions cancelled out almost immediately by induced increases in other prices and wages.) People and institutions with market power may, in our culture, be fairly sensitive to public opinion. To the extent that they are, an educated and mobilized public opinion may exert some restraining pressure to forestall or limit premature inflation.

The January 1962 guideposts were intended to be a step in the educational process. Whatever else they have accomplished, or not accomplished, I think they, and the discussion they aroused, have surely made a dent on public thinking about wage and price behavior. I give an example: In 1962 it was often said that if money wages rose at the same rate as productivity and the price level were constant, labor would in effect appropriate all of the gains in productivity. There may still be people who don't realize that the effect would actually be to increase aggregate wages and aggregate profits at the same rate, preserving their proportional relations to one another. But there must be many fewer such people now.

The object of the guideposts was and is to hold up to the public—and to those participants in wage and price decisions who can exercise some discretion—a summary picture of how wages and prices *would* behave in a fairly smoothly functioning competitive market economy subject neither to major excess demand nor major deficiency of demand. The hope was that active discussion of the issues might induce the participants, in effect, to imitate a little more closely a few aspects of competitive price and wage behavior. If that happened, the expansion of real demand and the production of real output might be able to go a little further before unacceptable increases in the general price level would begin.

I think it is fair to say that no one connected with the guideposts expects or ever expected that they could have any major role to play either under conditions of generalized excess demand or under conditions of substantial slack in the economy. When unemployment is heavy and excess capacity is widespread, wages and prices are likely to police themselves. To expect the price level as a whole to fall is probably too much, but it is unlikely to rise, and if it does, not very much. Similarly, when demand is excessive in broad sectors of the economy, it is idle to believe that the price level can be talked out of rising. The guidepost idea does rest on the presumption that somewhere in between there is a zone of economic conditions, neither too tight nor too slack, in which

there is some tendency toward inflation, but a weak enough tendency so that an informed and mobilized public opinion can have effect.

Have the Guideposts Had an Effect on Wages and Prices?

The most common criticism of dependence on wage-price guideposts is that they simply do not work and have no effect on either wages or prices. Some of these criticisms simply cancel one another: For every employer who complains that unions take the guidepost figure for a floor, there is a union leader who complains that employers take it for a ceiling. Such evidence is worth nothing. Better evidence can be had, but is in the nature of the case uncertain. We may not be able to tell whether the guideposts have had any influence on wage and price decisions: first because there is no way to measure the "intensity" with which the guideposts have been pressed; and second because we have no universally accepted quantitative doctrine about how prices and money wages are determined in the absence of guideposts.

The best such quantitative explanation I know is that of Professor George Perry [now of the Brookings Institution]. He reconstructs the percentage change in hourly wages in manufacturing from one quarter to the same quarter of the next year in terms of four determinants. The determinants are the unemployment rate, the accompanying change in the Consumer Price Index, the rate of profit on capital in manufacturing, and the change in the rate of profit. He finds, as you would expect, that wages in manufacturing will rise more rapidly the lower the unemployment rate; the faster the cost of living has been rising, the higher are profits, and the faster they have been rising. The precise relationship is based on the experience of the manufacturing sector from 1948 to 1960; it explains the course of money wages quite well during that period.

When Perry's relationship is used to explain wage changes in manufacturing after 1960, it tells an interesting story. In 1961 and the first half of 1962, wages rose faster than the theory would expect. Beginning with the third quarter of 1962, and without exception for the next fourteen quarters to the end of 1965, wages rose more slowly than the theory would expect. Runs in the residuals are not uncommon, but this run is uncommonly long. Moreover, although the overestimation of wage changes was initially small, it became substantial in 1964 and 1965. In 1965, the annual increase in wage rates was about 1.7 percent lower than the 1948–60 experience would lead one to expect.

Is all of this difference attributable to the influence of the guideposts? Is any? I don't suppose any definite answer can be given. The timing certainly suggests that the guideposts had something to do with it. But econometric inference is rarely completely solid, and I have no doubt that someone who wanted strongly to resist that conclusion could produce a statistical model giving different results.

What does seem fairly clear is that manufacturing wages have gone up relatively slowly during the past few years, given the unemployment rate actually ruling, the good profits actually earned, and the increase in consumer prices that actually occurred. It is not farfetched to believe that the guideposts might have been an important factor in this structural change.

The object of the guideposts is to stall off premature inflation. Wages themselves are a matter of concern only because they bulk so large in total costs. If the guideposts served only to damp the increase in wages without holding down the price level, then their main result would simply be a transfer of income from wages to profits, and that is not their purpose. So the question arises whether there has been any visible change in price behavior.

All of the obstacles to clear-cut measurement of the wage effects apply equally to the price effects. Moreover, I know of no basic study like Perry's to serve as a starting-point for price behavior. I can report, however, on one small scale and partial experiment.

Year-to-year changes in the wholesale price index for all manufactures, between 1954 and 1965, can be explained moderately well in terms of the McGraw-Hill index of capacity utilization, and the accompanying year-to-year changes in labor costs per unit of output in manufacturing. As one would expect, the price index rises faster the higher the utilization of capacity and the faster unit labor costs increase. If one amends the relation among these variables to allow for a structural shift after 1962, the data suggest that wholesale prices rose about 7/10 of a point a year more slowly after 1962 than before, for any given utilization rate and change in unit labor costs. (This suggestion just fails of statistical significance, but I

suspect that lengthening the period and refining the data would correct that.)

Although this is the most tentative sort of conclusion, it is double-barreled. Even if there were no structural change in price behavior after 1962, it would mean that any reduction or slowdown in unit labor costs achieved through the guideposts was being passed on into prices to the usual extent. If in fact there was a structural change, it means that over and above the effect through labor costs there was a further tendency for prices to rise more slowly than earlier experience would suggest.

There is, as I have said, no firm reason to attribute these shifts in behavior to the guideposts. Nor is there any reason not to.

Would the Guideposts Freeze the Distribution of Income and Interfere with Free Markets?

It is often remarked—as indeed I remarked earlier—that if wage rates on the average were to rise precisely as fast as productivity, while the price levels were to remain constant, then the proportions of the national income going to labor and to property would stay unchanged. To take some very round numbers, suppose production per man-year were $10,000 and the annual wage $7,500, so that $2,500 went to owners of capital. If productivity and the annual wage were both to rise by that famous 3.2 percent, and prices were unchanged, then output per man-year would go to $10,320 and the wage to $7,740. This would leave $2,580 in property income. Notice that the $320 of new output per man-year has been divided in the 75-25 proportions as the original $10,000, so that the overall proportional distribution of the national income is undisturbed.

This algebraic fact has led to criticism of the guidepost concept. The argument is not at all about the equity or justice of the current distribution of income. The argument is that the distribution of income—before taxes and transfers—is part of the market process in our economy. Changes in incomes are supposed to guide efficiently the allocation of resources. To freeze the distribution of income in a pattern that may be suitable to current conditions can lead to distortions and inefficiencies if economic conditions change and call for a changed distribution of income.

It seems to me that this argument has ro practical weight at all. It is rendered trivial by two facts. The first is that the division of the national income between labor and property incomes is among the slower-changing characteristics of our economy, or of any Western economy. The second is that neither the guideposts nor any other such quantitative prescription can be satisfied *exactly*. Suppose that wage rates do follow the guideposts exactly. Then if the price level, instead of remaining constant, goes up by, say, 1 percent in a year, the share of wages in national income will fall by 1 percent—that is, by about 3/4 of one percentage point. If, on the other hand, the price level should fall by 1 percent, the share of wages in national income would rise by 3/4 of 1 percentage point. That may not seem like much, but actually it is quite a lot, more than enough to provide all the flexibility that our economic system is likely to need.

In the twenty years since the end of the war, the proportion of "compensation of employees" to national income has moved about within a narrow range, say from 65 percent to 71 percent. There is no reason to suppose that market forces will always want to keep the figure within those bounds, but there is every reason to believe that market forces will never, or hardly ever, want to move the proportional distribution of income very rapidly. As the numerical example shows, if wages adhered to the guidelines, the distribution of income could get from one end of its postwar range to the other in about eight years, with an annual rate of inflation or deflation never exceeding one percent.

There is no practical question, then, of freezing the distribution of income. The normal amount of play in any such policy gives all the room needed for the market to operate. It would be possible to provide formally for more flexibility if that were needed. If the wages guideposts were expressed in terms of a fairly narrow range, say from 3.0 to 3.5 percent per year, this would serve two purposes. For one thing, it would more nearly express the uncertainty in any estimate of the trend increase in productivity. And secondly, it would permit the outcome to be nearer the bottom or the top of the range, depending on "market forces." Even a steady price level would then permit some drift in the distribution of income.

Even apart from this question of distribution, one hears it said that the guideposts are a dangerous interference in the free market, even a form of price control. At least this criticism is inconsistent with the other one that claims the guideposts to be ineffective. With some ingenuity, one could probably cook up a set of assumptions under which the guideposts had no effect on wage-price behavior, yet managed to do harm to the market economy. But this seems farfetched to me. If they are a real interference with the market, they must be partially effective.

I would contend that it is also farfetched to describe the wage-price guideposts as anything remotely like a system of wage and price controls. But in any case I am not concerned with the way the guideposts have been used by this President or that President, but with the way they were intended. They were intended, as I mentioned earlier, as a device for the education and mobilization of public opinion. It is no doubt inevitable that an activist President will want to help public opinion along. But that is still a far cry from wage and price control.

Moreover, by both intent and necessity, the guideposts can influence only those wage and price decisions in which the parties have a certain amount of discretion. Atomistic textbook competitors, having no discretion, will not be much influenced by either public opinion or the White House. But where there is enough market power, and hence enough discretion, for the guideposts to be a force, there is little or no reason to believe that the "free market" outcome will be in the public interest. The usual presumption against public interference in the market process does not hold. This conclusion does not depend on any very exact evaluation of the amount of competition to which the steel industry, or the aluminum industry, or the tobacco industry, or the United Automobile Workers, or the building trades unions are subject. It is enough that none of them is, and none of them thinks it is, selling against a nearly infinitely elastic demand curve.

Naturally, the fact that a concentrated industry and a strong union may make decisions not in the public interest does not automatically mean that what the guideposts suggest will be better. That question needs to be decided on its merits. Yet, the guideposts are intended to give a summary description of a well-functioning market economy; within limits they can be expected to represent the public interest fairly well. But it is much more important to realize that the public interest does need representation.

It is worth remembering, in this connection, that the guideposts are intended to have an effect on the general level of money wages and prices, not on relative wages and relative prices. Most of the things we expect free markets to accomplish are "real" things, more or less independent of the price level. Ideally, the guideposts should permit markets to allocate resources freely, insuring only that the price level not drift up in the process. The January 1962 Economic Report said: "It is desirable that labor and management should bargain explicitly about the distribution of the income of particular firms or industries. It is, however, undesirable that they should bargain implicitly about general price level." In practice, one must admit, the guideposts will operate unevenly; relative prices and resource allocation may thus be affected. One can hope that these effects are second-order.

Unevenness and Inequity

This inevitable unevenness in operation strikes me as the main weakness in the guideposts. Public opinion is bound to have its greatest impact on markets that are centralized and conspicuous. That may not be all bad; centralization and discretionary power over prices and wages may be correlated. But there are obvious instances in which the correlation is broken, in which considerable market power in local markets goes along with decentralization and near-immunity to pressure from public opinion. The construction industry and the building trades unions are the standard illustration; parts of trade and transportation may provide other examples.

This weakness must simply be admitted. It is dangerous not only because it invites inefficient relative price effects, but because policy that tries to mobilize public opinion on behalf of the public interest will inevitably find its foundations sapped by obvious inequity. There is probably no general solution to the problem. There may, however, be ad hoc solutions in special cases.

Another possible solution to the problem of uneven impact might be to formalize the guideposts into some sort of advance-notice and/or public hearing procedure, perhaps through a committee of Congress. I am opposed to this sort of development. It would be a move away from the original conception of the guideposts as an educational device, in the direction of a system of semiformal price controls. It is unlikely that Congress would favor that much of a break with the past; if we are to espouse unlikely legislation, I

would rather favor the promotion of competition and the reduction of tariff protection.

There is a different respect in which the involvement of Congress might be a good idea. Up to now, the burden of informing and mobilizing public opinion has fallen to the President and to the Chairman of the Council of Economic Advisers. This seems to be a mistake. The prestige of the President is probably too important a commodity to be spent in a way that invites occasional rebuff. And the prestige of the Council of Economic Advisers, taken by itself, is probably insufficient to carry the load. It might be helpful, therefore, if individual senators and congressmen would take part in the public debate, in their capacity as leaders and formers of public opinion. Even hearings are a possibility, provided they are hearings devoted to ordinary pieces of legislation —past or future—or to expert testimony and not to individual wage bargains or price decisions.

How Should the Guidepost Figure Be Set?

In principle, the guidepost figure for wages is supposed to be the trend-increase in productivity for the economy as a whole. This is a difficult thing to measure; indeed, the concept is not entirely free of ambiguity. For example, one clearly wants a figure free of the effects of short-term changes in capacity utilization in industry, because otherwise the result would be to transfer the risks of enterprise from profits to wages, and that is not the intent. This suggests using a long-run trend figure. On the other hand, it seems faintly ridiculous that the permissible wage increase today should be made to depend on what was happening to productivity a few decades ago. Actually, this particular problem is primarily a matter of measurement, not of ambiguity in principle. A group of technicians could probably come to reasonable agreement. The difficulty is, however, that this number produced by technicians needs to be believed and used by the public and others.

Consider the unedifying spectacle of earlier this year. Should the administration continue to promulgate last year's guidepost figure of 3.2 percent per year, or should it continue to use the method by which last year's figure was calculated, which would yield 3.6 percent for this year? The decision to stay with 3.2 percent was clearly the right one in substance; nobody with any sense believes that the steady-state rate of increase of output per man-hour in the private economy is now 3.6 percent annually. The whole difficulty was created by the explicit adoption of a five-year moving average as the "official" method for calculating the trend-increase in productivity. This is clearly not a technician's method; a technician would make a more explicit statistical decomposition into cyclical and secular productivity change. The five-year moving average was clearly a compromise expedient—a method anyone could understand, which happened to give the same numerical answer as the technicians' methods.

I am inclined to think that the technicians' methods should prevail. I realize that there are grave difficulties with this view. In the first place, the parties to collective bargaining are likely to resent being presented with a figure they had no part in setting. That is understandable. The trouble is that the parties' mutual relationship is naturally a bargaining one; presented with an opportunity to set or influence the guidepost figure, they will naturally bargain over it. But that would destroy any claim that the guidepost figure might have to be an objectively determined number. In the second place, I gather that some members of Congress would like to take a hand in guidepost-setting. Again, one can understand why. But in principle the guidepost figure is not something one sets, it is something that one finds out. Congress can investigate, of course, but it is far from clear that its methods are ideal for investigating the subtler

properties of economic time series. I can imagine that every so often Congress might like to hear expert testimony on how the exercise is being carried out; that would be salutary. But that would be different from an airing of predictable majority, minority, and interested-party views.

There is another sort of problem which is not open to technical solution and on which exchanges of opinion might be useful. It was easy to begin talking about wage-price guideposts in 1962 because the immediate history was one of approximate price stability. But suppose prices have been rising, and suppose that it is very unlikely that they can be made to level out in one year. Then it is difficult for labor to acquiesce in a figure for money wage increases which would give the right real-wage increase only if prices were constant.

That would be to acquiesce to a subnormal increase in real wages and a supernormal increase in profits. On the other hand, to add the current rate of price increase to the rate of productivity increase would be to throw the entire burden onto profits or, more likely, guarantee that prices will continue to rise. What is needed is some target pace for slowing down the price trend over a couple of years. One can imagine rational discussion of such a problem in a small country with centralized and enlightened trade union and employer association leadership. (Even then I'm not sure one can imagine anything actually being accomplished on so difficult a matter.) It is less easy to imagine such discussion in the United States.

PART FOUR

Economic Growth and the Environment

During much of the 1960s, most countries, including the United States, regarded economic growth as a major social goal. At the start of the decade, John F. Kennedy ran for President on a platform emphasizing the importance of economic growth. But, during the 1970s, many politicians and not a few economists have questioned the desirability of further economic growth. In the opening article, E.J. Mishan argues that "continued economic growth by Western societies is more likely on balance to reduce rather than increase social welfare." Indeed, he characterizes the American economy "as a spectacle of growing resources pressing against limited wants."

Another group, composed principally of engineers, is concerned about the desirability of further economic growth because they feel that we will run out of raw materials. In particular, the Club of Rome's study of "The Limits to Growth," carried out by Dennis Meadows and his colleagues, concludes that continued economic growth is impossible because of the drain on our raw materials and the increases in pollution and population. Most economists disagree with this conclusion. As Robert Solow points out in the next paper, there are many inadequacies in the Meadows model, the most notable defect being the absence of any recognition of the workings of the price system. Also, Solow points out some of the factors leading a great many economists to oppose Mishan's position.

Population growth can have an important impact on the rate of economic growth; and the next article, taken from Thomas Malthus's famous *Essay on the Principle of Population*, presents his ideas concerning the tendency of population to increase beyond the available food supplies. Economic growth is due in considerable measure to productivity growth and technological change. The National Productivity Commission, in the following selection, describes the changes over time in U.S. labor productivity, compares labor productivity in the United States with that in other countries, and discusses policies to raise productivity in this country. In the next paper, the editor summarizes what is known about the relationship between research and development (R and D) on the one hand, and the rate of economic growth and productivity increase on the other. Because R and D can result in external economies, it is often argued that a market economy will tend to underinvest in R and D. The evidence bearing on this issue, as well as the relevant theory, is discussed in this paper.

One reason why there is less enthusiasm than formerly for economic growth is that economic growth tends to be associated with increases in pollution. The more goods and services that we produce, the more wastes that we must dispose of. In the next selection, Edwin S. Mills describes how excessive pollution arises in a market economy due to the existence of external diseconomies with respect to the disposal of wastes. In addition, he describes various ways of controlling pollution, including direct regulation, subsidies, and effluent fees, and he makes a tentative proposal concerning public policy regarding air pollution. Finally, in the last paper in this part, the Council of Economic Advisers discusses some of the problems involved in devising a set of economic rules to safeguard the environment. This article includes both a description of the relevant theory and the practical considerations involved in applying this theory to the American economy.

29

The Case against Economic Growth

E. J. MISHAN

E. J. Mishan is Professor of Economics at the London School of Economics and Political Science. This selection is taken from his book The Costs of Economic Growth, *published in 1967.*

The notion of economic expansion as a process on balance beneficial to society goes back at least a couple of centuries, about which time, however, the case in favor was much stronger than it is today when we are not only incomparably wealthier but also suffering from many disagreeable by-products of rapid technological change. Yet so entrenched are the interests involved, commercial, institutional, and scientific, and so pervasive the influence of modern communications, that economic growth has embedded itself in the ethos of our civilization. Despite the manifest disamenities caused by the postwar economic expansion, no one today seeking to advance his position in the hierarchy of government or business fails to pay homage to this sovereign concept.

[My own] general conclusion is that the continued pursuit of economic growth by Western societies is more likely on balance to reduce rather than increase social welfare. And some additional light on the pattern of arguments employed is shed by enumerating the set of conditions that, if met, would ensure a positive relation between economic growth and welfare.

First, that the economy be highly competitive in structure in all its branches, or else so organized that in all sectors the outputs of goods are such that their prices tend to equal their corresponding marginal costs.

Second, that all the measurable effects on other people or firms arising in the production and use of any good—other than those effects which already register on the market mechanism in the form of alterations in product and factor prices—be brought into the cost calculus.

Third, that in increasing *per capita* output over time the process of economic growth does not bring about a less equitable distribution of income.

Fourth, that the consuming public be fully conversant with the comparative qualities and performances of all new goods coming on to the market.

Fifth, that the public, regarded as producers, become no worse off in adapting themselves to new techniques of production.

Sixth, that the so-called relative income hypothesis does not hold; or, less stringently, that an overall increase in real income *per capita* will have more than negligible effects in making some people feel better off without making others feel worse off.

Seventh, that the welfare experienced by men from sources other than goods produced by the economic system is small enough to be neglected.

Though it goes without saying that none of these conditions is likely to be met in today's wealthy societies, some of the conditions are more important than others. Observations, both slight and significant on each of the first six conditions, may be found in the professional literature. Since it lends itself to elegant formulation, the first condition is the one treated in most detail. Indeed, owing to the traditional presumption in favor of competition and free trade, measures of the degree of monopoly in the economy and, occasionally, of allocative waste associated therewith, are of continued interest to economists. Yet the scope for improvements in welfare by policies designed to increase competition is, I should think, very slight in comparison with the losses of welfare from neglect of the other conditions. The concern with external effects, relevant to the second condition, is hardly less pronounced. A good deal of the interest in these external effects, however, may be imputed to the intellectual fascination with optimality problems—not alas, to universal alarm at what is happening to our environment. I have suggested that the potential contribution to social welfare of adopting a policy of correcting outstanding external diseconomies is vastly underrated, and this for several reasons: (1) because of the present difficulties of measurement; (2) because of the mistaken view that the disamenities inflicted are limited, since there appear to be incentives to voluntary agreement for their control; and (3) because of a sense of resignation induced by the slippery problems connected with hypothetical and actual compensation. To these professional reasons we may add the popular impression—which in consequence of the above reasons also appeals to many economists—that economic growth provides a more direct and certain means of advancing welfare.

In illustrating some of the chief sources of external diseconomies no attempt was made to disguise the author's conviction that the invention of the private automobile is one of the great disasters to have befallen the human race. Given the absence of controls, the growth of population and its increased wealth and urbanization would, in any case, have produced overgrown cities. Commercial and munici-

pal greed, coupled with architectural apathy, share the responsibility for a litter of shabby buildings. But it needed the motor-car to consummate these developments, to fill our days with clamor and fumes, to suburbanize the countryside and to subutopianize suburbia, and to ensure that any resort which became accessible should simultaneously become unattractive. The motor industry has come to dominate the economy as brazenly as its products dominate our physical environment, and our psychology. The common sight today, of street after street strewn thick with layabout cars, no longer dismays us.

The other two rapidly growing sources of disamenity used in illustrating the external diseconomies thesis were air travel and tourism. No effective legislation putting the onus on airlines has been contemplated. The noise created is limited only by what the authorities believe people can be made to put up with. And the public may be conditioned over time to bear with increasing disturbance simply (1) because of the difficulties and cost of organizing protests; (2) because of the apparent hopelessness of prevailing upon the authorities to put the claims of the residents before the claims of "progress," that is, the airlines; and (3) because of the timidity felt in pressing one's claims against so effective a retort as "the national interest." If there is a national interest, however, our discussion reveals the case for the Government's bearing the cost of its safeguard; not the unfortunate victims of aerial disturbance. The least that should be done to promote social welfare is to extend to the public some choice in the matter by legislating for wholly noise-free zones— zones that are, however, desirable in other respects and easily accessible.

As for the rapid destruction by mass tourism of the world's dwindling resources of natural beauty, a small contribution towards preservation could be made by the prohibition of motorized vehicles within selected areas and by the discontinuing of air services to such areas. Once the public becomes aware of the spread of devastation, international agreement on more radical measures may be forthcoming—if by then there is anything left worth preserving.

In sum, [my] thesis is that if men are concerned primarily with human welfare, and not primarily with productivity conceived as a good in itself, they should reject economic growth as a prior aim of policy in favor of a policy of seeking to apply more selective criteria of welfare. Such a policy would involve (1) legislation recognizing the individual's right to amenity, which legislation would spearhead the attack on much of our postwar blight; and (2) a substantial diversion of investible resources from industry to the task of replanning our towns and cities—in general, to direct our national resources and our ingenuity to recreating an environment that will gratify and inspire men. Finally, if public opinion cannot, for the present, be swung overwhelmingly towards this alternative view of the primary ends of policy, any regard at all to the declared doctrine of increasing the range of choices available to men warrants an extension to existing minorities of separate facilities in matters both large and small—though especially in respect of viable areas wherein a man of moderate means may choose to dwell unmolested by those particular features of modern technology that most disturb his equanimity.

If the moving spirit behind economic growth were to speak, its motto would be "Enough does not suffice." The classical description of an economic system makes sense in today's advanced economy only when stood on its head. Certainly the American economy presents us with a spectacle of growing resources pressing against limited wants. Moreover, the pace of change in the patterns of people's wants destroys the base on which the economist's comparison of social welfare is raised: if all seven conditions mentioned were met, the mere fact of continually changing tastes alone would prevent the economist from inferring that economic growth *per capita* increased welfare. Moreover, the vagaries of fashion can become burdensome and the multiplication of goods disconcerting.

Once we move away from the economist's frame of reference, other factors bearing on social welfare loom large. Expanding markets in conditions of material abundance depend upon men's dissatisfaction with their lot being perpetually renewed. Whether individual campaigns are successful or not, the institution of commercial advertising accentuates the materialistic tendencies in society and promotes the view that the things that matter most are the things money will buy—a view to which the young, who have plenty of

need of the wherewithal, if they are to avail themselves of the widely advertised opportunities for fast living and cool extravagance, are peculiarly vulnerable, and which explains much of their vociferous inpatience and increasing violence.

These and other informal considerations lead to pessimistic conclusions. Technological innovations may offer to add to men's material opportunities. But by increasing the risks of their obsolescence it adds also to their anxiety. Swifter means of communications have the paradoxical effect of isolating people; increased mobility has led to more hours commuting; increased automobilization to increased separation; more television to less communication. In consequence, people know less of their neighbors than ever before in history.

The pursuit of efficiency, itself regarded as the lifeblood of progress, is directed towards reducing the dependence of people on each other, and increasing their dependence on the machine. Indeed, by a gradual displacement of human effort from every aspect of living, technology will eventually enable us to slip swiftly through our allotted years with scarce enough sense of physical friction to be certain we are still alive.

Considerations such as these, which do not lend themselves to formal treatment, are crucial to the issue of human welfare. And the apparent inevitability of technological advance does not thereby render them irrelevant. Death too is inevitable. But one does not feel compelled to hurry towards it on that account. Once we descry the sort of world towards which technological growth is bearing us, it is well worth discussing whether humanity will find it more congenial or not. If, on reflection, we view the prospects with misgivings, we are, at least, freed from the obligation to join in the frequent incantations of our patriotic growthmen. More positively, we have an additional incentive to support the policy of reducing industrial investment in favor of large-scale replanning of our cities, and of restoring and enhancing the beauty of many of our villages, towns and resorts.

30

The Limits to Growth

DONELLA MEADOWS, DENNIS
MEADOWS, J. RANDERS,
and WILLIAM BEHRENS

Donella Meadows, Dennis Meadows, J. Randers, and William Behrens carried out the well-known study of the limits of economic growth for the Club of Rome. The following article is from their book The Limits to Growth, *published in 1972.*

I do not wish to seem overdramatic, but I can only conclude from the information that is available to me as Secretary-General, that the Members of the United Nations have perhaps ten years left in which to subordinate their ancient quarrels and launch a global partnership to curb the arms race, to improve the human environment, to defuse the population explosion, and to supply the required momentum to development efforts. If such a global partnership is not forged within the next decade, then I very much fear that the problems I have mentioned will have reached such staggering proportions that they will be beyond our capacity to control.

U THANT, 1969

The problems U Thant mentions—the arms race, environmental deterioration, the population explosion, and economic stagnation—are often cited as the central, long-term problems of modern man. Many people believe that the future course of human society, perhaps even the survival of human society, depends on the speed and effectiveness with which the world responds to these issues. And yet only a small fraction of the world's population is actively concerned with understanding these problems or seeking their solutions.

Human Perspectives

Every person in the world faces a series of pressures and problems that require his attention and action. These problems affect him at many different levels. He may spend much of his time trying to find tomorrow's food for himself and his family. He may be concerned about personal power or the power of the nation in which he lives. He may worry about a world war during his lifetime, or a war next week with a rival clan in his neighborhood.

These very different levels of human concern can be represented on a graph like that in Figure 1. The graph has two dimensions, space and time. Every human concern can be located at some point on the graph, depending on how much geographical space it includes and how far it extends in time. Most people's worries are concentrated in the lower left-hand corner of the graph. Life for these people is difficult, and they must devote nearly all of their efforts to providing for themselves and their families, day by day. Other people think about and act on problems farther out on the space or time axes. The pressures they perceive involve not only themselves, but the community with which they identify. The actions they take extend not only days, but weeks or years into the future.

A person's time and space perspectives depend on his culture, his past experience, and the immediacy of the problems confronting him on each level. Most people must have successfully solved the problems in a smaller area before they move their concerns to a larger one. In general the larger the space and the longer the time associated with a problem, the smaller the number of people who are actually concerned with its solution.

There can be disappointments and dangers in limiting one's view to an area that is too small. There are many examples of a person striving with all his might to solve some immediate, local problem, only to find his efforts defeated by events occurring in a larger context. A farmer's carefully maintained fields can be destroyed by an international war. Local officials' plans can be overturned by a national policy. A country's economic development can be thwarted by a lack of world demand for its products. Indeed there is increasing concern today that most personal and national objectives may ultimately be frustrated by long-term, global trends such as those mentioned by U Thant.

Are the implications of these global trends actually so threatening that their resolution should take precedence over local, short-term concerns?

Is it true, as U Thant suggested, that there remains less than a decade to bring these trends under control?

If they are not brought under control, what will the consequences be?

What methods does mankind have for solving global problems, and what will be the results and the costs of employing each of them?

These are the questions that we have been investigating in the first phase of The Club of Rome's Project on the Predicament of Mankind. Our concerns thus fall in the upper right-hand corner of the space-time graph.

Problems and Models

Every person approaches his problems, wherever they occur on the space-time graph, with the help of models. A model is simply an ordered set of assumptions about a complex system. It is an attempt to understand some aspect of the infinitely varied world by selecting from perceptions and past experience a set of general observations applicable to the problem at hand. A farmer uses a mental model of his land, his assets, market prospects, and past weather conditions to decide which crops to plant each year. A surveyor constructs a physical model—a map—to help in planning a road. An economist uses mathematical models to understand and predict the flow of international trade.

Decision-makers at every level unconsciously use mental models to choose among policies that will shape our future world. These mental models are, of necessity, very simple when compared with the reality from which they are abstracted. The human brain, remarkable as it is, can only keep track of a limited number of the complicated, simultaneous interactions that determine the nature of the real world.

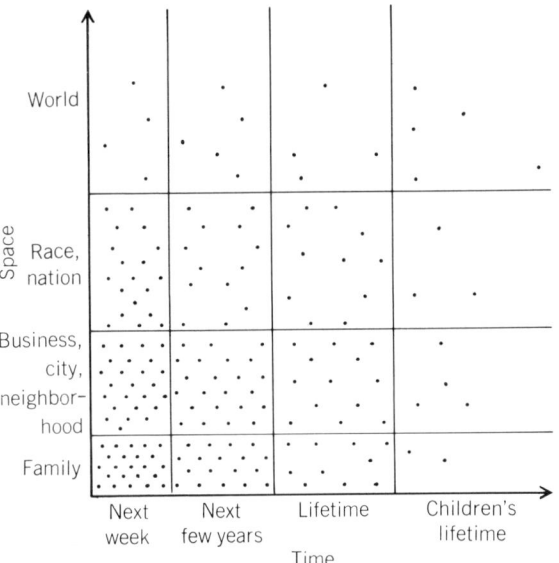

Figure 1. **Human Perspectives**

Although the perspectives of the world's people vary in space and in time, every human concern falls somewhere on the space-time graph. The majority of the world's people are concerned with matters that affect only family or friends over a short period of time. Others look farther ahead in time or over a larger area—a city or a nation. Only a very few people have a global perspective that extends far into the future.

We, too, have used a model. Ours is a formal, written model of the world.[1] It constitutes a preliminary attempt to improve our mental models of long-term, global problems by combining the large amount of information that is already in human minds and in written records with the new information-processing tools that mankind's increasing knowledge has produced—the scientific method, systems analysis, and the modern computer.

Our world model was built specifically to investigate five major trends of global concern—accelerating industrialization, rapid population growth, widespread malnutrition, depletion of nonrenewable resources, and a deteriorating environment. These trends are all interconnected in many ways, and their development is measured in decades or centuries, rather than in months or years. With the model we are seeking to understand the causes of these trends, their interrelationships, and their implications as much as one hundred years in the future.

The model we have constructed is, like every other model, imperfect, oversimplified, and unfinished. We are well aware of its shortcomings, but we believe that it is the most useful model now available for dealing with problems far out on the space-time graph. To our knowledge it is the only formal model in existence that is truly global in scope, that has a time horizon longer than thirty years, and that includes important variables such as population, food production, and pollution, not as independent entities, but as dynamically interacting elements, as they are in the real world.

Since ours is a formal, or mathematical, model it also has two important advantages over mental models. First, every assumption we make is written in a precise form so that it is open to inspection and criticism by all. Second, after the assumptions have been scrutinized, discussed, and revised to agree with our best current knowledge, their implications for the future behavior of the world system can be traced without error by a computer, no matter how complicated they become.

We feel that the advantages listed above make this model unique among all mathematical and mental world models available to us today. But there is no reason to be satisfied with it in its present form. We

intend to alter, expand, and improve it as our own knowledge and the world data base gradually improve.

In spite of the preliminary state of our work, we believe it is important to publish the model and our findings now. Decisions are being made every day, in every part of the world, that will affect the physical, economic, and social conditions of the world system for decades to come. These decisions cannot wait for perfect models and total understanding. They will be made on the basis of some model, mental or written, in any case. We feel that the model described here is already sufficiently developed to be of some use to decision-makers. Furthermore, the basic behavior modes we have already observed in this model appear to be so fundamental and general that we do not expect our broad conclusions to be substantially altered by further revisions.

We have used a computer as a tool to aid our own understanding of the causes and consequences of the accelerating trends that characterize the modern world, but familiarity with computers is by no means necessary to comprehend or to discuss our conclusions. The implications of those accelerating trends raise issues that go far beyond the proper domain of a purely scientific document. They must be debated by a wider community than that of scientists alone. Our purpose here is to open that debate.

The following conclusions have emerged from our work so far. We are by no means the first group to have stated them. For the past several decades, people who have looked at the world with a global, long-term perspective have reached similar conclusions. Nevertheless, the vast majority of policy-makers seems to be actively pursuing goals that are inconsistent with these results.

Our conclusions are:

1. If the present growth trends in world population, industrialization, pollution, food production, and resource depletion continue unchanged, the limits to growth on this planet will be reached sometime within the next one hundred years. The most probable result will be a rather sudden and uncontrollable decline in both population and industrial capacity.

2. It is possible to alter these growth trends and to establish a condition of ecological and economic stability that is sustainable far into the future. The state of global equilibrium could be designed so that the basic material needs of each person on earth are satisfied and each person has an equal opportunity to realize his individual human potential.

---

[1]The prototype model on which we have based our work was designed by Professor Jay W. Forrester of the Massachusetts Institute of Technology. A description of that model has been published in his book *World Dynamics* (Cambridge, Mass.: Wright-Allen Press, 1971).

3. If the world's people decide to strive for this second outcome rather than the first, the sooner they begin working to attain it, the greater will be their chances of success.

These conclusions are so far-reaching and raise so many questions for further study that we are quite frankly overwhelmed by the enormity of the job that must be done. We hope that people in many fields of study and in many countries of the world, will raise the space and time horizons of their concerns and join us in understanding and preparing for a period of great transition—the transition from growth to global equilibrium.

31

Is the End of the World at Hand?

ROBERT M. SOLOW

Robert M. Solow is Professor of Economics at Massachusetts Institute of Technology. This article was published in Challenge *in 1973.*

I was having a hard time figuring out how to begin when I came across an excerpt from an interview with my MIT colleague Professor Jay Forrester, who is either the Christopher Columbus or the Dr. Strangelove of this business, depending on how you look at it. Forrester said he would like to see about 100 individuals, the most gifted and best qualified in the world, brought together in a team to make a psychosocial analysis of the problem of world equilibrium. He thought it would take about ten years. When he was asked to define the composition of his problem-solving group, Forrester said: "Above all it shouldn't be mostly made up of professors. One would include people who had been successful in their personal careers, whether in politics, business, or anywhere else. We should also need radical philosophers, but we should take care to keep out representatives of the social sciences. Such people always want to go to the bottom of a particular problem. What we want to look at are the problems caused by interactions."

I don't know what you call people who believe they can be wrong about everything in particular, but expect to be lucky enough somehow to get it right on the interactions. They may be descendants of the famous merchant Lapidus, who said he lost money on every item he sold, but made it up on the volume. Well, I suppose that as an economist I am a representative of the social sciences; and I'm prepared to play out the role by talking about first principles and trying to say what the Growth vs. No-Growth business is really about. This is going to involve me in the old academic ploy of saying over and over again what I'm not talking about before I ever actually say what I think I am talking about. But I'm afraid that some of those boring distinctions are part of the price you have to pay for getting it right.

First of all, there are (at least) two separate questions you can ask about the prospects for economic growth. You can ask: Is growth desirable? Or you can ask: Is growth possible? I suppose that if continued economic growth is not possible, it hardly matters whether or not it's desirable. But if it is possible, it's presumably not inevitable, so we can discuss whether we should want it. But they are separate questions, and an answer to one of them is not necessarily an answer to the other. My main business is with the question about the possibility of continued growth; I want to discuss the validity of the negative answer given by the "Doomsday Models" associated with the names of Forrester and Meadows (and MIT!) and, to a lesser extent, with the group of English scientists who published a manifesto called "Blueprint for Survival." The main concern of Dr. E.J. Mishan, on the other hand, was with the desirability of continued economic growth (and, at least by implication, with the desirability of past economic growth). If I spend a few minutes poaching on his territory, it is mainly because that seems like a good way to get some concepts straight, but also just to keep a discussion going.

Sorting Out the Issues

Arguments about the desirability of economic growth often turn quickly into arguments about the "quality" of modern life. One gets the notion that you favor growth if you are the sort of person whose idea of heaven is to drive at ninety miles an hour down a six-lane highway reading billboards, in order to pollute the air over some crowded lake with the exhaust from twin 100-horsepower outboards, and whose idea of food is Cocoa Krispies. On the other hand, to be against economic growth is to be a granola-eating, backpacking, transcendental-meditating canoe freak. That may even be a true statistical association, but I will argue that there is no necessary or logical connection between your answer to the growth question and your answer to the quality-of-life question. Suppose there were no issue about economic growth; suppose it were impossible; suppose each man or each woman were equipped to have only two children (one bomb under each wing); suppose we were stuck with the technology we have now and had no concept of invention, or even of increased mechanization through capital investment. We could still argue about the relative merits of cutting timber for building houses or leaving it stand to be enjoyed as forest. Some people would still be willing to breathe carbon monoxide in big cities in return for the excitement of urban life, while others would prefer cleaner air and fewer TV channels. Macy's would still not tell Gimbel's. Admen would still try to tell you that all those beautiful women are actually just looking for somebody who smokes Winchesters, thus managing to insult both men and women at once. Some people

would still bring transistor radios to the beach. All or nearly all of the arguments about the quality of life would be just as valid if the question of growth never arose.

I won't go so far as to say there is no connection. In particular, one can argue that if population density were low enough, people would interfere much less with each other, and everyone could find a part of the world and style of civilization that suited him. Then differences of opinion about the quality of life wouldn't matter so much. Even if I grant the truth of that observation, it is still the case that, from here on out, questions about the quality of life are separable from questions about the desirability of growth. If growth stopped, there would be just about as much to complain about; and, as I shall argue later on, one can imagine continued growth that is directed against pollution, against congestion, against sliced white bread.

I suppose it is only fair to admit that if you get very enthusiastic about economic growth you are likely to be attracted to easily quantifiable and measurable things as objects of study, to point at with pride or to view with alarm. You are likely to pay less attention to important, intangible aspects of the standard of living. Although you can't know whether people are happier than they used to be, you can at least determine that they drink more orange juice or take more aspirin. But that's mere weakness of imagination and has nothing to do in principle with the desirability of economic growth, let alone with its possibility.

There is another practical argument that is often made; and although it is important, it sometimes serves as a way of avoiding coming to grips with the real issues. This argument says that economic growth, increasing output per person, is the only way we are likely to achieve a more equitable distribution of income in society. There is a lot of home truth in that. It is inevitably less likely that a middle-class electorate will vote to redistribute part of its own income to the poor than that it will be willing to allocate a slightly larger share of a growing total. Even more pessimistically, I might suggest that even a given relative distribution of income, supposing it cannot be made more nearly equal, for political or other reasons, is less unattractive if the absolute standard of living at the bottom is fairly high than it is if the absolute standard at the bottom is very low. From this point of view, even if economic growth doesn't lead to more equity in distribution, it makes the inequity we've got more tolerable. I think it is one of the lessons of history as recent as the McGovern campaign that this is a realistic statement of the prospects.

It is even clearer if one looks, not at the distribution of income within a rich country like the U.S., but at the distribution of income between the developed countries of the world and the underveloped ones. The rich Western nations have never been able to agree on the principle of allocating as much as one percent of their GNP to aid underveloped countries. They are unlikely to be willing to share their wealth on any substantial scale with the poor countries. Even if they were, there are so many more poor people in the world that an equally shared income would be quite low. The *only* prospect of a decent life for Asia, Africa, and Latin America is in more total output.

But I point this out only to warn you that it is not the heart of the question. I think that those who oppose continued growth should in honesty face up to the implications of their position for distributional equity and the prospects of the world's poor. I think those who favor continued growth on the grounds that only thus can we achieve some real equality ought to be serious about that. If economic growth with equality is a good thing, it doesn't follow that economic growth with a lot of pious talk about equality is a good thing. In principle, we can have growth with or without equity; and we can have stagnation with or without equity. An argument about first principles should keep those things separate.

What Has Posterity Done for Us?

Well, then, what is the problem of economic growth all about? (I'm giving a definition now, not stating a fact, so all I can say is that I think this way of looking at it contributes to clarity of thought.) Whenever there is a question about what to do, the desirability of economic growth turns on the claims of the future against the claims of the present. The pro-growth man is someone who is prepared to sacrifice something useful and desirable right now so that people should be better off in the future; the anti-growth man is someone who thinks that is unnecessary or undesirable. The nature of the sacrifice of present enjoyment for future enjoyment can be almost anything. The classic example is investment: We can use our labor and our resources to build very durable things like roads or subways or factories or blast furnaces or dams that will be used for a long time by people who were not even born when those things were created, and so

will certainly have contributed nothing to their construction. That labor and those resources can just as well be used to produce shorter-run pleasures for us now.

Such a sacrifice of current consumption on behalf of the future may not strike you as much of a sacrifice. But that's because you live in a country that is already rich; if you had lived in Stalin's Russia, that need to sacrifice would be one of the reasons you would have been given to explain why you had to live without comfort and pleasures while the Ministry of Heavy Industry got all the play. If you lived in an underdeveloped country now you would face the same problem: What shall you do with the foreign currency earned by sales of cocoa or copper or crude oil—spend it on imports of consumer goods for those alive and working now, or spend it on imports of machinery to start building an industry that may help to raise the standard of living in thirty years' time?

There are other ways in which the same choice can be made, including, for instance, the direction of intellectual resources to the invention of things (like the generation of electricity from nuclear fusion) that will benefit future generations. Paradoxically, one of the ways in which the present can do something for the future is to conserve natural resources. If we get along with less lumber now so that there will be more forests standing for our grandchildren, or if we limit the present consumption of oil or zinc so that there will be some left for the twenty-first century, or if we worry about siltation behind dams that would otherwise be fun for fishermen and water-skiers, in all those cases we are promoting economic growth. I call that paradoxical because I think most people identify the conservation freak with the antigrowth party whereas, in this view of the matter, the conservationist is trading present satisfaction for future satisfaction, that is, he is promoting economic growth. I think the confusion comes from mixing up the quality-of-life problem with the growth problem. But it is nonetheless a confusion.

Why should we be concerned with the welfare of posterity, given the indubitable fact that posterity has never done a thing for us? I am not anthropologist enough to know how rare or common it is that our culture should teach us to care not only about our children but about their children, and their children. I suppose there are good Darwinian reasons why cultures without any future-orientation should fail to survive very long in the course of history. (But remember that they had a merry time of it while they lasted!) Moreover, we now enjoy the investments made by our ancestors, so there is a kind of equity in passing it on. Also, unless something terrible happens, there will be a lot more future than there has been past; and, for better or worse—probably worse—there will be more people at each future instant than there are now or have been. So all in all, the future will involve many more man-years of life than the present or the past, and a kind of intergenerational democracy suggests that all those man-years-to-be deserve some consideration out of sheer numbers.

On the other hand, *if* continued economic growth is possible—which is the question I'm coming to—then it is very likely that posterity will be richer than we are even if we make no special efforts on its behalf. If history offers any guide, then, in the developed part of the world at least, the accumulation of technological knowledge will probably make our great-grandchildren better off than we are, even if we make no great effort in that direction. Leaving aside the possibility of greater equality—I have already discussed that—there is hardly a crying need for posterity to be on average very much richer than we are. Why should we poor folk make any sacrifices for those who will in any case live in luxury in the future? Of course, if the end of the world is at hand, if continued economic growth is *not* possible, then we ought to care more about posterity, because they won't be so well off. Paradoxically, if continued growth is not possible, or less possible, then we probably ought to do more to promote it. Actually, there's no paradox in that, as every student of economics will realize, because it is a way of saying that the marginal return on investment is high.

Overshoot, Collapse, Doom

There is, as you know, a school of thought that claims that continued economic growth is in fact not possible anymore, or at least not for very long. This judgment has been expressed more or less casually by several observers in recent years. What distinguishes the "Doomsday Models" from their predecessors is that they claim to much more than a casual judgment: they deduce their beliefs about future prospects from mathematical models or systems analysis. They don't merely say that the end of the world is at hand—they can show you computer output that says the same thing.

Characteristically, the Doomsday Models do more than just say that continued economic growth is impossible. They tell us why: in brief, because (a) the earth's natural resources will soon be used up; (b) increased industrial production will soon strangle us in pollution; and (c) increasing population will eventually outrun the world's capacity to grow food, so that famine must eventually result. And, finally, the models tell us one more thing: the world will end with a bang, not a whimper. The natural evolution of the world economy is not at all toward some kind of smooth approach to its natural limits, wherever they are. Instead, it is inevitable—unless we make drastic changes in the way we live and organize ourselves—that the world will overshoot any level of population and production it can possibly sustain and will then collapse, probably by the middle of the next century.

I would like to say why I think that the Doomsday Models are bad science and therefore bad guides to public policy.

The first thing to realize is that the characteristic conclusion of the Doomsday Models is very near the surface. It is, in fact, more nearly an assumption than a conclusion, in the sense that the chain of logic from the assumptions to the conclusion is very short and rather obvious.

The basic assumption is that stocks of things like the world's natural resources and the waste-disposal capacity of the environment are finite, that the world economy tends to consume the stock at an increasing rate (through the mining of minerals and the production of goods), and that there are no built-in mechanisms by which approaching exhaustion tends to turn off consumption gradually and in advance. You hardly need a giant computer to tell you that a system with those behavior rules is going to bounce off its ceiling and collapse to a low level. Then, in case anyone is inclined to relax into the optimistic belief that maybe things aren't that bad, we are told: Imagine that the stock of natural resources were actually twice as big as the best current evidence suggests, or imagine that the annual amount of pollution could be halved all at once and then set to growing again. All that would happen is that the date of collapse would be postponed by T years, where T is not a large number. But once you grasp the quite simple essence of the models, this should come as no surprise. It is important to realize where these powerful conclusions come from, because, if you ask yourself "Why didn't I realize earlier that the end of the world was at hand?" the answer is not that you weren't clever enough to figure it out for yourself. The answer is that the imminent end of the world is an immediate deduction from certain assumptions, and one must really ask if the assumptions are any good.

It is a commonplace that if you calculate the annual output of any production process, large or small, and divide it by the annual employment of labor, you get a ratio that is called the productivity of labor. At the most aggregative level, for example, we can say that the GNP in 1971 was $1,050 billion and that about 82 million people were employed in producing it, so that GNP per worker or the productivity of a year of labor was about $12,800. Symmetrically, though the usage is less common, one could just as well calculate the GNP per unit of some particular natural resource and call that the productivity of coal, or GNP per pound of vanadium. We usually think of the productivity of labor as rising more or less exponentially, say at 2 or 3 percent a year, because that is the way it has in fact behaved over the past century or so since the statistics began to be collected. The rate of increase in the productivity of labor is not a constant of nature. Sometimes it is faster, sometimes slower. For example, we know that labor productivity must have increased more slowly a long time ago, because if we extrapolate backward at 2 percent a year, we come to a much lower labor productivity in 1492 than can possibly have been the case. And the productivity of labor has risen faster in the past twenty-five years than in the fifty years before that. It also varies from place to place, being faster in Japan and Germany and slower in Great Britain, for reasons that are not at all certain. But it rises, and we expect it to keep rising.

Now, how about the productivity of natural resources? All the Doomsday Models will allow is a one-time hypothetical increase in the world supply of natural resources, which is the equivalent of a one-time increase in the productivity of natural resources. Why shouldn't the productivity of most natural resources rise more or less steadily through time, like the productivity of labor?

Of course it does for some resources, but not for others. Real GNP roughly doubled between 1950 and 1970. But the consumption of primary and scrap iron increased by about 20 percent, so the productivity of iron, GNP per ton of iron, increased by about 2.5 percent a year on the average during those twenty years. The U.S. consumption of manganese rose by 30 percent in the same period, so the productivity of manganese went up by some 70 percent in twenty

years, a bit under 2.25 percent a year. Aggregate consumption of nickel just about doubled, like GNP, so the productivity of nickel didn't change. U.S. consumption of copper, both primary and secondary, went up by a third between 1951 and 1970, so GNP per pound of copper rose at 2 percent a year on the average. The story on lead and zinc is very similar, so their productivity increased at some 2 percent a year. The productivity of bituminous coal rose at 3 percent a year.

Naturally, there are important exceptions, and unimportant exceptions. GNP per barrel of oil was about the same in 1970 as in 1951: no productivity increase there. The consumption of natural gas tripled in the same period, so GNP per cubic foot of natural gas fell at about 2.5 percent a year. Our industrial demand for aluminum quadrupled in two decades, so the productivity of aluminum fell at a good 3.5 percent a year. And industrial demand for columbium was multiplied by a factor of twenty-five: in 1951 we managed $2.25 million of GNP (in 1967 prices) per pound of columbium, whereas in 1970 we were down to $170 thousand of GNP per pound of columbium. On the other hand, it is a little hard to imagine civilization toppling because of a shortage of columbium.

Obviously many factors combine to govern the course of the productivity of any given mineral over time. When a rare natural resource is first available, it acquires new uses with a rush; and consumption goes up much faster than GNP. That's the columbium story, no doubt, and, to a lesser extent, the vanadium story. But once the novelty has worn off, the productivity of a resource tends to rise as better or worse substitutes for it appear, as new commodities replace old ones, and as manufacturing processes improve. One of the reasons the productivity of copper rises is because that of aluminum falls, as aluminum replaces copper in many uses. The same is true of coal and oil. A resource, like petroleum, which is versatile because of its role as a source of energy, is an interesting special case. It is hardly any wonder that the productivity of petroleum has stagnated, because the consumption of energy—both as electricity for domestic and industrial use and in the automobile —has recently increased even faster than GNP. But no one can doubt that we will run out of oil, that coal and nuclear fission will replace oil as the major sources of energy. It is already becoming probable that the high-value use of oil will soon be as feed stock for the petrochemical industries, rather than as a source of energy. Sooner or later, the productivity of oil will rise out of sight, because the production and consumption of oil will eventually dwindle toward zero, but real GNP will not.

So there really is no reason why we should not think of the productivity of natural resources as increasing more or less exponentially over time. But then overshoot and collapse are no longer the inevitable trajectory of the world system, and the typical assumption-conclusion of the Doomsday Models falls by the wayside. We are in a different sort of ball game. The system might still burn itself out and collapse in finite time, but one cannot say with any honesty that it must. It all depends on the particular, detailed facts of modern economic life as well as on the economic policies we and the rest of the world pursue. I don't want to argue for any particular counterstory; all I want to say now is that the overshoot-collapse pattern is built into the models very near the surface, by assumption, and by implausible assumption at that.

Scarcity—and High Prices

There is at least one reason for believing that the Doomsday story is almost certainly wrong. The most glaring defect of the Forrester-Meadows models is the absence of any sort of functioning price system. I am no believer that the market is always right, and I am certainly no advocate of laissez-faire where the environment is concerned. But the price system is, after all, the main social institution evolved by capitalist economies (and, to an increasing extent, socialist economies too) for registering and reacting to relative scarcity. There are several ways that the working of the price system will push our society into faster and more systematic increases in the productivity of natural resources.

First of all, let me go back to the analogy between natural resources and labor. We are not surprised to learn that industry quite consciously tries to make inventions that save labor, i.e., permit the same product to be made with fewer man-hours of work. After all, on the average, labor costs amount to almost three-fourths of all costs in our economy. An invention that reduces labor requirements per unit of GNP by 1 percent reduces all costs by about 0.75 percent. Natural resource costs are a much smaller

proportion of total GNP, something nearer 5 percent. So industry and engineering have a much stronger motive to reduce labor requirements by 1 percent than to reduce resource requirements by 1 percent, assuming—which may or not be true—that it is about as hard to do one as to do the other. But then, as the earth's supply of particular natural resources nears exhaustion, and as natural resources become more and more valuable, the motive to economize those natural resources should become as strong as the motive to economize labor. The productivity of resources should rise faster than now—it is hard to imagine otherwise.

There are other ways in which the market mechanism can be expected to push us all to economize on natural resources as they become scarcer. Higher and rising prices of exhaustible resources lead competing producers to substitute other materials that are more plentiful and therefore cheaper. To the extent that it is impossible to design around or find substitutes for expensive natural resources, the prices of commodities that contain a lot of them will rise relative to the prices of other goods and services that don't use up a lot of resources. Consumers will be driven to buy fewer resource-intensive goods and more of other things. All these effects work automatically to increase the productivity of natural resources, i.e., to reduce resource requirements per unit of GNP.

This is not an argument for laissez-faire. We may feel that the private decisions of buyers and sellers give inadequate representation to future generations. Or we may feel that private interests are in conflict with a distinct public interest—strip-mining of coal is an obvious case in point, and there are many others as soon as we begin to think about environmental effects. Private market responses may be too uncoordinated, too slow, based on insufficient and faulty information. In every case there will be actions that public agencies can take and should take; and it will be a major political struggle to see that they are taken. But I don't see how one can have the slightest confidence in the predictions of models that seem to make no room for the operation of everyday market forces. If the forecasts are wrong, then so are the policy implications, to the extent that there are any realistic policy implications.

Every analysis of resource scarcity has to come to terms with the fact that the prices of natural resources and resource products have not shown any tendency to rise over the past half-century, relative to the prices of other things. This must mean that there have so far been adequate offsets to any progressive impoverishment of deposits—like improvements in the technology of extraction, savings in end uses, or the availability of cheaper substitutes. The situation could, of course, change; and very likely some day it will. If the experienced and expert participants in the market now believed that resource prices would be sharply higher at some foreseeable time, prices would *already* be rising, as I will try to explain in a moment. The historical steadiness of resource prices suggests that buyers and sellers in the market have not been acting as if they foresaw exhaustion in the absence of substitutes, and therefore sharply higher future prices. They may turn out to be wrong; but the Doomsday Models give us absolutely no reason to expect that—in fact, they claim to get whatever meager empirical basis they have from such experts.

Why is it true that if the market saw higher prices in the future, prices would already be rising? It is a rather technical point, but I want to explain it because, in a way, it summarizes the important thing about natural resources: conserving a mineral deposit is just as much of an investment as building a factory, and it has to be analyzed that way. Any owner of a mineral deposit owns a valuable asset, whether the owner is a private capitalist or the government of an underdeveloped country. The asset is worth keeping only if at the margin it earns a return equal to that earned on other kinds of assets. A factory produces things each year of its life, but a mineral deposit just lies there: its owner can realize a return only if he either mines the deposit or if it *increases in value*. So if you are sitting on your little pile of X and confidently expect to be able to sell it for a very high price in the year 2000 because it will be very scarce by then, you must be earning your 5 percent a year, or 10 percent a year, or whatever the going rate of return is, each year between now and 2000. The only way this can happen is for the value of X to go up by 5 percent a year or 10 percent a year. And that means that anyone who wants to use any X any time between now and 2000 will have to pay a price for it that is rising at that same 5 percent or 10 percent a year. Well, it's not happening. Of course, we are exploiting our hoard of exhaustible resources; we have no choice about that. We are certainly exploiting it wastefully, in the sense that we allow each other to dump waste products into the environment without full accounting for costs. But there is very little evidence that we are exploiting it too fast.

Crowding on Planet Earth

I have less to say about the question of population growth, because it doesn't seem to involve any difficult conceptual problems. At any time, in any place, there is presumably an optimal size of population—with the property that the average person would be somewhat worse off if the population were a bit larger, and also worse off if the population were a bit smaller. In any real case it must be very difficult to know what the optimum population is, especially because it will change over time as technology changes, and also because it is probably more like a band or zone than a sharply defined number. I mean that if you could somehow plot a graph of economic welfare per person against population size, there would be a very gentle dome or plateau at the top, rather than a sharp peak. . . .

At the present moment, at least for the United States, the danger of rapid population growth seems to be the wrong thing to worry about. The main object of public policy in this field ought to be to ensure that the choice of family size is truly a voluntary choice, that access to the best birth-control methods be made universal. That seems to be all that is needed. Of course, we know very little about what governs voluntary fertility, about why the typical notion of a good family size changes from generation to generation. So it is certainly possible that these recent developments will reverse themselves and that population control will again appear on the agenda of public policy. This remains to be seen.

In all this I have said nothing about the Doomsday Models because there is practically nothing that needs to be said. So far as we can tell, they make one very bad mistake: in the face of reason, common sense, and systematic evidence, they seem to assume that at high standards of living, people want more children as they become more affluent (though over most of the observed range, a higher standard of living goes along with smaller families). That error is certainly a serious one in terms of the recent American data—but perhaps it explains why some friends of mine were able to report that they had run a version of the Forrester World Dynamics Model starting with a population of two people and discovered that it blew up in 500 years. Apart from placing the date of the Garden of Eden in the fifteenth century, what else is new?

There is another analytical error in the models, as Fred Singer has pointed out. Suppose resource exhaustion or increased pollution conspires to bring a reduction in industrial production. The model then says that birth rates will rise because, in the past, low industrial output has been associated with high birth rates. But there is nothing in historical evidence to suggest that a once-rich country will go *back* to high birth rates if (as I doubt will happen) its standard of living falls from an accustomed high level. Common sense suggests that a society in such a position would fight to preserve its standard of living by reducing the desired family size. In any case, this is another example of a poorly founded—or unfounded—assumption introduced to support the likelihood of overshoot-and-collapse.

Paying for Pollution

Resource exhaustion and overpopulation: that leaves pollution as the last of the Doomsday Devils. I think that what one gets from the Doomsday literature is the notion that air and water and noise pollution are an inescapable accompaniment of economic growth, especially industrial growth. If that is true, then to be against pollution is to be against growth. I realize that in putting the matter so crudely I have been unjust; nevertheless, that is the message that comes across. I think that way of looking at the pollution problem is wrong.

A correct analysis goes something like this. Excessive pollution and degradation of the environment certainly accompany industrial growth and the increasing population density that goes with it. But they are by no means an inescapable by-product. Excessive pollution happens because of an important flaw in the price system. Factories, power plants, municipal sewers, drivers of cars, strip-miners of coal and deep-miners of coal, and all sorts of generators of waste are allowed to dump that waste into the environment, into the atmosphere and into running water and the oceans, without paying the full cost of what they do. No wonder they do too much. So would you, and so would I. In fact, we actually do—directly as drivers of cars, indirectly as we buy some products at a price which is lower than it ought to be because the producer is not required to pay for using the environment to carry away his wastes, and even more indirectly as we buy things that are made with things that pollute the environment.

This flaw in the price system exists because a scarce resource (the waste-disposal capacity of the environment) goes unpriced; and that happens because it is owned by all of us, as it should be. The flaw can be corrected, either by the simple expedient of regulating the discharge of wastes to the environment by direct control or by the slightly more complicated device of charging special prices—user taxes—to those who dispose of wastes in air or water. These effluent charges do three things: they make pollution-intensive goods expensive, and so reduce the consumption of them; they make pollution-intensive methods of production costly, and so promote abatement of pollution by producers; they generate revenue that can, if desired, be used for the further purification of air or water or for other environmental improvements. Most economists prefer this device of effluent charges to regulation by direct order. This is more than an occupational peculiarity. Use of the price system has certain advantages in efficiency and decentralization. Imposing a physical limit on, say, sulfur dioxide emission is, after all, a little peculiar. It says that you may do so much of a bad thing and pay nothing for the privilege, but after that, the price is infinite. Not surprisingly, one can find a more efficient schedule of pollution abatement through a more sensitive tax schedule.

But this difference of opinion is minor compared with the larger point that needs to be made. The annual cost that would be necessary to meet decent pollution-abatement standards by the end of the century is large, but not staggering. One estimate says that in 1970 we spent about $8.5 billion (in 1967 prices), or 1 percent of GNP, for pollution abatement. An active pollution abatement policy would cost perhaps $50 billion a year by 2000, which would be about 2 percent of GNP by then. That is a small investment of resources: you can see how small it is when you consider that GNP grows by 4 percent or so every year, on the average. Cleaning up air and water would entail a cost that would be a bit like losing one-half of one year's growth, between now and the year 2000. What stands between us and a decent environment is not the curse of industrialization, not an unbearable burden of cost, but just the need to organize ourselves consciously to do some simple and knowable things. Compared with the possibility of an active abatement policy, the policy of stopping economic growth in order to stop pollution would be incredibly inefficient. It would not actually accomplish much, because one really wants to reduce the amount of, say, hydrocarbon emission to a third or a half of *what it is now*. And what no-growth would accomplish, it would do by cutting off your face to spite your nose.

32

The Principle of Population

THOMAS MALTHUS

Thomas Malthus was one of the great figures of economics. This article comes from his famous Essay on the Principle of Population, *published in 1798.*

In an inquiry concerning the improvement of society, the mode of conducting the subject which naturally presents itself is:

1. To investigate the causes that have hitherto impeded the progress of mankind towards happiness; and,

2. To examine the probability of the total or partial removal of these causes in the future.

To enter fully into this question, and to enumerate all the causes that have hitherto influenced human improvement, would be much beyond the power of an individual. The principal object of the present essay is to examine the effects of one great cause intimately united with the very nature of man; which, though it has been constantly and powerfully operating since the commencement of society, has been little noticed by the writers who have treated this subject. The facts which establish the existence of this cause have, indeed, been repeatedly stated and acknowledged; but its natural and necessary effects have been almost totally overlooked; though probably among these effects may be reckoned a very considerable portion of that vice and misery, and of that unequal distribution of the bounties of nature, which it has been the unceasing object of the enlightened philanthropist in all ages to correct.

The cause to which I allude, is the constant tendency in all animated life to increase beyond the nourishment prepared for it.

It is observed by Dr. Franklin, that there is no bound to the prolific nature of plants or animals but what is made by the crowding and interfering with each other's means of subsistence. Were the face of the earth, he says, vacant of other plants, it might be gradually sowed and overspread with one kind only, as, for instance, with fennel: and were it empty of other inhabitants, it might in a few ages be replenished from one nation only, as, for instance, with Englishmen.

This is incontrovertibly true. Throughout the animal and vegetable kingdoms Nature has scattered the seeds of life abroad with the most profuse and liberal hand; but has been comparatively sparing in the room and the nourishment necessary to rear them. The germs of existence contained in this earth, if they could freely develop themselves, would fill millions of worlds in the course of a few thousand years. Necessity, that imperious, all-pervading law of nature, restrains them within the prescribed bounds. The race of plants and the race of animals shrink under this great restrictive law; and man cannot by any efforts of reason escape from it.

In plants and irrational animals, the view of the subject is simple. They are all impelled by a powerful instinct to the increase of their species, and this instinct is interrupted by no doubts about providing for their offspring. Wherever, therefore, there is liberty, the power of increase is exerted, and the superabundant effects are repressed afterwards by want of room and nourishment.

The effects of this check on man are more complicated. Impelled to the increase of his species by an equally powerful instinct, reason interrupts his career, and asks him whether he may not bring beings into the world for whom he cannot provide the means of support. If he attend to this natural suggestion, the restriction too frequently produces vice. If he hear it not, the human race will be constantly endeavouring to increase beyond the means of subsistence. But as, by that law of our nature which makes food necessary to the life of man, population can never actually increase beyond the lowest nourishment capable of supporting it, a strong check on population; from the difficulty of acquiring food, must be constantly in operation. This difficulty must fall somewhere, and must necessarily be severely felt in some or other of the various forms of misery, or the fear of misery, by a large portion of mankind.

That population has this constant tendency to increase beyond the means of subsistence, and that it is kept to its necessary level by these causes, will sufficiently appear from a review of the different states of society in which man has existed. But, before we proceed to this review, the subject will perhaps be seen in a clearer light, if we endeavor to ascertain what would be the natural increase of population, if left to exert itself with perfect freedom; and what might be expected to be the rate of increase in the productions of the earth, under the most favourable circumstances of human industry.

It will be allowed that no country has hitherto been known, where the manners were so pure and simple, and the means of subsistence so abundant, that no check whatever has existed to early marriages from the difficulty of providing for a family, and that no waste of the human species has been occasioned by vicious customs, by towns, by unhealthy occupations, or too severe labour. Consequently in no state that we have yet known, has the power of population been left to exert itself with perfect freedom.

Whether the law of marriage be instituted or not, the dictate of nature and virtue seems to be an early attachment to one woman; and where there were no impediments of any kind in the way of a union to which such an attachment would lead, and no causes of depopulation afterwards, the increase of the human species would be evidently much greater than any increase which has been hitherto known.

In the northern states of America, where the means of subsistence have been more ample, the manners of the people more pure, and the checks to early marriages fewer, than in any of the modern states of Europe, the population has been found to double itself, for above a century and a half successively, in less than twenty-five years. Yet, even during these periods, in some of the towns, the deaths exceeded the births, a circumstance which clearly proves that, in those parts of the country which supplied this deficiency, the increase must have been much more rapid than the general average.

In the back settlements, where the sole employment is agriculture, and vicious customs and unwholesome occupations are little known, the population has been found to double itself in fifteen years. Even this extraordinary rate of increase is probably short of the utmost power of population. Very severe labour is requisite to clear a fresh country; such situations are not in general considered as particularly healthy; and the inhabitants, probably, are occasionally subject to the incursions of the Indians, which may destroy some lives, or at any rate diminish the fruits of industry.

According to a table of Euler, calculated on a mortality of one in thirty-six, if the births be to the deaths in the proportion of three to one, the period of doubling will be only twelve years and four-fifths. And this proportion is not only a possible supposition, but has actually occurred for short periods in more countries than one.

Sir William Petty supposes a doubling possible in so short a time as ten years.

But, to be perfectly sure that we are far within the truth, we will take the slowest of these rates of increase, a rate in which all concurring testimonies agree, and which has been repeatedly ascertained to be from procreation only.

It may safely be pronounced, therefore, that population, when unchecked, goes on doubling itself every twenty-five years, or increases in a geometrical ratio.

The rate according to which the productions of the earth may be supposed to increase, will not be so easy to determine. Of this, however, we may be perfectly certain, that the ratio of their increase in a limited territory must be of a totally different nature from the ratio of the increase of population. A thousand millions are just as easily doubled every twenty-five years by the power of population as a thousand. But the food to support the increase from the greater number will by no means be obtained with the same facility. Man is necessarily confined in room. When acre has been added to acre till all the fertile land is occupied, the yearly increase of food must depend upon the melioration of the land already in possession. This is a fund, which, from the nature of all soils, instead of increasing, must be gradually diminishing. But population, could it be supplied with food, would go on with unexhausted vigour; and the increase of one period would furnish the power of a greater increase the next, and this without any limit.

From the accounts we have of China and Japan, it may be fairly doubted whether the best directed efforts of human industry could double the produce of these countries even once in any number of years. There are many parts of the globe, indeed, hitherto uncultivated and almost unoccupied; but the right of exterminating, or driving into a corner where they must starve, even the inhabitants of these thinly peopled regions, will be questioned in a moral view. The process of improving their minds and directing their industry would necessarily be slow; and during this time, as population would regularly keep pace with the increasing produce, it would rarely happen that a great degree of knowledge and industry would have to operate at once upon rich unappropriated soil. Even where this might take place, as it does sometimes in new colonies, a geometrical ratio increases with such extraordinary rapidity, that the advantage could not last long. If the United States of America continue increasing, which they certainly will do, though not with the same rapidity as formerly, the Indians will be driven farther and farther back into the country, till the whole race is ultimately exterminated, and the territory is incapable of further extension.

These observations are, in a degree, applicable to all the parts of the earth where the soil is imperfectly cultivated. To exterminate the inhabitants of the greatest part of Asia and Africa, is a thought that could not be admitted for a moment. To civilise and direct the industry of the various tribes of Tartars and Negroes, would certainly be a work of considerable time, and of variable and uncertain success.

Europe is by no means so fully peopled as it might be. In Europe there is the fairest chance that human industry may receive its best direction. The science of agriculture has been much studied in England and Scotland; and there is still a great portion of uncultivated land in these countries. Let us consider at what rate the produce of this island (Great Britain) might be supposed to increase under circumstances the most favourable to improvement.

If it be allowed that by the best possible policy, and great encouragements to agriculture, the average produce of the island could be doubled in the first twenty-five years, it will be allowing, probably, a greater increase than could with reason be expected.

In the next twenty-five years, it is impossible to suppose that the produce could be quadrupled. It would be contrary to all our knowledge of the properties of land. The improvement of the barren parts would be a work of time and labour; and it must be evident to those who have the slightest acquaintance with agricultural subjects, that in proportion as cultivation extended, the additions that could yearly be made to the former average produce must be gradually and regularly diminishing. That we may be the better able to compare the increase of population and food, let us make a supposition, which, without pretending to accuracy, is clearly more favourable to the power of production in the earth than any experience we have had of its qualities will warrant.

Let us suppose that the yearly additions which might be made to the former average produce, instead of decreasing, which they certainly would do, were to remain the same; and that the produce of this island might be increased every twenty-five years, by a quantity equal to what it at present produces. The most enthusiastic speculator cannot suppose a greater increase than this. In a few centuries it would make every acre of land in the island like a garden.

If this supposition be applied to the whole earth, and if it be allowed that the subsistence for man which the earth affords might be increased every twenty-five years by a quantity equal to what it at present produces, this will be supposing a rate of increase much greater than we can imagine that any possible exertions of mankind could make it.

It may be fairly pronounced, therefore, that considering the present average state of the earth, the means of subsistence, under circumstances the most favourable to human industry, could not possibly be made to increase faster than in an arithmetical ratio.

The necessary effects of these two different rates of increase, when brought together, will be very striking. Let us call the population of this island eleven millions, and suppose the present produce equal to the easy support of such a number. In the first twenty-five years the population would be twenty-two millions, and the food being also doubled, the means of subsistence would be equal to this increase. In the next twenty-five years, the population would be forty-four millions, and the means of subsistence only equal to the support of thirty-three millions. In the next period the population would be eighty-eight millions, and the means of subsistence just equal to the support of half that number. And, at the conclusion of the first century, the population would be a hundred and seventy-six millions, and the means of subsistence only equal to the support of fifty-five millions, leaving a population of a hundred and twenty-one millions totally unprovided for.

Taking the whole earth, instead of this island, emigration would of course be excluded; and, supposing the present population equal to a thousand millions, the human species would increase as the numbers, 1, 2, 4, 8, 16, 32, 64, 128, 256; and subsistence as, 1, 2, 3, 4, 5, 6, 7, 8, 9. In two centuries the population would be to the means of subsistence as 256 to 9: in three centuries as 4096 to 13, and in two thousand years the difference would be almost incalculable.

In this supposition no limits whatever are placed to the produce of the earth. It may increase for ever, and be greater than any assignable quantity; yet still the power of population being in every period so much superior, the increase of the human species can only be kept down to the level of the means of subsistence by the constant operation of the strong law of necessity acting as a check upon the greater power.

33

Productivity Growth in the United States

THE NATIONAL COMMISSION ON

PRODUCTIVITY AND WORK QUALITY

This piece is taken from the Fourth Annual Report of the National Commission on Productivity and Work Quality, published in 1975.

U.S. productivity performance over the long term is of considerable importance because it is the major factor determining the growth of real earnings and the standard of living. In the long run, a principal way to offset the impact of drastic increases in the prices of energy and other basic materials is to maintain or increase the economy's productivity growth rate.

Post-War Retardation

Productivity in the private economy grew over the post-war period at a rate of 3.1 percent per year. But this is an average for the entire period. Examination of the figures plotted in Chart 1 reveals a somewhat higher rate in the earlier post-war years, and a somewhat lower rate in the more recent years (even after allowing for the severe drop in the last year). In other words, there is evidence of retardation: the rate of growth has tended to decline from decade to decade.

The average rate of growth, determined by fitting a trend line to the quarterly data, is about 3.6 percent per year at the beginning of the post-war period. It is about 3.0 percent in the middle as well as over the whole post-war period. It is about 2.4 percent at the end of the period. The average rate of retardation, then, was about 0.04 percentage points per year over the 27-year period covered.

The individual industries which make up the total private economy experienced widely varied post–World War II rates of productivity increase. The average rate of growth in the total was closely matched by relatively few industries. In fact, over half the industries for which separate information is available increased their productivity at annual rates that exceeded or fell short of the rate for the total private economy by as much as a full percentage point—a considerable difference. However, the majority of individual industries show long-term rates of productivity growth with some degree of retardation during the post-war period. According to the Bureau of Labor Statistics (BLS), more than two-thirds of the industries had lower rates of productivity gain during 1966–73 than during a preceding comparable period (generally 1947–66).

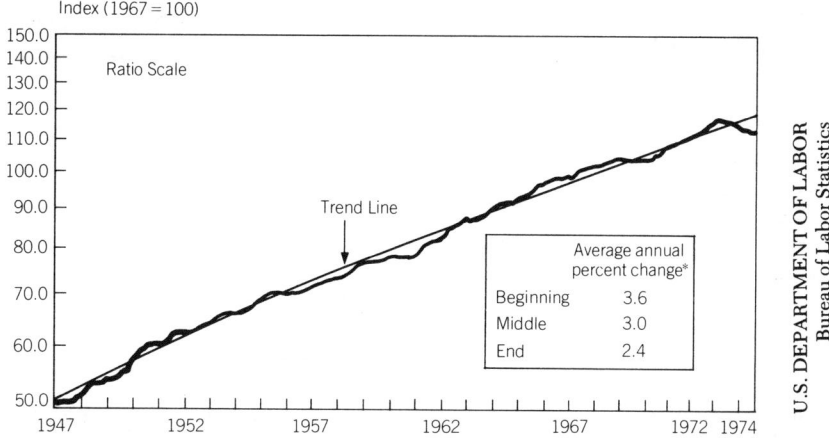

Index (1967 = 100)

Ratio Scale

Trend Line

	Average annual percent change*
Beginning	3.6
Middle	3.0
End	2.4

U.S. DEPARTMENT OF LABOR
Bureau of Labor Statistics

*Computed from trend line fitted to quarterly data for private economy.

Chart 1. **Output per Man-Hour Growth Rate Has Tended to Slow Down over the Post-War Period**

Perspective on Post-War Trend

The significance of this apparent retardation becomes clearer when the whole post-war trend is viewed against a broad historical background. Annual estimates available on a calendar-year basis as far back as 1889 provide the longer perspective.

The first feature of this history is the pronounced upward sweep of productivity. Output per man-hour did decline from time to time, but the declines took place in only a fifth of the years covered. These, together with the occasional slowdowns in other years, do not change the impression of a strong upward trend in productivity. On the average, output per man-hour rose at a rate of as much as 2.4 percent per year (compounded annually). By 1974 output per man-hour was six or seven times that of 85 years earlier.

A second outstanding feature is the greater stability in the rate of increase in productivity in the post–World War II period. While, as already noted, fluctuations in the rate of growth are found in all periods, the fluctuations were far more pronounced in the period up through the middle 1930s than in that following the reconversion period after World War II, or even in the longer period which includes the 1940s. Except for the decline during 1973 and 1974, the upward sweep of productivity in recent decades seems marred by a mere ripple when viewed against the background of the strong fluctuations characteristic of earlier years. The 1973–74 decline stands out so clearly precisely because it is an exception.

A third prominent feature is the speedier rate of growth since World War II than in any of the earlier periods of roughly corresponding length and phase of business cycle, namely, 1890–1907, 1907–29, and 1929–48. In fact, a similar upward shift in the rate of productivity growth following World War II seems to have been a worldwide phenomenon. However, the shift was even greater in many countries abroad, which rose from a pre-war rate below that of the United States to a post-war rate above the United States.

The post-war U.S. output per man-hour trend has often been interpreted as indicating a tendency of productivity to accelerate. However, projections into the future of changes in trends are dangerous. We know that during the past quarter-century there has been no pronounced tendency to a gradual speeding up of the rate of productivity growth; instead, as pointed out earlier, the evidence indicates some retardation since World War II.

The historical record also shows that, in addition to the short-term fluctuations in productivity growth, there are, as well, longer-term fluctuations, extending over a decade or more. The statistics suggest five long waves in the trend rate of change in productivity. The rates of increase ranged from a low of about 1-percent growth per year during the 10- or 15-year period centered around 1910 or 1915, to a high of about 3.5 percent per year during the decade immediately following World War II.

In the most recent decade the annual rate of increase in productivity has fallen to below 3 percent. In

Table 1. Manufacturing Output per Man-Hour in Seven Countries, Average Annual Percent Change, Selected Periods, 1950–74

Country	1950–74	1960–74	1950–66	1966–74	1966–70	1970–74
United States	2.9	3.3	2.7	3.6	2.2	4.8
Canada	4.1	4.3	4.0	4.4	4.7	4.2
Japan	9.5	10.5	8.4	11.1	13.9	9.5
France	5.4	6.0	4.8	6.0	6.6	6.0
Germany	6.0	5.8	6.2	5.4	5.8	5.7
Italy	5.9	6.4	5.9	6.1	5.4	8.3
United Kingdom	3.4	3.9	2.9	3.6	3.5	4.3

Source: U.S. Department of Labor, Bureau of Labor Statistics.
Note: Data for Italy cover periods ending with 1973. U.S. estimates for 1974 are based on data for full year; estimates for France are based on two quarters; and estimates for remaining countries are based on three quarters.

the light of historical experience it would be risky to extrapolate a further decline in the rate. The current period of slow growth in productivity—slow only by comparison with the earlier post-war rates, not by comparison with the longer experience—may well be succeeded by a period of higher growth. In fact, the objective of productivity policy is to do what is possible to ensure that this does happen.

Comparison with Productivity Trends Abroad

Comparisons of productivity changes in the United States with those in other countries are hazardous be cause of gaps and incomparabilities in the available statistics. Studies by the International Labor Office and the Organization for Economic Cooperation and Development, as well as by individual scholars, have made one thing quite clear: during the post–World War II period, output per man-hour in the U.S. economy rose less rapidly on the average than in most oth er industrial countries.

Between 1950 and 1974, according to the BLS's compilation of productivity in manufacturing of seven major industrial countries, output per man-hour in U.S. manufacturing rose less rapidly than in any of the other countries. (See Table 1.) The picture is much the same for various periods within the 24-year period, except for 1970–74, when the rate of productivity increase here was better than in two of the six countries. However, in a comparison between 1973 and 1974 among the six major industrial countries,

the BLS finds the U.S. below four of the five others in the rate of increase in manufacturing productivity.

The level of output per man-hour in the United States has been higher than in other countries for a very long time, in manufacturing and most other industries, and in the private economy at large. (See Chart 2.) This output per man-hour continues to be higher. But our productivity lead has been substantially diminished during the post-war period, even after allowance for the recovery in the early post-war period from the distortions and other severe effects of the war in Europe and Japan. Other countries have been catching up and closing the gap.

Productivity Growth Ahead

Considerable concern is expressed about the apparent tendency of productivity to "flatten out" in the past decade.

Attention has been focused on a number of possible factors. One is retardation in the majority of the industries making up the economy, as briefly described earlier. Each industry has its own story. In some cases "maturation," with little new technology or investment, may be the reason. The slowdown in long-term growth of demand, as in tobacco, probably accounts for retardation in some sectors. In mining industries, it becomes more and more difficult to increase per man-hour output as measured in recoverable mineral content as lower-quality ores are mined.

The increasing relative importance of the service industries, which is characterized by comparatively low

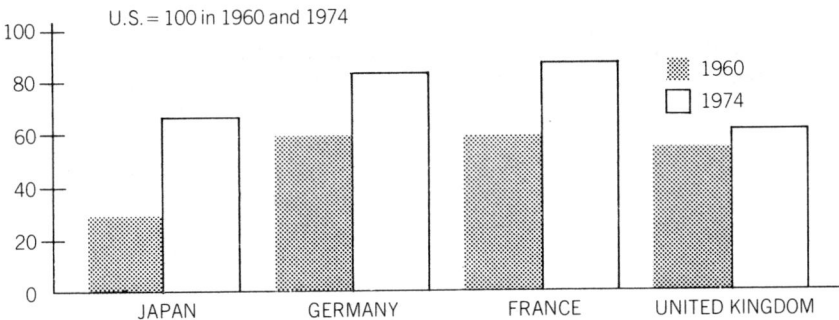

U.S. = 100 in 1960 and 1974

▨ 1960
☐ 1974

JAPAN   GERMANY   FRANCE   UNITED KINGDOM

U.S. DEPARTMENT OF LABOR
Bureau of Labor Statistics

Chart 2.   **Level of U.S. Productivity Remains High Relative to Major Countries, But the Gap Is Closing**

levels and low growth rates of productivity as conventionally measured, is also considered a dampening factor. The increase in government employment is, in addition, measured at zero productivity growth. If technological, organizational, and managerial innovations in government and in such service industries as retail food, hospitals, and banks were to be applied more extensively to result in a faster rate of increase in productivity, the effect of the shift to services on the average rate for the private sector would be lessened.

Another reason for retardation is the cessation of the employment decline in agriculture. The massive shift of agricultural labor to industry, with a relatively high level of productivity, contributed to increasing the post-war rate of productivity growth in the private economy by about 10 percent. However, employment in agriculture, now accounting for only about 4 percent of civilian employment, is not expected to continue to decline at the same rate in the future. As a result, we can no longer count on agriculture as a source of gain in the economy's productivity growth.

The influx of a large number of new, inexperienced (though well-educated) young people has also had some impact. According to some researchers, this influx tended to depress productivity in the late 1960s. However, these unusual demographic factors will no longer dominate. Over the next 10 years, the youngest age group in the labor force will diminish in relative importance, and the fastest growing group, in relative terms, will be more experienced (age 20 to 34). This trend would affect productivity positively.

The trend in the amount of capital per worker or man-hour has been another pertinent factor in the long-term increase in output per man-hour, but the uncertainty in recent statistics on trends makes it difficult to assess its impact with any confidence. BLS estimates that the capital/labor ratio grew more rapidly from 1966 to 1972 than from 1947 to 1966 in the private economy and the nonfarm and manufacturing sectors. However, other statisticians, using different concepts, show little change in the capital/labor ratio between 1966 to 1972 and a slightly higher change between 1950 and 1966.

Comparative data on capital investment in the United States and other major countries suggest a possible reason for the lower growth rate of U.S. manufacturing productivity relative to other countries. Among the five major nations, the United States invested the smallest proportion of GNP in plant and equipment over the 1960–73 period. Output also increased less rapidly in the United States.

As we look to the future, it appears likely that capital spending for modernization and expansion of plant and equipment will be increasingly in competition for available funds with programs for expanding energy supplies, improving the quality of the environment, and meeting housing and other social needs.

There is speculation about the effect on productivity of such factors as the deterioration of workers' attitudes; the devaluation of technology and growth; a tendency toward slackness on the part of management; impediments to savings, investment, and enterprise created by the tax system; government "interference"; and imperfections of competition. Another matter of concern is the long-run implication of a decline in the proportion of GNP being spent on R & D and an increase in such expenditures in Japan, Germany, and the USSR.

The complexity of the factors affecting productivity and the inadequacy of data about those factors make projections of future trends uncertain. It would be risky to extrapolate from the post-war trend, but the available figures put us on notice that things have not gone as well as we would like. They oblige us to pay attention and give positive support to factors favorable to higher productivity.

Policies to Raise Productivity

While business recovery probably will restore the rate of productivity growth approximately to its historic trend, long-term growth is not preordained. Public and private policies which foster advance must be considered in relation to what is known about the main sources of long-term growth and the major obstacles to improvement.

Sources of Long-Term Growth in Productivity

Nationally, productivity has tended to rise persistently. It has also tended to rise in virtually all sectors of our economy in the long run. The key question is: Why has the increase in output per man-hour been so widespread?

A basic reason lies in the incentives that impel people everywhere in our economy to strive constantly to advance themselves and their enterprises. To raise their standard of living, they tax themselves for their own education and training and that of their families. They save to increase the tangible capital of their own businesses or professions or their investment in businesses in which they can acquire shares. They devise new techniques and shortcuts in old methods; they improve old products and invent new products; they seek better sources of supply of old materials and develop new materials. For some people, technology affords opportunities to increase their income; for others, it offers a chance to satisfy their instinct for workmanship.

Some of the forces making for an increase in tangible and intangible capital per worker and efficiency operate through the markets for labor and capital. Thus, when savings make tangible capital plentiful in relation to labor and the services of labor become more expensive than the services of tangible capital, managers find it profitable or economical to increase the volume of tangible capital per worker. When education levels rise as private expenditures on education are lifted by higher incomes and expanded government support, the relative prices of high-quality labor tend to fall and industry finds it profitable to seek ways to put the improved labor to use.

Another source of growth is wide diffusion of new products by the market system. When technological developments are potentially versatile enough to be put to use in different industries, sooner or later the profit motive and competitive pressures see to it that they are used in different industries. In all these industries, then, technology, wherever it may originate, helps to raise efficiency in the use of labor and capital. Because many technological developments must be embodied in equipment or other tangible capital and operated by trained people, these developments also add inducements to increase capital per worker, to employ better educated workers, and to train them on the job.

Knowledge—of innovations in production processes, or materials, or marketing methods, or business organization—which initially appears to be of use only in a few industries may sooner or later be adapted to the peculiar conditions of other industries. This is the history of the steam engine, the principle of interchangeable parts, scientific management, the electric motor, and plastics. Today, the output of R & D—the industry of discovery—is disseminated widely by an active industry of diffusion, made up of firms and consultants whose business it is to convey and adapt new knowledge.

The forces that make for an increase in labor productivity operate broadly across the entire economy and affect different industries at different times and in different degrees. Although the revolutionary changes are better known, most industries must content themselves with the host of small technological innovations which crop up almost continuously over the full range of economic activity.

In explaining the tendency of productivity to rise throughout the economy, three main groups of productivity factors have been identified—the quality of labor, the tangible capital with which labor is equipped, and the efficiency with which management utilizes labor and capital. These factors are not entirely independent of one another. For example, education which affects the quality of labor can raise the capacity of labor to produce without increasing the level of technology and with a given volume of tangible capital. But education can also influence the speed with which new techniques are put into use, thereby affecting efficiency.

In short, the high productivity of the American

economy is the end result of a great many different activities involving decisions by millions of scientists, engineers, and technicians in laboratories and industry; educators in schools, universities, and training centers; managers and owners of production facilities; and workers and their unions. Productivity cannot be increased simply by government fiat and exhortation. An increase of this country's output per man-hour over the long run will be the result of the energy, ingenuity, and skill with which we as a nation manage all our resources of production.

Productivity and Employment in the Long Run

One of the most significant sources of resistance to productivity improvement is the widespread association of the concept with the loss of jobs and unemployment. The question of labor displacement has troubled people since the early days of the machine age. A decade ago automation and the possibility of mass unemployment (which did not materialize) caused intense concern.

There is no doubt that automation, mechanization, or any advance which makes for higher labor productivity can wipe out jobs. The immediate effect of increases in output per man-hour is to reduce employment per unit of output. If output is unchanged and hours of work remain the same, this reduction in employment per unit makes for a reduction in the industry's aggregate employment. However, if output is increased, employment can remain the same or be expanded.

Important indirect effects of productivity increases can result in such output increases. A rise in an industry's productivity also presses down on the price of the industry's product. If productivity rises rapidly, reduction in production costs and in selling prices will follow. With demand responding to the reduction in price, output will rise and thus partially or wholly offset the effect of higher output per man-hour on employment. If demand is sufficiently responsive to the decline in price, the resulting rise in output could even exceed the rise in output per man-hour. The number of man-hours worked in the industry would then go up, not down.

The historical record shows that this event is not infrequent. In the long run, industries whose productivity has risen more rapidly than in the whole economy have often raised their employment by a larger percentage than industry generally, and not by a smaller percentage, as might be supposed. Correspondingly, industries whose productivity has seriously lagged, such as footwear, have often raised their employment less than industry generally or have actually cut employment.

On the other hand, in some industries, relatively rapid increases in productivity have been accompanied by relative or even absolute declines in employment. Farming is the outstanding example of our generation. Other examples include industries where output rose little or not at all, such as railroads and coal mining.

Another important fact stands out in the historical records. While output per man-hour rose more rapidly after than before World War II, the rate of unemployment of the labor force as a whole averaged less after the war than before it. It is also noteworthy that Japan and many European countries have substantially lower rates of unemployment but faster rates of productivity increase.

The course of employment in an industry also reflects what has been happening to productivity in the country at large. The increase in national productivity and the higher income it has brought have tended to raise the demand for workers in individual industries with increasing productivity. This often offsets the direct adverse effects of the industries' own productivity changes on employment.

The effects of increased income were especially great on the output and employment of industries which produce the goods and services that people buy more freely as they become more affluent and are able to pay higher prices. Increased national productivity helped sustain and often raise employment in these lower-productivity industries. Many of the health service industries provide examples of rising prices accompanied by rising rather than falling demand.

Further, unemployment is not necessarily created by declining employment in an industry, for when the pace of decline is slow enough, normal attrition by retirement can contribute to avoiding displacement. In addition, although technological change may destroy jobs, it also creates new jobs. Workers are often attracted to these by better pay, and go off to them voluntarily even before their old jobs have become obsolete. In an expanding economy, such shifts can be made with a minimum of lost time.

Yet it is a fact that technological and other changes within an industry can create serious problems of personal adjustment. Not everybody whose job has become obsolete is ready for retirement, or can move off to a new job elsewhere at the same rate of pay and fringe benefits. The introduction of a machine may create new jobs for computer programmers, but not for the people whose skills or specialties have become obsolete. Thus, the effects of technological change on particular groups of workers can be serious, even if total employment in an industry is little changed. The problems of adjustment depend not only on the rate of technological development but also on the capacity of the country to adjust. There is evidence that this capacity has grown on net balance. A higher level of education, better transportation and communications, a greater reserve in the form of savings—all identified among the sources of higher productivity—also help to ease the problem of adjustment.

In addition, improvement has occurred in aids to adjustment, including unemployment insurance, employment services, retraining programs, public service employment, and pension vesting. There has also been improvement in private arrangements, worked out in labor-management agreements, to study and ease the problems of adjustment to technological change; for example, by avoiding worker displacement, mitigating financial loss to individual workers, and assisting workers in securing alternative work. Through collective bargaining, programs have been adopted for manpower planning for attrition, advance notice of change, employee reassignment and retraining, protection of pay rate, severance pay and retirement, and separation programs which provide benefits in case of involuntary early termination.

Therefore, rather than responding to adjustment problems by impeding technological development or the other factors which make for higher productivity, arrangements must be made whereby society as a whole, which benefits from these changes, helps to shoulder the problems of adjusting to rising productivity. Higher productivity is the source of our nation's greater economic welfare. We must see to it that the burdens resulting from this higher productivity are not borne exclusively by those who are immediately affected.

34

Contribution of
Research and Development to
Economic Growth in the United States

EDWIN MANSFIELD

Edwin Mansfield is Professor of Economics at the Wharton School of the University of Pennsylvania. This excerpt comes from a paper commissioned by the National Science Foundation and published in Science *in 1972.*

Technological change is clearly an important factor in economic growth, both in the United States and in other countries, both now and in the past. In recent years—after neglecting the study of technological change for a long time—economists have shown a considerable interest in examining the relationship between research and development (R and D), on the one hand, and the rate of economic growth and productivity increase, on the other. In addition, there have been a number of discussions of whether we, as a nation, are underinvesting in certain kinds of R and D.

At the outset, two important points should be noted. First, by focusing attention on the economic effects of R and D, I am not implying that only these effects of R and D are important. On the contrary, increased knowledge is clearly of great importance above and beyond its strictly economic benefits. Second, by looking at our nation's rate of economic growth and productivity increase, I am not assuming explicitly or implicitly that economic growth is, in some simple sense, what public policy should attempt to maximize. Clearly, the desirability of a particular growth rate depends on the way it is achieved, how the

extra production is distributed, how growth is measured, and many other things.

R and D and Economic Growth

The pioneering studies of the relationship between technological change and economic growth occurred in the mid-1950s. Assuming that there were constant returns to scale, that capital and labor were paid their marginal products, and that technological change was neutral, Robert Solow attempted to estimate the rate of technological change for the nonfarm American economy during the period from 1909 to 1949. His findings suggested that, for the period as a whole, the average rate of technological change was about 1.5 percent per year. More precisely, the output that could be derived from a fixed amount of inputs increased at about 1.5 percent per year.

Based on these findings, he concluded that about 90 percent of the increase in output per capita during this period was attributable to technological change, whereas only a minor proportion of the increase was due to increases in the amount of capital employed

193

per worker. This conclusion received a great deal of attention—and caused some consternation among economists who had focused much more attention on the factors underlying the amount of capital employed per worker than on those underlying the rate of technological change. A flurry of papers followed Solow's, each modifying his techniques slightly or using a somewhat different data base.

After the first wave of papers in the mid-1950s, investigators began to feel increasingly uneasy about the basic methodology used in these studies. In essence, this methodology was the following. Economists, who view the total output of the economy as being due to various inputs of productive services into the productive process, began by specifying these inputs as labor and capital and by attempting to estimate the contribution of these inputs to the measured growth of output. Then, whatever portion of the measured growth of output that could not be explained by these inputs was attributed to technological change. The crudeness of this procedure is obvious. Since the effect of technological change is equated with whatever increase in output is unexplained by other inputs, the resulting measure of the effect of technological change does not isolate the effects of technological change alone. It also contains the effects of whatever inputs are excluded—which, depending on the study, may be economies of scale, improved allocation of resources, changes in product mix, increases in education, or improved health and nutrition of workers.

To remedy some of these limitations, a number of additional studies were carried out in the early 1960s, the most comprehensive and influential one being by Edward Denison. Denison attempted to include many inputs—particularly changes in labor quality associated with increases in schooling—that had been omitted, largely or completely, in earlier studies. Since it was relatively comprehensive, his study resulted in a relatively low residual increase in output unexplained by the inputs included. Specifically, Denison concluded that the "advance of knowledge"—his term for the residual—was responsible for about 40 percent of the total increase in national income per person employed during 1929–1957.

Of course, technological change can stem from sources other than organized R and D, as evidenced by the findings of Jewkes *et al.* concerning the importance of independent investors as a source of major inventions, and the findings by Hollander and others concerning the importance of technological changes that depend in no significant way on formal R and D. Denison estimates that about one-fifth of the

contribution to economic growth of "advance of knowledge" in 1929–1957 can be attributed to organized R and D. But this is the roughest kind of guess, and Denison himself would be the first to admit that this estimate is based largely on conjecture.

Fundamental Problems of Measurement

How firmly based is the current state of the art in this area? In others words, how reliable are the estimates of the contribution of R and D to economic growth in the United States? I have already indicated some of the difficulties present in these estimates. Unfortunately, there are a number of additional problems of a fundamental nature that must be understood as well. First, the measured rates of growth of output on which these estimates are based suffer from a very important defect because, to a large extent, they fail to give proper credit and weight to improvements in the quality of goods and services produced, and these improvements are an important result of R and D. For example, the growth rate would have been the same whether antibiotics were developed or not, or whether we devoted the resources used to reach the moon to public works. In general, only those changes in technology that reduce the costs of end products already in existence have an effect on measured economic growth. Unfortunately, the measured growth of national income fails to register or indicate the effects on consumer welfare of the increased spectrum of choice arising from the introduction of new products.

Second, the models on which these estimates are based may not take into account the full complexity of the relationships among the various inputs. In particular, if the returns to some input are dependent on the rate of technological change, and if this is not recognized explicitly, some of technology's contribution to economic growth will be attributed incorrectly to other inputs. This may be the case with education, since the returns to education would probably have been less if technological change had occurred at a slower pace. It may also be the case with "the reallocation of resources," a factor sometimes used to explain part of the residual increase in output.

Third, it is not clear how one can get from an estimate of the contribution to economic growth of technological change (or advance of knowledge, in Denison's terms) to an estimate of the contribution to economic growth of R and D. Clearly, there is no reason that these two estimates should be the same; on the contrary, one would expect the latter estimate to be smaller than the former. But the estimate that results from the models discussed above is the former estimate, not the latter—which is the one we want. As pointed out, Denison does make an attempt to derive the latter estimate from the former, and to do so, he is forced to make extremely rough assumptions. To a certain extent, numbers must simply be pulled out of the air.

Fourth, there are difficulties in measuring inputs, the measurement of aggregate capital being a particularly nettlesome problem. Since errors in the measurement of inputs will result in errors in the estimated contribution of these inputs to economic growth, these errors will also be transmitted to, and will affect, the residual unexplained increase in output, which is used to measure the contribution of technological change to economic growth. Also, it is difficult to adjust for quality changes in inputs, and there are problems in constructing proper price deflators.

Fifth, difficulties are caused by the fact that much of the nation's R and D is devoted to defense and space purposes. For example, some observers note the tremendous increase in expenditures on R and D in the postwar period and conclude that, because productivity has not risen much faster in this period than it did before the war, the effect of R and D on economic growth must be very small. What these observers forget is that the bulk of the nation's expenditures on R and D has been devoted to defense and space objectives and that the contribution of such expenditures to economic growth may have been limited. Moreover, they fail to realize that improvements in defense and space capability per dollar spent will not show up in measures of output because government output is valued at cost. (Also, they fail to recognize the fact that product improvements and new products often fail to register in output measures and that the effects of R and D often occur with a considerable lag.)

Based on this catalog of problems and limitations, it is clear that the current state of the art in this area is not strong enough to permit very accurate estimates of the contribution of R and D to the economic growth of the United States. At best, the available estimates are rough guidelines. In no sense is this a criticism of the economics profession or of the people working in this area. On the contrary, a great deal of progress has been made since the pioneering ventures into this area a little over a decade ago. Given the small number of people working in this area and the inherent difficulty of the problem, it is hard to see how much more could have been achieved.

R and D and Productivity Increase in Individual Industries

During the late 1950s, important work concerning the rate of productivity increase in various industries was going on at the National Bureau of Economic Research. As part of this work, Terleckyj carried out a study of the relationship between an industry's rate of increase of total factor productivity during the period from 1919 to 1953 and various industry characteristics. According to his results, an industry's rate of growth of total factor productivity was related in a statistically significant way to its ratio of R and D expenditures to sales, its rate of change of output level, and the amplitude of its cyclical fluctuations. Specifically, the rate of growth of total factor productivity increased by about 0.5 percent for each tenfold increase in the ratio of R and D expenditures to sales and by about 1 percent for every 3 percent increase in the industry's growth rate.

Subsequently, two other papers appeared on this topic, one pertaining to agriculture, one pertaining to manufacturing. The agricultural study by Zvi Griliches investigated the relationship in various years between output per farm in a given state and the amounts of land, labor, fertilizer, and machinery per farm, as well as average education and expenditures on research and extension in a given state. The results indicate that, holding other inputs constant, output was related in a statistically significant way to the amount spent on research and extension. Moreover, the regression coefficient of this variable remains remarkably stable when cross sections are deleted or added and when the specification of the model is changed somewhat.

The manufacturing study by Edwin Mansfield was based on data regarding ten large chemical and petroleum firms and ten manufacturing industries in the postwar period. Both for firms and for industries, the measured rate of productivity change was related in a statistically significant way to the rate of growth of cumulated R and D expenditures made by the firm or industry. The specific form of the relationship depends somewhat on whether technological change is assumed to be disembodied (better methods and organization that improve the efficiency of both old capital and new) or capital embodied (innovations that must be embodied in new equipment if they are to be utilized). When technological change was disembodied, the average effect of a 1 percent increase in the rate of growth of cumulated R and D expenditures was a 0.1 percent increase in the rate of productivity increase. When technological change was capital embodied, it was a 0.7 percent increase in the rate of productivity increase.

Evaluation of Productivity Studies

How reliable are these estimates of the relationship between R and D and productivity increase in individual industries? Clearly, one advantage of these studies is that the effect of R and D is not derived indirectly as a residual. Instead, an industry's—or a firm's or area's—R and D expenditures are introduced as an explicit input in the productive process. Thus, it is possible to obtain explicit relationships between R and D and productivity increase; it is no longer necessary to attribute to technology or R and D whatever cannot be explained by other factors. This is a real advantage.

But a number of important problems remain. First, too little is known about the characteristics of the activities that firms call "research and development."

Second, even if one were sure that R and D figures were reliable, there would still be the possibility of spurious correlation. Firms and industries that spend relatively large amounts on R and D may tend to have managements that are relatively progressive and forward looking. To what extent is the observed relationship between R and D and productivity increase due to this factor rather than to R and D?

Third, a large percentage of the R and D carried out by many industries is directed at productivity increase in *other* industries. Consequently, relationships between R and D in an industry or firm and productivity increase in the *same* industry or firm catch only part of the effects of R and D.

Fourth, there is a host of technical problems. To what extent is technological change disembodied, and to what extent is it capital embodied? If R and D is treated as investment in new knowledge—as it is in most of these studies—what depreciation rate should be used? Also, there is the perennial problem of how R and D expenditures should be deflated, as well as the problem of the form of the production function that should be used in particular cases.

Fifth, studies of the relationship between R and D and productivity increase in individual industries suffer, of course, from a number of the same problems that beset studies of the contribution of R and D to economic growth. Some of these problems are inadequacies of the output measures used, poor specification of the relationship among inputs, and difficulties in measuring inputs.

Externalities, Riskiness, and Investment in R and D

At this point, I turn to the question of whether or not, from a purely economic point of view, the United States is underinvesting in R and D. Certain propositions bearing on this question are widely accepted by economists and should be set forth at the beginning of this discussion. The first proposition is that, because the results of research are often of little direct value to the sponsoring firm but of great value to other firms, there is good reason to believe that, left to its own devices, the market would allocate too few resources to R and D—and that the shortfall would be particularly great at the more basic end of the R and D spectrum. The reason for this is fairly obvious: the market operates on the principle that the benefits go to the person bearing the costs, and vice versa. If a firm or individual takes an action that contributes to society's welfare, but it cannot appropriate the full gain, then it obviously is less likely to take this action than would be socially desirable.

The second proposition is that, because R and D is risky for the individual form, there is good reason to believe that the market, left to its own devices, would allocate too few resources to R and D. Of course, the risk to the individual investor in R and D is greater than the risk to society, since the results of the R and D may be useful to someone else, not to himself, and he may be unable to obtain from the user the full value of the information. Because the economic system has limited and imperfect ways of shifting risks, there would be an underinvestment in R and D. For this reason, too, one would expect the underinvestment to be greatest at the more basic end of the R and D spectrum.

These defects of the market mechanism in allocating resources to R and D have long been recognized. Moreover, they have been recognized in the realm of practical affairs and of social organization, as well as in the realm of social science. Our society, taking account of these defects of the market mechanism, does not depend exclusively on the market for an investment in R and D. On the contrary, a very large proportion of the nation's expenditures on R and D stems from government agencies, private foundations, and universities, all of which supplement the R and D supported through the market mechanism. Thus, the relevant question is not whether the market mechanism requires supplementing, but whether the type and extent of supplementary support provided at present is too large or too small, and whether it is allocated properly.

Salient Characteristics of the Nation's Investment in R and D

Before discussing the above question, several important characteristics of the nation's investment in R and D must be noted. First, as is well known, the nation's investment in R and D is focused very strongly on defense and space technology. During the early 1960s, over 55 percent of the nation's R and D expenditures were for these purposes. With the passage of time, this percentage has decreased, but even in 1970, about 43 percent of the nation's investment in R and D was for these purposes. The relevance to economic growth of much of this huge investment in defense and space R and D has been questioned by many economists.

Numerous groups within the government have been interested in the extent of the benefits to civilian technology—the "spillover" or "fallout"—from military and space R and D. Obviously, the extent of this spillover has implications regarding the extent to which the investment in defense and space R and D has relevance for economic growth. It is perfectly clear that the value of the spillover that has occurred in the past has been substantial—the computer, numerical control, integrated circuits, atomic energy, and many other significant advances having stemmed at least partly from military R and D. However, it is also clear that the contribution of a dollar of military and space R and D to economic growth is considerably less than the contribution of a dollar of civilian R and D. Moreover, in the opinion of some observers, the spillover per dollar of military-space R and D is unlikely to be as great as it was in the past, because the capabilities that are being developed and the environment that is being explored are less closely connected with civilian pursuits than they were in the past.

Second, just as the government's expenditures on R and D are concentrated largely in a few agencies (the Department of Defense, the National Aeronautics and Space Administration, and the Atomic Energy

Commission) with defense and space missions, so industry's expenditures on R and D are concentrated in a few industries. In 1969, 82 percent of all industrial R and D expenditures took place in only five industries—aerospace, electrical equipment and communication, chemicals (including drugs), machinery, and motor vehicles. Of course, this concentration is due in part to the fact that these industries perform a great deal of R and D for the federal government. But if one looks only at company-financed R and D, the concentration is nearly the same, with these five industries accounting in 1969 for 75 percent of all company-financed R and D expenditures. Moreover, this concentration seems to be increasing.

Industry's R and D expenditures are also concentrated largely on products, not processes. For example, according to a survey of business firms carried out in the early 1960s, about 47 percent of the firms reported that their main purpose was to develop new products, and about 40 percent reported that it was to improve existing products: only 13 percent reported that it was to develop new processes. However, lest there be any misunderstanding, it should be recognized that one industry's products may be part of another industry's processes. Thus, when a machinery producer improves its products or when a chemical producer improves its products, the result may be an improvement in the processes of industries that buy and use the machinery or chemicals.

Third, this nation's investment in R and D is focused very strongly on development, not research. The distinction between research and development, although hazy and indistinct in some cases, is important. Research is aimed primarily at the search for new knowledge, whereas development is aimed at the reduction of research findings to practice. In 1970, according to estimates made by the National Science Foundation, about two-thirds of the nation's investment in R and D went for development, only about one-third for research. Much of the development work carried out by industry and government is aimed at very specific objectives and involves large expenditures on prototypes and pilot plants. It is important to avoid the (unfortunately common) mistake of confusing this activity with research.

Moreover, it is important to recognize that much of the R and D carried out by industry is aimed at fairly modest advances in the state of the art. Studies seem to indicate that the really major inventions seldom stem from industrial laboratories of major firms, which are primarily contributors of minor "improvement" inventions. Also, surveys indicate that firms exphasize relatively short payout periods for R and D, this emphasis being another indication that most R and D carried out by the responding firms is aimed at improvements or minor changes in existing products. In addition, detailed studies of the characteristics of the R and D portfolio of a number of industrial laboratories provide direct evidence that the bulk of the work involves rather small technical risks.

Nature of the Evidence

A number of economists have been concerned with the question of whether or not the R and D support that society presently gives to supplement the market mechanism is adequate in total and allocated properly. They generally seem to be of the opinion that the nation's investment in R and D may be too small, but this opinion is often characterized as little more than a hunch. They are much more confident that, whether or not the total investment in R and D is too small, the investment is not properly allocated, there being too little R and D devoted to (1) more ambitious attempts to place the technology of various industries on a stronger scientific base; (2) urban transportation, pollution control, and housing; and (3) more competitive and fragmented industries.

What sorts of evidence are these conclusions based on? First, some of these studies rely largely on judgment combined with economic theory.

Second, these studies rely on the results of several econometric investigations which indicate that, for the industries and fields under investigation, the marginal rate of return from an investment in R and D has been very high.

Finally, based on computations for the economy as a whole, Edward Denison concluded that the rate of return from R and D was about the same as the rate of return from investment in capital goods. His estimate of the returns from R and D was lower than the estimates of other investigators, perhaps because he assumed no lag between R and D expenditures and their contribution to economic growth. The calculated rate of return on R and D could be much higher if R and D's contribution occurred only with a lag. In his 1969 presidential address to the American Economic Association, William Fellner estimated the average social rate of return from technological-progress activities and concluded that it is "substantially in excess" of 13 or 18 percent, depending on the cost base, and that this is much higher than the marginal rate of return from physical investment at a more or less given level of knowledge.

Evaluation of the Evidence

How conclusive is the evidence described above? First, consider the judgmental approach. Clearly, this approach, although sensible and frequently used in all fields, is limited by the large subjective component that inevitably must enter the calculations. It is very difficult to estimate the extent of the external economies arising from particular types of R and D, or to determine whether incentive modifications are small relative to the gap between private and social returns, or to tell whether supplementary R and D provided by government and nonprofit institutions is small relative to the scope of socially desirable work. The weight one places on this evidence must depend on the confidence one puts in the judgment and objectivity of the investigators.

Second, consider the econometric approach. This approach is more objective in many respects. Certainly the assumptions underlying the estimates are specified clearly, and one can see how sensitive the results are to changes in these assumptions. But this does not mean that the results can be accepted uncritically. On the contrary, since most of these estimates depend on, and are derived from, the studies of R and D and productivity growth in individual industries, they are subject to many of the limitations of these studies.

Yet, having taken pains to point out the limitations of the individual bits of evidence that have been amassed, we must not lose sight of an impressive fact: no matter which of the available studies one looks at (other than Denison's), the conclusions seem to point in the same direction. In the case of those using the judgmental approach, there is considerable agreement that we may be underinvesting in particular types of R and D in the civilian sector of the economy. In the case of the econometric studies, every study of which I am aware indicates that the rate of return from additional R and D in the civilian sector is very high.

35

Economic Incentives
in Air-Pollution Control

EDWIN S. MILLS

Edwin S. Mills is Professor of Economics at Princeton University. This selection appeared in The Economics of Air Pollution, *edited by H. Wolozin and published in 1966.*

Smoke is one of the classic examples of external diseconomies mentioned in the writings of Alfred Marshall and his followers. Generations of college instructors have used this form of air pollution as an illustration to help their students to understand conditions under which competitive markets will or will not allocate resources efficiently. By now, the theoretical problems have been explored with the sharpest tools available to economists. The consensus among economists on the basic issue is overwhelming, and I suspect one would be hard-pressed to find a proposition that commands more widespread agreement among economists than the following: The discharge of pollutants into the atmosphere imposes on some members of society costs which are inadequately imputed to the sources of the pollution by free markets, resulting in more pollution than would be desirable from the point of view of society as a whole.

In spite of the widespread agreement on the fundamental issues regarding externalities such as air pollution, there have been remarkably few attempts in the scholarly literature to carry the analysis beyond this point. Most writers have been content to point out that the free market will misallocate resources in this respect, and to conclude that this justifies intervention. But what sort of intervention? There are many kinds, and some are clearly preferable to others.

Too often we use the imperfect working of a free market to justify *any* kind of intervention. This is really an anomalous situation. After all, markets are man-made institutions, and they can be designed in many ways. When an economist concludes that a free market is working badly—giving the wrong signals, so to speak—he should also ask how the market may be restructured so that it will give the right signals.

Thus, in the case of air pollution, acceptance of the proposition stated above leads most people to think entirely in terms of direct regulation—permits, registration, licenses, enforcement of standards, and so on. I submit that this is rather like abandoning a car because it has a flat tire. Of course, in some cases the car may be working so badly that the presence of a flat tire makes it rational to abandon it, and correspondingly the inadequacies of some market mechanisms may make abandonment desirable. Nevertheless, I submit that the more logical procedure is to ask how a badly functioning market may be restructured so as to preserve the clear advantages of free and decentralized decision-making, but to remedy its defects. Only when there appears to be no feasible way of structuring a market so that it will give participants the right signals, should it be given up in favor of direct regulation.

Technical Factors

Technical questions arise with regard to both the sources and the effects of air pollution. Unfortunately, much less is known about the sources and effects of air pollution than about those of water pollution.

Although a large number of substances can pollute the air, it seems that almost all air-pollution problems result from the direct or indirect effects of from five to ten substances. Candidates for inclusion in this group are particulate matter (smoke and dust), sulfur dioxide, carbon monoxide, hydrocarbons, nitrogen oxides, carbon dioxide, hydrogen sulfide, hydrogen fluoride, and lead. Some experts might add one or two others, and some might delete one or two. Most sources of these substances can apparently be identified, and the amounts can be metered, at least on a sample basis, in ways that are not extremely expensive. For most pollutants, there are a large number of control methods, some of which are more effective than others, and some of which are more costly than others. Take sulfur dioxide as an example. Its major source is burning fossil fuels. It can be removed from smokestack gases in a variety of more or less effective ways. Or it can be removed from the fuel before burning (*e.g.*, in the refining process). In addition, fuels with low sulfur dioxide content can be substituted for fuels with high sulfur dioxide content. The time pattern of burning can be altered so that relatively little fuel is burned at times when pollution is serious. The level or location of the activity for which the fuel is burned can be changed. Finally, it can be dispersed by high smokestacks.

These methods of control differ greatly in effectiveness and cost. Some may be more appropriate in one set of conditions that in others. The moral is: There are a large number of ways of doing almost anything, and air-pollution abatement is no exception.

Technical questions also arise regarding the effects of air pollution. Pollution may damage property (including crops and livestock); it may injure people's health; or it may be aesthetically displeasing. Property damage should not be particularly difficult to estimate, but I have seen no very careful attempts to do so. Health damage is much harder to estimate because of the chronic nature of the suspected damage. The aesthetic damage is measured by the number of dollars people are willing to pay to reduce the aesthetic displeasure from air pollution. Like other subjective magnitudes, it is difficult to estimate.

The relevance of the above considerations is, of course, that the extent to which it is in society's interests to abate pollution depends on the benefits and costs of doing so.

It is easy to state the principle by which the socially desirable amount of pollution abatement should be determined: Any given pollution level should be reached by the least costly combination of means available; the level of pollution should be achieved at which the cost of a further reduction would exceed the benefits.

To clothe the bare bones of this principle with the flesh of substance is a very tall order indeed. In principle, if every relevant number were known, an edict could be issued to each polluter specifying the amount by which he was to reduce his discharge of pollutants and the means by which he was to do so. In fact, we are even farther from having the right numbers for air pollution than we are from having those for water pollution.

In this situation, I suggest that any scheme for abatement should be consistent with the following principles:

1. It should permit decision-making to be as decentralized as possible. Other things being equal, a rule that discharges must be reduced by a certain amount is preferable to a rule that particular devices be installed, since the former permits alternatives to be considered that may be cheaper than the devices specified in the latter.

2. It should be experimental and flexible. As experience with abatement schemes accumulates, we will gain information about benefits and costs of abatement. We will then revise our ideas about the desirable amount and methods of abatement. Control schemes will have to be revised accordingly.

3. It should be coupled with careful economic research on benefits and costs of air-pollution abatement. Without benefit-cost calculations, we cannot determine the desirable amount of abatement. We can, however, conjecture with confidence that

more abatement is desirable than is provided by existing controls. Therefore, our present ignorance of benefits and costs should not be used as an excuse for doing nothing. I would place great emphasis on doing the appropriate research as part of any control scheme. A well-designed scheme will provide information (*e.g.*, on the costs of a variety of control devices) that is relevant to the benefit-cost calculations.

Means of Control

We are now in a position to evaluate a variety of schemes that are in use or have been proposed to control or abate air pollution.

1. *Direct Regulation.* In this category, I include licenses, permits, compulsory standards, zoning, registration, and equity litigation.

2. *Payments.* In this category I include not only direct payments or subsidies, but also reductions in collections that would otherwise be made. Examples are subsidization of particular control devices, forgiveness of local property taxes on pollution-control equipment, accelerated depreciation on control equipment, payments for decreases in the discharge of pollutants, and tax credits for investment in control equipment.

3. *Charges.* This category includes schedules of charges, or fees, for the discharge of different amounts of specified pollutants, and excise or other taxes on specific sources of pollution (such as coal).

My objection to direct regulation should be clear by now. It is too rigid and inflexible, and loses the advantages of decentralized decision-making. For example, a rule that factories limit their discharges of pollutants to certain levels would be less desirable than a system of effluent fees that achieved the same overall reduction in pollution, in that the latter would permit each firm to make the adjustment to the extent and in the manner that best suited its own situation. Direct restrictions are usually cumbersome to administer, and rarely achieve more than the grossest form of control. In spite of the fact that almost all of our present control programs fall into this category, they should be tried only after all others have been found unworkable.

Thus, first consideration ought to be given to control schemes under the second and third categories.

Many of the specific schemes under these two categories are undesirable in that they involve charges or payments for the wrong thing. If it is desired to reduce air pollution, then the charge or payment should depend on the amount of pollutants discharged and not on an activity that is directly or indirectly related to the discharge of pollutants. For example, an excise tax on coal is less desirable than a tax on the discharge of pollutants resulting from burning coal because the former distorts resource use in favor of other fuels and against devices to remove pollutants from stack gases after burning coal. As a second example, a payment to firms for decreasing the discharge of pollutants is better than a tax credit for investment in pollution-control devices because the latter introduces a bias against other means of reducing the discharge of pollutants, such as the burning of nonpolluting fuels. Thus, many control schemes can be eliminated on the principle that more efficient control can normally be obtained by incentives that depend on the variable it is desired to influence rather than by incentives that depend on a related variable.

Many of the specific schemes under *Payments* can be eliminated on the grounds that they propose to subsidize the purchase of devices that neither add to revenues nor reduce costs. Thus, if a pollution-control device neither helps to produce salable products nor reduces production costs, a firm really receives very little incentive to buy the device even if the government offers to pay half the cost. All that such subsidy schemes accomplish is to reduce somewhat the resistance to direct controls. Of course, some control devices may help to recover wastes that can be made into salable products. Although there are isolated examples of the recovery of valuable wastes in the process of air-pollution control, it is hard to know whether such possibilities are extensive. A careful survey of this subject would be interesting. However, the key point is that, to the extent that waste recovery is desirable, firms receive the appropriate incentive to recover wastes by the use of fees or payments that are related to the discharge of effluents. Therefore, even the possibility of waste recovery does not justify subsidization of devices to recover wastes.

The foregoing analysis creates a presumption in favor of schemes under which either payments are made for reducing the discharge of pollutants or charges are made for the amount of pollutants discharged. The basic condition for optimum resource allocation can in principle be satisfied by either scheme, since under either scheme just enough incentive can be provided so that the marginal cost of further abatement approximates the marginal benefits of further abatement. There are, however, three reasons for believing that charges are preferable to subsidies:

1. There is no natural "origin" for payments. In principle, the payment should be for a reduction in the discharge of pollutants below what it would have been without the payment. Estimation of this magnitude would be difficult and the recipient of the subsidy would have an obvious incentive to exaggerate the amount of pollutants he would have discharged without the subsidy. The establishment of a new factory would raise a particularly difficult problem. The trouble is precisely that which agricultural policy meets when it tries to pay farmers to reduce their crops. Jokes about farmers deciding to double the amount of corn not produced this year capture the essence of the problem.

2. Payments violate feelings of equity which many people have on this subject. People feel that if polluting the air is a cost of producing certain products, then the consumers who benefit ought to pay this cost just as they ought to pay the costs of labor and other inputs needed in production.

3. If the tax system is used to make the payments, e.g., by permitting a credit against tax liability for reduced discharge of pollutants, a "gimmick" is introduced into the tax system which, other things being equal, it is better to avoid. Whether or not the tax system is used to make the payments, the money must be raised at least partly by higher taxes than otherwise for some taxpayers. Since most of our taxes are not neutral, resource misallocation may result.

I feel that the above analysis creates at least a strong presumption for the use of discharge or effluent fees as a means of air-pollution abatement.

A Tentative Proposal

It is not the purpose of this paper to make detailed proposals of an institutional or legal nature. Nevertheless, implementation of any scheme of air-pollution abatement requires an institutional framework, and some discussion of criteria for such a framework seems desirable. Briefly, the proposal is that air pollution control authorities be created with responsi-bility to evaluate a variety of abatement schemes, to estimate benefits and costs, to render technical assistance, to levy charges for the discharge of effluents, and to adopt other means of abatement.

Serious problems of air pollution are found mostly in urban areas of substantial size. Within an urban area, air pollution is no respecter of political boundaries, and an authority's jurisdiction should be defined by the boundaries of a metropolitan air shed. Although difficult to identify precisely, such air sheds would roughly coincide with Standard Metropolitan Statistical Areas. Except in a few cases, such as the Chicago–Gary and the New York–Northern New Jersey areas, jurisdiction could be confined to a single metropolitan area. In a number of instances, the authority would have to be interstate. In many large metropolitan areas, the authority would have to be the joint creation of several local governments. There would presumably be participation by state governments and by the Federal Government at least to the extent of encouragement and financial support.

Each authority would have broad responsibility for dealing with air pollution in its metropolitan air shed. It would institute discharge fees and would be mainly financed by such fees. It would have the responsibility of estimating benefits and costs of air-pollution abatement, and of setting fees accordingly. It would have to identify major pollutants in its area and set fees appropriate to each significant pollutant. The authority could also provide technical advice and help concerning methods of abatement.

Although there would be great uncertainty as to the appropriate level of fees at first, this should not prevent their use. They should be set conservatively while study was in progress, and data on the responses of firms to modest fees would be valuable in making benefit-cost calculations. Given present uncertainties, a certain amount of flexible experimentation with fees would be desirable.

Questions will necessarily arise as to just what kinds and sources of pollutants would come under the jurisdiction of the proposed authority. I do not pretend to have answers to all such questions. Presumably, standard charges could be set for all major pollutants, with provision for variation in each metropolitan air shed to meet local conditions. It is clear that provision should be made for the possibility of varying the charge for a particular pollutant from air shed to air shed. The harm done by the discharge of a ton of sulfur dioxide will vary from place to place, depending on meteorological and other factors. It is probably less harmful in Omaha than in Los Angeles. It is important that charges reflect these differences, so that locational decisions will be appropriately affected.

Consideration would also have to be given to the appropriate temporal pattern of charges. In most cities, pollution is much more serious in summer than at other times. Charges that were in effect only during summer months might induce a quite different set of adjustments than charges that were in effect at all times.

No one should pretend that the administration of an effective air pollution control scheme will be simple or cheap. Measurement and monitoring of discharges are necessary under any control scheme and can be expensive and technically difficult. Likewise, whatever the control scheme, finding the optimum degree of abatement requires the calculation of benefits and costs; these calculations are conceptually difficult and demanding.

The point that needs to be emphasized strongly is that the cost of administering a control scheme based on effluent fees will be less than the cost of administering any other scheme of equal effectiveness. An effluent-fee system, like ordinary price systems, is largely self-administering.

The point is important and is worth stating in detail. First, consider an effluent-fee system. Suppose a schedule of fees has been set. Then firms will gradually learn the rate of effluent discharge that is most profitable. Meanwhile, the enforcement agency will need to sample the firm's effluent to insure that the firm is paying the fee for the amount actually discharged. However, once the firm has found the most profitable rate of effluent discharge, and this is known to the enforcing agency, the firm will have no incentive to discharge any amount of effluent other than the one for which it is paying. At this point the system becomes self-administering and the enforcement agency need only collect bills. Second, consider a regulatory scheme under which the permissible discharge is set at the level that actually resulted under the effluent-fee scheme. Then the firm has a continuing incentive because of its advantage on the costside to exceed the permissible discharge rate so as to increase production. Monitoring by the enforcement agency therefore continues to be necessary.

Of course, under either a regulatory or an effluent-fee scheme, a change in conditions will require the search for a new "equilibrium." Neither system can be self-enforcing until the new equilibrium has been found. The point is that the effluent-fee system becomes self-enforcing at that point, whereas the regulatory system does not.

36

Safeguarding the Environment

COUNCIL OF
ECONOMIC ADVISERS

This article is taken from the 1971 Annual Report *of the
Council of Economic Advisers.*

As the economy grows, more waste of various types is produced. This does not cause major problems as long as the population is widely dispersed and the environment is not overloaded. As the population is increasingly concentrated in urban areas, however, the assimilative capacity of the environment in these areas tends to be exceeded. It then becomes more and more important that these limited environmental resources be used to the best advantage.

While it might be tempting to say that no one should be allowed to do any polluting, such a ban would require the cessation of virtually all economic activity. Since society places a value both on material goods and on clean air and water, arrangements must be devised that permit the value we place on each to determine our choices. Additional industrial development, increased use of pesticides on farms, and a growing volume of municipal sewage mean dirtier water downstream and fewer opportunities for recreation. On the other hand, stricter rules for pollution control generally mean either higher taxes or higher prices for goods. What we seek, therefore, is a set of rules for use of the environment which balances the advantages of each activity against its costs in other activities forgone. We want to eliminate pollution only when the physical and aesthetic discomfort it creates and its damage to people and things are more costly than the value of the good things—the abundance of industrial or farm products and efficient transportation—whose production has caused the pollution.

One of the ways that the competing claims on environmental resources could be balanced is through the development of "new towns" and resort communities. In these cases, a developer essentially buys title to a whole community's environment. He then has an economic incentive to avoid excessive damage to that environment. If, for example, he lets a factory buy the right to locate in the community even though it would substantially damage the community's environment, the value of potential residential property will thereby be lowered. Only when the advantages of industrial activity, such as increased income, outweigh the environmental disadvantages would the developer permit the factory to locate there. The same incentives would operate to limit pollution from such activities as municipal waste disposal.

The concept of unified development does not provide much guidance for solving pollution problems in areas that are already developed. With substantial capital invested in existing industrial facilities, a company that must pay large additional costs for pollution control may find continuing operations economically infeasible. A major change in liability for pollution costs may, in effect, expropriate the capital of some even while it enhances that of others. Nearby homeowners, on the other hand, may feel that pollution has always been harmful, and that its existence in the past does not justify its continuation.

This kind of dispute is central to the pollution problem and has become increasingly widespread as the various users of air and water seek to assert their claims to the limited environmental resources. A solution requires procedures and rules for the use of clean air and water that permit an orderly settlement of the competing claims on these limited resources, and that take account of the fact that these resources are not inexhaustible. The homeowner, the factory owner, and the farmer cannot simultaneously enjoy unlimited use of air and water. Industry and agriculture must recognize the new sense of urgency and concern about environmental problems. At the same time we must not overlook the fact that people also want more and more of the jobs and products of farms and factories.

Social Role of Property Rights

Problems similar to those arising from pollution have frequently been handled by granting private title to limited resources. Agricultural and forest land were once common property with poorly defined usage rights. As demands on these resources grew, their use by one party inflicted damage on others. The adjudication of conflicting claims to these resources by granting private title to them served the important social purpose of providing an incentive for these resources to be used more efficiently.

Air and water resources are harder to divide into meaningful private parcels than land. If each landowner had title to clean air around his property, a factory in New York that would emit air pollutants might have to deal with eight million "property owners," making it difficult to operate any factories at all.

Because private property arrangements cannot be applied generally to our air and water resources,

environmental problems connected with their use have to be solved within a framework of common property. The procedures and rules that we develop for resources regarded as common property must encourage their efficient use, just as would be true if they were private property.

A set of rules for the efficient use of air and water should not only permit no more fouling of air and water than we wish to tolerate, but it should also ensure that the tolerated degree of pollution occurs for the most productive reasons. The rules should also encourage the use of resources to limit the damage done by the pollution that is allowed. Finally, the rules and procedures should not themselves entail a higher cost of administration and enforcement than the cost of having no rules.

Specific Rules

As our society has become increasingly aware of the conflicting claims on air and water, specific rules have been developed for the use of these resources that recognize their limited nature. As early as 1899 a Federal law was passed regulating the disposal of waste in rivers and harbors. However, only with recent legal opinions and legislation has it become clear that the law could be used to reduce pollution, and the President has recently issued an Executive Order to use the law in this way.

Two problems must be faced in setting up rules for use of the environment. First, it must be decided how much pollution, if any, will be tolerated and under what circumstances changes in this amount will be permitted. Toward this end, the Federal Government has established the Environmental Protection Agency. This Agency, together with State and local authorities, develops standards for ambient air and water quality. These standards are statements of environmental quality goals considered desirable for particular areas or for the Nation as a whole. Since past arrangements, which imposed no cost on those who polluted the environment, led to excessive pollution, these air and water quality goals have uniformly sought reduction of pollution. Once such goals are developed, the next problem is to devise a system of rules for attaining them. Particular polluters must be led to change their actions so that, in fact, less pollution is produced. The Federal Government and other authorities have also been active in devising rules to implement attainment of environmental goals.

Foremost among the new rules has been the setting

of Government standards applicable to particular pollution sources. Under this system, the Government requires that each source reduce its emissions of pollutants by an amount sufficient to keep the total of all emissions within the environmental quality standard. All sources are ordinarily required to reduce emissions by the same percentage. While such Government standards have been applied most extensively to automobiles, similar standards are now being developed and implemented for other pollution sources.

This system of Government standards provides one mechanism for attaining environmental goals that recognizes the increasing scarcity of environmental resources. If this system is to generate efficient results, the goal must, of course, be appropriate. That is, the control of emissions that is required at each source must produce a high enough quality of air and water so that further improvements are not worth the costs of further control. If Government standards are to achieve the best use of environmental resources, there must also be substantial uniformity of the cost of control among pollution sources. Where these costs differ, the same environmental quality could be attained more cheaply by having the source with low control costs undertake more control than the source with high costs; but this would not occur if uniform standards were applied to all sources. The standards might, of course, be made nonuniform to account for differences in control cost, but only at considerable administrative cost because the Government agency setting the standards would need detailed knowledge about many different pollution-causing activities. It is also difficult politically to set variable standards. Many, including of course the owner, would think it unfair to penalize a plant with low control costs for its efficiency in pollution control by imposing an especially tough standard on such a plant.

Differences in control cost were perhaps an unimportant problem when attention focused on automobile exhausts. While there are some differences among types of cars in the cost of controlling exhaust emissions, the common technology of the internal combustion engine limited these differences and seemed to justify the application of common standards to all cars. In other cases a pollutant may prove so damaging that a common standard, namely, an outright ban on all discharges, would also be called for even if there are differences in control costs. However, as attention focuses on industrial and agricultural pollutants that are not to be eliminated completely, differences in control cost will prove to be

more of a problem. Particular pollutants are emitted from sources with diverse processes, sizes, and ages; and large differences in the cost of control can be expected. For example, sulphur oxides, which are one of the most damaging pollutants of the air, are emitted by electric powerplants, steel mills, nonferrous metal smelters, and home-heating systems. The differences in the size of these sources and the diversity of their processes make it almost certain that a given reduction of sulphur oxides cannot be accomplished at the same cost at each source. It is already known that there are economies of scale in sulphur oxide abatement, so that, for example, a given degree of control could be attained less expensively at one large powerplant than in many home-heating systems.

One way that differences in control costs could be taken into account would be to set "prices" for the use of the air and water. If each potential polluter were faced with a price for each unit of pollutant he discharged, he would have to compare this with the costs of pollution control in his particular circumstance. If control costs were relatively low, he would engage in extensive control to avoid paying the price being charged for polluting. If control costs were high, less control would be undertaken. Since sources with low control costs would carry out more than average control and those with high control costs less than average, a given level of environmental quality could be attained with expenditure of less productive resources than if all sources had to meet a common standard. At the same time, discovery of new techniques to control pollution would be encouraged, because every reduction in pollution would lower the payments for the right to emit pollutants. Of course, a price system, like a system of standards must be employed in a way that is consistent with environmental goals. The right to use air and water must be priced high enough so that the abatement encouraged improves the quality of the environment enough to justify the abatement expenses, while further improvement would not be worth additional expenditures.

There are three methods by which prices may be established for use of air and water: subsidies for control of pollution, charges for emissions of pollution (also called effluent fees), and sales of transferable environmental usage rights.

In the case of pollution abatement subsidies, the "price" paid by the polluter is the subsidy he forgoes. The more he fouls the air and water, the less he receives in subsidies. This approach can attain the efficiency inherent in a price system, but it entails substantial administrative as well as fiscal costs. In order to keep its subsidy payments down, the Government agency will have to incur the expense of ascertaining the level of pollution that would have occurred without any pollution control. As new products and processes are developed, this administrative task would grow more expensive, because in their case no record of past pollution would be available.

Alternatively charges could be levied on pollution. A charge on emissions of harmful substances would limit the amount of emissions indirectly. The higher the charge, the more a polluter would be willing to spend to avoid contaminating the environment (and thereby avoiding the charge). Another alternative would be an environmental usage certificate system. It would limit the amount of pollutants directly, but allow the price for pollution to be set indirectly. Under this system, as under a system of pollution standards, a Government agency would set a specific limit on the total amount of pollutants that could be emitted. It would then issue certificates which would each give the holder the right to emit some part of the total amount. Such certificates could be sold by the Government agency at auction and could be resold by owners. The Government auction and private resale market would thus establish a price on use of the environment. The more pollution a user engaged in, the more certificates he would have to buy. Groups especially concerned about the environment, such as conservation groups, would have a direct method of affecting the environment. They could themselves buy and hold some of the certificates, thus directly reducing the amount of emissions permitted and increasing the cost of pollution.

In general, any choice between emission charges and usage certificates should depend on which is easier to determine: the right price for pollution or the right quantity. If the amount of damage done by a pollutant can be measured easily and it appears that each unit of pollutant does roughly the same damage, an emission charge would be called for. If the damage per unit of pollutant may rise substantially with higher total emissions, a usage certificate system would be in order. Both the charge and the certificate approach would, like a system of standards, reduce the total amount of air and water pollution. However, by introducing a price mechanism, charges or certificates would allow the limited amount of tolerable pollution to be allocated efficiently when differences in the cost of control are present. Such efficiency would reduce the resource cost of pollution control and would therefore enable us to afford cleaner air and water

than we could if common standards were imposed in the face of differences in control costs.

While transferable environmental usage certificates have the same kind of efficiency advantages as emission charges, they have not yet been applied to the solution of environmental problems. One area where their use may merit attention is the control of offshore dumping of waste, which constitutes a growing hazard to the environment. It is feared that damage, especially to food sources, may escalate sharply unless steps are taken to limit the waste dumped into the ocean. At the same time, the cost of alternative means of waste disposal differs among the many current users of the ocean. Ocean dumping could be limited and individual differences in the cost of control of dumping taken into account under a certificate system. This would require that anyone who wished to dump wastes in the ocean have a Government license to do so. The license would specify the amount and type of material that could be dumped at a particular ocean site, and the number of such licenses would be limited to permit no more dumping activity than is considered safe. These licenses could be auctioned off by the Government, and sold later by a purchaser who no longer required them.

The Administration has proposed legislation under which licenses will be required for ocean dumping. A possibility worth considering is to make such licenses transferable. If this were done, prospective ocean dumpers would either have to pay the going price for licenses or find a cheaper way of disposing of their waste products. Those who were able to find such alternatives would not buy the licenses; those for whom alternatives were very costly would purchase them. The Government's prime concern should, of course, be limited to the total amount and kind of dumping, not who is doing it.

As choices are made between applying Government standards and instituting prices, the grounds on which the choice is made must be kept clear. Prices for pollution have, for example, been regarded by some as a form of evasion of standards, as a "license to pollute." Actually every system of rules for use of the environment, other than outright and total prohibition of certain uses, involves granting someone the right or "license" for some polluting. The amount of pollution that results does not depend on which system of rules is adopted, but on how each is administered.

It is sometimes said that administration of emission charges is unduly complicated, since they must be varied continually as pollution damages change, and they require close measurement of the pollution against which the charge is to be made. When damage estimates can change frequently, administration of a system of charges can become costly, and a certificate or standard system would save this cost. However, the cost of measuring pollution is not unique to a charge or certificate system. It would be just as great if standards are to be enforced. If measurement of pollution is too expensive to permit an effective system of standards, charges, or licenses, we face a choice between outright prohibition of the pollution, tolerating the present level, or requiring adoption of some conventional control procedure.

Problems in the Application of Rules

As rules for the use of common property are developed, whether these are embodied in Government standards, emission charges, or usage certificates, several problems will have to be resolved. We shall, for example, have to decide at what level of Government the rules will be made. Since these rules require that the gains and losses entailed by different levels of environmental quality be weighed, the Government agency making the rules must be responsive to those who bear the gains and losses. This is especially important because part of the damage from pollution cannot be measured directly but depends on such things as the aesthetic preferences of those affected. As a practical matter, much of the damage from pollution will be "measured" by political pressures from those damaged. Many, though not all, pollution problems are local in character, and therefore determination of the appropriate level of environmental quality in these cases is likely to be more accurate if it is done locally rather than by the Federal Government.

Where the environmental effects of a particular activity are in fact nationwide, as is true when poisons enter the food chain in a river and eventually damage fish caught in a distant waterway, the Federal Government must ensure that certain minimum standards are set. Some degree of uniformity may also be desirable where the cost of altering a given production process or product to meet differing local standards is great. It is not clear, however, that the Federal role should extend beyond the setting of such minimum standards where most benefits and costs of pollution are borne locally. In such cases, a pollution source generates income as well as pollution damage in the community where it is located. The seriousness of the damage will depend in part on such local factors as topography, wind patterns, and population density; and the right amount of control will depend on how much income would be lost to achieve abatement. It would not be sensible to impose the same abatement costs on a factory or farm located in a lightly populated area or where the environment has substantial assimilative capacity as on one in an area without these favorable characteristics.

Where environmental damage crosses local political boundaries but is not national in scope, the appropriate Federal role might be to foster the creation of interstate agencies, such as regional air quality boards and river basin authorities, which would be responsible to residents of areas affected by common environmental problems.

New rules for use of the environment are bound to affect competitive relationships within and among industries, localities, and nations. As industries are forced to bear the costs of using the environment, those who have high costs will lose part of their market to those with lower costs of using the environment. Inevitably, there will be pressures for Government action to prevent this reallocation of production. It should be realized, however, that such reallocation is necessary if environmental resources are to be used efficiently. Government interference with this process should therefore be limited to mitigating the transitional effects.

The same considerations apply internationally as well as domestically. Our high level of material wealth has caused us to place a higher value on clean air and water than they are assigned in countries which have lower incomes or where clean air and water may still be abundant. As this value becomes reflected in the costs imposed on our producers, those for whom the costs of pollution control are high will find it harder to compete with producers in countries where clean air and water are less valuable or where pollution is lower. The resulting reallocation of production among nations should benefit all nations. We will tend to concentrate on the production of goods which make small added demands on our valuable environmental resources, while other countries will produce goods which increase the use of their relatively abundant environmental resources or whose lower incomes make growing industrialization more urgent than extensive control of damage to their environment. International agreements to restrict this reallocation would, however, be desirable when pollutants emitted in one country damage residents of another.

PART FIVE

International Economics

In recent years, the headlines have trumpeted that the major trading nations of the world have been experiencing difficulties in keeping international trade and financial relationships in effective working order. In the opening selection, Hendrik S. Houthakker discusses the competitive position of the United States in world trade; he points out that, contrary to some popular opinion, we are not being flooded with imports, and we can compete with low-wage foreign labor. Richard Cooper, in the next article, discusses the relationship between technology and world trade. He stresses that technological innovation, and the international diffusion of innovations, have an important impact on a country's competitive position, and that differences among nations in technological capability are responsible for a substantial amount of international trade.

An important feature of the postwar world economy has been the growth of multinational corporations. Lawrence B. Krause, in the next article, describes the effects of multinational firms on product markets, input markets, technology gaps, and the international monetary system. He concludes that "there is little question that multinational corporations have benefited the international economy, but they have been a mixed blessing for many countries." Marxist Paul A. Baran's view of the multinational corporation is quite different from Krause's. Baran argues that "the principal impact of foreign enterprise on the development of the underdeveloped countries lies in hardening and strengthening the sway of merchant capitalism, in slowing down and indeed preventing its transformation into industrial capitalism." There has been a tendency in recent years for Congressmen and others to look with more favor on the regulation of multinational corporations and on the imposition of import quotas for many manufactured products. Walter Adams, in the next selection, argues against protectionist measures of this sort.

Irving Kravis argues in the following article that "the interests of the U.S. lie in the direction of freer trade. The arguments for a contrary policy . . . are based on incorrect assessments of the facts. . . ." James McCarthy then provides some empirical findings concerning the effectiveness of trade adjustment assistance, a feature of both the Trade Expansion Act of 1962 and the Trade Act of 1974.

In the area of international finance, no issue has received more attention, and generated more controversy, than the question of whether exchange rates should be fixed or flexible. Milton Friedman, in the next article, presents the case for flexible exchange rates. He argues that flexible exchange rates can allow international adjustments to take place with fewer undesirable internal adjustments and that they would allow us to "become masters in our own house." Henry C. Wallich, in the following selection, presents the case for fixed exchange rates. He says that flexible exchange rates would lead to a worldwide acceleration of inflation, and that "their successful functioning would require more self-discipline and mutual forbearance than countries today are likely to muster."

The less-developed countries contain the bulk of the world's population. In the next article, Barbara Ward describes the characteristics of these countries and some of the changes that have been going on in them. She stresses the difficulties involved in raising their economic growth rate, and chides the rich nations for being relatively unconcerned about the fate of the poor nations. Simon Kuznets, in the next selection (which is taken from his Nobel Memorial Lecture), goes further in describing the characteristics of the less-developed countries, and concludes that "substantial economic advance in the less-developed countries may require modification in the available stock of material technology, and probably even greater innovations in political and social structure."

Angus Maddison takes a more cheerful view of economic progress in the less-developed countries: based on a study of the experience of twenty-two developing countries in the 1950s and 1960s, he concludes in the next article that "the developing world has moved decisively into a new era." Hans J. Morgenthau, in the following selection, presents a rather skeptical view of what foreign aid can achieve. In his opinion, it "has a chance to be successful only within relatively narrow limits which are raised by cultural and political conditions impervious to direct outside influence."

37

America's Competitive
Position in World Trade

HENDRIK S. HOUTHAKKER

*Hendrik S. Houthakker is Professor of Economics at Harvard
University. During the early years of the Nixon administra-
tion, he was a member of the Council of Economic Advisers.
The following selection is taken from his testimony before the
Senate Subcommittee on Foreign Trade in 1971.*

The notion of competitiveness is a somewhat elusive
one and the question of whether we are competitive
does not admit of a precise answer, although some
indications can be given. As a first approximation we
may say that a nation is competitive if it is able,
through its exports and other activities, to earn the
foreign exchange it needs for imports and other
purposes. In fact, if we can abstract from capital
movements for the moment, a nation may be called
competitive if its current account balance—covering
goods, services, transportation, and unilateral transfers—is zero at full employment and in the absence of
quantitative restrictions. Thus, if this abstraction from
capital movements were legitimate, the United States
would be competitive at the present time, for our
current account balance has generally had a small
surplus. We do not yet have any figures for the first
quarter of 1971, but for 1970 as a whole the current
account surplus was $638 million. It is true that there
are restrictions on imports from the United States in
certain foreign countries, and that we also have
restrictions on certain classes of imports. The severity
of these restrictions is hard to measure, but in the

aggregate they probably come close to canceling each
other out as far as the current account balance is
concerned. Consequently, if we could consider only
the current account, our export prices would not be
too high, despite the fact that wages in the United
States are much higher than wages elsewhere. These
higher wages are generally offset by our much higher
productivity, which is itself the main cause of the
much higher wages prevailing in the United States.

This preliminary assessment of our overall position
does not mean that we are competitive in all
industries. If we were, we would not need any imports,
and foreigners would not have the dollars with which
to buy our exports. A country that engages in foreign
trade usually has a cost advantage in those commodities that it exports and a disadvantage in those that it
imports, though sometimes these advantages are
distorted by tariffs, subsidies, and other interferences
with trade. We have a cost advantage in agricultural
staples such as grains and cotton, where our costs are
kept low by our relatively abundant supply of land and
by the skill of our farmers, but if we tried to grow all of
the coffee or bananas consumed here we would find

211

that our costs would be far higher than those in certain tropical countries.

While in the case of agricultural and other primary products the relative cost advantages are strongly influenced by geographical and climatic factors, this is less true for manufactured products, where technology and the availability of capital, skilled labor, and management are likely to be more important. This implies that in manufactured products the pattern of relative advantages is more likely to change over time under the influence of trends in technology, transport costs, consumer demand, and other factors. For many years, for instance, the United States had a cost advantage in steel production, which made us net exporters. We apparently lost this advantage sometime in the late 1950s, when our trade balance in steel turned negative. On the other hand, our aircraft industry appears to have increased its cost advantage over the years.

These changes in the relative position of different industries sometimes cause difficult problems of adjustment. In the case of an industry that is losing its international competitiveness an increase in imports will be the first manifestation of what may be a much more deep-seated problem. Our steel industry, for instance, appears to be handicapped, among other things, by a lack of price competition among domestic producers. Since the demand for steel is subject to change over time, output has to vary excessively if prices are not allowed to help maintain equilibrium. This means that the industry must have excess capacity to be able to cope with demand at its peak. Most of the time, consequently, the industry is unable to use its capacity to full advantage and this keeps down its productivity and raises its costs. There are no doubt other important factors involved in the relative decline of our steel industry, and I mention this particular factor only as an example. The point I want to make is that imports not infrequently are blamed for developments of purely domestic origin.

In fact, there are relatively few important sectors of the economy where imports constitute a large enough percentage of supply to affect employment and profits to a serious extent. The notion that we are being flooded with imports will not bear examination. In 1967, there were only 25 four-digit manufacturing industries—out of a total of about 400—where imports accounted for 20 percent or more of total shipments; these 25 industries represented only 2.5 percent of the value of domestic shipments in all manufacturing.

There is no reason to think that these figures will be very different for more recent years.

Even though the impact of imports is frequently exaggerated, it remains true that the burden of adjustment may be too heavy for any particular industry to bear. This is why adjustment assistance may be necessary. In the last two years several groups of firms and workers have become eligible for such assistance, but more could be done if the law were changed. The President's trade bill of 1969 carried provisions for liberalizing it further. The great advantage of adjustment assistance is that, while sometimes costly in the short run, it promotes the adaptability to changing circumstances, both domestic and worldwide, that has long been one of the main strengths of our economy.

The argument is sometimes made that we cannot expose our workers to foreign competition because wages are much higher in this country than abroad. Protection, according to this argument, would be necessary to maintain the real income of workers. Apart from the difficulties of redeployment, which can be taken care of by adjustment assistance; this argument is without merit and indeed, the reverse of the truth. Our workers get high real income not because they are protected from foreign competition, but because they are highly productive, at least in certain industries. As a nation we have a high per capita real income because our output per capita is high. And our per capita output is high, among other things, because we use our labor force to good advantage. The fact that our wages are high does not prevent us from being net exporters in a number of industries, because productivity is high there, too. If we were to keep a larger proportion of our labor force in low-productivity industries, our per capita output would be reduced, and this would have an adverse effect on the real income of workers generally and of everybody else. Imports are also a significant factor in keeping domestic prices under control by stimulating competition and cost-saving innovations, and thus benefit us as consumers.

There are, of course, cases, especially those involving national security, where we may deliberately want to preserve domestic industries in the face of a cost disadvantage. Even in those national security cases, however, it should not be taken for granted that protection through quotas or otherwise is necessarily the best solution.

So far I have abstracted from capital movements

and talked only about the current account. Much of what I have said also applies to the more realistic situation where capital movements are present. The principal difference is that when there are capital movements the current account balance no longer has to be zero for a country to be competitive. Depending on whether there is an inflow or an outflow of capital, the current account balance will have to be negative or positive to achieve overall equilibrium in the balance of payments.

On the capital account it is useful to distinguish between short-term and long-term capital, and the latter can be further distinguished into direct investment and portfolio investment. We have had a large and growing outflow of capital on direct investment account for many years, while portfolio investment has been more erratic, with surpluses prevailing in recent years. For the sake of simplicity I shall ignore portfolio investment from here on, and leave short-term capital for later discussion. The outflow of funds for direct investment purposes would then have to be offset by a surplus on current account, but this has not happened in recent years. In fact, it is sometimes argued that the net outflow of direct investment funds by itself reflects a lack of competitiveness on our part, though it may also have something to do with the relative abundance of capital in different countries. The net outflow of direct investment means that more American businessmen find it profitable to invest abroad than foreign businessmen find it profitable to invest in the United States. However, direct investment is not always a reflection of relative cost differentials only; it may also be the result of import restrictions, differences in management skills, and technological advantages. Because of these several reasons more and more of our larger corporations have become multinational. While multinational corporations may raise certain problems for Government policy, there is no reason to believe that their existence invalidates the proposition that the best interest of all countries, including the United States, is normally served by unimpeded movement of goods and capital. What these corporations do, in fact, is to make within one firm the same cost comparisons that are also made by the free market, and in so doing they promote greater efficiency in the use of labor and capital everywhere.

I shall only say a few words about short-term capital, which is primarily a monetary phenomenon. The willingness of individuals and firms in different countries to give each other credit depends primarily on relative interest rates and expectations of future changes in exchange rates. Since the United States has a strong economy and a well-organized capital market, the dollar has become the principal reserve currency in the world. Many foreigners, both private and official, have been willing to hold substantial amounts of dollars at prevailing rates of interest in recent years, although occasionally this willingness is impaired by changes in international interest rate patterns or by fears of changes in parities.

Taking all these things—the current account, the long-term capital account, and the normal increase in short-term liabilities to be expected in a growing world economy—together it appears that the United States has often had some difficulty in attaining balance, though the shortfall has generally not been large. The large official settlements deficits that we have had in 1970 and in 1971 are attributable almost entirely to short-term capital movements of a transitory nature, but underlying this there may be a more fundamental problem of limited magnitude. Our imports increased more than our exports from 1964 to 1969, but the adverse effect on the current account was offset to some extent by an improvement in earnings on U.S. investment abroad, and more recently the growth in our exports has overtaken the growth in our imports. Once the expected revival of the domestic economy is realized, the current account may again become less favorable, but the long-term capital account may improve. I cannot definitely say, therefore, that at prevailing prices and exchange rates the United States is not competitive, but I would go so far as to say that it is more likely that we are less than competitive than that we are more than competitive.

In order to maintain and strengthen our competitive position in the future it is of the highest importance that we keep our domestic price level under control by appropriate fiscal and monetary policy. A continuation of present trends in prices and wages would almost certainly aggravate our international problems, even though our rates of increase do not necessarily compare unfavorably with those in other major countries. In addition, maintenance of a normal rate of productivity increase will obviously help our competitive position.

Finally, exchange rates are a significant determinant of competitiveness. Under the international monetary system as it has been operated until now there appears to be a bias toward devaluation of other currencies; moreover there is some evidence that foreign demand for our exports does not rise as rapidly as our own demand for imports, other factors remaining the same. Even though there is no firm evidence of an overall disequilibrium at the moment, it is, therefore necessary that the exchange rate mechanism possess sufficient flexibility to cope with whatever trends may emerge in the future. Greater U.S. competitiveness leading to a stronger export performance by our industries is probably the best defense against the understandable but shortsighted preoccupation with the transitory effects of imports that is now so widespread.

38

Technology and World Trade

RICHARD COOPER

Richard Cooper is Under Secretary of State in the Carter administration. The following article first appeared in Technology and World Trade, *published by the National Bureau of Standards in 1967.*

Most theoretical discussions of international trade involve what may be called traditional trade, the exchange of food for raw materials or for simple manufactures. David Ricardo, the English inventor of our theory of comparative advantage to explain trade flows, drew his example in terms of wine and cloth.

The United States imports coffee and exports wheat, both as a result of climatic and soil differences. Europe is often characterized as an importer of food, fuels and other raw materials, and an exporter of manufactures.

The composition and direction of trade depends, in the theory, largely on natural endowment, although occasionally special skills are also involved.

It is difficult to reconcile this theoretical picture of trade patterns to the patterns which have actually developed.

Manufactured products now account for nearly 60 percent of the value of world trade, up from 25 percent in the 1920s, and the proportion is still growing. Trade among major industrial countries now accounts for nearly half of world trade and the share of this trade which is manufactures has grown even more rapidly than is true for the world as a whole.

The growth in trade of manufactures does not reflect a need to pay more in manufactures for the food and raw materials needed by the industrial countries. It represents increasingly an exchange of manufactures for manufactures. The growth of this type of trade is due to a variety of factors, including the reduction in trade barriers over the last fifteen years, and the rising importance of brand name products in consumer purchases. But a key factor may also have been the rapid pace of technological innovation which has taken place. An innovation adds to the list of export products, at least temporarily, and trade is stimulated.

Quantifying the Effect of Technology on Trade

We have little quantitative information on the influence of technical change on trade. Nearly ten years ago, the Danish economist, Erik Hoffmeyer, studied the pattern of U.S. trade and found that the United States tended to specialize in what he called research-intensive goods. He found that U.S. exports of these research-intensive goods increased twenty times between the period just before World War I and the mid-fifties, while exports of traditional goods merely trebled.

More recently, several studies have shown that there is a striking relationship between U.S. export performance and several measurements we might think are related to technical change.

Donald Keesing has found, for example, a very high correlation, industry by industry, between research and development expenditures in relation to sales and the U.S. share of exports of manufactures by all the OECD countries. The relationship between U.S. export performance and share of industry employment occupied by scientists and engineers is similarly high. The weight of the evidence leaves little question that there is some relationship, at least for the United States, between export performance and industrial research and development.

This relationship deserves closer scrutiny. First, it should not blind us to the impact of technical change on more traditional forms of trade and, second, we should not take for granted the direction of causality in the relationship just noted.

As to the first point, the impact of technology is clearly not limited to the generation of new products which enter international trade. Our attention is usually focused on these—the visible products, the jet aircraft, the new computer, synthetic fibers, the new drugs. But the influence of technology is far more pervasive than that.

In addition to these product innovations, there are also important process innovations, improvements which lower the cost of producing and moving a wide variety of goods, including goods of the traditional type. Examples of such cost-reducing improvements come to mind in concentrating metal ores, producing steel, weaving cloth, harvesting grain, raising chickens.

Some innovations have a double role. They involve the new product and they lower costs in producing traditional products. The sewing machine and the mechanical reaper are now classic examples; the machinery industry is replete with current examples.

Sometimes the so-called traditional products are themselves improved through advances in technical knowledge. Selective breeding has increased both the yield and the quality of many agricultural products and has produced chickens and turkeys which far surpass their scrawny ancestors in edibility. Purity of refined metals has been increased. New alloys have greatly increased the performance of these metals, and so on through most products.

Furthermore, trade has been greatly encouraged by the impact of technological change on the transportation industry. The big change came in the nineteenth century with the railroad and the steamship, but these changes have not ceased. Ocean freight rates continue to decline relative to the value of goods shipped and large bulk carriers with specialized port facilities will make profitable the movement of large amounts of low value goods, many being the traditional products.

Air transport will come into range of an increasing number of goods as air cargo methods improve. International air freight rates have fallen 20 percent in the last decade while other prices were generally rising, and the trend will probably continue downward.

It is worth recalling, however, that not all technological advances stimulate trade. Some of the major developments have the opposite effect, as when nylon largely replaced silk, or when the Haber process permitted fixation of nitrogen from the air and reduced dependence on natural deposits.

Such developments reduce dependence on geography and substitute, as it were, technology for geography and climate, tending to lower imports.

For all these reasons, it is not possible to identify the impact of technology on trade by focusing on a short list of technologically visible goods. The impact is much more general, operating on production costs and transport costs as well as producing new products; and some improvements may inhibit rather than stimulate trade.

In view of this it may be asked, however, why on such measures as we have there is in fact such a close relationship, at least for the United States, between exports of certain goods and technological inputs into those industries. This close relationship has already been noted. I would suggest, however, that it requires an interpretation somewhat different from the one usually cited or implied. This latter interpretation treats R and D expenditures as largely autonomous, determined primarily, say, by government concern for national defense. But much R and D is itself responsive to commercial demands for new products as incomes grow and for new labor-saving techniques of production as wages increase and labor becomes more expensive. Technical improvements tend to respond to the demands primarily of the domestic market. Many of the resulting improvements also stimulate exports, either by creating new products or by lowering the cost of existing ones.

There is some evidence, at least within the electronics industry—I assume the same is true for other industries—that those firms whose research and development programs are geared toward commercial application, rather than government contract work, do much better, both in the home market and in foreign markets, than is true of firms whose research effort is oriented heavily toward special requirements of government contracts. These often involve very exacting requirements which dominate cost considerations. For commercial applications, cost considerations are important.

A Few Countries Are the Primary Technical Innovators

Domestic demand attracts private research, and research success satisfies new market demands, both at home and abroad. It is not surprising in view of the relationship between the domestic market and directed research, that the great majority of the innovations take place in half-a-dozen to a dozen countries, and that among these the United States plays a leading role.

Quite apart from the effect of size—the proportion of Nobel Laureates in the last fifteen years who have been American corresponds roughly to the U.S. share in free world industrial production, for instance—there are two reasons for supposing that the United States might generate a disproportionate share of commercial innovations. The U.S. economy is on the frontier of experience, as it were, in two respects: first, per capita incomes are higher in the U.S. than elsewhere and have continued so for a number of years; second, closely related to that, wage rates are substantially higher than elsewhere and are continuing to rise, so that American businessmen face before others the need to find new labor-saving techniques of production.

The first of these effects can be seen in a wide range of consumer products which were first produced on a massive scale in the United States—automobiles, household appliances, telephones, hi-fi sets, small boats, small aircraft. The potential demand for such products not only generates improvements in the products themselves, but also induces improvements in productive techniques to service the volume of demand and to bring the product within the reach of the mass consumer a bit sooner.

High Labor Cost as a Stimulus to Innovation

The second effect can be seen in the long history of U.S. innovations directed at the conservation of labor, which has always been high cost relative to other productive factors and which on some occasions has simply not been available in the quantity or quality required to satisfy domestic demand with old techniques of production.

The sewing machine, the linotype machine, the typewriter, shoe machinery, and down to data sorting machinery and the computer are only the best known of these labor-saving innovations.

Labor-saving innovations were often U.S. inventions. The need drew creative attention to possible solutions. Very often the inventions were made elsewhere but first widely used in the United States, where there was a wide receptivity to improvements in techniques.

A typical illustration of the importance of receptivity as distinguished from just the generation of new products is offered by the sewing machine, which in a primitive but effective form was invented by a Frenchman, Thimonnier, sixteen years before Elias Howe constructed his machine in the United States. It was actually used to mass produce uniforms for the French Army (an earlier example of government support for innovation), but the Parisian tailors formed mobs, smashed the machines, and forced Thimonnier to flee to Paris. The labor-short U.S. economy could not afford the luxury of forgoing an important labor-saving device.

Resistance to technological improvement is not absent today on either side of the Atlantic, but presumably it is not carried to the lengths of the Parisian tailors. So long as labor costs are highest in the United States, however, and are expected to rise further, the incentive to devise new labor saving techniques will be strongest there. As wages rise in Europe and elsewhere around the world, businessmen there will be passing through a range of experience already passed in the United States, and the possibility of borrowing labor-saving techniques rather than having to generate them will be much greater.

On both counts, high per capita incomes and high

and growing wage rates, innovation is therefore likely to be somewhat stronger in the United States until incomes elsewhere and labor costs rise to the U.S. level, a day that, at least for Europe, is still some distance off, but is at least within sight.

The choice of technology available to less developed countries will be even wider and it is at present a matter of considerable debate whether they should in general adopt techniques now obsolete in the major industrial nations but which are appropriate to the availability and cost of labor in those countries, or whether they should adopt the latest, most up-to-date techniques even though they are labor-saving.

The Stream of Innovations

Technological innovation can undoubtedly strengthen the competitive position of a country in which the innovation takes place, whether it be one which enlarges exports or displaces imports. However, technological advantage in any one product is transitory. Once a breakthrough has been made, the new information is typically spread widely. Underlying cost considerations will ultimately govern where it will be produced and where it will be used.

For the impact on trade, we must look not to the individual product (because of obsolescence it may not even be marketable long enough for basic cost considerations to come into play) but to the stream of new products and processes, each one often replacing previous ones.

The advantage which accrues to a country's trading position depends both on the intensity of the stream of innovations and on the rate at which new knowledge is put into use elsewhere, where the basic cost advantages lie.

Intensity of the stream is partly accidental, the product of individual and uncoordinated inventive effort, but it is increasingly the product of systematic and coordinated application of talent and resources to discovery.

What we may call the research and development industry, programmed expenditures for the development of new techniques and new products, absorbed in the United States only two-tenths of 1 percent of GNP in the early 1920s, but has grown to 2.8 percent of GNP in 1960 and must be 3 percent today. Even excluding government financed research and development, the expenditure grew sharply from the 20s to over 1 percent of GNP for commercially financed R and D today.

Business incentive to develop new products is strong as the public with steadily increasing incomes gets sated with the traditional necessities of life. Other countries have experienced a similarly rapid growth of programmed R and D expenditures over the same period.

Is Spill-Over a Significant Source of Innovation?

Not all of these expenditures contribute to the stream of commercially relevant innovations. Much R and D expenditure, especially in France, Britain, and the United States, is financed by the central government in pursuit of national defense. There is a lively debate about how important is the so-called spill-over from this military research. There are a few examples where military R and D has had clear commercial application, such as the jet engine. In other cases, military R and D has pioneered a field and led to further development work aimed at the civilian market. This was to some extent true of computers which started on government contract.

But students of these spill-overs in the United States find them to be surprisingly small. They are difficult to quantify but it is noteworthy that in the mid-fifties only 4 percent of all patent applications arose from defense contracts, even though the Defense Department financed roughly half of the total U.S. R and D. Furthermore, commercial utilization of private patents arising from government-financed R and D is only 13 percent, compared with around 60 percent for patents arising from private development work. One aerospace firm reported that out of 400 patent applications accumulated by the end of the 1950s, only three had commercial application.

Indeed, there is some concern in this country that very large government R and D programs may actually reduce the stream of commercial innovations by drawing away critical scientific and engineering talent into military and now space work to a greater extent than the pool of such skills is augmented by the attractions of these programs. Fewer men are available for commercial research and development.

Finally, even when there are spill-overs, much commercial R and D is often required to adapt them to the commercial requirements. It has often been firms other than those doing the military work which have made the products commercially successful. As noted above, export success, at least within some industries, seems much more closely related to privately financed research and development expenditures than to total research and development expenditures.

International Diffusion of Technology

The intensity of the stream of innovation is only one factor governing the trade advantage a country gains from technological change. The second important factor is the rate at which new knowledge is diffused abroad. Unless the innovating country enjoys a basic cost advantage in producing the new product, its trade position is enhanced only to the extent that there is a lag in time between its production of the product and new production in other, lower cost locations.

While the evidence we have is only fragmentary, it does not seem as though the international diffusion of new techniques of production or of new products is much more rapid today than it has ever been in the past.

The point is illustrated by the quip of a few years ago which went, "In January, an American invents a new product; in February, Tass announces that a Russian had invented this product thirty years ago; and by March, Japan is exporting the product to the United States."

In times past, great efforts were taken to prevent the diffusion of technological knowledge to preserve monopoly for those with the specialized knowledge. The secret of Tyrian purple was so tightly kept by the Phoenicians that it was lost in the course of time. England, seat of the industrial revolution, was much aware of the advantage it gained by the new machinery and took stringent measures in the eighteenth and early nineteenth centuries to prevent the export of machinery, especially of textile machinery. The export prohibitions on capital goods were not finally removed until 1843.

France has similar restrictions. Many Germans were worried about the export of capital goods right up to the eve of World War I out of fear that it would undercut their markets.

Knowledge can be transmitted through emigration as well as through the export of capital goods. The first spinning mill in the United States was set up by an Englishman, William Slater, in 1790, who had to memorize the machine design before he emigrated. Britain was very much aware of this possibility and imposed heavy fines on skilled English workmen who went abroad. Those who were abroad for more than six months, despite notification from the British Embassy to return, lost their British citizenship and all their property was confiscated.

This kind of impediment to the movement of knowledge was largely swept away by the free trade sentiment of the nineteenth century, and today such restrictions are generally limited to goods of military application. Even without such deliberate impediments to diffusion of technical improvements, diffusion has been slow, but it has been accelerating. The evidence we have is largely anecdotal, but as an illustration consider the typewriter, which was invented in the United States in 1868 and by the mid-eighties had quite a large market in this country. It first appears as a separate entry in U.S. export statistics in 1897 with exports amounting to $1.4 million. A report of 1908, eleven years later, indicates that American typewriting machines had only German competitors in Europe. Actually by that time there were also two British firms with exports of $90,000, a negligible amount compared with U.S. exports of $6-1/2 million. Broadly speaking, it took twenty years from the time of heavy marketing in the U.S. to the time of modest exports by the few leading competitors, Britain and Germany.

Compare this with more recent developments. Within a year of the introduction of stainless steel razor blades by Wilkinson Sword, a British firm, several American firms had competing blades on the market. This was a defensive response and it was rapid. The inauguration of new techniques has only been slightly less spectacular in other areas. Float glass was produced in the United States only four years after the pioneering production began in England. Many computers have been produced in Europe within a relatively few years after they were first marketed in the United States.

Even where international trade is not directly involved, new technology moves quickly. For instance, U.S. firms introduced much more efficient methods for generating electricity from coal in 1949. By 1956, seven years later, all new French generating capacity incorporated the new technology and a substantial part of new British capacity did.

We have other indications of the rapid diffusion of technical knowledge. One is the so-called international patent crisis, where the number of cross-filings has increased to such an extent that most national patent offices are in heavy arrears in their work. A second is the great expansion of patent licensing across national frontiers. The United States alone earned more than $1 billion from foreigners last year in royalties, license fees, and management fees—exports of knowledge, disembodied from exports of goods and even, in many cases, from exports of capital.

Finally, there has been a large and growing amount of direct foreign investment abroad—the creation of the multinational firm. Such investment tends to diffuse technical knowledge and management skills as well as, or even perhaps more than, capital.

Leads or Lags?

I will close by venturing some speculation on these trends. In the first place, they offer some partial explanation for the baffling conjunction of two arguments, one on the eastern side of the Atlantic, that the so-called technological lead of the United States is increasing, and the other on this side of the Atlantic, and with some vigor only a few years ago, that the U.S. competitive position in world markets is being weakened because of a diminution in technological lead. In fact, both arguments probably represent unwarranted generalizations from particular examples and, of course, both tendencies can be observed simultaneously by looking at different industries.

A more sophisticated reconciliation would refer to the two basic dimensions that I have just been discussing. The intensity of the stream of innovations from the United States may have increased—we still await evidence on whether that is acutally so—but at the same time, the rate of diffusion of this knowledge to other countries has also increased. From the viewpoint of competitiveness in international trade, it is the product of these two factors which is important, neither one alone.

Speculating on the Future Basis of Trade

The very rapid diffusion of new technological knowledge along with the great accumulation of capital which is taking place in most countries suggests a deeper irony. It is that most large countries will become more alike over the course of time in their structure of production and levels of income, and they can become economically more self-sufficient. The basis for trade among them will be undercut. There is already some evidence that most Western countries do look more alike in the structure of their production, particularly in manufacturing production, than they did in the past.

Trade has certainly not diminished among these countries, even relative to output, but even while technological change throws up new products for trade, rapid diffusion of this knowledge reduces the underlying basis for trade.

One can even speculate—idly, for most of us—that in the course of time there will be a swingback in relative importance to the traditional trade with which we started out—trade in food and raw materials, whose production costs are rooted in climate and natural endowments—while advances in technology and rapid dissemination of new knowledge permit many countries or small groups of countries to produce their own requirements of the other commodities or services.

Perhaps this is one of those historical reversals to which Professor McLuhan has referred, like the complete cycle from a tailor-made service economy through mass production and back again.

39

The International Economic System and the Multinational Corporation

LAWRENCE B. KRAUSE

Lawrence B. Krause is an economist at the Brookings Institution. This article first appeared in the Annals of the American Academy of Political and Social Science *in 1972.*

The multinational corporation is now having a revolutionary effect upon the international economic system, but ironically, it is neither a very new development in itself, nor an unknown phenomenon in economic history. The consequences can properly be described as revolutionary because the growth of international transactions of multinational corporations has already overwhelmed the more traditional forms of international trade and capital flows for some countries, and has become much more important to the world economy in general. But multinational corporations are not new. Some currently operating companies were already in existence and conducting international business in the early 1900s. Furthermore, the major elements of such operations were functioning even before 1860, and by stretching a point or two, one could trace the origin back to the Muscovy Company chartered in 1555. Also, previous economic developments entirely within single nations were quite similar in kind to the international phenomenon now being observed. In principle, therefore, it should be possible to research this phenomenon in terms of its own development and by

analogy to other known experiences, and to devise appropriate public policy to keep this revolution from devouring its young or whatever else unconstrained revolutions are alleged to do.

The Essence of a Multinational Corporation

A number of characteristics are used to identify the multinational corporation, but the essential element of such a firm is that it makes direct investments in other countries and thereby extends the organic operations of the firm across national borders.[1] The transplanted organism is specific to a particular industry and combines a collection of attributes, including equity capital, managerial talent, industrial

[1]Real distinctions exist among multinational companies depending on whether they produce manufactured products, develop natural resources, or engage in trade of goods or services. For expositional brevity, these distinctions will not be recognized.

technology, and other productive knowledge, distribution channels, and marketing ties, which give a competitive margin over economic rivals. Firms making such investments are usually not small, nor do they operate in markets characterized by many buyers and many sellers. In other words, the economist's model of pure competition doesn't apply; rather a model of monopolistic competition is required.

The multinational corporation may have a profound effect upon the economy of the country in which it operates and to a lesser extent on the parent and third countries as well. It works to break down the isolation of individual economies and to intergrate them into a world system. In this respect the phenomenon of the multinational corporation is analogous to the development of national corporations in the United States in the 1880s and 1890s. Despite the fact that the Constitution guaranteed an absence of trade barriers, before 1880 product markets were not unified within the United States, and labor and capital markets were even more fragmented. Essentially the United States consisted of a series of interconnected regional markets with quite distinctive characteristics.

The rise of national corporations reduced the distortions arising from separation of regional markets and thus increased economic efficiency within the United States. With improvements in communications via railroads, the telegraph, and telephone, firms could expand the area within which they could effectively manage their operations. Since wages were higher in the New England, Middle Atlantic, and Western states than in the South or Midwest, firms moved facilities or directed their expansion to these areas to take advantage of cheaper labor. Capital could be borrowed more efficiently and at lower interest rates in financial centers such as New York, Philadelphia, Boston, and Chicago; so firms borrowed in those centers, but utilized the money elsewhere in the country. Firms increased their own efficiency and improved factor markets by bringing capital and technology to labor because labor was the more difficult factor of production to move. By producing near regional centers of population, firms often reduced the costs of shipping products to markets. Striving to develop brand-name consciousness across the entire country, firms utilized nationwide advertising and thereby created truly national markets.

The rise of national corporations in the United States, however, was a mixed blessing. Some purely local or regional firms found that they could no longer

compete successfully and either died or were absorbed by larger firms. Local banks found they could no longer completely control the economic life of their locale and had to settle for a much smaller role. Many observers began to worry about the future of market competition in the country both because of the power of a few firms and because of the business tactics being utilized by them. What resulted was the development of institutions to regulate the activities of firms based on antitrust laws.

The Multinational Corporation and the World Economy

What the national corporation did for the U.S. economy, the multinational corporation is doing for the world economy. Some quantitative dimensions are helpful in coming to a qualitative judgment regarding the importance of multinational firms. The United States is the largest parent of multinational companies, and U.S. data provide the best available evidence concerning their operations. First, between 1950 and 1970, the book value of U.S. direct investment abroad increased from $11.8 billion to $78.1 billion—close to a sevenfold increase. A comparable concept for corporate investment in the United States increased by less than fivefold over this same period (net value of corporate structures, plant, and equipment calculated at historical costs). Second, there is some evidence that the value of exports of multinational firms to their affiliates is expanding at a faster rate than total U.S. exports. Official figures available for only a few years in the mid 1960s confirm the trend, and this conclusion is supported by a special survey of seventy-four multinational firms for the entire decade of the 1960s. Furthermore, these exports have been growing at a faster rate than the gross national product (GNP) of the United States. Third, imports by multinational parents from their affiliates within recent years have been increasing more rapidly than total imports or the GNP, as indicated by this same survey.

American-based multinational companies have been a major instrument through which the United States has become more closely integrated with other countries, and, as an indirect result, the other countries have become more closely integrated with each other. The firms have transferred American technology, management, and capital to other countries in such quantities as to make their foreign operations an important determinant of the health of the U.S. economy and of many other countries as well. It has been estimated that earnings from these foreign operations by 1970 contributed between 20 and 25 percent of total U.S. corporate profits after taxes, a very considerable magnitude indeed. An example of comparable figures in the United Kingdom indicates a similar order of magnitude. Furthermore, through their exporting and importing activities, multinational corporations have been leaders in making available the fruits of American labor to foreigners, and of foreigners to Americans.

These magnitudes relate to the United States, but Americans are by no means alone in forming and operating multinational companies. While the data are not available to prove the point, obtainable evidence indicates that foreign-owned multinational companies are growing as fast or faster than their American counterparts. For instance, Japanese direct investment abroad has recently been increasing by more than 30 percent per year and reached a book value of more than $3 billion by March 1971—fiscal year 1970. Among *Fortune*'s list of the world's five hundred largest corporations are now found 200 non-American firms, and they have been increasing in number. Since foreign investment is related to and postively correlated with size, this suggests that the economies of other countries might also be in the process of being integrated into a world system through the activities of their own multinational companies. A more conclusive statement, however, must wait upon direct measurements.

World Product Markets

The most visible consequence of multinational corporations is the integration of product markets; indeed, a product like Coca-Cola is bottled and consumed almost everywhere. The major welfare gains from unifying product markets come from making goods that were not previously offered for sale not only available to consumers, but at prices not much different from their point of origin. To a degree this can be accomplished through international trade, and, as noted above, multinational corporations are active traders. But often foreign production is required, and it is the foreign production of multina-

tional corporations that gives them their distinctive character. As economists discovered their inability to make useful normative judgments concerning future sources of comparative advantage, they have come to recognize that previously held theories concerning international trade are no longer adequate in view of multinational companies and their effects on production of manufactured goods.

In response to perceived possibilities and needs in their home markets, business firms develop new products and processes. Innovations are likely to be initiated by large firms, for they can command the resources to undertake research and development expenditures, make large capital investments, and shoulder substantial risks of failure. For American firms, the new products are usually those which appeal to high-income consumers, and the processes, those that replace high-priced labor in general and scarce labor skills in particular. If the product or process is successful, the firm will expand its productive capacity at home to serve the domestic market. Shortly thereafter, foreign sales will be attempted, based on the success at home. At this stage, foreign markets will be supplied through exports from the United States, particularly if domestic productive capacity is developed beyond domestic demand.

In time, however, the firm's position in the foreign market for the product will be threatened if demand in particular markets expands to such an extent that economies of scale can be captured through local production. At this point, the firm may itself invest in production facilities abroad to pre-empt potential competition. Foreign production in addition usually provides some cost savings through lower transport costs, lower wages, avoidance of tariffs, and other cost-reduction factors. Thus, foreign markets are served increasingly from foreign production sites and decreasingly by U.S. exports. Some exports of raw materials and intermediate products from parent to affiliate may continue, however, on a permanent basis.

If no further improvements are made in the product or process in the United States, the firm may find that its foreign plants can produce the good more cheaply than its American plants—because of lower wages if for no other reason. If foreign costs are enough below domestic costs to compensate for added transporting expense and the American tariff, the firm may start importing the product from its foreign affiliate to serve its domestic market. Thus the product cycle is completed; however, by then the firm might well have developed an even newer or more advanced product to start the cycle over again.

The multinational corporation has an important role in the product cycle model; its managers are the ones that read market forces and make the decisions to move production from one site to another. There is some evidence that the decision-making process has improved to such an extent that firms are capable of world scanning. They can seek out the lowest cost site for even individual components of products and cross-haul them to various assembly points. Such a high degree of specialization and exchange would have warmed the heart of Adam Smith, and it is possible mainly because it is done within a single enterprise.

Multinational companies have overcome both natural and man-made barriers that have separated product markets in the past. They have almost destroyed the natural barriers of distance and ignorance and have surmounted man-made tariff walls through local production. In so doing they have improved economic efficiency, but like the national corporation, the multinational corporation has raised the fear of possible excessive market power. Protecting competition is a many-faceted problem which needs much more attention.

Transfer of Technology

Observers have noted that there are some U.S. industries, like steel, in which multinational firms do not operate other than obtaining raw materials, even though the domestic firms are themselves quite large and presumably could command the resources to extend themselves to other countries. What appears to distinguish these industries is the absence of technological leadership. Without the advantage of superior technology, foreign firms can seldom compete successfully with domestically owned firms because the foreigner is producing in an alien environment. Ignorance of local factors, existence of natural prejudice of customers for local firms, and other handicaps reduce the foreigner's chance of attaining commercial success. Thus the multinational firm needs to develop some advantage over its local rivals to produce successfully abroad, and superior technology is generally the means. Indeed, if the multinational

firm does not maintain its advantage through continuing technological improvement, it may lose out to local competitors or become a candidate for expropriation by local governments.

It would not be completely unfair to say that one of the major consequences of multinational corporations is the greater diffusion of new industrial technology around the world. It is true that even before multinational corporations became important, new technology did spread from country to country, but now this occurs more widely and with greater speed. One important consequence is the increase in payoff to research and development (R and D) within the multinational firm through higher earnings from successful innovations. Higher earnings stimulate even more R and D expenditures, and thus the process is reinforcing.

Another consequence is that it substantially raises the level of technology in the country in which it is transplanted through direct and indirect effects. In order to utilize new technology, the multinational firm must train workers and managers who are primarily local citizens. This training invariably seeps beyond the enterprise because nonaffiliated firms that provide local services to the enterprise have to be made technologically competent. Also, local competitors may lure the trained workers and managers who will carry much industrial knowledge with them. Some technology is patentable and cannot legally be copied, but much cannot be protected and is fair game for competitors. Furthermore, local firms will be stimulated to increase their own R and D expenditures to maintain their competitive position. Thus an indirect consequence of the multinational corporations is a spurring of R and D effort generally throughout the host's economy. The aggregative effect of this spread is to reduce the technological gap among nations and thereby reduce income differentials. Countries obtain newest technology much faster, and it becomes more widely adopted throughout the industry.

Economists have faced a dilemma over the question of technical knowledge. On the one hand, once technology is developed, it is not consumed by use, and thus its marginal social cost is zero and its price should also be zero. But, on the other hand, if private firms are not permitted to earn a return on technology, they lose the incentive to invest in the R and D expenditures that create the technology originally. Thus economists have supported patent laws, although they reduce competition and interfere with marginal cost pricing. Similarly, the rewards earned by multinational firms can be justified on the grounds that large profits encourage the development of socially desirable new technology, and the benefits reach many countries. The present process can be considered a compromise between mercantilist ideas that would bar all technology from going abroad and the other extreme of free distribution of all knowledge.

The technological aspect of multinational companies has also caused a dilemma for some governments. In countries where economic self-sufficiency is an important goal, officials may prefer domestic industry to be locally owned in order to maintain independence, but they are hesitant to restrict multinational companies for fear of becoming technologically backward. However, they also fear that once multinational firms obtain a foothold within the economy, locally owned firms will never catch up. Can an electronics firm compete in third- or fourth-generation computers if it has not learned the lessons from producing the first two generations? Furthermore, multinational firms may do their research at home, and thus local citizens are not encouraged to become scientists or engineers, or even worse, they may emigrate to other countries after local training. A simpleminded solution of insisting that multinationals undertake some research locally may make the situation worse, since the multinationals would then absorb the often scarce scientific talent, making it even more difficult for local firms to compete. Clearly, the supply of locally available scientific talents must be increased faster than the demand for it by multinational firms in order to promote R and D in locally owned firms, and this requires more complex policies.

Basically, countries must accept the risks of an interdependent world or give up its benefits. For a while, the Japanese appeared to have solved the dilemma by encouraging the rental and purchase of foreign technology by Japanese companies, while not permitting foreign firms to operate directly in Japan. Once the Japanese economy reached an advanced stage, however, foreign firms would no longer cooperate and insisted on equity participation. Furthermore, it is unlikely that the multinational firms will ever be willing to repeat the Japanese experience elsewhere because, from their point of view, they helped create formidable competitors to themselves for very meager returns.

Integration of Capital Markets

One of the most far-reaching effects of multinational companies is on world capital markets. Governments have often desired to keep domestic capital markets separated, but multinational companies have made this all but impossible. The linkages of capital markets go far beyond the original equity investment, although this transnational flow of funds by multinational corporations is important in itself. Actually, every transaction between a parent firm and its affiliate either contains elements of a capital flow or can easily be made to encompass such effects.

In the absence of major distortions in both capital markets and foreign exchange markets, economic welfare is improved by multinational firms transferring capital from countries in which rates of return are low to countries where the return is higher. Furthermore, these firms improve the capital market of host countries by mobilizing local sources of capital. Frequently the segmentation of capital markets within individual countries can be overcome with the entrance of major new firms into the economy, and once joined, capital markets are usually improved for both domestic borrowers and domestic savers.

Even after a foreign venture is operating, firms have periodic need for new capital. Much of the continuing equity financing is done through reinvested earnings, but other types of long-term investment are also needed. Spurred by multinational firms, an active international bond market has developed outside the United States. As recently as 1963, only half a billion dollars was raised through new international bond flotations outside the United States, and 90 percent was for governments or international organizations. By 1971, new flotations exceeded five billion dollars, with over half by private companies. This improved bond market makes long-term debt financing available to companies of many countries—only one-quarter of the 1971 flotations were initiated by American companies—and in many different currencies, so that investors can choose their portfolio in ways that match their individual preferences.

Multinational firms also participate in the short-term capital market and sometimes upset government economic strategies through their actions. Because these firms operate in many countries, they have knowledge of and financial ties to all major money markets and most smaller ones as well. Corporate treasurers will shift their liquid funds from country to country in response to interest rate incentives and also will take positions in currencies in expectation of adjustments in exchange rates. Thus if the interest rate in one money market, for example Frankfort, is higher than another one, perhaps New York, then firms will shift funds from the United States to West Germany. Likewise, if one currency is thought to be a candidate for devaluation and another for revaluation, firms will move funds from the weaker into the stronger currency. If both factors combine, as they did in the spring of 1971, a tremendous amount of funds will be moved—as in the gigantic flow from the United States to West Germany which precipitated the floating of the deustche mark on May 5, 1971.

Since multinational firms enter equity, debt, and short-term capital markets, they almost fully integrate world capital markets. This has profound effects upon the economies of most countries, the effectiveness of national monetary policies, and the workings of the international monetary system. By joining capital markets, firms help spread economic impulses from one country to another. Furthermore, the independence of national monetary authorities is undermined. If the central bank tries to enforce tight money to fight inflation, firms borrow abroad and avoid the restraint. If the authorities try to stimulate their economy through easy money policies, they may have their efforts frustrated as firms utilize their liquidity to invest abroad for higher rates of return. Attempts by central banks to achieve domestic monetary objectives by exchange controls are also frustrated by multinational firms, which can transfer capital in different ways to avoid controls. Since these flows also affect the balance of payments to which governments respond, all governments have lost some of their sovereignty in economic policymaking to the private sector, although the United States, because of its large size, has lost less than others.

The large short-term capital movements of 1971 finally called into question the adequacy of the entire international monetary system. While weaknesses have long been recognized, it wasn't until the monetary crisis of 1971 and the New Economic Policy of the United States that governments became convinced that the system needed to be changed. Thus the reform of Bretton Woods must take into account the reality of short-term capital movements, a reality that was mainly created through the actions of multinational corporations.

Other Factor Markets

Multinational firms also have an impact on labor markets in general and the market for management services in particular. Since, where possible, firms attempt to utilize cheaper sources of labor, wage differentials in the same industry across borders tend to be reduced—wages in low-wage areas tend to rise much faster than in high-wage areas. The U.S.-Canadian situation in automobiles may be a special and extreme situation, but it is indicative nonetheless. The Canadian employees of American automobile companies demanded and more or less obtained wage parity with their American counterparts, a demand made credible because the same union represented workers in both countries. Wage inflation may have been stimulated throughout the Canadian economy as one union tried to match the gains of another. In general, unions in individual countries lose bargaining strength vis-a-vis employers as firms improve their ability to shift production to other countries. Thus the two effects of multinational firms on labor markets are the reduction of wage differentials and the undermining of the monopolistic power of unions.

For corporate managers, being employed by a multinational firm may be greatly different from working for a purely domestic firm. Success comes from an ability to adjust to many unique situations. These include a willingness to travel and be domiciled in foreign countries, a capacity to suppress nationalistic prejudices, and a proficiency in picking up political nuances. All of these talents must be combined with usual management skills. As multinational firms grow, a cadre of managers having these skills is being created. The full economic, social, and political consequences of such a management class are hard to predict, but could be quite important.

Stresses on the International System

As noted above, multinational firms cause certain problems for countries, and taken together, they cause considerable stress upon the international economy. Most immediate concern is about international monetary arrangements. The old Bretton Woods system, based on fixed exchange rates with narrow bands of fluctuations in which parities were adjusted only through large, discrete changes, cannot function well when national money markets are closely integrated and governments try to follow independent monetary policies—and multinational firms have insured that money markets are closely integrated. Furthermore, these firms keep capital controls from being very effective. Thus designs for a new monetary system will have to take into account the existence of these firms. Basically, to achieve national stability, the new system will have to utilize market forces to which firms respond, and this means wider permissible fluctuations of market exchange rates plus smaller and possibly more frequent changes in parities. Also, facilities need to be provided for financing large short-term capital flows among countries, since there will be times when it will be neither desirable nor possible to prevent the flows. Furthermore, countries will have to develop more responsive fiscal policy instruments to achieve domestic stabilization objectives in view of the undermining of monetary independence. Finally, governments will have to find a method to coordinate better their individual economic policies. Through coordination, each country's policies can be made to meet its individual needs more effectively.

Another major fear of many governments is that multinational companies will become so powerful that they will destroy the desirable degree of competition in world markets, that they will be more powerful than the governments trying to control or regulate them, and that individual firm decisions may not correspond to the needs or desires of countries. These fears are fed by some naive extrapolations that suggest a handful of companies could control most of the world's industrial ouput within this generation. While such forecasts no doubt greatly exaggerate both the present and likely future role of multinational firms, the point that a great deal of power will be held in private hands, albeit still subject to national laws, deserves attention. Some governments have attempted to force multinational firms to adopt a national viewpoint by insisting on local participation through joint ventures. Joint ventures may be desirable on a number of grounds, but they also tend to reduce rather than increase the number of actual or potential competitors in the market.

At present there is no administrative or legal authority that is charged with protecting competition from a worldwide point of view. Some countries have domestic antitrust laws, and the European Economic Community has a code for the whole Common Market, but these laws do not apply to international competition—and often through specific exclusions. United States laws theoretically include extraterritorial applications, but attempts by American courts to extend their jurisdiction abroad is generally resisted by other countries as an infringement upon their sovereignty. Clearly a new approach is required to deal with the threat by multinational corporations to effective world competition. Countries must first agree on what needs to be done and then create an authority to investigate and, if necessary, take appropriate action. This may well require a new forum to exchange views and negotiate solutions—possibly a new international institution.

Still another source of international stress comes from potential differences of view among countries concerning the division of economic gains that come from the operations of multinational companies. At the government-to-government level, questions can arise over the division of taxes; the U.S. Congress apparently is going to review our own laws on this subject. Also a question can arise over the division of profits: should domestic investors have the right to share in the profits of a local subsidiary of a multinational firm? Insisting on some local participation would accomplish this result. In the extreme, a government can completely take over a local subsidiary through expropriation—a rather frequent occurrence in recent years. What international rules should apply in such circumstances remains to be seen, since the right of full and prompt compensation to owners is seldom honored. This is yet another area where neither an international forum nor authority exists to deal with the issues. Governments must begin to discuss multinational solutions to these issues, which are unlikely to stay buried for very much longer.

Stresses in the international system are all reflected within individual countries where they are viewed from a national perspective. Multinational firms pose domestic economic and political problems additional to and interacting with the international ones. The undermining of domestic policies and the threatening of domestic elites fall within this category. Pressures for new policies and new approaches may also arise as individual countries seek national solutions to their problems.

Conclusion

There is little question that multinational corporations have benefited the international economy, but they have been a mixed blessing for many countries. By integrating the economies of different countries into a worldwide system, they have reduced the distortions erected by man and nature. New products have been introduced to consumers, and prices on existing products have been reduced. Methods of production have been improved through the spread of technology and industrial knowledge. Capital markets of most countries have been linked, improving the world distribution of financial resources. An international market has been created for labor skills, which has benefits for relatively backward areas. The totality of these effects improves economic welfare by stimulating growth and efficiency. The stimulus comes directly from the activities of multinational corporations and also indirectly from local business firms striving to compete with them.

In the wake of the changes brought by multinational corporations, new problems have been created for the international system, and some existing difficulties have been exacerbated. Out-of-date international monetary arrangements were made almost inoperative as multinational firms learned to move massive amounts of short-term capital from country to country in response to interest rate incentives and prospects for speculative windfalls. Present attempts to reform the Bretton Woods system are in response to this threat. The extensive market power of multinational firms has challenged governments to devise an internationally viable antitrust strategy. As yet none has been developed. Nor have governments created a mechanism for resolving grievances that arise over the operations of multinational companies—grievances that can affect government-to-government relations as well as business-government concerns.

The difficulties arising from these international problems are reinforced by national problems also created or intensified by multinational firms. National economic policy instruments such as monetary restraints or industrial policy are undermined or weakened. The multinational firms may also constitute a threat to the economic power or well-being of certain domestic groups such as labor unions and local competitors. Political and cultural problems are also created because of the threat multinational firms pose for local managers, landed oligarchies, and intellectual elites. In the extreme, multinational firms can be a source of political instability if they attempt to interfere in local politics, and sometimes their mere presence may unhinge the political process.

Thus, it will take much ingenuity to meet the myriad of challenges posed by the multinational corporation. Solutions to problems must be found which meet the needs of national interest without constraining the process or destroying the benefits of multinational firms, as in the case of confiscatory taxation. Because of the benefits of multinational firms, the search for appropriate solutions to these problems should be well worthwhile. The greatest danger to the international system may result from apathy. Governments seldom face up to international problems until some sort of crisis occurs, and then it is frequently too late to reach otpimum outcomes. The machinery for negotiations that is being created to deal with international monetary problems could be retained, even after those decisions are made, and be put to other uses; such a suggestion at least deserves consideration.

40

The Multinational Firm and Imperialism

PAUL A. BARAN

Paul A. Baran was Professor of Economics at Stanford University. This article comes from his book, The Political Economy of Growth, *published in 1957.*

The principal impact of foreign enterprise on the development of the underdeveloped countries lies in hardening and strengthening the sway of merchant capitalism, in slowing down and indeed preventing its transformation into industrial capitalism.

This is the really important "indirect influence" of foreign enterprise on the evolution of the underdeveloped countries. It flows through a multitude of channels, permeates all of their economic, social, political, and cultural life, and decisively determines its entire course. There is first of all the emergence of a group of merchants expanding and thriving within the orbit of foreign capital. Whether they act as wholesalers—assembling, sorting, and standardizing commodities that they purchase from small producers and sell to representatives of foreign concerns—or as suppliers of local materials to foreign enterprises, or as caterers to various other needs of foreign firms and their staffs, many of them manage to assemble vast fortunes and to move up to the very top of the underdeveloped countries' capitalist class. Deriving their profits from the operations of foreign business, vitally interested in its expansion and prosperity, this comprador element of the native bourgeoisie uses its considerable influence to fortify and to perpetuate the *status quo.*

There are secondly the native industrial monopolists, in most cases interlocked and interwoven with domestic merchant capital and with foreign enterprise, who entirely depend on the maintenance of the existing economic structure, and whose monopolistic status would be swept away by the rise of industrial capitalism. Concerned with preventing the emergence of competitors in their markets, they look with favor upon absorption of capital in the sphere of circulation, and have nothing to fear from foreign export-oriented enterprise. They too are stalwart defenders of the established order.

The interests of these two groups run entirely parallel with those of the feudal landowners powerfully entrenched in the societies of the backward areas. Indeed, these have no reason for complaints about the activities of foreign enterprise in their countries. In fact, these activities yield them considerable profits. Frequently they provide outlets for the produce of landed estates, in many places they raise the value of land, often they offer lucrative employment opportunities to members of the landed gentry.

What results is a political and social coalition of wealthy compradors, powerful monopolists, and large landowners dedicated to the defense of the existing feudal-mercantile order. Ruling the realm by no matter what political means—as a monarchy, as a military-fascist dictatorship, or as a republic of the Kuomintang variety—this coalition has nothing to hope for from the rise of industrial capitalism which would dislodge it from its positions of privilege and power. Blocking all economic and social progress in its country, this regime has no real political basis in city or village, lives in continual fear of the starving and restive popular masses, and relies for its stability on Praetorian guards of relatively well kept mercenaries.

In most underdeveloped countries social and political developments of the last few decades would have toppled regimes of that sort. That they have been able to stay in business—for business is, indeed their sole concern—in most of Latin America and in the Near East, in several "free" countries of Southeast Asia and in some similarly "free" countries of Europe, is due mainly if not exclusively to the aid and support that was given to them "freely" by Western Capital and by Western governments acting on its behalf. For the maintenance of these regimes and the operations of foreign enterprise in the underdeveloped countries have become mutually interdependent. It is the economic strangulation of the colonial and dependent countries by the imperialist powers that stymied the development of indigenous industrial capitalism, thus preventing the overthrow of the feudal-mercantile order and assuring the rule of the comprador administrations. It is the preservation of these subservient governments, stifling economic and social development and suppressing all popular movements for social and national liberation, that makes possible at the present time the continued foreign exploitation of underdeveloped countries and their domination by the imperialist powers.

Foreign capital and the governments by which it is represented have steadily kept their part of the bargain to this very day. Although official opinion at the present time, while admitting that "colonial powers added the weight of government proscription and discouragement to the economic forces handicapping industrial expansion in raw materials producing areas," feels strongly that "those days . . . are gone forever," unhappily nothing could be a more egregious misreading of current history. Whether we look at the British proceedings in Kenya, in Malaya, or in the West Indies, at French operations in Indo-China and North Africa, at the United States' activities in Guatemala and the Philippines, or whether we consider the somewhat "subtler" United States transactions in Latin America and the Far East and the still more complex Anglo-American machinations in the Near East, very little of the *essence* of the imperialism "of those days" can be said to have "gone forever."

To be sure, neither imperialism itself nor its *modus operandi* and ideological trimmings are today what they were fifty or a hundred years ago. Just as outright looting of the outside world has yielded to organized trade with the underdeveloped countries, in which plunder has been rationalized and routinized by a mechanism of impeccably "correct" contractual relations, so has the rationality of smoothly functioning commerce grown into the modern, still more advanced, still more rational system of imperialist exploitation. Like all other historically changing phenomena, the contemporary form of imperialism contains and preserves all its earlier modalities, but raises them to a new level. Its central feature is that it is now directed not solely towards the rapid extraction of large sporadic gains from the objects of its domination, it is no longer content with merely assuring a more or less steady flow of those gains over a somewhat extended period. Propelled by well-organized, rationally conducted monopolistic enterprise, it seeks today to rationalize the flow of these receipts so as to be able to count on it in perpetuity. And this points to the main task of imperialism in our time: to prevent, or, if that is impossible, to slow down and to control the economic development of underdeveloped countries.

That such development is profoundly inimical to the interests of foreign corporations producing raw materials for export can be readily seen. There is of course the mortal threat of nationalization of raw materials producing enterprises that is associated with the ascent to power of governments in backward countries that are determined to move their nations off dead center; but, even in the absence of nationalization, economic development in the source countries bodes nothing but evil to Western capital. For whichever aspect of economic development we may consider, it is manifestly detrimental to the prosperity of the raw materials producing corporations. As under conditions of economic growth employment opportunities and productivity expand in other parts of the economy, and the class consciousness and bargaining power of labor increase, wages tend to rise in the raw materials producing sector. While in some lines of output—on plantations primarily—those increased costs can be offset by the adoption of improved techniques, such mechanization involves capital outlays that are obviously repugnant to the corporations involved. And in mining and petroleum operations even this solution is hardly possible. These in general employ the same methods of production that are in use in the advanced countries, so that the technological gap that could be filled is accordingly very small. With the prices of their products in the world markets representing a fixed datum to the individual companies—at least in the short run—increased labor costs combined with various fringe benefits resulting from growing unionization, as well as rising costs of other local supplies, must lead necessarily to a reduction of profits. If thus the longer-run effects of economic development cannot but be damaging to the raw materials exporting corporations, the immediate concomitants of economic development are apt to be even more disturbing. They will be, as a rule, higher taxes and royalties imposed on the foreign enterprises by the local government seeking revenue to finance its developmental ventures, foreign exchange controls designed to curtail the removal of profits abroad,

tariffs rendering the importation of foreign-made equipment more expensive or raising the prices of imported wage goods, and others—all inevitably interfering with the freedom of action of foreign enterprise and encroaching upon its profitability.

Small wonder that under such circumstances Western big business heavily engaged in raw materials exploitation leaves no stone unturned to obstruct the evolution of social and political conditions in underdeveloped countries that might be conducive to their economic development. It uses its tremendous power to prop up the backward areas, comprador administrations, to disrupt and corrupt the social and political movements that oppose them, and to overthrow whatever progressive governments may rise to power and refuse to do the bidding of their imperialist overlords. Where and when its own impressive resources do not suffice to keep matters under control, or where and when the costs of the operations involved can be shifted to their home countries' national governments—or nowadays to international agencies such as the International Bank for Reconstruction and Development—the diplomatic, financial and, if need be, military facilities of the imperialist power are rapidly and efficiently mobilized to help private enterprise in distress to do the required job.

41

The New Protectionism

WALTER ADAMS

Walter Adams is Distinguished University Professor and former President of Michigan State University. This article first appeared in Challenge *in 1973.*

"The lessons of history," said Franklin D. Roosevelt in 1935, "show conclusively . . . that continued dependence on relief induces a spiritual and moral disintegration fundamentally destructive to the national fiber. To dole out relief . . . is to administer a narcotic, a subtle destroyer of the human spirit." Society, Roosevelt argued, has an obligation to care for its citizens who cannot care for themselves. For others the overriding aim should be to provide an opportunity to work, not an opportunity to avoid it. The goal must be rehabilitation rather than relief.

President Nixon would heartily endorse this view. This is the Protestant work ethic—an indelible part of Americana. It is the criterion we use to judge welfare programs for the poor, the disadvantaged, the underprivileged. Curiously enough, it is *not* the standard employed in evaluating welfare programs for the rich, the powerful, the vested interests of corporate America. Thus we bail out Lockheed. We rescue the Penn-Central. We subsidize the oil moguls. We protect the lethargic, somnolent steel oligopoly from foreign competition. Welfare programs, it would seem, are not instituted evenhandedly.

The Burke-Hartke Bill

The issue of corporate welfarism will once again be joined when the Burke-Hartke bill reaches the floor of Congress.[1] In addition to regulating multinational corporations, the bill would impose mandatory import quotas on a wide range of manufactured products whenever an American industry or its workers could claim to be suffering from "undue" foreign competition. The bill, which some consider the most restrictive trade legislation since the Embargo Act of 1807, represents a high watermark of the new protectionism—what *Barron's* calls "the protection racket." It is aggressively backed, not only by politically influential big business industries but also by George Meany and his AFL-CIO.

What has given the Burke-Hartke initiative additional impetus, of course, is the recent deterioration in the U.S. trade balance and the embattled state of the U.S. dollar. By 1971, merchandise imports exceeded

[1]As of October 1, 1973, the Burke-Hartke bill was pending in the House Ways and Means Committee.

exports by $2.7 billion—the first officially reported trade deficit since 1893. This alarming trend, said the Administration, would be counteracted by the Smithsonian accord (hailed by Mr. Nixon as "the greatest monetary agreement in history") and the devaluation of the dollar. Making the dollar cheaper, it was said, would stimulate exports and discourage imports, thus correcting or reversing the trade deficit. But nothing of the sort happened. By the end of 1972, the U.S. trade balance had worsened—running at an annual rate of $7 billion—necessitating yet another devaluation of the dollar in February of this year. Obviously, a quite different kind of economic medicine was called for.

To the proponents of Burke-Hartke, the answer is clear: if only imports can effectively be curtailed, a trade deficit can easily be turned into a surplus. Imports, they say, are not only a drain of dollars from the United States: they also threaten the profitability and the very existence of major domestic industries. They undermine the jobs and incomes of the workers employed in these import-impacted industries. At stake, says George Meany, "are the American standard of living and America's prospects for remaining an industrial nation with a wide range of industries, products, and employment."

I don't happen to view imports in the same light. In some cases, I think, imports are merely the symptom of the declining competitiveness of an American industry so long corrupted by a permissive oligopolistic environment that it has become lazy, lethargic, inefficient, and technologically backward. And when an industry has led the quiet life for prolonged periods, in control of a lucrative continental-sized market and insulated from competition, it eventually tends to fall prey to the erosion of that market by imports and substitutes while pricing itself out of world markets and triggering a decline in its export trade. Shutting off imports, or curtailing them substantially by quotalike restrictions, does nothing to cure the underlying disease. It only makes the disease more virulent and debilitating, requiring ever-mounting doses of protectionism for survival. Moreover, it has indirect effects on other domestic industries, which have to pay higher prices for the protected products and thus find their export potential artificially diminished. This has the effect of further straining our balance of trade. Finally, and be no means least important, protectionism adds unneeded fuel to the cost-push inflation which seems to have become endemic in the American economy.

Let me illustrate these points with reference to two major industries—steel and oil. These case studies demonstrate why voluntary quotas where now in effect should not be made mandatory, and why mandatory quotas should be repealed rather than imposed on additional industries.

Steel

The U.S. steel industry is a classic, textbook oligopoly. Domestic producers do not compete among themselves in terms of price. It is simply not the custom of the industry. Instead of price competition, they follow a regime of strict price leadership and followership—more often than not in a monotonously upward direction.

Since the end of World War II, the industry's notorious policy of constant price escalation has contributed a prime stimulus to successive inflationary movements. Thus, between 1947 and 1951, according to the Council of Economic Advisers, "the average increase in the price of basic steel products was 9 percent per year, twice the average increase of all wholesale prices. The unique behavior of steel prices was most pronounced in the mid-1950s. While the wholesale price index was falling an average of 0.9 percent annually from 1951 to 1955, the price index for steel was rising an average of 4.8 percent per year. From 1955 to 1958, steel prices were increasing 7.1 percent annually, or almost three times as fast as wholesale prices generally. No other major sector shows a similar record." After a quiescent stage during the early 1960s, characterized by the moral suasion and "jawboning" of the Kennedy Administration, steel prices resumed their upward movement in 1964—on a gradual, selective, product-by-product basis at first, and on a general across-the-board basis in 1969. The imposition of "voluntary" import quotas in January 1969 and the Nixon Administration's refusal to engage in government-industry confrontations simply accelerated the trend.

The one factor which dampened the industry's enthusiasm for marching in lockstep toward constantly higher price levels was the burgeoning of import competition. Thus, between January 1960 and December 1968, a period of nine years, the composite steel price index increased 4.1 points—or 0.45 points per year. Starting in January 1969, however, after the U.S. State Department had successfully persuaded the Europeans and Japanese to accept "voluntary" quotas on their sales to the United States (i.e., to enter into an informal international steel cartel), imports were cut back drastically and the domestic steel prices resumed their pre-1960 climb. In the four years between January 1969 and December 1972, the steel price index rose 26.7 points—or 6.67 points per year. Put differently, steel prices increased at an annual rate fourteen times greater after the import quotas went into effect than in the previous nine years. All this in the face of recession, low volume, and the idleness of roughly 25 percent of the nation's steel capacity.

As if the import quotas—supplemented by "Buy American" regulations and assorted trade barriers —were not enough to insulate the steel industry from competition, President Nixon approved (and later withdrew) a temporary 10 percent surcharge on imports, including steel. In doing so, he perverted the "infant industry" argument for the benefit of lusty steel giants whose rambunctious excesses had wreaked havoc with past attempts at inflation control. With his arsenal of import restraints, he neutralized the perhaps most effective lid on steel pricing and, at the same time, built up additional steam in an already overheated pressure cooker. He also penalized such major steel-consuming industries as automobiles, construction equipment, and agricultural implements, which found it increasingly difficult to absorb the higher prices for an essential raw material while trying to maintain their competitiveness in domestic and foreign markets.

The case study of steel yields some incontrovertible conclusions. Giantism in this industry is the result of massive mergers of the past. The dominant firms are neither big because they are efficient nor efficient because they are big. Their technological lethargy, especially during the 1950s, when they lagged in introducing the basic oxygen process, continuous casting, and direct reduction of steel, put them at a comparative disadvantage in world competition. Their insensitive, extortionate, oligopolistic price policy displaced American steel from world markets and opened the U.S. market to erosion by imports and substitutes. And, finally, the mercantilist protectionism of the federal government compounded the problems of the industry and the nation's economy and gave legitimacy and endurance to a cartel which could not survive without government succor and support.

Oil

The pattern of protectionism in the petroleum industry is both older and more pervasive. Under the antitrust laws, it is an offense for private firms to fix prices or allocate markets, yet in the name of conservation the government does for the oil companies what they could not legally do for themselves. The process is familiar. The Bureau of Mines in the Department of the Interior publishes monthly estimates of the market demand for petroleum, at current prices, of course. Under the Interstate Oil Compact, approved by Congress, these estimates are broken down into quotas for each of the oil-producing states, which, in turn, through various prorationing devices, allocate so-called allowable production to individual wells. Oil produced in violation of these prorationing regulations is branded "hot oil," and the federal government prohibits its shipment in interstate commerce. Also, to buttress this government-sanctioned cartel against potential competition, oil imports by sea are limited by a tariff, in effect since 1943, and by a mandatory import quota, in effect since 1963.[2]

Finally, to top off these indirect subsidies with more visible favors, and to provide the proper "incentives" for an industry crucial to the national defense, the government authorizes oil companies to charge off a 22 percent depletion allowance against their gross income. In all, the industry is receiving special favors variously estimated at from $3.5 to $7 billion annually—this in addition to having a government-sanctioned cartel provide the underpinning for its control of markets and prices.

The artificially high price of petroleum in the United States has an injurious effect not only on the ultimate consumer but also on those American industries which use it as a raw material and must then try to sell their finished products in competitive world markets. Not long ago, for example, Japanese manufacturers were able to buy Iranian heavy crude oil at a price of $1.35 per barrel. That same oil could have been transported to the U.S. East Coast at a delivered price of $2.10 per barrel before payment of tariff. U.S. manufacturers, however, were compelled to buy their crude oil at an East Coast-delivered price of $3.42 per barrel—i.e., at a differential of $1.32 per

[2]This paper was written prior to the cessation of the oil import quota in 1973 and to the Arab oil embargo in late 1973 and 1974.

barrel before the tariff and $1.22 after the tariff. Such a differential obviously could not exist except for the penalties imposed on U.S. manufacturers by the import quota program.

Major American chemical companies—du Pont, Union Carbide, Dow Chemical, and others—have estimated that domestic oil prices on the East Coast average $1.25 per barrel more than elsewhere in the world; this amounts to 3 cents a gallon, or 60 percent above the world price. This quota-protected price differential, they point out, can be critical, if not fatal, in petrochemical production, in which, in many cases, raw material costs account for more than 50 percent of the cost of the basic product. "Furthermore," they say, "U.S. petrochemical products have only a shrinking level of tariff protection in the domestic market. Foreign petrochemicals, on the other hand, need no import quotas for their shipments to the U.S. market and are not restricted in their access to the low-cost oil of the Middle East, Africa, and South America."

Clearly, the continued growth of our petrochemical industry—which contributes about $1.0 billion to our balance of trade—is vitally dependent on access to competitively priced feedstocks. Its competitive posture in world markets depends on the transformation or total elimination of oil import restrictions and other government price-support programs for the domestic oil industry.

Professor Wayne Leeman has well summarized this aspect of the problem: "So the oil we keep out of the United States benefits our most important competitors. Manufacturers in Japan and Western Europe buy energy, industrial heat, and petrochemical feedstocks at prices which give them a competitive advantage over U.S. producers. And they have this competitive advantage partly because import quotas give U.S. firms only limited access to cheap foreign oil and partly because oil shut out of the Unites States depresses the prices they pay.

But what about national security? Is it not vital to protect the domestic oil industry from foreign competition in order to assure ourselves uninterrupted access to petroleum and petroleum products in times of war or emergency? Are not the current restrictions on oil imports imperative to safeguard the national security? Quite the opposite is true.

First, the only safe and low-cost storage for oil is underground. If domestic oil reserves are to be conserved for use in an emergency, therefore, they should be kept intact rather than depleted by artificial stimulation of domestic production.

Second, to the extent that domestic oil reserves are in scarce supply, we should resist the temptation to deplete them in peacetime and maximize our peacetime reliance on foreign sources—especially those which might be beyond our reach in the event of military conflict.

Third, it seems to me that national security could be much better served by R and D support for developing the technology to convert our gargantuan deposits of oil shale into a cost-competitive fuel—rather than by subsidizing excess developmental drilling that uses up supply instead of preserving it.

In short, as a general guideline we should import low-cost foreign oil at a time when we have free access to it, and conserve our own reserves for such times as foreign oil may no longer be available to us. In this, as in other cases, the imperatives of national security and the dictates of rational economic policy would seem to coincide.

One final observation. If, as some argue, the United States is in the midst of an energy crisis, can we seriously defend the honeycomb of import restrictions which artificially curtail supplies and thus become the pretext for maintaining and escalating domestic prices? All the available evidence points in the opposite direction.

The Protection Racket Has No Winners

In summary, import quotas are inimical to the public interest. Quotas undermine the competitive discipline of the marketplace. They encourage price escalation and cost-push inflation. They penalize industries using quota-protected products as raw materials, thereby reducing the cost- and price-competitiveness of those industries in domestic and world markets. Finally, like any scheme of protectionism, quotas have a narcotic effect on the patient they are ostensibly designed to help. A sick industry no longer has to face up to its problems—to reform if it is to survive. Under a quota system, it can luxuriate in inefficiency and backwardness without penalty, knowing that a permissive government will support its catatonic refusal to face up to reality.

In the long run, this is not sound public policy. It condemns the protected industries to the fate of our coddled railroads. It exposes labor to job and income losses as export-related industries find themselves incapable of absorbing the constantly rising cost burden and as direct foreign investment therefore becomes progressively more attractive. Finally, protectionism saddles the nation with an inefficient, noncompetitive industrial structure, a declining posture in world markets, mounting trade deficits, and a currency increasingly vulnerable to successive devaluations.

42

The Current Case for Import Limitations

IRVING KRAVIS

Irving Kravis is Professor of Economics at the University of Pennsylvania. This piece comes from United States International Policy in an Interdependent World, *published in 1971.*

A new wave of sentiment in favor of import limitations has brought forward some new arguments for import limitations and revived some old ones. The fundamental fact remains that every restriction of supply, whether it be applied to supply of domestic or foreign origin, helps the producers of the restricted products but only at the expense of everyone else. Every current claim for protection, no matter what its guise, is a claim for special preference at the general expense. Let us take the main current arguments for import limitations one by one.

U.S. Imports Have Risen More Rapidly than Exports in Recent Years; Our Trade Surplus Is Much Reduced, and May Even Be Eliminated or Turned into a Deficit

It is not at all clear that the U.S. balance of payments should in the long run have a trade surplus or that a trade surplus needs to be an objective of U.S. Government policy, but even if these points are granted they do not establish the case for import restrictions. Import restrictions will bring retaliation that will reduce the level of trade without any predictable effect on the trade balance. Furthermore, even if other countries were to permit the U.S. to improve its trade surplus through import limitation, item-by-item restrictions would provide neither an equitable nor efficient method. Discriminatory tariff increases or quotas favor the domestic producers of some goods over the domestic producers of others. They also require that the Government rather than the market place determine which imports will be reduced.

If the objective is really to improve the trade balance, a uniform ad valorem tariff surcharge and an export subsidy of the same amount would be more equitable and efficient. Other measures that would accomplish the same result include a depreciation of the dollar and the restriction of the U.S. price level to lower rates of increase than foreign price levels.

The United States Has, over the Years, Given Many One-Sided Trade Concessions That Have Opened Its Markets to Foreigners While U.S. Exporters Find Themselves under Serious Handicaps in Foreign Markets

The pervasiveness of this view in the U.S. is remarkable in view of the almost absolute lack of evidence to support it. The available evidence does not indicate that U.S. tariff levels are now substantially lower than those of other major industrial countries or that they have been so reduced in recent years as to enhance substantially the price competitiveness of foreign goods in the U.S. market place. Certainly the disappearance of the U.S. trade surplus since 1964 cannot be explained on these grounds. Tariff changes have had on the average small effects on the landed dollar prices of foreign goods and have been accompanied by roughly equal advantages for U.S. exporters. Much has been made of non-tariff barriers, but, if anything, U.S. non-tariff barriers have increased since 1964 relative to foreign non-tariff barriers. Furthermore, the only attempt to estimate the overall level of effective protection inclusive of tariff and non-tariff barriers, made for the U.S. and the U.K., does not show any great difference between the two countries. This is not to deny that non-tariff barriers have been growing in importance, both at home and abroad, relative to tariffs, nor is it to claim that the non-tariff barriers of Japan and the EEC are not more restrictive than those of the U.S. It is to say that claims that foreigners have one-sided access to the U.S. market are at the minimum grossly exaggerated.

Imports Have an Unfavorable Impact on Employment, Particularly Since They Tend to Be Concentrated in Labor-Intensive Products

It is true that international trade enables us to export the goods of 1,000 manhours and receive back goods that would require more than 1,000 manhours to produce. This is our gain from trade. Every internal improvement has the same effect; we get more goods per manhour. The optimum way to full employment does not lie in make-work policies such as excluding labor-intensive imports or forbidding new labor-saving machines. Protection of labor-intensive industries is certainly not in the best interests of U.S. labor in any long run sense; it leads to the preservation of low-wage jobs which would disappear in a free market and be replaced by higher wage jobs. In my home state of Pennsylvania, the textile workers of yesterday were injured when the textile industry moved south but their successors today are better off than they would be if there had been government intervention to keep the textile industry in Pennsylvania; they are working at better paying jobs in new or expanded industries that are competitive and can export different products to the rest of the U.S. and to the world.

Foreign Competition Is Unfair Because It Is Based on Low Wages

The wage advantage that foreign industries enjoy is no more unfair in a relevant economic sense than is the advantage of superior capital resources or of sophisticated technology enjoyed by many U.S. industries. No sound policy can be based on the principle of eradicating all the economic advantages possessed by any contestant in order to run a sports-like competition that gives an equal chance to all entrants. It is precisely by capitalizing upon the special advantages enjoyed by workers and producers everywhere that we can maximize output per unit of input.

The Advent of the Multinational Corporation Has So Changed the Nature of Trade Relations That the Case for Freer Trade Has Been Made Irrelevant

There is no evidence that the multinational corporation is immune from the economic forces that determine which goods can be most cheaply produced in which countries. On the contrary, it seems likely that the multinational corporation provides decision-makers with better information about the most advantageous location of production than was previously available. Components, such as the Ford engine for the Pinto, are produced abroad when they can be made cheaper.

The effects of multinational corporations on the U.S. trade balance are very difficult to estimate, but multinational corporations can hardly be held responsible for import problems in textiles and a number of other areas where the domestic industry has been in difficulty and has sought protection. In most of the areas in which multinational corporations are important, the U.S. has a strong export position.

In any case, the injury to U.S. interests of which multinational corporations are accused by those seeking trade restrictions is not different from others independently claimed as a basis for import limitations nnd already discussed—e.g., a reduced U.S. trade surplus and job displacement.

The National Security of the United States Requires That Some Industries Be Protected

The national security argument is sometimes applied to natural resource products such as petroleum and sometimes to fabricated products such as steel.

In the case of a natural resource product, it has never been satisfactorily explained how a program which encourages the use of domestic reserves rather than the use of the foreign product will assure adequate domestic supplies in case of an emergency. If national security is dependent upon the ready domestic availability of large quantities of petroleum, what is really called for is a program of subsidization for the exploration of petroleum reserves in the United States and a program that would restrict domestic production to the levels necessary to keep a domestic petroleum industry operational and capable of sudden and large expansion in the event of necessity.

In the case of a manufacturing industry, such as the steel industry, it is argued that protection is necessary to maintain skills that would be lost were the industries subject to unrestricted import competition. In fact, the wartime experience of the United States, like that of every other country, including England, Germany, and Japan, demonstrates very clearly that human skills and ingenuity manage very quickly to produce whatever is needed in wartime.

The national security argument is also weakened by the diminished likelihood of a large-scale conventional war of long duration. A major nuclear war would be brief and horrible and its outcome would not be affected by the size of particular domestic industries such as oil or steel. Non-nuclear wars restricted to particular regions are unlikely to leave the U.S. cut off from all foreign sources of supply.

Protection for national security purposes is also counterproductive politically and diplomatically. Further action to limit steel imports, for example, would strengthen the divisive forces affecting our relations with friendly countries.

The national interests of the U.S. lie in the direction of freer trade. The arguments for a contrary policy, it has been shown, are based on incorrect assessments of the facts, draw unwarranted conclusions from true statements of fact, or stress benefits that may be real and important but either incapable of achievement or can be attained only at large economic and political cost.

The costs include the reduction to the stimulus to innovation, less consumer choice, higher prices, lower exports owing to higher costs and to the exclusion of the U.S. from the growing volume of intra-industry trade, and the deterioration of our relations with friendly countries.

Import limitations involve the use of government power to promote special interests at the general expense.

43

Contrasting Experiences with Trade Adjustment Assistance

JAMES E. McCARTHY

James E. McCarthy is an economist at the Conference Board. This article appeared in the Monthly Labor Review *in 1975.*

The Trade Expansion Act of 1962, which authorized U.S. participation in the Kennedy Round of trade negotiations, also authorized this country's first experiment with trade adjustment assistance. The legislation provided that firms or groups of workers which could demonstrate to the Tariff Commission that they had suffered injury from increased imports, as defined in the act, could qualify for assistance. Assistance for workers consisted of (1) trade readjustment allowances, which supplement unemployment compensation; (2) the provision of testing, counseling, placement, and training services by State Divisions of Employment Security; and/or (3) relocation for new employment. Assistance for firms consisted of tax assistance, technical assistance, and loans or loan guarantees. On April 3, 1975, new trade legislation, the Trade Act of 1974, provided for similar but expanded trade adjustment assistance.

Adjustment assistance has been of interest to economists and policymakers for a number of reasons. It promised aid to groups which would otherwise suffer as a result of freer trade. Unlike the escape clause or other broad forms of protection given to an entire industry, adjustment assistance would be given only to those within the industry who genuinely needed help. Instead of forcing consumers to subsidize all firms in an industry by means of tariffs or quotas, government funds would be spent to increase the efficiency of failing firms and to assist the functioning of labor markets.

The shoe industry in Massachusetts has been one of the few industries which has been able to qualify for adjustment aid. As of December 31, 1972, when this study was begun, a total of 68 cases of worker adjustment assistance involving 30,651 workers from all industries and States had been certified eligible. Both in number of cases (24) and in number of workers (6,505) the nonrubber footwear industry ranked first. About half the footwear certifications (13 cases and 2,989 workers) were from Massachusetts. Thus, it seemed that a case study of worker assistance in the Massachusetts shoe industry would yield some indication as to the program's effectiveness.

To study the worker program, a random sample of 200 workers, stratified by city and by firm, was chosen. Workers from 12 firms were included. Each of these workers was interviewed to obtain information concerning personal characteristics, the job lost due to imports, and the adjustment experience of the individual since layoff. The workers lost their jobs between January 1969 and August 1971. The fieldwork was done between March and July 1973. Information was also collected from the claimant files of the Massachusetts Division of Employment Security.

Worker Assistance

Eleven of the 12 firms represented in the survey shutdown and permanently laid off all their workers. Most of the workers (71.4 percent) had a month or less notice of layoff. The other company received firm assistance and was still in business at the time interviews were conducted. Sample members from this firm had been temporarily laid off for varying lengths of time, but most had been recalled.

Our study found that the permanently laid-off workers as a group had severe adjustment problems. One-fourth of those laid off never found another job. At the time of interview (an average 3 years and 3 months after layoff), half were not employed full time. And real wages for those employed had declined 17.9 percent from prelayoff levels. Yet of the 185 workers who were laid off, only one had participated in a government training program, one had received a relocation allowance, and only five had been placed in jobs by the Massachusetts Division of Employment Security. For most workers, assistance consisted only of trade readjustment allowances (TRA), a supplement to unemployment insurance. Sample members received an average of $1,072 in trade readjustment allowances in addition to a mean $1,635 in regular and extended unemployment benefits.

Little Use of Adjustment Services

Despite the difficult adjustment which most workers faced, there were at least four reasons why the adjustment services authorized by the Trade Expansion Act

---

Worker Adjustment Assistance under the Trade Act of 1974

The new Trade Act, which became effective April 3, 1975, provides for expanded adjustment assistance to American workers who have lost their jobs because of import competition. The law also provides for improved access to the assistance.

To expedite certification of eligibility and delivery of services, workers who believe they have been or will be injured by increased import competition may simply petition the Secretary of Labor, seeking certification of eligibility to apply for adjustment assistance. No longer do the workers need to establish a link between the injury and an earlier tariff concession. Nor do they have to prove that imports were the major factor causing injury. If the workers' petitions show that increased imports have contributed importantly to their unemployment and to a decrease in sales or production of the firm(s) from which they have become unemployed, the Secretary of Labor may declare them eligible for adjustment assistance.

The expanded assistance available under the new law includes cash trade allowances amounting to 70 percent (up from 65 percent) or a worker's average weekly wage, not to exceed the national average weekly manufacturing wage (approximately $180 a week in 1974) for up to 52 weeks. An additional 26 weeks of allowances was available to complete approved training. Workers age 60 or older may also receive up to 26 additional weeks of allowances, but no worker may receive more than 78 weeks of allowances. There are also provision for training, counseling, testing, placement services, and other services through cooperating state agencies.

Workers who cannot expect to find suitable employment within their own commuting area may qualify for job search and relocation allowances. Eighty percent of necessary job search expenses, up to $500, may be reimbursed. Workers who relocate may be reimbursed for 80 percent of moving expenses plus a lump sum (up to $500) equal to three times their average weekly wage.

To be eligible for adjustment assistance under the new law a worker must have been employed for 26 weeks out of the 52 weeks prior to layoff at a firm or plant certified as affected by import competition. He must have earned $30 or more per week.

were not used. First, the time lag between application for and receipt of benefits was so long that most applicants were forced to adjust on their own. Workers in our sample waited an average of 19.4 months from date of layoff to receipt of their first TRA check. Much of the delay was the result of the cumbersome procedures required by the Trade Expansion Act.

Second, knowledge of available benefits was not widespread. In our survey, fewer than 70 percent of TRA recipients knew that they were also eligible to receive retraining or relocation benefits. A more detailed survey of worker knowledge, undertaken by the Bureau of International Labor Affairs, found even less awareness: more than 60 percent of those potentially eligible for benefits were unaware of the training, placement, and relocation aspects of adjustment assistance.

Third, many affected workers were simply not interested in the services. In addition to the few who did retrain or relocate only 17 percent of our sample members expressed any interest in retraining and less than 7 percent an interest in relocation.

Fourth, those workers who were interested in the services often faced insurmountable administrative obstacles in trying to obtain them. Manpower Development and Training Act training classes had long waiting lists, and single referral training was generally available only in Boston, outside the commuting area of most sample members. Relocation allowances were available only to heads of families who obtained employment or received a bona fide offer of employment outside the commuting area, and only if the Secretary of Labor determined that the worker could not reasonably be expected to secure suitable employment within the commuting area. Under these conditions, few even applied.

It should be noted that in most cases the Massachusetts Division of Employment Security did not make much of an effort to provide special services to trade-affected workers. Most claimants only dealt with the unemployment insurance side of the Division. The employment service, which would provide counseling, refer individuals to training, or provide other services, was a separate branch, sometimes in a different building. Unemployment insurance personnel did refer some individuals for counseling by the employment service, but unless the person was young and unemployed at the time he filed for trade readjustment allowances, he was generally not referred for such counseling.

A Contrasting Case

The experiences of the workers with regard to receipt of noncash adjustment services were not atypical compared to the experiences of most groups in other States, but there were a few other groups which had far different experiences. One of these was a group in neighboring Rhode Island, whose experiences were described in *Industrial Gerontology*. Seven hundred fifty-five workers, employees of the Uniroyal Co. in Woonsocket, lost their jobs in April 1970 as a result of increased imports of rubber and canvas footwear. In many respects these workers were similar to those in our case study: women made up 68 percent of the group, the average age was 47 years, and average length of employment with Uniroyal was over 20 years. In addition, since they represented 10.1 percent of the community's manufacturing jobs, it was difficult for the labor market to absorb them quickly and they faced severe adjustment problems.

The company had announced its intention to close the plant in August 1969, 8 months before the closing, and had announced a definite closing date January 21, 1970, 2.5 months before production was to cease. Because of this advance notice, the Rubber Workers' union was able to apply for adjustment assistance before the plant closed. The petition was approved by the Tariff Commission on April 20 and certified by the Secretary of Labor on May 13, only a month after the layoffs. The State's Department of Employment Security also became involved relatively early. Officials of the Department wrote the plant management offering to provide job placement and training, and later met with union and management officials to draw up a plan of action. The results were in marked contrast to the experiences of our sample.

> During the month of July 1970, the Rhode Island State Department of Employment Security transferred three staff members to the Woonsocket office to perform counseling duties and to interview the 755 displaced Uniroyal employees. This staff interviewed 738 individuals in a total of 2,019 counseling interviews to determine specific employment needs and training aspirations. As a result of these interviews, 105 persons were subsequently placed in other positions, and training proposals were prepared and submitted to the Labor Department in conjunction with the State Division of Vocational Education for an additional 313 persons.

Despite delays due to lack of facilities in the area and unwillingness of workers to take training outside the immediate vicinity, 119 people were enrolled in private training during November 1970, and within a year of the plant closing, a total of 305 had been enrolled in some type of training. By use of private as well as government facilities, a wide range of training options was made available. Course titles ranged alphabetically from air-conditioning mechanic to welder; they were concentrated in mechanical, medical, and clerical occupations. Of the 305 who entered training, 253 (83 percent) completed it, and 224 (88.5 percent of those) were placed in jobs, at least 170 of them in training-related jobs.

All of the factors which we listed as limiting the use of adjustment services by our survey subjects were overcome in this instance. There was advance notice of layoff and cooperation among the various groups involved, so that much of the delay in authorizing assistance was overcome. Counseling sessions with 738 of 755 workers eliminated the problem of ignorance about available services. The Rhode Island Department of Employment Security undertook a massive effort to train and place the affected workers. And, as a result, disinterest of individuals in training, such as we found, appears not to have been a factor. All of this combined to produce massive use of adjustment services by the Uniroyal workers.

The effects of adjustment assistance in this case, however, have not been studied. Whether training led to stable employment and higher wages, whether benefits justified costs, and how the experience of workers trained and placed compared with that of others in the group is not known. A more thorough study of this case could help us judge the potential of trade adjustment assistance.

Conclusion

The experiences of shoe workers in Massachusetts with trade adjustment assistance leads to four conclusions: (1) Adjustment assistance, in most cases, consisted entirely of trade readjustment allowances, a supplement to unemployment insurance. While this may have helped to compensate workers for loss of a job, it did nothing to improve their chances of future employment. (2) The slowness of the program effectively precluded the use of adjustment services by most workers. Even a more timely program would have to deal with workers' ignorance of benefits or disinterest in them, and the administrative obstacles which often made benefits unobtainable. Overcoming these factors requires special effort on the part of State Divisions of Employment Security. (3) Workers most in need of adjustment services were women and older workers, especially those with seniority or long experience in the industry. High or increasing unemployment rates in local labor markets and the absence of employment opportunities in the same industry nearby hindered adjustment. (4) Firm assistance appears to have brought significant benefits to workers in the one case where its effects were studied. The effectiveness of this assistance in solving the long-run problems of firms themselves, however, has yet to be proven.

44

The Case for Flexible Exchange Rates

MILTON FRIEDMAN

Milton Friedman is Professor of Economics at the University of Chicago. The following article is taken from his testimony before the Joint Economic Committee in 1963.

Discussions of U.S. policy with respect to international payments tend to be dominated by our immediate balance-of-payments difficulties. I should like to approach the question from a different, and I hope more constructive, direction. Let us begin by asking ourselves not merely how we can get out of our present difficulties but instead how we can fashion our international payments system so that it will best serve our needs for the long pull; how we can solve not merely this balance-of-payments problem but the balance-of-payments problem.

A shocking, and indeed, disgraceful feature of the present situation is the extent to which our frantic search for expedients to stave off balance-of-payments pressures has led us, on the one hand, to sacrifice major national objectives; and, on the other, to give enormous power to officials of foreign governments to affect what should be purely domestic matters. Foreign payments amount to only some 5 percent of our total national income. Yet they have become a major factor in nearly every national policy.

I believe that a system of floating exchange rates would solve the balance-of-payments problem for the United States far more effectively than our present arrangements. Such a system would use the flexibility and efficiency of the free market to harmonize our small foreign trade sector with both the rest of our massive economy and the rest of the world; it would reduce problems of foreign payments to their proper dimensions and remove them as a major consideration in governmental policy about domestic matters and as a major preoccupation in international political negotiations; it would foster our national objectives rather than be an obstacle to their attainment.

To indicate the basis for this conclusion, let us consider the national objective with which our payments system is most directly connected: the promotion of a healthy and balanced growth of world trade, carried on, so far as possible, by private individuals and private enterprises with minimum intervention by governments. This has been a major objective of our whole postwar international economic policy, most recently expressed in the Trade Expansion Act of 1962. Success would knit the free world more closely together, and, by fostering the international division of labor, raise standards of living throughout the world, including the United States.

Suppose that we succeed in negotiating far-reaching reciprocal reductions in tariffs and other trade barriers with the Common Market and other countries. To simplify exposition I shall hereafter refer only to tariffs, letting these stand for the whole range of barriers to trade, including even the so-called voluntary limitation of exports. Such reductions will expand trade in general but clearly will have different effects on different industries. The demand for the products of some will expand, for others contract. This is a phenomenon we are familiar with from our internal development. The capacity of our free enterprise system to adapt quickly and efficiently to such shifts, whether produced by changes in technology or tastes, has been a major source of our economic growth. The only additional element introduced by international trade is the fact that different currencies are involved, and this is where the payment mechanism comes in; its function is to keep this fact from being an additional source of disturbance.

An all-around lowering of tariffs would tend to increase both our expenditures and our receipts in foreign currencies. There is no way of knowing in advance which increase would tend to be the greater and hence no way of knowing whether the initial effect would be toward a surplus or deficit in our balance of payments. What is clear is that we cannot hope to succeed in the objective of expanding world trade unless we can readily adjust to either outcome.

Many people concerned with our payments deficits hope that since we are operating further from full capacity than Europe, we could supply a substantial increase in exports whereas they could not. Implicitly, this assumes that European countries are prepared to see their surplus turned into a deficit, thereby contributing to the reduction of the deficits we have recently been experiencing in our balance of payments. Perhaps this would be the initial effect of tariff changes. But if the achievement of such a result is to be *sine qua non* of tariff agreement, we cannot hope for any significant reduction in barriers. We could be confident that exports would expand more than imports only if the tariff changes were one sided indeed, with our trading partners making much greater reductions in tariffs than we make. Our major means of inducing other countries to reduce tariffs is to offer corresponding reductions in our tariff. More generally, there is little hope of continued and sizable liberalization of trade if liberalization is to be viewed simply as a device for correcting balance-of-payments difficulties. That way lies only backing and filling.

Suppose then that the initial effect is to increase our expenditures on imports more than our receipts from exports. How could we adjust to this outcome?

One method of adjustment is to draw on reserves or borrow from abroad to finance the excess increase in imports. The obvious objection to this method is that it is only a temporary device, and hence can be relied on only when the disturbance is temporary. But that is not the major objection. Even if we had very large reserves or could borrow large amounts from abroad, so that we could continue this expedient for many years, it is a most undesirable one. We can see why if we look at physical rather than financial magnitudes.

The physical counterpart to the financial deficit is a reduction of employment in industries competing with imports that is larger than the concurrent expansion of employment in export industries. So long as the financial deficit continues, the assumed tariff reductions create employment problems. But it is no part of the aim of tariff reductions to create unemployment at home or to promote employment abroad. The aim is a balanced expansion of trade, with exports rising along with imports and thereby providing employment opportunities to offset any reduction in employment resulting from increased imports.

Hence, simply drawing on reserves or borrowing abroad is a most unsatisfactory method of adjustment.

Another method of adjustment is to lower U.S. prices relative to foreign prices, since this would stimulate exports and discourage imports. If foreign countries are accommodating enough to engage in inflation, such a change in relative prices might require merely that the United States keep prices stable or even, that it simply keep them from rising as fast as foreign prices. But there is no necessity for foreign countries to be so accommodating, and we could hardly count on their being so accommodating. The use of this technique therefore involves a willingness to produce a decline in U.S. prices by tight monetary policy or tight fiscal policy or both. Given time, this method of adjustment would work. But in the interim, it would exact a heavy toll. It would be difficult or impossible to force down prices appreciably without producing a recession and considerable unemployment. To eliminate in the long run the unemployment resulting from the tariff changes, we should in the short run be creating cyclical unemployment. The cure might for a time be far worse than the disease.

This second method is therefore also most unsatisfactory. Yet these two methods—drawing on reserves and forcing down prices—are the only two methods available to us under our present international payment arrangements, which involve fixed exchange rates between the U.S. dollar and other currencies. Little wonder that we have so far made such disappointing progress toward the reduction of trade barriers, that our practice has differed so much from our preaching.

There is one other way and only one other way to adjust and that is by allowing (or forcing) the price of the U.S. dollar to fall in terms of other currencies. To a foreigner, U.S. goods can become cheaper in either of two ways—either because their prices in the United States fall in terms of dollars or because the foreigner has to give up fewer units of his own currency to acquire a dollar, which is to say, the price of the dollar falls. For example, suppose a particular U.S. car sells for $2,800 when a dollar costs 7 shillings, tuppence in British money (i.e., roughly £1 = $2.80). The price of the car is then £1,000 in British money. It is all the same to an Englishman—or even a Scots-man—whether the price of the car falls to $2,500 while the price of a dollar remains 7 shillings, tuppence, or, alternatively, the price of the car remains $2,800 while the price of a dollar falls to 6 shillings, 5 pence (i.e., roughly £1 = $3.11). In either case, the car costs the Englishman £900 rather than £1,000, which is what matters to him. Similarly, foreign goods can become more expensive to an American in either of two ways—either because the price in terms of foreign currency rises or because he has to give up more dollars to acquire a given amount of foreign currency.

Changes in exchange rates can therefore alter the relative price of U.S. and foreign goods in precisely the same way as can changes in internal prices in the United States and in foreign countries. And they can do so without requiring anything like the same internal adjustments. If the initial effect of the tariff reductions would be to create a deficit at the former exchange rate (or enlarge an existing deficit or reduce an existing surplus) and thereby increase unemployment, this effect can be entirely avoided by a change in exchange rates which will produce a balanced expansion in imports and exports without interfering with domestic employment, domestic prices, or domestic monetary and fiscal policy. The pig can be roasted without burning down the house.

The situation is, of course, entirely symmetrical if the tariff changes should initially happen to expand our exports more than our imports. Under present circumstances, we would welcome such a result, and conceivably, if the matching deficit were experienced by countries currently running a surplus, they might permit it to occur without seeking to offset it. In that case, they and we would be using the first method of adjustment—changes in reserves or borrowing. But again, if we had started off from an even keel, this would be an undesirable method of adjustment. On our side, we should be sending out useful goods and receiving only foreign currencies in return. On the side of our partners, they would be using up reserves and tolerating the creation of unemployment.

The second method of adjusting to a surplus is to permit or force domestic prices to rise—which is of course what we did in part in the early postwar years when we were running large surpluses. Again, we should be forcing maladjustments on the whole economy to solve a problem arising from a small part of it—the 5 percent accounted for by foreign trade.

Again, these two methods are the only ones available under our present international payments arrangements, and neither is satisfactory.

The final method is to permit or force exchange rates to change—in this case, a rise in the price of the dollar in terms of foreign currencies. This solution is again specifically adapted to the specific problem of the balance of payments.

Changes in exchange rates can be produced in either of two general ways. One way is by a change in an official exchange rate—an official devaluation or appreciation from one fixed level which the Government is committed to support to another fixed level. This is the method used by Britain in its postwar devaluation and by Germany in 1961 when the mark was appreciated. This is also the main method contemplated by the IMF which permits member nations to change their exchange rates by 10 percent without approval by the Fund and by a larger amount after approval by the Fund. But this method has serious disadvantages. It makes a change in rates a matter of major moment, and hence there is a tendency to postpone any change as long as possible. Difficulties cumulate and a larger change is finally needed than would have been required if it could have been made promptly. By the time the change is made, everyone is aware that a change is pending and is certain about the direction of change. The result is to encourage flight from a currency, if it is going to be devalued, or to a currency, if it is going to be appreciated.

There is in any event little basis for determining precisely what the new rate should be. Speculative movements increase the difficulty of judging what the new rate should be, and introduce a systematic bias, making the change needed appear larger than it actually is. The result, particularly when devaluation occurs, is generally to lead officials to "play safe" by making an even larger change than the large change needed. The country is then left after the devaluation with a maladjustment precisely the opposite of that with which it started, and is thereby encouraged to follow policies it cannot sustain in the long run.

Even if all these difficulties could be avoided, this method of changing from one fixed rate to another has the disadvantage that it is necessarily discontinuous. Even if the new exchange rates are precisely correct when first established, they will not long remain correct.

A second and much better way in which changes in exchange rates can be produced is by permitting exchange rates to float, by allowing them to be determined from day to day in the market. This is the method which the United States used from 1862 to 1879, and again, in effect, from 1917 or so to about 1925, and again from 1933 to 1934. It is the method which Britain used from 1918 to 1925 and again from 1931 to 1939, and which Canada used for most of the interwar period and again from 1950 to May 1962. Under this method, exchange rates adjust themselves continuously, and market forces determine the magnitude of each change. There is no need for any official to decide by how much the rate should rise or fall. This is the method of the free market, the method that we adopt unquestioningly in a private enterprise economy for the bulk of goods and services. It is no less available for the price of one money in terms of another.

With a floating exchange rate, it is possible for Governments to intervene and try to affect the rate by buying or selling, as the British exchange equalization fund did rather successfully in the 1930s, or by combining buying and selling with public announcements of intentions, as Canada did so disastrously in early 1962. On the whole, it seems to me undersirable to have government intervene, because there is a strong tendency for government agencies to try to peg the rate rather than to stabilize it, because they have no special advantage over private speculators in stabilizing it, because they can make far bigger mistakes than private speculators risking their own money, and because there is a tendency for them to cover up their mistakes by changing the rules—as the Canadian case so strikingly illustrates—rather than by reversing course. But this is an issue on which there is much difference of opinion among economists who agree in favoring floating rates. Clearly, it is possible to have a successful floating rate along with governmental speculation.

The great objective of tearing down trade barriers, of promoting a worldwide expansion of trade, of giving citizens of all countries, and especially the underdeveloped countries, every opportunity to sell their products in open markets under equal terms and thereby every incentive to use their resources efficiently, of giving countries an alternative through free world trade to autarchy and central planning—this great objective can, I believe, be achieved best under a regime of floating rates. All countries, and not just the United States, can proceed to liberalize boldly and confidently only if they can have reasonable assurance that the resulting trade expansion will be balanced and will not interfere with major domestic objectives. Floating exchange rates, and so far as I can see, only floating exchange rates, provide this assurance. They do so because they are an automatic mechanism for protecting the domestic economy from the possibility that liberalization will produce a serious imbalance in international payments.

Despite their advantages, floating exchange rates have a bad press. Why is this so?

One reason is because a consequence of our present system that I have been citing as a serious disadvantage is often regarded as an advantage, namely, the extent to which the small foreign trade sector dominates national policy. Those who regard this as an advantage refer to it as the discipline of the gold standard. I would have much sympathy for this view if we had a real gold standard, so the discipline was imposed by impersonal forces which in turn reflected the realities of resources, tastes, and technology. But in fact we have today only a pseudo gold standard and the so-called discipline is imposed by governmental officials of other countries who are determining their own internal monetary policies and are either being forced to dance to our tune or calling the tune for us, depending primarily on accidental political developments. This is a discipline we can well do without.

A possibly more important reason why floating exchange rates have a bad press, I believe, is a mistaken interpretation of experience with floating rates, arising out of a statistical fallacy that can be seen easily in a standard example. Arizona is clearly the worst place in the United States for a person with tuberculosis to go because the death rate from tuberculosis is higher in Arizona that in any other State. The fallacy in this case is obvious. It is less obvious in connection with exchange rates. Countries that have gotten into severe financial difficulties, for whatever reason, have had ultimately to change their exchange rates or let them change. No amount of exchange control and other restrictions on trade have enabled them to peg an exchange rate that was far out of line with economic realities. In consequence, floating rates have frequently been associated with financial and economic instability. It is easy to conclude, as many have, that floating exchange rates produce such instability.

This misreading of experience is reinforced by the general prejudice against speculation; which has led to the frequent assertion, typically on the basis of no evidence whatsoever, that speculation in exchange can be expected to be destabilizing and thereby to increase the instability in rates. Few who make this assertion even recognize that it is equivalent to asserting that speculators generally lose money.

Floating exchange rates need not be unstable exchange rates—any more than the prices of automobiles or of Government bonds, of coffee or of meals need gyrate wildly just because they are free to change from day to day. The Canadian exchange rate was free to change during more than a decade, yet it varied within narrow limits. The ultimate objective is a world in which exchange rates, while free to vary, are in fact highly stable because basic economic policies and conditions are stable. Instability of exchange rates is a symptom of instability in the underlying economic structure. Elimination of this symptom by administrative pegging of exchange rates cures none of the underlying difficulties and only makes adjustment to them more painful.

The confusion between stable exchange rates and pegged exchange rates helps to explain the frequent comment that floating exchange rates would introduce an additional element of uncertainty into foreign trade and thereby discourage its expansion. They introduce no additional element of uncertainty. If a floating rate would, for example, decline, then a pegged rate would be subject to pressure that the authorities would have to meet by internal deflation or exchange control in some form. The uncertainty about the rate would simply be replaced by uncertainty about internal prices or about the availability of exchange; and the latter uncertainties, being subject to administrative rather than market control, are likely to be the more erratic and unpredictable. Moreover, the trader can far more readily and cheaply protect himself against the danger of changes in exchange rates, through hedging operations in a forward market, than he can against the danger of changes in internal prices or exchange availability. Floating rates are therefore more favorable to private international trade than pegged rates.

Though I have discussed the problem of international payments in the context of trade liberalization, the discussion is directly applicable to the more general problem of adapting to any forces that make for balance-of-payments difficulties. Consider our present problem, of a deficit in the balance of trade plus long-term capital movements. How can we adjust to it? By one of the three methods outlined: first, drawing on reserves or borrowing; second, keeping U.S. prices from rising as rapidly as foreign prices or forcing them down; third, permitting or forcing exchange rates to alter. And, this time, by one more method: by imposing additional trade barriers or their equivalent, whether in the form of higher tariffs, or smaller import quotas, or extracting from other countries tighter "voluntary" quotas on their exports, or "tieing" foreign aid, or buying higher priced domestic goods or services to meet military needs, or imposing taxes on foreign borrowing, or imposing direct controls on investments by U.S. citizens abroad, or any one of the host of other devices for interfering with the private business of private individuals that have become so familiar to us since Hjalmar Schacht perfected the modern techniques of exchange control in 1934 to strengthen the Nazis for war and to despoil a large class of his fellow citizens.

Fortunately or unfortunately, even Congress cannot repeal the laws of arithmetic. Books must balance. We must use one of these four methods. Because we have been unwilling to select the only one that is currently fully consistent with both economic and political needs—namely, floating exchange rates—we have been driven, as if by an invisible hand, to employ all the others, and even then may not escape the need for explicit changes in exchange rates.

We affirm in loud and clear voices that we will not and must not erect trade barriers—yet is there any doubt about how far we have gone down the fourth route? After the host of measures already taken, the Secretary of the Treasury has openly stated to the Senate Finance Committee that if the so-called interest equalization tax—itself a concealed exchange control and concealed devaluation—is not passed, we shall have to resort to direct controls over foreign investment.

We affirm that we cannot drain our reserves further,

yet short-term liabilities mount and our gold stock continues to decline.

We affirm that we cannot let balance-of-payments problems interfere with domestic prosperity, yet for at least some four years now we have followed a less expansive monetary policy than would have been healthy for our economy.

Even all together, these measures may only serve to postpone but not prevent open devaluation—if the experience of other countries is any guide. Whether they do, depends not on us but on others. For our best hope of escaping our present difficulties is that foreign countries will inflate.

In the meantime, we adopt one expedient after another, borrowing here, making swap arrangements there, changing the form of loans to make the figures look good. Entirely aside from the ineffectiveness of most of these measures, they are politically degrading and demeaning. We are a great and wealthy nation. We should be directing our own course, setting an example to the world, living up to our destiny. Instead, we send our officials hat in hand to make the rounds of foreign governments and central banks; we put foreign central banks in a position to determine whether or not we can meet our obligations and thus enable them to exert great influence on our policies; we are driven to niggling negotiations with Hong Kong and with Japan and for all I know, Monaco, to get them to limit voluntarily their exports. Is this posture suitable for the leader of the free world?

It is not the least of the virtues of floating exchange rates that we would again become masters in our own house. We could decide important issues on the proper ground. The military could concentrate on military effectiveness and not on saving foreign exchange; recipients of foreign aid could concentrate on how to get the most out of what we give them and not on how to spend it all in the United States; Congress could decide how much to spend on foreign aid on the basis of what we get for our money and what else we could use it for and not how it will affect the gold stock; the monetary authorities could concentrate on domestic prices and employment, not on how to induce foreigners to hold dollar balances in this country; the Treasury and the tax committees of Congress could devote thier attention to the equity of the tax system and its effects on our efficiency, rather than on how to use tax gimmicks to discourage imports, subsidize exports, and discriminate against outflows of capital.

A system of floating exchange rates would render the problem of making outflows equal inflows unto the market where it belongs and not leave it to the clumsy and heavy hand of Government. It would leave Government free to concentrate on its proper functions.

The price of gold should be determined in the free market, with the U.S. Government committed neither to buying gold nor to selling gold at any fixed price. This is the appropriate counterpart of a policy of floating exchange rates. With respect to our existing stock of gold, we could simply keep it fixed, neither adding to it nor reducing it; alternatively, we could sell it off gradually at the market price or add to it gradually, thereby reducing or increasing our governmental stockpiles of this particular metal. In any event, we should simultaneously remove all present limitations on the ownership of gold and the trading in gold by American citizens. There is no reason why gold, like other commodities, should not be freely traded on a free market.

45

The Case for Fixed Exchange Rates

HENRY C. WALLICH

Henry C. Wallich is a member of the Federal Reserve Board. The following article is taken from his testimony before the Joint Economic Committee in 1963.

Flexible rates have achieved a high measure of acceptance in academic circles, but very little among public officials. This raises the question whether we have a parallel to the famous case of free trade: almost all economists favor it in principle, but no major country ever has adopted it. Does the logic of economics point equally irrefutably to flexible rates, while the logic of politics points in another direction?

The nature of the case, I believe, is fundamentally different. Most countries do practice free trade within their borders, although they reject it outside. But economists do not propose flexible rates for the states of the Union, among which men, money, and goods can move freely, and which are governed by uniform monetary, fiscal, and other policies. Flexible rates are to apply only to relations among countries that do not permit free factor movements across their borders and that follow, or may follow, substantially different monetary and fiscal policies. It is the imperfections of the world that seem to suggest that flexible rates, which would be harmful if applied to different parts of a single country, would do more good than harm internationally.

It is quite arguable that the Appalachian area would benefit if it could issue a dollar of its own, an Appalachian dollar which in that case would sell, probably, at 60 or 90 cents. Exports from that region would increase, and unemployment would diminish. A great many good things would happen, but we are also aware of what it would do to the economy of the United States—and, therefore, we do not propose that solution. The question is, Do we want to look upon the world as quite different from the United States, as hopelessly divided into self-contained units where cooperation and efforts to coordinate policies are doomed to frustration? In that case, flexible rates may be the best way to avoid a very bad situation. But should we not try to establish within the world something that begins to approximate the conditions that prevail within a country, in the way of coordination of policies, freer flow of capital and of goods and so try to achieve the benefits of one large economic area within the world? This is what we should try for.

The proponents of flexible rates argue, in effect, that flexible rates can help a country get out of almost any of the typical difficulties that economies experience. This is perfectly true. If the United States has a balance-of-payments deficit, a flexible exchange rate allows the dollar to decline until receipts have risen and payments fallen enough to restore balance. If the United States has unemployment, flexible rates can protect it against the balance-of-payments consequences of a policy of expansion. We would then have less unemployment. If the United States has suffered inflation and fears that it will be undersold internationally, flexible rates can remove the danger.

All of these advantages are quite clear.

Other countries have analogous advantages. If Chile experiences a decline in copper prices, flexible rates can ease the inevitable adjustment. If Germany finds that other countries have inflated while German prices have remained more nearly stable, flexible rates could help to avoid importing inflation. If Canada has a large capital inflow, a flexible rate will remove the need for price and income increases that would otherwise be needed to facilitate the transfer of real resources.

There are other adjustments, however, that must be made in all of these cases. If a country allows its exchange rate to go down, some price adjustments still remain to be made. Furthermore, each time a country makes this kind of adjustment, allowing its exchange rate to decline, other countries suffer. If the U.S. dollar depreciates, we undersell the Europeans. It could be argued that if the U.S. price levels go down instead of the exchange rate, we also undersell the Europeans, and if because of a declining price level we have unemployment we would be buying still less from them. Nevertheless, there is a difference. A price adjustment tends to be slow and is likely to be no greater than it need be and tends to be selective for particular commodities. In contrast, an exchange rate movement is unpredictable. It can be large—we could easily have a drop of 10 or 20 percent in an exchange rate. It comes suddenly. And it compels other countries to be on their guard.

Why, given the attractions of flexible rates, should one advise policymakers to stay away from them? Since the dollar problem is the concrete situation in which flexible rates are being urged today, it is in terms of the dollar that they must be discussed. In broadest terms, the reason why flexible rates are inadvisable is that their successful functioning would require more self-discipline and mutual forbearance than countries today are likely to muster. Exchange rates are two sided—depreciation for the dollar means appreciation for the European currencies. To work successfully, a flexible dollar, for instance, must not depreciate to the point where the Europeans would feel compelled to take counteraction. I believe that the limits of tolerance, before counteraction begins today are narrow and that a flexible dollar would invite retaliation almost immediately.

In the abstract, the European countries perhaps ought to consider that if the United States allows the dollar to go down, it is doing so in the interests of all-round equilibrium. They ought perhaps to consider that with a stable dollar rate the same adjustment might have to take place through a decline in prices here and a rise in prices there. In practice, they are likely to be alive principally to the danger of being undersold by American producers if the dollar goes down, in their own and third markets. The changing competitive pressure would fall unevenly upon particular industries, and those who are hurt would demand protection.

The most likely counteraction might take one of two forms. The Europeans could impose countervailing duties, such as the United States also has employed at times. They could alternately also depreciate European currencies along with the dollar or, what would amount to almost the same thing, prevent the dollar from depreciating. This might involve the European countries in the purchase of large amounts of dollars. If they are to peg the dollar, they could minimize their commitment by imposing a simple form of exchange control that the Swiss practiced during the last war. The Swiss purchased dollars only from their exporters, also requiring their importers to buy these dollars thereby stabilizing the trade dollar, while allowing dollars from capital movements—finance dollars—to find their own level in the market.

The large volume of not very predictable short-term capital movements in the world today makes such reactions under flexible rates particularly likely.

A sudden outflow of funds from the United States, for instance (because of the fear of budget deficits or many other things that could happen), would tend to drive the dollar down. As a result, American exporters could undersell producers everywhere else in the world. It seems unlikely that foreign countries would allow a fortuitous short-term capital movement to have such far-reaching consequences. It would not even be economically appropriate to allow a transitory fluctuation in the capital account of the balance of payments to have a major influence on the current account. Such a fluctuation should not alter the pattern of trade, because the situation is likely to be reversed. Other countries therefore would probably take defensive action to make sure that no industry is destroyed and after several years may have to be rebuilt because of the ups and downs of short-term capital movements.

It can be argued that under flexible rates the effects of such a movement would be forestalled by stabilizing speculation on a future recovery of the dollar. This is possible. It is possible also, however, that speculation would seek a quick profit from the initial drop in the dollar, instead of a longer run one from its eventual recovery. Then short-run speculation would drive the dollar down farther at first. In any case there is not enough assurance that speculators will not make mistakes to permit basing the world's monetary system upon the stabilizing effects of speculation.

In the case of countries which import much of what they consume, such as England, a temporary decline in the local currency may even be self-validating. If the cost of living rises as the currency declines, wages will rise. Thereafter, the currency may never recover to its original level.

This points up one probable consequence of flexible exchange rates: a worldwide acceleration of inflation. In some countries the indicated ratchet effect of wages will be at work. If exchange rates go down, wages will rise, and exchange rates cannot recover. In the United States the rise in the cost of imports would not be very important. But the removal of balance-of-payments restraints may well lead to policies that could lead to price increases. The American inflation of the 1950s was never defeated until the payments deficit became serious. Elsewhere, the removal of balance-of-payments disciplines might have the same effect. Rapid inflation in turn would probably compel governments to intervene drastically in foreign trade and finance.

I am aware that there is a choice to be made here—more employment or more stable prices. If we pursued more sensible policies and exerted a little more self-restraint, this choice would not be upon us. But if we insist on raising costs and raising prices in the presence of unemployment then this unpleasant choice must be made. As Mr. Friedman has said, it is quite clear that the discipline of the balance of payments has made for a more restrictive policy in this country than would have been followed in the absence of this discipline. It is quite conceivable that the

absence of balance-of-payments disciplines would have strong inflationary effects in some countries. In that case governments would be compelled immediately to intervene drastically in foreign trade and finance; in other words, flexible exchange rates would contribute to their own extinction or to exchange control.

The prospect that flexible rates would greatly increase uncertainty for foreign traders and investors has been cited many times. It should be noted that this uncertainty extends also to domestic investment decisions that might be affected by changing import competition or changing export prospects. It has been argued that uncertainties about future exchange rates can be removed by hedging in the futures market. This, however, involves a cost even where cover is readily available. The history of futures markets does not suggest that it will be possible to get cover for long-term positions. To hedge domestic investment decisions that might be affected by flexible rates is in the nature of things impracticable.

The picture that emerges of the international economy under flexible rates is one of increasing disintegration. Independent national policies and unpredictable changes in each country's competitive position will compel governments to shield their producers and markets. The argument that such shielding would also automatically be accomplished by movements in the affected country's exchange rate underrates the impact of fluctuations upon particular industries, if not upon the entire economy. That international integration and flexible rates are incompatible seems to be the view also of the European Common Market countries, who have left no doubt that they want stable rates within the EEC. The same applies if we visualize the "Kennedy round" under the Trade Expansion Act. I think if we told the Europeans that, after lowering our tariffs, we were going to cast the dollar loose and let it fluctuate, we would get very little tariff reduction. They would want to keep up their guard.

If the disintegrating effects of flexible rates are to be overcome, a great deal of policy coordination, combined with self-discipline and mutual forbearance, would be required. The desired independence of national economic policy would in fact have to be foregone—interest rates, budgets, wage and prices policies would have to be harmonized. If the world were ready for such cooperation, it would be capable also of making a fixed exchange rate system work. In that case, flexible rates would accomplish nothing that could not more cheaply and simply be done with fixed rates. It seems to follow that flexible rates have no unique capacity for good, whereas they possess great capacity to do damage.

A modified version of the flexible rates proposal has been suggested. This version would allow the dollar and other currencies to fluctuate within a given range, say 5 percent up and down. This "widening of the gold points" is believed to reduce the danger of destabilizing speculation. It might perhaps enlist speculation on the side of stabilization, for if the dollar, say, had dropped to its lower limit, and if the public had confidence that that limit would not be broken, the only movement on which to speculate would be a rise. The spectacle of a currency falling below par may induce, according to the proponents, a strong political effort to bring it back.

This proposal likewise strikes me as unworkable. For one thing, I doubt that people would have a great deal of confidence in a limit of 5 percent below par, if par itself has been given up. Political support for holding this second line would probably be less than the support that can be mustered to hold the first. For another, the execution of the plan would still require the maintenance of international reserves, to protect the upper and lower limits. But with fluctuating rates, dollar and sterling would cease to be desirable media for monetary reserves. International liquidity would become seriously impaired. A third objection is that under today's conditions, the complex negotiations and legislation required, in the unlikely event that the plan could be negotiated at all, could not go forward without immediate speculation against the dollar before the plan goes into effect.

It remains only to point out that, even in the absence of a high degree of international cooperativeness, a system of fixed exchange rates can be made to work. It can be made to work mainly because it imposes a discipline upon all participants, and because within this discipline there is nevertheless some room for adjustment. The principal sources of flexibility are productivity gains and the degree to which they are absorbed by wage increases. Wages cannot be expected to decline. But their rise can be slowed in relation to the rate of productivity growth, in which case prices would become more competitive relative to other countries. With annual productivity gains of 2 to 3 percent in the United States and more abroad, it would not take many years to remove a temporary imbalance.

46

The Poor Nations

BARBARA WARD

Barbara Ward is the former Albert Schweitzer Professor of International Economic Development at Columbia University. This selection is taken from her book The Rich Nations and the Poor Nations, *published by W. W. Norton in 1962.*

How are we to define the "poor" nations? The phrase 'underdeveloped' is not very satisfactory for it groups together very different types of underdevelopment. India and Pakistan, for instance, are heirs of a great and ancient civilization and have many of the other attributes—in art, literature, and administration—of developed states, even though they are also very poor. Other areas—one thinks of the Congo—are developed in virtually no sense at all. I think, therefore, that perhaps the most satisfactory method of defining poverty at this stage is to discuss the question simply in terms of per capita income—the average income available to citizens in the various countries. If you fix the level of wealth of 'wealthy' communities at a per-capita income of about $500 a year, then 80 percent of mankind lives below it. The mass of mankind live well below the income level of $500 per head a year; and in some countries—one thinks particularly of India—per capita income may be as low as $60. Yet between 400 and 500 million people live in India—something like two-fifths of all the poor people in the uncommitted world. So the gap between rich and poor is tremendous and, as we have already noticed, it is tending to widen further.

What is the cause of this? Why is there this great blanket of poverty stretched across the face of the globe? Before we attempt an answer, we should, I think, remember that ours is the first century in which such a question can even be put. Poverty has been the universal lot of man until our own day. No one asked fundamental questions about a state of affairs which everyone took for granted. The idea that the majority could have access to a little modest affluence is wholly new, the breakthrough of whole communities to national wealth totally unprecedented.

To return to our question: the contrast between the wealth of the West and the poverty of nearly everybody else does have some puzzling features. For centuries, for millennia, the East had been the region of known and admired wealth. It was to the Orient that men looked when they spoke of traditional forms of riches: gold and diamonds, precious ointments, rare spices, extravagant brocades, and silks. In fact, for over a thousand years, one of the great drives in the Western economy was to open trade with the wealthier East. And one of the problems facing that trade—as far in the past as in the days of imperial Rome—was the West's inability to provide very much in return. It is hard to sell bear rugs to merchants at Madras, especially during the monsoon. Nor is the contrast between the East's endowment and the relative poverty of the West simply a matter of history. Today, for instance, Indonesia seems obviously better endowed in a whole range of ways than are some European countries—one might perhaps pick Norway.

In spite of these puzzles, there are some underlying physical causes which explain why some countries have been left behind in the world's present thrust towards greater wealth. Many of the tropical soils have been submitted to millennia of leaching under the downpour of heavy rains and are precarious soils for agriculture. Nor is the climate of tropical regions precisely designed for work. When the temperature rises to ninety degrees and the humidity to 90 percent, you do not feel like rushing out and solving one of the first problems in Euclid. Even less do you want to cut a tree—favourite occupation of Victorian gentlemen—or dig a ditch.

Wherever the monsoon is the rain-bringing force, there is an underlying element of instability in farming. The concentration of rain in a few months creates expensive problems of control and storage. Rivers vary from raging torrents to dry beds. And if the monsoons fail in India or Southeast Asia, then there is quite simply no agriculture because there is no water.

Another fact making for poverty is that the great tropical belt stretching round the world has only limited sources of energy: no coal and not too much oil outside the Middle East, Venezuela, and Indonesia. One must conclude, therefore, that certain original differences exist in the actual endowment of resources in the advancing Northern Hemisphere and the relatively stagnant South. Nonetheless, I think the profound reason for the contrast of wealth and poverty lies in the fact that the various revolutions which have swept over the face of the Western world in the last hundred years exist at only a chaotic or embryonic stage among the poorer states.

The biological revolution of more rapid growth in population is on the way in these areas. But the other vast changes—an intellectual revolution of materialism and this-worldliness, the political revolution of equality, and above all the scientific and technological revolution which comes from the application of savings and the sciences to the whole business of daily life—are only beginning the process of transforming every idea and institution in the emergent lands. The revolution of modernization has not yet driven these states into the contemporary world. The greatest drama of our time is that they will be swept onwards. But we are still uncertain over the form these revolutions will finally take. Everywhere they have started; nowhere are they yet complete; but the trend cannot be reversed. The modernizing of the whole world is under way.

Millennia ago, hunting and food-gathering began to give way before the advance of settled agriculture. So today the transformation of society by the application of reason, science, and technology is thrusting the old static subsistence economies to the backwaters of the world. The world is, in fact, involved in a single revolutionary process of which our four dominant themes are all a part. In the wealthier lands, the first stage of this transformation has been completed in the emergence of the modern, wealthy, reasonably stable, technologically adept capitalist state. In the poorer lands, the first stage only has opened. The contrast between world wealth and world poverty largely turns upon this lag in time.

Now we must examine the impact of the four changes upon emergent lands—and we should remember again the distinction between poorer lands such as India which are at the same time rich in culture, history, and tradition, and tribal lands, whether in Africa, Australia, or Latin America, which lack even the rudiments of a developed tradition. The biological revolution brought about by a sudden acceleration of the birthrate could not take place in these countries until colonial rule abolished local wars and until modern medical science and modern sanitation began to save babies and lengthen life. That these changes were introduced *before* the establishment of a modern economy is one of the most fateful differences between East and West, and one to which we will return. But until the second half of the nineteenth century most of these lands still followed the old millennial pattern of a population rising to the limits of production and then falling back into violence, struggle, and death where the limits were surpassed. In tribal life, for instance, when the tribe had eaten up the resources available in its hunting grounds, it had no alternative but to reduce its numbers by malnutrition and starvation or break out and conquer the lands of other tribes, thereby diminishing the numbers on both sides. This cycle was one of the perennial causes of tribal war.

Even in a great settled civilization like China, history has given us a kind of physical representation of the "melancholy wheel" of fate in the pressure of population rising to the limit of resources, and there precipitating violence, despair, banditry, civil war, and invasion. Then, under tribulations of all kinds, the population falls back again to numbers which the food supply can carry, only to rise once more as peace is restored—a kind of self-perpetuating cycle in which the wheel of fate is driven by pressure of population into a constant alternation of peaceful growth and violent diminution. This, until the day before yesterday, seemed to be the fundamental fatality of man's existence.

Now let us turn to the second force: the new revolutionary emphasis on work and effort devoted to the things of *this* world, the drive of interest devoted to changing and bettering man's physical environment. In traditional or tribal societies, this force is, in the main, lacking. Very largely, the material organization of life and, above all, the natural sequence of birth and death, of the seasons, of planetary change, have been taken as given: they were not the subject of speculative activity. In primitive tribal society one can say that nature is very largely accepted as impenetrable by reason. It can be propitiated. It can be worked on by human will through magic. A flood may be diverted by drowning a male child. But no one connects the precipitation of rain at the head of the watershed with the expected annual flow and devises earthworks to avert disaster. Life is lived in the midst of mystery which cannot be manipulated, beyond very narrow limits, in answer to human needs.

In the great archaic societies—of Babylon, of Egypt, of the Indus Valley, or of the Yellow River—both the exploration of reality and the use of technology registered a formidable advance. Irrigation works such as those of ancient Egypt demanded elaborate scientific calculation, accurate observation of nature, and efficient, large-scale administration. And societies which evolved astronomy and the mathematical sciences to the levels achieved by the Persians or the Greeks achieved a penetration of matter by the human intellect unequalled until our own day. But the dynamism of our modern interest in created things was lacking. In some societies, as we shall see, the lack followed from a certain scientific indifference; in others, from a dissociation between the understanding of natural law and any idea of using the laws as tools for experimental work; and in all societies from a static concept of life in which the chief means of subsistence—agriculture—provided daily bread for the many and magnificence for the few, but was not a capital resource to be steadily extended by further

investment. And, in truth, once the limits of land and water were reached, lack of scientific experiment inhibited further expansion.

In short, the chief aims of these societies were not this-worldly in our modern sense. Take, for instance, the significant Victorian phrase "making good." We understand it in terms of making money, of achieving material success in the broadest sense. In premodern society no such meaning could possibly have been attached to any activity thought of as being 'good.' In tribal society, approved behaviour implies strict observance of tribal laws and customs. In archaic civilization, the good man, the man of wisdom, is the man who observes the rules and duties of his way of life: the rich man, in magnificence, affability, and alms-giving; the poor man, in work and respect. No group, except the despised merchant, devotes his life to accumulation. And even the merchant tends, as he did in China, to turn his wealth into land and leave the life of capital formation behind as soon as his fortune permits the change. Such societies incline of their very nature to be backward-looking, to preserve rather than to create, and to see the highest wisdom in the effort to keep things as they are. Under these conditions no underlying psychological drive impels people to work and accumulate for the future. Wisdom is to wait on Providence and follow in the ways of your forefathers, ways of life compatible with great serenity, great dignity, profound religious experience, and great art, but not with the accumulation of material wealth for society as a whole.

The lack of the third revolution—equality—has worked in the same sense. There was no concept of equality in traditional society. As one knows from still-existing tribal societies, leadership lies with the old men of the tribe. There is no way for the "young men" to claim equality. They simply have to wait for the years to pass. Seniority (as in the American Senate) also ensures that the leaders are men who respect the backward-looking traditions of the group and have a vested interest in the unequal prestige conferred by advancing years. It is the inescapable recipe for extreme conservatism.

When tribal society is left behind, the values supported by the leaders are still conservative. They are fixed by an inviolate upper order. Save in times of immense upheaval, the peasant does not reach the throne. King, warrior, landlord form a closed order to which recruitment is in the main by birth. In India the fixedness of the pattern extended to everyone. A man is born to his caste and to no other. The very idea of equality is almost meaningless since you are what you are and you cannot measure yourself against other men who are entirely different by birth and by caste. Caste thus reinforced the inability of the merchant class to achieve greater influence and status. The merchant remained a Vaishya—the merchant caste—and money-making was not considered a valuable enough occupation to warrant any increase in status or esteem. Thus the Indian merchant did not achieve the political breakthrough which launched the rising power of the middle classes in Western Europe.

Another facet of equality—a vital facet for economic growth—was lacking: since there was no national community as we understand it, competitive drives based on national equality were also absent. The tribe is a sort of tiny nation, a nation in embryo, but it cannot exercise the same economic influence as the modern nation because it is too small to be a significant market. In any case, tribal agriculture is devoted to subsistence, not to exchange.

The larger post-tribal political units were, in the main, dynastic or imperial units—one thinks of such loose structures as the India of the Guptas or of China's gigantic bureaucracy—in which there was little interconnection between the scattered cities and the great mass of people living their isolated, subsistence village lives. Certainly there was not enough economic and social coherence to define a market in such terms that a merchant would feel himself in competition with other vigorous national markets and could operate with driving energy to defend national interests against the rival national interests of others. The competitive "equality" of Western Europe's commerce was wholly absent. As one sees again and again in human history—or in daily life—people do not begin to act in new ways until they have formulated the idea of such ways in their minds. The idea of the nation was immensely reinforced—but also in part created—by the rivalry of commercial interests in Western Europe.

Now we turn to the last and most pervasive of the revolutions, the crucial revolution of science and saving. There is virtually no science in tribal society. There is a good deal of practical experience, skilled work, and early technique. It seems possible, for instance, that primitive farming developed as a result of close observation of nature's cycle of seed and harvest and its imitation in fertility rites and religious festivals. But the idea of controlling material things by grasping the inner law of their construction is absent.

An underlying sense of the mysteriousness of things explains, as we have noticed, the use of magic. But magic depends on the force of a man's will, not upon the nature of the things upon which he tries to exercise his will. And since the human will is a very potent force, one occasionally encounters some very strange and unaccountable results which seem inexplicable in ordinary terms. Few travelers return from Africa without some sense of having brushed the uncanny fringes of a world where some of the ordinary rules do not apply. Nonetheless, primitive society lacks the sustained and purposive manipulation of matter for human ends which becomes possible once you grasp the laws to which matter responds.

In great traditional civilizations such as India and China, there certainly was enough intellectual ferment for a vast scientific breakthrough to be theoretically possible. Many of the most acute minds in those societies devoted themselves to systematic thought for generations. In the Eastern Mediterranean, among the Chaldeans and the Egyptians, some of the basic mathematical tools of science had been forged long before the Christian era. Yet the breakthrough never came. In India, there could be no obsessive research into material things since many of the finest spirits thought of the natural world as in some sense an illusion with no fundamental significance for human beings. In China, for a rather different reason, science failed to achieve the preeminence one might have expected in one of the most brilliantly intellectual societies of all time; and one in which printing—and gunpowder—were invented far ahead of the West. The reason is one more illustration of the degree to which revolutions begin—or fail to begin—in the minds of men. The Confucian gentleman who dominated the official thinking of Chinese society thought science an occupation for charlatans and fools and, therefore, not really respectable. One need hardly add that if the best brains do not think a pursuit respectable, the best brains do not devote their time to it.

The Confucians had an excuse for their prejudice. In Europe, the medieval alchemists spent much of their time and energy trying to discover the "philosopher's stone"—the catalyst which would turn base metals into gold. In the course of their futile search they made many sound experimental discoveries about the properties of metals and some people regard them as precursors of the inductive and experimental methods upon which modern science is based.

In China the "philosopher's stone" took another

form—the "elixir of life." China's emperors did not want gold. They wanted immortality and at their courts the Taoists, followers of a mystical and metaphysical religious 'way,' conducted practical experiments with plants and chemicals to see if the elixir could be produced in a test tube. To the Confucians, the folly of the aim overshadowed the potential value of the means. They turned their backs on experiment and, in doing so, on science as well. So in China, for all the ancient glory of its culture, for all the force and vitality of its intellectual tradition, the scientific breakthrough could not occur.

Primitive and archaic societies match their lack of scientific *élan* by an equal lack of sustained saving. Every society saves something. Saving is, after all, not consuming. If everything were consumed, men would be reduced to hunting and fishing—and even these occupations require rods and spears. But in settled agricultural societies, seed cord is set aside for the next harvest and men do the hedging and ditching and field-levelling needed to carry production forward year by year. Probably such saving for maintenance and repair—and more occasionally by land-clearing and irrigation, for expansion—does not surpass 4 or 5 percent of national income in any year.

The savings which make possible a general change in the techniques of productivity—more roads, more ports, more power, more education, more output on the farms, new machines in the factories—must rise dramatically above the 5 percent level. Economists fix a level of about 12 to 15 percent of national income as the range needed to cover all possible increases in population, some increase in consumption, and a high, expanding level of investment. And no traditional society ever reached this level.

One reason for this fact takes us back to the revolution of equality. The merchant in the Orient never achieved decisive political influence. There were no city corporations, no charters based on autonomous rights. As a result, the merchant never achieved full security either. The government of kings and emperors was a government above the law, depending upon the monarch's whim. There is a brilliant phrase used by one of the young gentlemen of the East India Company to describe the uncertainties of the commercial calling in India. He describes the monarch and his tax-gatherers as bird's-nesters who leave a merchant to accumulate a nestful of eggs and then come to raid them all. One can well understand that under such conditions the stimulus to sustained capital accumulation is fairly marginal. On the contrary, the tendency is to put money that is earned from trade—and a great deal of money was earned—either into hoards of currency that can be hidden or else into jewels which are easily transportable and easily hid. But neither of these reserves makes for the expansion of productive enterprise.

In short, the chief point that distinguishes tribal and traditional society is that all the internal impulses to modernization have been largely lacking. And yet today these societies are everywhere in a ferment of change. How has this come about? Where did the external stimulus come from? There is only one answer. It came, largely uninvited, from the restless, changing, rampaging West. In the last 300 years, the world's ancient societies, the great traditional civilizations of the East, together with the pre-Iberian civilizations of Latin America and the tribal societies of Africa, have all, in one way or another, been stirred up from outside by the new, bounding, uncontrollable energies of the Western powers which, during those same years, were undergoing concurrently all the revolutions—of equality, of nationalism, of rising population, and of scientific change—which make up the mutation of modernization.

The great worldwide transmitter of the modernizing tendency has been without doubt—for good and evil—Western colonialism. It is typical, I think, of the way in which the changes have come about that, again and again, Western merchants were the forerunners of upheaval. They went out to bring back the spices and silks and sophistications of the Orient to cold and uncomfortable Europe. At first, they had no intentions of conquering anything. They simply tried to establish monopoly positions for themselves—hardly surprising when you could earn a 5,000-percent profit on a shipload of nutmeg making landfall in Europe—and to drive the traders of other nations away. They fought each other ferociously at sea but on land controlled only "factories"—clusters of warehouses, port installations, and dwelling houses held on sufferance from the local ruler. And so the position might have remained. But Dutch pressure was too great for the frail political structure of Java in the seventeenth century and little by little, by backing compliant sultans and deposing sullen ones, the Dutch became political masters of all the rich "spice islands."

In the following century, the Mogul superstructure collapsed in India and in their maneuvering to destroy French influence the British found themselves assuming power by a similar route, first backing local contenders, then, saddled with them as puppets or incompetents, gradually assuming the power which slipped from their enfeebled grip. The Europeans had come out to trade. Imperial control was a by-product—and an increasingly ruinous one in commercial terms—yet as late as 1850 the nominal ruler in India was still a merchant corporation—"John Company," the East India Company.

Colonial control, developing from its origins in trade, began to set the whole revolution of modernization into motion. It launched the radical changes brought about by a rapidly increasing growth in population. Western control introduced the beginnings of medical science. It ended internal disorder. A crowding into the big cities began. There were some attempts at more modern sanitation.

Towards the close of the nineteenth century a spurt of population began throughout India and the Far East. But this spurt had a different consequence from the comparable increase in the West. Western lands were relatively underpopulated—North America absolutely so—when the processes of modernization began. The growth in numbers was a positive spur to economic growth; it brought labourers into the market and widened the market. At the same time the new machines, the new developing economy based on rising productivity, expanded the possibilities of creating wealth in a way that more than outstripped the growth in population. But in the Far East, in India, where population was already dense, the effect of the colonial impact was to increase the rate of the population's growth without launching a total transformation of the economy. More births, longer lives, sent population far beyond the capabilities of a stumbling economy. Today the grim dilemma has appeared that population is so far ahead of the means of satisfying it that each new wave of births threatens in each generation to wipe out the margin of savings necessary to sustain added numbers. The West, where growth in population acted as a spur to further expansion, has not faced this dilemma, and in the East it is not yet clear how so grave a dilemma *can* be faced.

Colonial rule brought in the sense of a this-worldly concern for the advantages of material advance by the simplest and most direct route—the "demonstration effect." The new merchants, the new administrators, lived better, lived longer, had demonstrably more materially satisfying lives. The local people saw that this was so and they began to wonder why and whether others might not live so too. Above all, the

local leaders saw vividly that the new scientific, industrial, and technological society enjoyed almost irresistible power. This, too, they naturally coveted.

At the same time, the colonial system did set in motion some definite beginnings in the processes of technical change and economic growth. There was some education of local people in the new techniques of Western life. Some merchants in the old societies, the Compradors in China, for instance, or the Gujaratis in India, began to exercise their talents as entrepreneurs in a new, settled, commercial society. Some of the preliminaries of industrialization—railways, ports, roads, some power—the preliminaries we call 'infrastructure'—were introduced to the benefit of the new colonial economy. Some export industries expanded to provide raw materials for the West. Virtually nothing was done about basic agriculture; but plantation systems did develop agricultural products—tea, pepper, ground-nuts, jute—for the growing markets of Europe.

Above all, the new political ideas streamed in. Western education gave an *élite* a first look at Magna Charta. In their school books in India the sons of Indians could read Edmund Burke denouncing the depradations of Englishmen in India. The new sense of equality, inculcated by Western education, was reinforced by the daily contrast between the local inhabitants and the colonial representatives who claimed to rule them. Personal equality fused with the idea of national equality, with the revolt educated men increasingly felt at being run by another nation. The whole national movement of anticolonialism was stirred up by Western ideas of national rights and national independence, and by the perpetual evidence that the rights were being denied.

Everywhere there was ferment; everywhere there was the beginning of change; everywhere a profound sense that the old ways were becoming inadequate, were in some way no longer valid or viable for modern man. And this feeling stirred up an equally violent reaction. Men rose up to say that the old ways were better and that the new-fangled fashions would destroy all that was valuable and profound in indigenous civilization. Between the modernizers and the traditionalists, between the young men who wanted to accept everything and the old men who wanted to reject everything, the local community threatened to be distracted by contradictory leadership. A crisis of loyalty and comprehension superimposed itself on all the other crises. It was rare for a country to achieve the national coherence that was achieved in India under the leadership of Gandhi in whom ancient vision and the modern idea of equality could coexist, and around whom old and new were thus able to unite.

The important point to remember, however, if one wishes to grasp the present contrast between the rich nations and the poor, is that all these changes, introduced pell-mell by colonialism, did not really produce a new and coherent form of society, as they had done in the West. There was no "take-off," to use Professor Rostow's phrase, into a new kind of society. The colonial impact introduced problems that seemed too large to be solved, or, at least, problems that offered immense difficulty to any solution. Take, for instance, the problem of population. You could not deny medicine; you could not resist sanitation; yet all the time life lengthened, the birthrate went on going up, and you could almost watch population beginning to outstrip resources that were not growing in proportion because saving and capital formation were still inadequate. Yet the rising population continuously made saving more difficult.

This small level of saving meant that all economic developments under colonialism—or semicolonialism—were on too small a scale to lead to a general momentum. China is a good example. After the Opium Wars the British compelled the crumbling Manchu Empire to open its ports to Western trade. In the so-called treaty ports, quite a rapid rate of economic and industrial expansion took place. Europeans brought in capital. Some Chinese entrepreneurs joined them. International trade soared. The customs, also under European control, grew to be an important source of revenue. Plans for building railways were prepared. Meanwhile, however, the desperate, overcrowded countryside where the bulk of the people lived slipped steadily down into deeper ruin. Little economic activity could spread beyond the Westernized areas; for there were no markets, no savings, no initiative—only the dead weight of rural bankruptcy.

Similarly, in India the only areas where anything like a sustained 'take-off' began to occur were in the neighbourhood of Bombay with its shrewd merchants and great port, among the Scottish jute-growers round Calcutta, and with the lively adaptable farmers of the Punjab. Elsewhere, the countryside was largely unaffected by the new economic forces.

The same patchiness affected social life and education. All over Asia the educational system began to produce an *élite* who believed in Western ideas of law, Western ideas of liberty, of constitutional government. But behind them there was little general change among the people at large and, above all, no trace of change in the vast number—80 or more percent of the population—who lived on the land where the old, unchanged, subsistence agriculture went on as before. And so there came about what one can only call a kind of dual society, in which the scattered growing points of a modern way of life were restrained almost to the pitch of immobility by enormous forces of inertia inherent in the old framework of society.

When, for instance one reads of the attempts made by small groups of Chinese merchants in the late nineteenth century to transform their economy in such a way that they could withstand the commercial and political pressure of the West, one confronts again and again the fact that the real society simply had not changed enough to go along with them. The Court was backward-looking. The Confucian bureaucracy was still utterly unchanged. Worse still, the merchants themselves were still divided in their own minds. They still hankered for the days when a successful merchant naturally put all his capital into land and became a member of the landed gentry. At every point, there were psychological blocks in men's minds when it came to completing the changes they had been ready to start. In a very real sense societies like China or India in the last century were caught between a world that had died and a new world that could not yet be born—and this is, of course, the perfect recipe for maximum psychological and social strain.

Perhaps one can best judge the entent of the inhibitions by examining the opposite example of Japan. There, an extraordinarily efficient and ruthless ruling class determined, after the forced opening of their ports by the Western powers, to transform their country completely on the modern Western model. They decided that nothing short of almost total technical transformation would give them power to resist the West. So they forced through the reform of agriculture, the imposition of savings on the people, the absolute liquidation of all forms of the feudal economy. They introduced industry, sent many men to train abroad, and set in motion a drive for universal literacy. Although, unhappily, they also borrowed from the contemporary West a spirit of imperialism also present in their own traditions, they were able to transform their society radically in about thirty years and eliminated the social blocks and psychic inhibitions which held the other societies miserably suspended between contradictory worlds.

But elsewhere throughout the uncommitted world, in the traditional societies of China and India, in large parts of Latin America, and in the primitive emergent countries of Africa, old and new remained locked in a kind of battle, stuck fast in an apparently unbreakable deadlock. And how to break out of it; how to get the forces of modernization flowing through all of society; how to change leadership; how to get the new cadres in education; how to stimulate massive saving; how to get agriculture transformed: all these urgent and irresistible problems of the new society still wait to be answered.

This is a fact which the West cannot ignore. Most of the dilemmas of the underdeveloped areas have been stirred up by Western impact. Yet I think it is not entirely untrue to say that the Western powers are not looking very hard to find answers to these dilemmas. And this, I think, is for a very good reason. They have largely forgotten about their own transition. They are not conscious of the fact that a hundred years ago, even fifty years ago, many of them were struggling with just these problems of changing leadership, of developing new social groups, giving rights to new classes, finding methods of achieving greater saving, and securing a technological breakthrough on a massive scale. We take our development so much for granted that we hardly understand the dilemmas of those who have not yet travelled so far.

Another reason for our relative indifference is that owing to the relative underpopulation of our part of the world and owing to the scale of latent resources waiting to be developed in the Atlantic world, we in the West had not too difficult a passage to modernity; certainly nothing compared with the really appalling dilemmas that are faced by the underdeveloped world today. So, although we are perhaps beginning to see that they face almost insurmountable problems, I do not think that we have worked out our response or even perhaps fully measured our responsibility. Yet there is no human failure greater than to launch a profoundly important endeavour and then leave it half done. This is what the West has done with its colonial system. It shook all the societies in the world loose from their old moorings. But it seems indifferent whether or not they reach safe harbour in the end.

This is one difficulty; but there is another, a greater one. While we face these dilemmas, another set of answers to them has been formulated—also in the West. It claims to go to the heart of all these revolutions and offer a surer route to equality, to material well-being, to the achievement of technology, science, and capital. Communism claims to be the pattern of the future and to hold the secret of the next phase of history for mankind. In one sense, the claim is serious. Communism is a sort of résumé of the revolutions that make up modernization and it offers a method of applying them speedily to societies caught fast in the dilemmas of transition. We must, therefore, admit that, at the present moment, the poor nations, the uncommitted nations, face a double challenge. They face an enormous challenge of change. But, in addition, they face an equally vast challenge of choice.

47

The Less-Developed Countries: Observations and Implications

SIMON KUZNETS

Simon Kuznets is George E. Baker Professor of Economics Emeritus at Harvard University. This selection is taken from his Nobel Memorial Lecture, December 11, 1971.

Two major groups of factors appear to have limited the spread of modern economic growth. First, such growth demands a stable, but flexible, political and social framework, capable of accommodating rapid structural change and resolving the conflicts that it generates, while encouraging the growth-promoting groups in society. Such a framework is not easily or rapidly attained, as evidenced by the long struggles toward it even in some of the presently developed countries in the nineteenth and early twentieth centuries. Japan is the only nation outside of those rooted in European civilization that has joined the group of developed countries so far. Emergence of a modern framework for economic growth may be especially difficult if it involves elements peculiar to European civilization for which substitutes are not easily found. Second, the increasingly national cast of organization in developed countries made for policies toward other parts of the world that, while introducing some modern economic and social elements, were, in many areas, clearly inhibiting. These policies ranged from the imposition of colonial status to other limitations on political freedom, and, as a result,

political independence and removal of the inferior status of the native members of the community, rather than economic advance, were given top priority.

Whatever the weight of the several factors in explaining the failure of the less-developed countries to take advantage of the potential of modern economic growth, a topic that, in its range from imperialist exploitation to backwardness of the native economic and social framework, lends itself to passionate and biased polemic, the factual findings are clear. At present, about two-thirds or more of world population is in the economically less-developed group. Even more significant is the concentration of the population at the low end of the product per capita range. In 1965, the last year for which we have worldwide comparable product estimates, the per capita Gross Domestic Product (at market prices) of 1.72 billion out of a world population of 3.27 billion, was less than $120, whereas 0.86 billion in economically developed countries had a per capita product of some $1,900. Even with this narrow definition of less-developed countries, the intermediate group was less than 0.7 billion, or less than 20 percent of the world total. The preponderant population was thus divided between the very low and the rather high level of per capita economic performance. Obviously, this aspect of modern economic growth deserves our greatest attention, and the fact that the quantitative data and our knowledge of the institutional structures of the less-developed countries are, at the moment, far more limited than our knowledge of the developed areas, is not reason enough for us to ignore it.

Several preliminary findings, or rather plausible impressions, may be noted. First, the group of less-developed countries, particularly if we widen it (as we should) to include those with a per capita product somewhat larger than $120 (in 1965 prices), covers an extremely wide range in size, in the relation between population and natural resources, in major inherited institutions, and in the past impact upon them of the developed countries (coming as it did at different times and from different sources). There is a striking contrast, for example, in terms of population size, between the giants like Mainland China and India, on the one hand, and the scores of tiny states in Africa and Latin America; as there is between the timing of direct Western impact on Africa and of that on many countries in Latin America. Furthermore, the remarkable institutions by which the Sinic and East Indian civilizations produced the unified, huge societies that dwarfed in size any that originated in Europe until recently, bore little resemblance to those that structured the American Indian societies or those that fashioned the numerous tribal societies of Africa.

Generalizations about less-developed countries must be carefully and critically scrutinized in the light of this wide variety of conditions and institutions. To be sure, their common failure to exploit the potential of modern economic growth means several specific common features: a low per capita product, a large share of agriculture or other extractive industries, a generally small scale of production. But the specific parameters differ widely, and because the obstacles to growth may differ critically in their substance, they may suggest different policy directions.

Second, the growth position of the less-developed countries today is significantly different, in many respects, from that of the presently developed countries on the eve of their entry into modern economic growth (with the possible exception of Japan, and one cannot be sure even of that). The less-developed areas that account for the largest part of the world population today are at much lower per capita product levels than were the developed countries just before their industrialization; and the latter at that time were economically in advance of the rest of the world, not at the low end of the per capita product range. The very magnitudes, as well as some of the basic conditions, are quite different: no country that entered modern economic growth (except Russia) approached the size of India or China, or even of Pakistan and Indonesia; and no currently developed country had to adjust to the very high rates of natural increase of population that have characterized many less-developed countries over the last two or three decades. Particularly before World War I, the older European countries, and to some extent even Japan, relieved some strains of industrialization by substantial emigration of the displaced population to areas with more favorable opportunities—an avenue closed to the populous less-developed countries today. Of course, the stock of material and social technology that can be tapped by less-developed countries today is enormously larger than that available in the nineteenth and even early twentieth centuries. But it is precisely this combination of greater backwardness and seemingly greater backlog of technology that makes for the significant differences between the growth position of the less-developed countries today and that of the developed countries when they were entering the modern economic growth process.

Finally, it may well be that, despite the tremendous accumulation of material and social technology, the stock of innovations most suitable to the needs of the less-developed countries is not too abundant. Even if one were to argue that progress in basic science may not be closely tied to the technological needs of the country of origin (and even that may be disputed), unquestionably the applied advances, the inventions and tools, are a response to the specific needs of the country within which they originate. This was certainly true of several major inventions associated with the Industrial Revolution in England, and illustrations abound of necessity as the mother of invention. To the extent that this is true, and that the conditions of production in the developed countries differed greatly from those in the populous less-developed countries today, the material technology evolved in the developed countries may not supply the needed innovations. Nor is the social technology that evolved in the developed countries likely to provide models of institutions or arrangements suitable to the diverse institutional and population-size backgrounds of many less-developed countries. Thus, modern technology with its emphasis on labor-saving inventions may not be suited to countries with a plethora of labor but a scarcity of other factors, such as land and water; and modern institutions, with their emphasis on personal responsibility and pursuit of economic interest, may not be suited to the more traditional life patterns of the agricultural communities that predominate in many less-developed countries. These comments should not be interpreted as denying the value of many transferable parts of modern technology; they are merely intended to stress the possible shortage of material and social tools specifically fitted to the different needs of the less-developed countries.

If the observations just made are valid, several implications for the growth problems of the less-developed countries follow. I hesitate to formulate them explicitly, since the data and the stock of knowledge on which the observations rest are limited. But at least one implication is sufficiently intriguing, and seems to be illuminating of many recent events in the field, to warrant a brief note. It is that a substantial economic advance in the less-developed countries may require modifications in the available stock of material technology, and probably even greater innovations in political and social structure. It will not be a matter of merely borrowing existing tools, material and social, or of directly applying past patterns of growth, merely allowing for the difference in parameters.

The innovational requirements are likely to be particularly great in the social and political structures. The rather violent changes in these structures that occurred in those countries that have forged ahead with highly forced industrialization under Communist auspices, the pioneer entry going back over forty years (beginning with the first Five Year Plan in the U.S.S.R.), are conspicuous illustrations of the kind of social invention and innovation that may be involved. And the variants even of Communist organization, let alone those of democracy and of non-Communist authoritarianism, are familiar. It would be an oversimplification to argue that these innovations in the social and political structures were made primarily in response to the strain between economic backwardness and the potential of modern economic growth or to claim that they were inexorable effects of antecedent history. But to whatever the struggle for political and social organization is a response, once it has been resolved, the results shape significantly the conditions under which economic growth can occur. It seems highly probable that a long period of experimentation and struggle toward a viable political framework compatible with adequate economic growth lies ahead for most less-developed countries of today; and this process will become more intensive and acute as the *perceived* gap widens between what has been attained and what is attainable with modern economic growth. While an economist can argue that some aspects of growth must be present because they are indispensable components (i.e., industrialization, large scale of production, etc.), even their parameters are bound to be variable; and many specific characteristics will be so dependent upon the outcome of the social and political innovations that extrapolation from the past is extremely hazardous.

48

Economic Growth
in the Developing Countries

ANGUS MADDISON

Angus Maddison, currently with the Development Advisory Service of Harvard University, was formerly Director in the Development Department of the Organization for Economic Cooperation and Development. This article is taken from his book Economic Progress and Policy in Developing Countries, *published in 1970.*

It is easy to be pessimistic about economic development. Three-quarters of the world's population lives in a degree of poverty which rich countries have not known for generations, and the income gap has widened in spite of $80 billion of foreign aid. In the past twenty years, many panaceas have been suggested and found inadequate. Land reform, community development, planning, creation of social overhead capital, technical assistance, a take-off engendered by foreign aid, development of human resources and education, a 'green revolution' in agriculture have all inspired hope and enthusiasm. Each in turn has led to some degree of disillusionment. Since the mid 1960s, there has been a new wave of pessimism. India, which was so often regarded as a test case for the success of aid and development policy, has been in a mess. The harvests failed in 1965 and 1966 on a massive scale, and the country came close to famine. The balance of payments crisis was so severe that an important part of the industrial sector was left idle for lack of supplies. The investment rate dropped as the government diverted resources to military purposes. Faith in

planning was shaken as a series of government inquiries and the International Bank for Reconstruction and Development (IRBD) reports showed the inefficiency of the control mechanism and of government enterprises. The Fourth Plan was three years late in appearing and is still very tentative. The whole of Indian economic policy is undergoing an agonizing reappraisal and the political system is showing dangerous cracks. Another disturbing feature is that nearly all the wars of the past twenty years have taken place in the developing world, and their incidence and violence has been particularly severe since 1965 in Vietnam, in the Middle East, in India, Pakistan and Nigeria. Rates of population growth have steadily increased and the Malthusian spectre of large-scale famine has claimed increasing public attention. Foreign aid appropriations have been cut substantially in the U.S. and none of the ambitious aid targets of the United Nations Conference on Trade and Development (UNCTAD) has been met.

Discouragement is compounded by some of the propagandists for the developing world. Some are so gloomy about past achievements that they argue as if the living standards of developing countries were decreasing in absolute terms. This is as false as the now discarded Marxist doctrine of the absolute pauperization of the workers under capitalism. But it is repeated so often that it comes to be believed. Secondly, the blame for the alleged lack of progress is often laid entirely at the door of the developed world. It is true that developed countries could do a good deal more to help both with aid and trade, but continuous public castigation is not the best way to win concessions and this approach discourages an objective assessment of the real achievements of domestic policy.

Our own view of the development process and of future prospects is more cheerful. Even a brief survey makes it clear that the developing world has moved decisively into a new era. Political independence has permitted experiment with a wide variety of growth policies. Colonial types of exploitation have virtually disappeared. Aid has been outstandingly successful in countries where it was given in large quantities. If postwar performance is measured in the light of economic history, the acceleration of growth has been remarkable almost everywhere. Per capita income has risen about three times as fast as in the past, and progress has been significant enough for this generation to have experienced very tangible evidence of change for the better. Improvements in health, nutrition, and sanitation have lowered death rates dramatically. In a short leap the people of the developing world have jumped from a medieval to a modern life expectation. It is not possible to quantify this gain in economic terms but its importance is obvious when we recall how medieval Europe was haunted by ghoulish and macabre imagery—with images of death lavishly embellished on every cathedral door. There has also been a big improvement in education. The idea that these countries are predominantly illiterate is no longer true. The majority of working adults are now literate and although the content of schooling leaves a lot to be desired, it has contributed greatly to enrich the lives and social mobility of those who received it.

There has been genuine progress in development policy. Twenty years ago it was not at all clear how one should go about promoting economic development, and there was certainly no idea that such substantial results could be achieved. There was very little information about the economies of these countries and very few economists and statisticians to provide it.

Most economists in the developed world (including Keynes) had never given their problems serious thought. But the urgency and immensity of the problems has provoked a whole series of new models and ideas for policy. Some of these were ineffective or dangerous, but the ferment of controversy has created new dimensions in economic analysis and a much more realistic view of the policy problems.

On the political level there is increased sophistication, more pragmatism, and less emphasis on ideology. There also has been some convergence of views. In the 1950s, many of the new political leaders in Asia and Africa disliked capitalist solutions, curbed their own private sector, rejected foreign private capital, and pursued a "socialist" course with emphasis on planning and state industries (though none of them used Stalinist techniques of resource mobilization). In Latin America there was disillusion with the international economy, and with liberal capitalism which had broken down so decisively in 1929 and showed little sign of recovery during or immediately after the war. Therefore Latin America tended to follow inflationary and autarkic economic policies on the lines developed in Europe in the 1930s.

Public discussion of basic economic policy issues in the 1950s tended to be bitter, particularly when it involved confrontation between the developing world and Western countries or international organizations. Within the developed Western countries there had been a remarkable revival of economic liberalism and a dismantling of the controls and trade barriers erected in the 1930s. The stabilizing role of government was of course powerful, but the general tenor of policy was completely different from that of Latin American populism and Afro-Asian socialism.

As a result there was no possibility of dialogue between an old-school liberal economist like Per Jacobsen, as head of the International Monetary Fund, and the archetypal Latin American populist Kubitschek as President of Brazil. Similarly the U.S., although it was the major aid donor to India, refused to finance any of its "socialist" inspired state steel plants, even though it had earlier helped to finance state steel works in Brazil and Mexico—countries which in practice are no less "socialist" than India. There were also violent clashes between the U.S. and developing countries on questions of commodity stabilization and trade policy in the first session of UNCTAD.

By the end of the 1960s there were some notable changes in the situation. In Latin America, the deliberate attempt to promote growth by inflation has been abandoned. Three of the most inflationary countries. Argentina, Brazil, and Chile have made major efforts (not too successful as yet) at stabilization and more realistic exchange rates. They have also abandoned the extreme emphasis on import substitution and have made more of an effort to promote exports. In India there has been a slow conversion to the need to use the price mechanism more, to rely less on stifling controls and to run nationalized industries efficiently. There is also a clearer recognition of the potential role of the private sector and foreign capital. The so-called crisis in planning which has caused so much heart-searching amongst Indian economists, is in reality a move towards a more sophisticated policy mix in which the price mechanism is being restored to a more realistic role. It is a milder form of the same crisis which has affected Soviet planning and it is being resolved more successfully. The past two decades have been a period of *Sturm und Drang* for development policy and though this period is by no means concluded we are now in a position to put the achievements in perspective, and to assess the scope for further improvements.

In order to assess the actual and potential contribution of policy to growth we constructed a model and applied it to our sample of twenty-two countries. In spite of the crudeness of statistics and the necessarily simplified treatment involved in any model, it puts the performance of all countries within the same frame of reference and brings out clearly some of the major characteristics of postwar growth.

The average growth of our countries was 5.6 percent a year, which is better than the 5 percent target set by the United Nations for the development decade of the 1960s. The model suggests that about 2 percentage points of the annual growth since 1950 can reasonably be attributed to the domestic policy effort of governments. The rest is due to spontaneous growth forces of the type which operated in prewar years, and foreign aid has also made a significant contribution. The policy effort of most countries has been concentrated on resource mobilization, i.e. investment in physical capital and in human skills and training. There are a few countries where policy led to significant gains in efficiency, and many where resource allocation was inefficient. The model also shows that the growth potential depends on the level of development. The poorest countries have greater difficulty in raising savings and government revenue

than the richer ones, and this must be borne in mind when assessing the success of policy.

There are three ways in which domestic policy can contribute to accelerate the growth of income, i.e. by increased resource mobilization, increased efficiency, and population control.

The effort of resource mobilization has already been vast. The average proportion of income devoted to investment is now as high as in the U.S. and proportion collected in government revenue is close to Japanese levels. There is still scope for increased effort, particularly in the longer run, but the most promising prospects for higher growth lie in more efficient resource allocation.

If the effort of investment and taxation is to bear its proper fruits, there must be better management of the general level of demand with more attention to the dangers of inflation, better allocation of scarce capital resources, better provision for diffusing new inputs and technology to farmers, more regard to comparative advantage in choice of industries for development, and much more attention to export promotion. Increased efficiency will require more careful planning. There is need for better and more topical statistics, closer scrutiny of costs, better choice of technology, more attention to the economic value of research and education, better management of public enterprise and a closer link between the public and private sectors both in planning and implementation. A better mix of fiscal and monetary policy is required for stabilization purposes. There is need for greater use of the price mechanism to reinforce other weapons of policy. Efficiency is difficult to achieve if the rate of interest is too low, if the exchange rate is overvalued, if farm prices are set so low that farmers do not find it profitable to sell food to the towns, and if public enterprise sells electricity, transport, steel, and other products at a loss.

Efficient policy also requires a bigger effort to deal with payments problems. Developing countries are hampered because half of their exports consist of food and raw materials for which demand is expanding slowly and prices are weak. Their export earnings are much more unstable than those of developed countries. But, some payments difficulties have been self-inflicted. Inflation, overvalued exchange rates and highly protected home markets have discouraged exporters, and in several countries there have been disincentives due to government price controls, the tax system and other bureaucratic impediments. This is true of Argentina, Brazil, and India. A few countries have had great success in building up exports and have achieved a remarkable transformation in their structure. This is the case in Israel, Korea, Taiwan, and Yugoslavia. Trade performance is therefore capable of substantial improvement simply from domestic efforts.

Finally, per capita income growth can be accelerated by family planning. As a result of better health and nutrition, the death rate has fallen sharply. This is a major improvement in welfare as parents no longer see most of their children dying at birth or in infancy. However, it is difficult to employ so many people given the shortage of capital, and the increased proportion of dependents reduces the capacity to save and invest. It is therefore necessary to match the decline in death rates by a reduction in birth rates. In the long run, the benefits of slower population growth will be enormous, but Asian countries are only just beginning to take effective action in this field, and in Africa and Latin America, most governments have done nothing. It is unlikely therefore that we will see any significant drop in population growth in developing countries as a whole until the 1980s.

Although there is considerable scope for improvement in economic policy in developing countries, it is also true that some of the criticism of their policy has been misplaced, and some of their mistakes were due to policy in developed countries.

There is a popular illusion that there has been widespread neglect of agriculture in developing countries, and that there is a Malthusian crisis of world hunger. In fact, agriculture has shared in the general postwar acceleration of growth, and most countries have consumption levels well above subsistence. We found only four cases where there was a serious failure of agricultural policy, i.e. in Argentina, Chile, India, and Pakistan. But the agrarian policy of these countries did not fail on the same scale as that of the U.S.S.R. in the 1930s, and was no worse than the opposite failings which have plagued the postwar policy of developed countries. Pakistan has demonstrated quite clearly that, with a change in policies, rapid increases in output can now be achieved by some of the poorest and most tradition-bound farmers in the world. The more recent change in Indian policy confirms this conclusion.

Almost all governments have given heavy emphasis to industrialization. In the mid-1960s, this strategy came in for a good deal of criticism, because it was felt that money had been wasted on costly ventures which were symbols of modernization whilst agriculture was neglected. But the basic strategy of concentrating on industry was justified on four main grounds. Firstly, the demand for industrial products is growing much more rapidly than that for food. Average food consumption in developing countries is almost half of that in the United States, whereas consumption of industrial goods is only a tenth of the U.S. level. Secondly, industrialization transforms the character of an economy, makes it more flexible, creates new skills and momentum for development. Its initial costs are high but are offset by economies of scale and learning which should make themselves felt at a later stage. Thirdly, industrialists have a high propensity to save, and a large part of profits are reinvested. Fourthly, it is easy for government to help industry. As developing countries are all large net importers of industrial products, rather simple measures of import restriction can create new markets for local entrepreneurs.

The real problem with industry is not that it received too high a priority over agriculture. This was true in Argentina, Chile, India, and Pakistan. But in practically all countries there has been substantial misallocation of resources *within* industry.

Protectionist weapons have been too crude and have given far too much emphasis to import substitution in all lines which the countries were physically capable of making. As a result there has been a proliferation of new high-cost industries and little competition. It is difficult to estimate the scale on which resources have been wasted, but a carefully documented study for Pakistan, where industry is still relatively small, suggests that it might be over 3 percent of GNP. Most countries need to reduce and rationalize their protective barriers, so that domestic industry is subjected to more competition. Export promotion needs much greater emphasis. A greater and more sophisticated use of foreign direct investment would help in solving technical problems, and in several countries the management and pricing policy of public enterprise need to be overhauled.

Some of the past errors in resource allocation have been fostered by policies of the developed world. Agricultural protection in developed countries is now more extreme than it has ever been before. European protection plus U.S. surplus food disposals deprive developing countries of export markets worth $2.7 billion. In the case of manufactured goods, protection blocks a smaller amount of trade at present, but if all countries were as liberal with their textile imports as the U.K., the developing world would probably sell another $1 billion worth of exports. The restrictions thus apply specially to goods in which developing countries have a strong comparative advantage. This protectionism of the developed world has reinforced the autarkic prejudices of developing countries and made them cynical about criticism of the way they allocate resources.

In this situation, action by developed countries to remove trade barriers could well be more useful than increased aid. It would, by itself, bring a considerable improvement in resource allocation and efficiency, but it would also encourage developing countries to reduce some of their own trade barriers and open their economies to the winds of competition. Financial help towards the creation of regional trade and payments arrangements would provide a very useful spur to cooperation between developing countries.

The allocation of aid has also been inefficient. The fact that a good deal of it has been given in the form of surplus food has weakened incentives to increase farm output. The earlier refusal of aid donors to help with programs of birth control and family planning and the attitude of the Vatican on this issue have retarded action. Aid donors have tended to prefer large-scale capital projects, some of which, particularly in the field of irrigation have had a low rate of return. They were reluctant to help current developmental expenditures on education or to provide general purpose funds for imports to keep the capital stock working. They have not been notably helpful in providing aid to strengthen export capacity or regional cooperation. Technical assistance to atomic energy has encouraged diversion of indigenous scientific resources away from more useful lines of research. Uncertainty about the size and duration of aid have contributed to the problem of instability and payments equilibrium.

In the postwar period, developing countries have received about $80 billion in official aid. This is about six times as big as the Marshall Plan for Western Europe. There has been disappointment that it has not had more dramatic results and that the need for funds shows no sign of drying up. However, the aid flow is not as impressive as it appears at first sight. It has been distributed among 1.5 billion people instead of the 250 million who received Marshall Aid, and prices have risen, so that in real per capita terms it has been smaller. Secondly the recipients of aid have an income level ranging downwards to a twentieth of that in the United States, whereas the income gap between Western Europe and the U.S. was about one to three, so the magnitude of the task is much greater. Thirdly aid has not been used as a spur to improved resource allocation. It is now so hamstrung with restrictionist clauses that it tends to foster a philosophy of autarchy and dirigisme. The genius of the Marshall Plan was that it acted as a catalyst to open up Europe's trade, free its payments and improve efficiency. Thus its indirect contribution to growth was greater and more permanent than its direct effects.

On average, aid has been equal to 1.5 percent of the income of developing countries and less than 0.5 percent of the income of the developed world. For most developing countries, it has been less important in the acceleration of their postwar growth than improvements in their own policy. The biggest beneficiaries have been Greece, Israel, South Korea, and Taiwan. In these countries external finance averaged about 10 percent of Gross Domestic Product (GDP) and was a major reason for rapid growth. Their real output grew by 8 percent a year compared with 5 percent elsewhere, and most of the difference was due to bigger aid.

There have been a number of attempts to develop allocation criteria to determine aid "needs." The theory has been that developing countries should be supplied with aid up to the limits of their "absorptive" capacity, i.e. they should get as much as they could usefully invest. However, there is little evidence that the overall volume of aid has come close to these limits.

As aid is smaller than the amount which could usefully be absorbed, there is a strong case for allocating it more efficiently and for stimulating a bigger flow of private capital.

There are serious shortcomings in present aid doctrine and practice. The most obvious defect is that aid is conceived as a temporary proposition, and its supposed objectives are only obliquely related to the abolition of poverty. Aid is to be given only for the period in which a country achieves its take-off to self-sustained growth. It is supposed to provide countries with extra resources to use for investment and other development purposes so that they can break out of a situation of economic stagnation and set off a process of cumulative growth, i.e. a steady rise in real income per head. In fact, all of the countries we examined have made significant progress in this respect in the past twenty years. In spite of temporary setbacks, as in India in 1965–66, and in spite of accelerated population growth, it seems clear that domestic economic policy alone is now adequate to achieve continued increases in per capita income in future. The take-off has therefore been achieved, but is growth sulf-sustaining?

The concept of self-sustaining growth has been used in two rather different senses. In the first place it is used to describe a golden age in which the spontaneous growth forces in the private sector will be strong enough to propel the economy forward to higher income levels. This situation is different from that during the take-off in which government policy will have to drag the economy forward and break down the institutional obstacles and inertia of a stagnant economy. However, there has been a great increase in the degree to which even highly developed countries depend on active government policy and close intergovernmental cooperation in order to sustain their growth. All private enterprise economies now depend heavily on both spontaneous and on policy-induced growth, so that self-sustaining growth in this sense is no longer a very meaningful goal for any kind of country.

Self-sustained growth is also used to describe a situation in which a country can attain its full growth potential without balance of payments support, i.e. when it can finance all the imports it needs from its own export earnings and private capital receipts. Although a good many indicators have been devised which help to determine whether a country is moving towards this goal, it is doubtful wehther any country will ever actually reach a position in which foreign aid could not increase its growth rate. The U.K., for instance, has not been in a state of sulf-sustained growth in the postwar period, and the U.S. has also had a long-standing balance of payments deficit. This criterion is therefore so vague that it permits almost any country to make a case for aid.

The present criteria for allocating aid funds are not satisfactory either in identifying which countries should be helped or in demonstrating when aid should be ended. The primary purpose of aid should be to help countries which are poor to get richer. We should define potential aid recipients in terms which are objectively measurable and keep on helping them until they pass the poverty line. Our own suggestion for the poverty line is a per capita income of $500 when measured at 1965 U.S. prices. This is a lower definition of poverty than would be acceptable inside the U.S. itself, but it is near the income level in Taiwan to which the U.S. has ceased giving economic aid. The purpose of foreign aid is, of course, very different from domestic antipoverty programs. Foreign aid is not relief intended to bring up incomes to a minimum $500 level in order to boost consumption. On its present scale, aid is only big enough to provide an income supplement of around $3.50 a head and it must therefore be channelled into uses (mainly investment) which will raise production.

This approach involves a commitment to aid for an indefinite period of time. It will take several decades to raise all countries above the poverty line. But most rich countries have very extensive domestic welfare programs for their poorer citizens and the indefinite continuation of aid should be easier to accept now than it was in an era of more rugged individualism.

A major difficulty in aid allocation is to devise a system of rewards and penalities to ensure that it bears some relation to performance as well as to need. However, past experience suggests that attempts to scrutinize closely the use of aid have been cumbersome for both donors and recipients and they have only had a limited success. Aid is not the only element in development programmes, and overdetailed scrutiny of these particular resources may detract attention from overall growth strategy. The best way to ensure that it is used efficiently is to provide a mechanism for assessing whether overall economic policy is successful. But it is not politically acceptable that surveillance should be carried out by individual aid donors or even by aid donors acting collectively. The experience of developed countries has shown that the most effective check on the efficiency of economic policy is by a procedure of regular international review and consultation in an organization where countries do not feel any tutelary constraints. It is highly desirable that similar regional organizations be built up within the developing world, and these organizations should themselves be used as a channel for aid in order to get them started successfully.

The definition of a poverty line at $500 per capita will leave an intermediate group of countries between this level and the $1,400 level which presently constitutes the threshold of the "developed world." Countries in this position will generally still be capital importers, but they should get their capital on commercial terms. The knowledge that they are no longer candidates for aid should help sharpen their efforts to make better use of the international capital market and to follow sounder economic policies. The experience of Greece, Israel, and Spain demonstrates that countries in this position can attract a good deal of foreign private capital and enjoy fast rates of growth. However, a good deal still remains to be done to foster their access to private capital markets, and more serious attention should be given to the Horowitz plan for using public guarantees to support loans issued on the private market, particularly where this enables the financing burden to be shifted to countries with payments surpluses, like Germany.

Finally, there is need for greater precision about the content of aid. An appreciable part of "aid" has been given in the form of loans. Loans are aid only to the extent that the terms are more favourable than those on private capital markets. It is necessary that this be made clearer to legislators who vote on aid programs. In cases where legislatures falter in their commitment to new aid funds, it is also desirable to explore the possibilities for debt cancellation. In this way, past loans can be converted into aid which is often more useful to the recipient than new funds.

49

Foreign Aid: A Skeptical Appraisal

Hans J. Morgenthau is a professor of political science at the City University of New York. This article comes from his testimony before the Joint Economic Committee in 1970.

The burden of my argument is twofold. First, one must distinguish sharply between foreign aid for political purposes and foreign aid for economic development. Second, foreign aid for economic development has a chance to be successful only within relatively narrow limits which are raised by cultural and political conditions impervious to direct outside influence.

Foreign Aid for Political Purposes

Foreign aid for political purposes is about as old as foreign policy itself. Bribes proffered by one government to another for political advantage were, until the beginning of the nineteenth century, an integral part of the armory of diplomacy. It was proper and common for a government to pay the foreign minister or ambassador of another country a pension. Nor was it regarded less proper or less usual for a government to compensate foreign statesmen for their cooperation in the conclusion of treaties. The Prussian Ambassador in Paris summed up well the main rule of this

game when he reported to his government in 1802: "Experience has taught everybody who is here on diplomatic business that one ought never to give anything before the deal is definitely closed, but it has only proved that the allurement of gain will often work wonders."

Much of what goes by the name of foreign aid today is in the nature of bribes. The transfer of money and services from one government to another performs here the function of a price paid for political services rendered or to be rendered by the recipient. These bribes differ from the traditional ones in two respects: They are justified primarily in terms of foreign aid for economic development, and money and services are transferred through elaborate machinery fashioned for genuine economic aid. In consequence, these bribes are a less effective means for the purpose of purchasing political favors than were the traditional ones.

The compulsion to substitute for the traditional businesslike transmission of bribes the pretense and elaborate machinery of foreign aid for economic results from a climate of opinion which accepts as universally valid the proposition that the highly developed industrial nations have an obligation to transfer money and services to underdeveloped nations to foster economic development. Thus, aside from humanitarian and military foreign aid, the only kind of transfer of money and services that seems to be legitimate is the one made for the purpose of economic development. Economic development has become an ideology by which the transfer of money and services from one government to another is rationalized and justified.

However, the present climate of opinion assumes not only that affluent industrial nations have an obligation to extend foreign aid for economic development to nations of the third world. It also assumes as a universally valid proposition that economic development can actually be promoted through such transfer of money and services. Thus economic development as an ideology requires machinery that makes plausible the assumption of the efficacy of the transfer of money and services for the purpose of economic growth. The government of Nation A, trying to buy political advantage from the government of Nation B for, say, the price of $20 million, not only must pretend, but also must act out in elaborate fashion the pretense, that what it is actually doing is giving aid for economic development to the government of Nation B.

The practice of giving bribes as though they were contributions to economic development necessarily creates expectations, in the donor and the recipient, which are bound to be disappointed. Old-fashioned bribery is a straightforward transaction: Services are to be rendered at a price, and both sides know what to expect. Bribery disguised as foreign aid for economic development makes of donor and recipient actors in a play which in the end they can no longer distinguish from reality. In consequence, both expect results in economic development which, in the nature of things, could not have been forthcoming. Thus both are bound to be disappointed, the donor blaming the recipient for his inefficiency and the recipient accusing the donor of stinginess.

Foreign aid for military purposes is a traditional means for nations to buttress their alliances. Rome used to receive tribute from its allies for the military protection it provided. The seventeenth and eighteenth centuries were the classic period of military subsidies, by which especially Great Britain endeavored to increase the military strength of her continental allies. This traditional military aid can be under-

stood as a division of labor between two allies who pool their resources, one supplying money, material, and training. the other providing primarily manpower.

In contrast to traditional practice, military aid is today extended not only to allies but also to certain uncommitted nations. The purpose here is not so much military as political, for political advantage is sought in exchange for military aid. This kind of aid obligates the recipient to the donor. The latter expects the former to abstain from a political course that might put in jeopardy the continuation of military aid, which is thus really in the nature of a bribe.

What appears as military aid may also be actually in the nature of prestige aid, to be discussed below. The provision of jet fighters and other modern weapons for certain underdeveloped nations can obviously perform no genuine military function. It increases the prestige of the recipient nation both at home and abroad. Being in the possession of some of the more spectacular instruments of modern warfare, a nation can at least enjoy the illusion that it has become a modern military power.

As bribery appears today in the guise of aid for economic development, so does aid for economic development appear in the guise of military assistance. In the session of 1967, Congress, for instance, appropriated $600 million for economic aid to strategic areas, and it is likely that in the total appropriations for military aid in excess of $1 billion other items of economic aid were hidden. This mode of operation results from the reluctance of Congress to vote large amounts for economic aid in contrast to its readiness to vote for military purposes. Yet the purposes of aid for economic development are likely to suffer when they are disguised as military assistance, as we saw the purposes of bribery suffer when disguised as aid for economic development. The military context within which such aid is bound to operate, even though its direct administration may be in the hands of the civilian authorities, is likely to deflect such aid from its genuine purposes. More particularly, it strengthens the ever-present tendency to subordinate the requirements of aid for economic development to military considerations.

Prestige aid has in common with modern bribes that its true purpose, too, is concealed by the ostensible purpose of economic development. The unprofitable or idle steel mill, the highway without traffic and leading nowhere, the airline operating with foreign personnel and at a loss but under the flag of the recipient country—they ostensibly serve the purposes of economic development and under different circumstances could do so. Actually, however, they perform no positive economic function. They owe their existence to the penchant, prevalent in many underdeveloped nations, for what might be called "conspicuous industrialization," and industrialization that produces symbols of, and monuments to, industrial advancement rather than satisfying the objective economic needs of the country.

For many of the underdeveloped nations the steel mill, the highway, the airline, the modern weapons perform a function that is not primarily economic or military but psychological and political. They are sought as symbols and monuments of modernity and power. Nehru is reported to have said, when he showed Chou En-lai a new dam: "It is in these temples that I worship."

The advantage for the donor of prestige aid is threefold. He may receive specific political advantages in return for the provision of aid, very much after the model of the advantage received in return for a bribe. The spectacular character of prestige aid establishes a patent relationship between the generosity of the giver and the increased prestige of the recipient: the donor's prestige is enhanced, as it were, by the increase of the recipient's prestige. Finally, prestige aid comes relatively cheap. A limited commitment of resources in the form of a spectacular but economically useless symbol of, or monument to, modernity may bring disproportionate political dividends.

It is in the nature of prestige aid that it is justified by the prospective recipient in terms of genuine economic development. The prospective donor, unaware of the distinction, is likely to fall into one of two errors. By mistaking prestige aid for aid for economic development, he will either waste human and material resources in support of the latter, while the purpose of prestige aid could have been achieved much more simply and cheaply. Or else he will reject out of hand a request for prestige aid because it cannot be justified in terms of economic development, and may thereby forego political advantages he could have gained from the provision of the aid requested.

Foreign Aid for Economic Development

These different types of foreign aid require the same kind of political judgment as do the other, more obvious methods of foreign policy, such as diplomatic inducements or military pressure. When we try to develop a sensible foreign-aid policy for economic development, we must take into account two other factors: the cultural and political conditions in the recipient country.

Since Western economic development, from the first Industrial Revolution onward, has been the result of the formation of capital and the accumulation of technical knowledge, we have tended to assume that these two factors would by themselves provide the impetus for the economic development of the underdeveloped nations of Asia, Africa, and Latin America. This tendency has been powerfully supported by the spectacular success of the Marshall Plan, conceived and executed as a strictly economic measure for the provision of capital and technological know-how. Yet it is not always recognized that this success was made possible only by the fact that, in contrast to the underdeveloped nations of Asia, Africa, and Latin America, the recipients of Marshall aid were among the leading industrial nations of the world, whose economic systems were only temporarily in disarray.

By contrast, many of the underdeveloped nations suffer from cultural and political disabilities which stand in the way of economic development and which cannot be removed by foreign aid. A civilization, for instance, which depreciates success in this world because it stands in the way of success in the other world, which is the only success that counts, puts a cultural obstacle in the path of industrial development which foreign aid by itself cannot overcome. Saving —that is, the accumulation of capital or goods for future use—has become so integral a part of our economic thought and action that it is hard for us to realize that there are hundreds of millions of people in the underdeveloped areas of the world who are oblivious to this mode of operation, indispensable to economic development. We have come to consider the productive enterprise as a continuum in which the individual owner or manager has a personal stake. Yet in many underdeveloped areas the productive enterprise is regarded primarily as an object for financial exploitation, to be discarded when it has performed its function of bringing the temporary owner a large financial return in the shortest possible time. Foreign aid poured into such a precapitalistic and even prerational mold is not likely to transform the mold, but rather it will be forced by it into channels serving the interests of a precapitalistic or prerational society.

The economic interests that stand in the way of

foreign aid being used for economic development are typically tied in with the distribution of political power in underdeveloped societies. The ruling groups in these societies derive their political power in good measure from the economic status quo. The ownership and control of arable land, in particular, is in many of the underdeveloped societies the foundation of political power. Land reform and industrilization are therefore an attack upon the political status quo. In the measure that they are successful, they are bound to affect drastically the distribution of economic and political power. According to the *New York Times* of March 11, 1970, the head of the Indian Affairs Department of Salta Province in Argentina was dismissed because "I stepped on the toes of too many landholders and others who benefit from Indian poverty." Even illiteracy which we tend to attribute to poverty, is frequently a weapon in defense of the status quo. It is perpetuated on purpose, for illiterates are more likely to be quiescent than people who are able to absorb ideas by reading and disseminate them by writing.

Yet the beneficiaries of both the economic and political status quo are the typical recipients of foreign aid given for the purpose of changing the status quo! Their use of foreign aid for this purpose requires a readiness for self-sacrifice and a sense of social responsibility that few ruling groups have shown throughout history. Foreign aid proffered under such circumstances is likely to fail in its purpose of economic development and, as a bribe to the ruling group, rather will strengthen the economic and political status quo. It is likely to accentuate unsolved social and political problems rather than bring them closer to solution. A team of efficiency experts and public accountants might well have improved the operations of the Al Capone gang; yet, by doing so, it would have aggravated the social and political evils that the operations of that gang brought forth.

Given this likely resistance of the ruling group to economic development, foreign aid requires drastic political change as a precondition for its success. Foreign aid must go hand in hand with political change, either voluntarily induced from within or brought about through pressure from without. The latter alternative faces the donor nation with a dual dilemma. On the one hand, to give foreign aid for economic development without stipulating conditions that maximize the chances for success maximizes the chances for failure. On the other hand, to give aid "with strings" arouses xenophobic suspicions and

nationalistic resentments, to be exploited both by the defenders of the *status quo* and by the promoters of revolution.

The promotion of drastic social change on the part of the donor nation creates the precondition for economic development, but it also conjures up the specter of uncontrollable revolution. In many of the underdeveloped nations, peace and order are maintained only through the ruthless use of the monopoly of violence by the ruling group. Determined and skillful foreign intervention may not find it hard to weaken the power of the ruling group or to remove it from power altogether. Where it may be able to control events up to this point—that is, to instigate drastic reform and revolution—it may well be unable to control the course of the revolution itself.

Successful foreign aid for economic development may have similar unsettling political results. Economic development, especially by way of industrialization, is likely to disrupt the social fabric of the underdeveloped nation. By creating an urban industrial proletariat, it loosens and destroys the social nexus of family, village, and tribe, in which the individual had found himself secure. And it will not be able, at least not right away, to provide a substitute for this lost social world. The vacuum thus created will be filled by social unrest and political agitation. Furthermore, it is not the downtrodden masses living in a static world of unrelieved misery who are the likely protagonists of revolution, but rather those groups that have begun to rise in the social and economic scale but not enough to satisfy their aroused expectations. Thus, economic development is bound to disturb not only the economic status quo but, through it, the political status quo as well. If the change is drastic enough, the social and political effects of economic development may well amount to a prerevolutionary or revolutionary situation. And while the United States may have started the revolutionary process, it has no control over the auspices under which it will be ended.

Thus we arrive at the disconcerting conclusion that successful foreign aid for economic development can be counterproductive if the donor nation's goal is the recipient's social and political stability. In some cases at least, the failure of American aid for economic development may have been a blessing in disguise in that it did not disturb a status quo whose continuing stability was our main interest.

Foreign aid for economic development, then, has a very much smaller range of potentially successful operation than is generally believed, and its success depends in good measure not so much upon its soundness in strictly economic terms as upon intellectual, moral, and political preconditions, which are not susceptible to economic manipulation, if they are susceptible to manipulation from the outside at all. Furthermore, the political results of successful foreign aid for economic development may be either unpredictable or counterproductive in terms of the goals of the donor nation. In any event, they are in large measure uncontrollable. Foreign aid proffered and accepted for purposes of economic development may turn out to be something different from what it was intended to be, if it is not oriented toward the political conditions within which it must operate. Most likely, it will turn out to be a bribe or prestige aid, or else a total waste. To do too much may here be as great a risk as to do too little, and "masterly inactivity" may sometimes be the better part of wisdom.